Praise for *In*

"Ayaan Hirsi Ali is one of Europe's most controversial political figures and a target for terrorists. A notably enigmatic personality whose fierce criticisms of Islam have made her a darling of . . . conservatives . . . and . . . popular with leftists . . . Soft-spoken but passionate."

—*The Boston Globe*

"Brave, inspiring, and beautifully written . . . Narrated in clear, vigorous prose, it traces the author's geographical journey from Mogadishu to Saudi Arabia, Ethiopia and Kenya, and her desperate flight to the Netherlands to escape an arranged marriage."

—*The New York Times*

"This woman is a major hero of our time. Please read her book and, if you like it as I do, recommend it to others."

—Richard Dawkins

"Crammed with harrowing details, Hirsi Ali's account is a significant contribution to our times."

—*Kirkus* (starred review)

"Her voice is forceful and unbowed—like Irshad Manji, she delivers a powerful feminist critique of Islam informed by a genuine understanding of the religion."

—*Publishers Weekly* (starred review)

"In Hirsi Ali's mesmerizing memoir . . . we're permitted to admire her courage and her prose, to marvel at her steely feminist self-creation, to mourn her sister, deplore her brother, and share her horror at true believers on a misogynistic rampage."

—*Harper's Magazine*

"But *Infidel* is not just a bitter manifesto against genital mutilation and holy terror. With her terrific ear for dialogue and her fine eye for detail, it's at times more like *Little Women* under the shade of the talal tree, mapping the stories of family life, a young girl's first kiss and 'old chants of war and death, raids, herding, green pastures, herds of many camels' against the soul-crushing backdrop of Somalia's bloody civil war."

—*San Francisco Chronicle*

"*Infidel* is a unique book, Ayaan Hirsi Ali is a unique writer, and both deserve to go far."

—*The Washington Post*

"A gifted writer and compassionate soul. . . . [R]eaders who crave well-told tales will want to listen."

—*People,* Critic's Choice, 4 stars

"A powerful, compelling read. . . . Put simply, this woman is a heroine."

—*The Christian Science Monitor*

"A profoundly moving memoir that celebrates triumph over adversity."

—*The New Yorker*

"The most remarkable, moving, eye-opening, can't-put-down book you'll read this year. You may not agree with every word, but Ayaan Hirsi Ali's story will haunt you for life."

—Alvin Toffler, author of *Future Shock* and coauthor with Heidi Toffler of *Revolutionary Wealth*

"A brave and elegant figure . . . an honest woman . . . No one who reads her [memoirs] will doubt the self-questioning and the rigorous honesty of her mind. Perhaps, as in Voltaire's short story 'L'Ingenu,' it is that too much honesty is sometimes unpalatable, even if it is couched in civil terms. . . . She has an open mind that has released itself from the old strait-jacketed frame of reference of Right and Left, she is instinctively deeply anti-authoritarian and she is unlikely to stick to straight ideological lines. She will go on asking difficult questions."

—*The Observer*

"Her mission is too large for any single party. She is urging the West to judge Islam by its own standards. She is urging the Islamic world to take a look at itself. What Islam needs, she feels, is a swift dose of eighteenth-century enlightenment—it's time to put down the Koran and pick up Voltaire."

—*Sunday Times Culture*

"A jaw-dropping account . . . freshly riveting. . . . A candid and compelling narrative of survival, personal growth, and cosmopolitan achievement against all odds, *Infidel* is . . . noteworthy for its passionate insistence that so-called Western values such as free speech and gender equality are fundamental and universal rights—rights still denied to millions of men and, especially, women around the world today."

—*Elle*

"It's a page-turner, almost novelistic, the story of a metamorphosis from young girl born to be forced into marriage and subjugated, to an interpreter, to a graduate student in political science, then to a representative [in Parliament]. . . . Beyond the account of Ayaan's own emancipation, this book is a terrifying exploration of the situation of women in Islamic countries, and a plea for their sexual liberation."

—*Elle* (France)

"Hirsi Ali's spirited recollections and defense of women's rights to independence and self-expression are inspiring to women of all cultures."

—*Booklist*

"One marvels at the tenacity of Ayaan Hirsi Ali, the Somali 'slave' turned Dutch MP and now fugitive Muslim feminist . . . If there is one book that really addresses the existential issues of our civilisation, then Ali's autobiography is it. That it is brilliantly and soberly written is a bonus. That at thirty-eight she has plenty of time for more books—maybe about her impressions of America—leads to keen anticipation."

—*Sunday Telegraph,* lead review

"Intelligent, passionate, beautiful. And living in fear of her life . . . How she went from devout believer to fearless opponent, from a loyal clan member to being renounced by her family, from Africa to Europe, and from blind faith to unbending reason is the compelling story she tells in her new autobiography entitled, with characteristic bluntness, *Infidel* . . . Her combination of elegance and eloquence would be impressive in any circumstances. Under threat of death, it is nothing short of incredible."

—*Observer Review,* front cover

"A charismatic figure . . . of arresting and hypnotizing beauty . . . [who writes] with quite astonishing humor and restraint."

—Christopher Hitchens, *Slate*

"A remarkable book . . . *Infidel* shows that a determined woman can change much more history than her own."

—Christopher Hitchens, *The Sunday Times,* front cover

"Ayaan Hirsi Ali is a maverick, bravely defying the Netherlands' political correctness to address Europe's growing cultural rifts . . . the former Dutch politician is a master of self-reinvention. . . . It's all retold in her eloquent new memoir."

—*New York* magazine

"Hirsi Ali is a tractarian and a memoirist. . . . Her entire purpose in fleeing to the Netherlands, as she explained eloquently and at length, was to escape a life of submitting to other people's reactionary opinions and to go bang the table on behalf of individual freedom, and here she is doing what she has intended to do. . . . In her books, . . . she dedicates herself mostly . . . to [describing] and to [decrying] the miseries of women in the . . . Muslim world that she knows best. . . . These passages express . . . a visceral anger at oppression. A moral indignation, and not just a wistful pragmatism . . . Hirsi Ali's books raise the issue of women's rights, and not from an outsider's point of view. . . . Here is the actual insider; the real thing. . . . Hirsi Ali's writings have the effect of making a large number of nuanced subtleties look ridiculous. . . . [Her] critics have lost the ability to distinguish between a fanatical murderer and a rational debater."

—Paul Berman, "Who's Afraid of Tariq Ramadan," *The New Republic*

"Ayaan Hirsi Ali is one of the outstanding figures of our time. She is a luminous example of enlightenment and courage, and an emblem of hope not just for women in Islam but for women and men everywhere in all circumstances, because she shows that an undaunted spirit always achieves victory, no matter what. She is a human being of the present and future, who shows how to stand up as a free agent, shaking off the shackles of the past and all its rooted injustices and oppressions. Her experience and how she has transcended it shows the way to far better possibilities for human flourishing. Her autobiography is an education and an inspiration: it should be required reading for everyone everywhere."

—A. C. Grayling

"*Infidel* is a riposte, controversial and compelling, to all her critics. Ali has invited them to walk a mile in her shoes. Most wouldn't last 100 yards."

—*Evening Standard*

"*Infidel* is the autobiography of a woman who has battled to free herself from enslavement to Islam, carried along almost entirely by her own impetus to become an individual. . . . What stands out the most is the personal integrity that has allowed her to distance herself first from Islamic fundamentalism and then from European political correctness. Through her direct, clear, convincing and intelligent written style, the former MP in her book unveils the dramatic story of a personal revolution."

—*El País*

"As a woman whom radical Muslims have marked for death, her message deserves every American's attention."

—*National Review Online*

"Ayaan Hirsi Ali is a crusader . . . an Infidel indeed. . . . This articulate autobiography is worth reading for both its political and religious perspectives and because Hirsi Ali's life is so fascinating."

—*The Age*

"The death threat received by Ayaan Hirsi Ali demanded to be taken more seriously, mostly because of its mode of delivery: staked to the dying body of Theo Van Gogh, her collaborator in producing the film *Submission, Part One,* which depicted abused women with verses from the Koran inscribed on their semi-naked bodies. Van Gogh's murder provides Hirsi Ali's autobiography with an arresting opening and lends moral weight to her unrelenting critique of Islam."

—*The Weekend Australian*

"This is the extraordinary story of a woman born into a family of desert nomads, circumcised as a child, educated by radical imams in Kenya and Saudi Arabia, taught to believe that if she uncovered her hair, terrible tragedies would occur. . . . She now espouses a controversial conclusion: that Islam is in a period of transition and that as practised now it is often incompatible with modernity and democracy so must radically transform itself to become so."

—*Australian Financial Review*

"Ayaan Hirsi Ali has survived genital mutilation, civil war, a forced marriage and numerous death threats but she won't be silenced. *Infidel* is the story of her life and is one of the most absorbing books I have read in a long time. . . . Her book offers an illuminating look at Islam, and emphasises the view that religious tolerance should never come at the cost of basic human rights. *Infidel* is a must-read"

—*Sunshine Coast Daily*

"From her traditional Muslim childhood in Somalia to her rise as one of the world's most eloquent and determined champions of free speech, this enlightening memoir of an admired and controversial political figure reveals how Hirsi Ali developed her beliefs and maintains her resolve to fight injustice and change the world."

—*Weekend Gold Coast Bulletin*

"Too many people still don't understand what our country is up against. They might if they read [Hirsi Ali's] book."

—Fred Thompson, former U.S. Senator and author
of *At That Point in Time*

Also by Ayaan Hirsi Ali

The Caged Virgin:
An Emancipation Proclamation for Women and Islam

INFIDEL

❧

Foreword by Christopher Hitchens

Ayaan Hirsi Ali

FREE PRESS

New York   London   Toronto   Sydney

*f***P**

FREE PRESS
A Division of Simon & Schuster, Inc.
1230 Avenue of the Americas
New York, NY 10020

First Free Press trade paperback edition April 2008

For reasons of privacy, certain names in this book have been changed.

For information about special discounts for bulk purchases,
please contact Simon & Schuster Special Sales at
1-800-456-6798 or business@simonandschuster.com

DESIGNED BY ERICH HOBBING

Manufactured in the United States of America

9   10   8

The Library of Congress has cataloged the hardcover edition as follows:
Hirsi Ali, Ayaan.
Infidel / Ayaan Hirsi Ali.
p. cm.
1. Politicians—Netherlands—Biography. 2. Muslims—Netherlands—Biography.
3. Refugees—Netherlands—Biography. I. Title.

DJ292.H57 A3 2007
949.207'3092 B 22   2006049762

ISBN-13: 978-0-7432-8968-9
ISBN-10:   0-7432-8968-4
ISBN-13: 978-0-7432-8969-6 (pbk)
ISBN-10:   0-7432-8969-2 (pbk)

To Abeh, Ma, Ayeeyo (Grandma), Mahad
And in loving memory of Haweya

Contents

Foreword

The volume that you hold in your hands is really two books. The first is a fascinating memoir of participation in one of the modern world's most imposing new realities: cross-border and cross-cultural migration. Tens of millions of people, for reasons of either dislocation or aspiration, now live far from their country of origin. This displacement involves not just a journey in miles but also a journey in time: citizens born in the conditions of the medieval village work amid European and American skyscrapers. Ayaan Hirsi Ali grew up in circumstances that would be unimaginable to most inhabitants of the "developed" world; she even wonders at one point how many of the girl babies born on the same day as she was, in the same hospital, have survived, let alone flourished as she has. A few lucky accidents, a tenacious mother, and, in my opinion, her early acquisition (while in Kenya) of the English language have made the crucial difference. Not only does the author relate her own escape from one sphere to another, but she also describes how she tried to help others to manage the transition and, ultimately, how her past tried to pursue her into her future.

Onto the "Third World" conditions of warfare, clan rivalry, scarcity, and repression are superimposed the man-made tyrannies of religion and superstition. Ayaan—as I shall call her from now on, proud as I am to be counted as her friend—was while still a child subjected to the gross torture of genital mutilation. Numerous were the men (and older women) who had the right to beat her, and who exercised that right with gusto. Denied autonomy even in respect to her own private parts, she was also expected to acquiesce in any arrangements for her own nuptials that others might determine for her. And all of this had to be accepted fatalistically, because it was the will of a supreme being. Thus the other journey described here, and a no less arduous one, is the gradual emancipation of the self from the "mind-forged manacles" of theocracy. Ayaan used to believe in the existence of *djinns* and devils, in the workings of an international Jewish conspiracy, in the literal truth of a single book, and in the necessity of covering female limbs and faces. It is inspiring to read of her gradual liberation from these delusions, and of her eventual rejection of belief in the supernatural altogether.

In a conversation that we had in the fall of 2007, I asked Ayaan about the good-humored tone of this book, remarkably free as it is of the rancor that might, given the story it tells, have been forgiven. Her response was twofold. First, she said, she felt on balance fortunate. She was, after all, alive to tell the tale. Second, she had seen what anger had done to her mother, a woman "imprisoned" in resentment at the many ways that life had maltreated her. (You will be meeting this unusual woman in the following pages and perhaps imagining what a brilliant mother she could have been in more propitious conditions.)

We then discussed the triad of mentalities that, in my opinion, go to make up Islamist fundamentalism. These are self-righteousness, self-pity, and self-hatred. "In the Muslim world there is hardly a self," was her first comment, "because the only real human moments are stolen ones. This leads to hypocrisy, which is the main cause of self-righteousness." A strong feature of this book is the clear-eyed approach that it takes to matters of sex. Ayaan believes that sexual repression is at the root of all the related problems, because "without sexual freedom there is no self." The corollary to this is that anybody who wants to possess sexual self-respect will have to embark on a collision course with religious orthodoxy. The cult of virginity, which is one of the centerpieces of the Quran, absolutely mandates both male supremacy and female misery. She talked quietly and demurely but graphically of the ways this cult makes the lives of women a misery, either by depriving them of a sex life altogether or by forcing them into expedients (painful anal penetration, the resealing of the hymen) that are dangerous as well as unpleasant and degrading.

One of the many ways this book succeeds is in reconstructing the confused mentality of a young girl who was bewildered by the endless demands of a cruel faith. "One of my first moments of alarm," she told me, "was when I was five or six years old and found my granny with her bottom in the air, talking to herself and addressing somebody. I thought it was a game and started to play around, and she told me I was an evil girl. The thing was—I could swear that though she was talking to someone, there was nobody there." (I told her the old joke: when people say they talk to god, we may call that prayer. When people say that god talks to them—that's schizophrenia.) Religious cults often emphasize the role of the precocious child who utters words of wisdom, but it is equally true that children can be quick to see through the devices of religion. "Islam is so crude because it insists on such strict prayer routines and exercises. I had to attend but I couldn't concentrate and so I felt guilty." Here is the very encapsulation of the sado-masochism of religion: it makes impossible demands on people and then convicts them of original sin when they fail to live up to them.

The fear of eternal punishment is a wicked thing to inflict on a child. Ayaan told me that she wasn't completely free of her repressive upbringing until she had lost her terror of hell. "In Muslim teaching, hell is intensely real and very close. You could be feeling the flames at any moment." To throw off this reign of mental terror isn't an easy matter. Some intelligent adults never quite lose their fear of damnation. It wasn't until she had crossed this Rubicon that she could declare her full independence. But this is perhaps to get slightly ahead of the story.

Medieval Christianity made the uncomfortable discovery that all absolutist belief systems have since had to make: it is impossible to be just a little bit heretical, or to permit just a little heresy. The rack and the stake and the thumbscrew are ultimately unavailing against this fact. Once admit any doubt, and the whole edifice is in danger of collapse. An excellent instance of such questioning occurs in the first third of this book, when Ayaan is sitting through yet another dull rant about the need to cover up all the distinctive features of the female, lest women commit the unpardonable sin of arousing male desire. She gets up to ask "What about the men? Shouldn't they cover? Don't women also have desire for male bodies? Couldn't they be tempted by the sight of men's skin?" Of course, this inescapable question is considered ridiculous, and, anyway, the Prophet didn't allow any latitude for it to be asked, so that must be the end of the matter. Ayaan tells us that she used to hear on all sides that work would come to a standstill if men could see female flesh: trucks would crash and all would be chaos. It was only when she got to Holland that she appreciated that coexistence on terms of gender equality and casual dress was possible. (The irony here, I must add, is slightly at her expense. I have seen grown men look really quite foolish when she comes into the room.)

Ever since the assault on civil society that was launched on September 11, 2001, much of the "Western" world has been on a frenzied quest for interlocutors with the Islamic world. How are we to "understand" Muslim demands and emotions? What have we done to merit such hatred? How can we come to terms with a society that appears to take religious preachments literally? In the pages of *Infidel,* the answers to these questions are fairly easily discoverable. The cause of backwardness and misery in the Muslim world is not Western oppression but Islam itself: a faith that promulgates contempt for Enlightenment and secular values. It teaches hatred to children, promises a grotesque version of an afterlife, elevates the cult of "martyrdom," flirts with the mad idea of forced conversion of the non-Islamic world, and deprives societies of the talents and energies of 50 percent of their members: the female half. One need look no further to explain the stultification of Afghanistan, Iran, Sudan, Pakistan, and Somalia. The corollary holds with some exactitude: those Muslim societies that are relatively open and prosperous—one might instance Indonesia, Turkey, and Tunisia—are precisely the ones that keep religion in bounds. And the line between a failed state and a "rogue" one thus becomes increasingly difficult to draw, because when Islamist societies fail (as they will, if they try to govern on the principles of *shari'a*) they are prevented by their own faith from making any self-critical inquiry. It cannot be because of Quranic fanaticism that our children's teeth rot, that disease and illiteracy are rampant, that nothing much (except the police system) seems to work. No: it is because of a conspiracy of Jews and Crusaders that we suffer! And thus the latent violence of the failed state is mobilized for export, and hysterical, impoverished crowds applaud the self-destructive actions of the ignorant, barbaric children they have raised.

A number of brave ex-Muslims have been warning us for many years that Islamist demands are *not* to be interpreted as some kind of "civil rights" claim. Even within the frontiers of Europe and North America, there are now "honor" killings, the mutilation of female genitalia, the imposition of veilings and beatings on wives and daughters and sisters, and calls for censorship and repression backed up by serious threats of violence. Several European capital cities, from London to Madrid, have shared the fate of New York and Washington in becoming the scene of random bombings. Nor have the cities of more "secular" Muslim countries, including the three I just mentioned, Indonesia, Turkey, and Tunisia, been exempt. Salman Rushdie, Taslima Nasrin, Hanif Kureishi, Nadeem Aslam, Monica Ali, and many others have tried to tell us what is under way, and what lies in our future. *Infidel* is one of the latest, and surely one of the most luminous, of these manifestos. You cannot read it and be content with the insipid and masochistic suggestions of "dialogue" that flow every day into our media from the pens of people like Karen Armstrong and John Esposito. You cannot read it and allow President Bush the least credit for intoning the weird idea that "Islam is a religion of peace."

Nor can you read it and expect to be confirmed in the rightness of your "own" religion as against the "other" one. Ayaan does not just speak out against female circumcision. She doesn't think that boy babies should have their genitals hacked in the name of god either. (For this, she has been compared to Hitler!) Christian groups trying to recruit her have been gently but firmly turned away. Her self-education has led her to adopt the skeptical, humanist tradition that was so much aided by the hospitality of Holland, a country that sheltered Spinoza and Pierre Bayle and other freethinkers who sought refuge from clerical tyranny, and which for a while lived up to this humanist tradition by giving her asylum as well.

The end of this book tells the story of the disappointment that followed, a disappointment we should all feel. An element in Dutch public life, and indeed Dutch public opinion, has decided that it prefers a quiet life to the adoption and protection of this outspoken young lady. Having promised one of its more talented parliamentarians indefinite security against the sadists and fanatics who butchered Theo van Gogh on an Amsterdam street, and who told Ayaan that she was next on the list, the government of the Netherlands abruptly announced in October 2007 that it would no longer guarantee her safety if she chose to continue living in America. (Having effectively forced her to leave for America after evicting her from her home and subjecting her to a trumped-up charge of falsifying her asylum papers, those who came up with this formula can be congratulated on the ingenuity of their sanctimoniousness.) The essential cowardice and hypocrisy of the maneuver is easily summarized: the cost of the protection is said to be too great, but it nevertheless can be borne, yet only if she continues to live in Holland, which has already said that it doesn't want her. Mr. Pecksniff himself could hardly have formulated it better.

Alas, this parochialism and provinciality is not solely a Dutch affair. Across the intellectual spectrum of the West, voices are raised to say that the problem is not the exorbitant demands made by Muslim bullies (which have recently included death threats against Danish cartoonists, announcements by Islamic taxi drivers that they will not carry "unclean" guide dogs for blind people, and a successful claim by a Muslim policeman in London that he should be exempt from guarding the embassy of Israel). No, the problem is that of people like Ayaan, who upset and "offend" the "faith community" of Islam. Let us be absolutely clear and state that this objection on their part is not to what she says, but to her very existence. To that extent, then, we ought to recognize that it is in the final analysis an objection to our existence, too.

It is very often said that we should not judge religion by the actions of its fringe extremists. This fair-seeming advice has led to the promotion of a new school of Muslim "moderates," most notably Tariq Ramadan, who have come to expect (and to receive) considerable deference from Western intellectuals. However, let us take just one aspect of Ayaan's case and see how well the "moderate" interpretation holds up. One reason why she herself is so hated, and why her life is considered forfeit, is that she is exactly what the title of this book proudly proclaims her to be: an apostate. She has exerted her right to abandon the religion in which she was brought up. But an immediate problem here presents itself. The Muslim *hadith,* which have canonical status along with the Quran, state plainly that the punishment for apostasy is death. In textual matters, embarrassed religious revisionists sometimes take refuge in metaphor or in variant readings of scriptural scholarship, but even that evasive tactic isn't available in this case. The injunction says what it says, no more and no less. The "fundamentalists," in other words, have the religious law on their side. I once had the chance to ask Tariq Ramadan what he thought of this, and he replied that in his view the killing of apostates was "unimplementable." *Unimplementable?* That may well—given the fast-growing number of ex-Muslims—be so. But the morally lazy term does not seem to carry anything much by way of, say, condemnation. (In another debate, this time with Nicolas Sarkozy before he became the president of France, Tariq Ramadan was induced to say that he thought the stoning of women for adultery should be subject to "a moratorium." In other words, Muslims might consider stopping it for a while.) So apparently Islam could suffer something worse than being judged by its extremists. It could, after all, be judged by its *moderates*.

Implied in all this dreary "dialogue," with its implication that Islam will reform itself very slowly, if at all, is the idea that in the meantime we must expect to adapt ourselves to its preachings and policies. There is another viewpoint that must be stated without equivocation: if Muslims want to immigrate to open and developed societies in order to better themselves, then it is *they* who must expect to do the adapting. We no longer allow Jews to run separate Orthodox courts in their communities, or permit Mormons to practice polygamy or racial discrimination or child marriage. That is the price of "inclusion," and a very reasonable one. The demand for special consideration for Islamists—even to the extent of press censorship, where they can claim "offense," and school segregation by sex, where they can invoke tradition—is the demand not to extend our multicultural and polyethnic culture, but rather the demand to *negate* it. Are we to admit to membership of the societal mosaic those who scream with hatred against immodest women, Jews, homosexuals, and Hindus (and this is not to exhaust the list)? If so, then we are knowingly admitting enemies on the same footing as friends. Relativism has no right to make such an exorbitant demand.

Enormous credit, then, should go to Ayaan Hirsi Ali, who worked these great questions out for herself in a crucible of personal experience. She is much wiser than many thousands of apologetic academics and pundits, and she is also, I want to say, much more tolerant and much more humane. It is impossible to imagine her disliking someone on the mere grounds of origin or faith, just as it is impossible to imagine her being reconciled to any dogma that forms its calcified opinion on that basis. To invoke Immanuel Kant's principle of universality, we might be able to say with a high degree of confidence that the world would be a better place if *her* ethos was to be the determining one. Can we say the same for those who play the dull game of temporizing, compromising, affectless moral equivalence? We are unlikely to arrive at a time when examples of individual moral courage and intellectual honesty are not the clue to a larger scheme of liberty. As long as we continue to value these qualities, *Infidel* will count as a rebuke to all those who claim to see no difference between secular civilization and clerical barbarism, and as an inspiration to all those who view this confrontation without apology as the defining struggle of our time.

Christopher Hitchens

Introduction

One November morning in 2004, Theo van Gogh got up to go to work at his film production company in Amsterdam. He took out his old black bicycle and headed down a main road. Waiting in a doorway was a Moroccan man with a handgun and two butcher knives.

As Theo cycled down the Linnaeusstraat, Muhammad Bouyeri approached. He pulled out his gun and shot Theo several times. Theo fell off his bike and lurched across the road, then collapsed. Bouyeri followed. Theo begged, "Can't we talk about this?" but Bouyeri shot him four more times. Then he took out one of his butcher knives and sawed into Theo's throat. With the other knife, he stabbed a five-page letter onto Theo's chest.

The letter was addressed to me.

Two months before, Theo and I had made a short film together. We called it *Submission, Part 1*. I intended one day to make *Part 2*. (Theo warned me that he would work on *Part 2* only if I accepted some humor in it!) *Part 1* was about defiance—about Muslim women who shift from total submission to God to a dialogue with their deity. They pray, but instead of casting down their eyes, these women look up, at Allah, with the words of the Quran tattooed on their skin. They tell Him honestly that if submission to Him brings them so much misery, and He remains silent, they may stop submitting.

There is the woman who is flogged for committing adultery; another who is given in marriage to a man she loathes; another who is beaten by her husband on a regular basis; and another who is shunned by her father when he learns that his brother raped her. Each abuse is justified by the perpetrators in the name of God, citing the Quran verses now written on the bodies of the women. These women stand for hundreds of thousands of Muslim women around the world.

* * *

Theo and I knew it was a dangerous film to make. But Theo was a valiant man—he was a warrior, however unlikely that might seem. He was also very Dutch, and no nation in the world is more deeply attached to freedom of expression than the Dutch. The suggestion that he remove his name from the film's credits for security reasons made Theo angry. He told me once, "If I can't put my name on my own film, in Holland, then Holland isn't Holland any more, and I am not me."

People ask me if I have some kind of death wish, to keep saying the things I do. The answer is no: I would like to keep living. However, some things must be said, and there are times when silence becomes an accomplice to injustice.

This is the story of my life. It is a subjective record of my own personal memories, as close to accurate as I can make them; my relationship with the rest of my family has been so fractured that I cannot now refresh these recollections by asking them for help. It is the story of what I have experienced, what I've seen, and why I think the way I do. I've come to see that it is useful, and maybe even important, to tell this story. I want to make a few things clear, set a certain number of records straight, and also tell people about another kind of world and what it's really like.

I was born in Somalia. I grew up in Somalia, in Saudi Arabia, in Ethiopia, and in Kenya. I came to Europe in 1992, when I was twenty-two, and became a member of Parliament in Holland. I made a movie with Theo, and now I live with bodyguards and armored cars. In April 2006 a Dutch court ordered that I leave my safe-home that I was renting from the State. The judge concluded that my neighbors had a right to argue that they felt unsafe because of my presence in the building. I had already decided to move to the United States before the debate surrounding my Dutch citizenship erupted.

This book is dedicated to my family, and also to the millions and millions of Muslim women who have had to submit.

PART I

My Childhood

CHAPTER 1

Bloodlines

"Who are you?"

"I am Ayaan, the daughter of Hirsi, the son of Magan."

I am sitting with my grandmother on a grass mat under the talal tree. Behind us is our house, and the branches of the talal tree are all that shields us from the sun blazing down on the white sand. "Go on," my grandmother says, glaring at me.

"And Magan was the son of Isse."

"And then?"

"Isse was the son of Guleid, was the son of Ali. Was the son of Wai'ays. Was the son of Muhammad. Ali. Umar." I hesitate for a moment. "Osman. Mahamud." I catch my breath, proud of myself.

"Bah?" asks my grandmother. "Which consort?"

"Bah Ya'qub, Garab-Sare." I name the most powerful of Osman Mahamud's wives: daughter of Ya'qub, she of the highest shoulder.

My grandmother nods, grudgingly. I have done well, for a five-year-old. I have managed to count my forefathers back for three hundred years—the part that is crucially important. Osman Mahamud is the name of my father's subclan, and thus my own. It is where I belong, who I am.

Later, as I grow up, my grandmother will coax and even beat me to learn my father's ancestry eight hundred years back, to the beginning of the great clan of the Darod. I am a Darod, a Harti, a Macherten, an Osman Mahamud. I am of the consort called the Higher Shoulder. I am a Magan.

"Get it right," my grandmother warns, shaking a switch at me. "The names will make you strong. They are your bloodline. If you honor them they will keep you alive. If you dishonor them you will be forsaken. You will be nothing. You will lead a wretched life and die alone. Do it again."

*   *   *

Somali children must memorize their lineage: this is more important than almost anything. Whenever a Somali meets a stranger, they ask each other, "Who are you?" They trace back their separate ancestries until they find a common forefather.

If you share a grandfather, perhaps even an eighth great-grandfather, with a Somali, the two of you are bound together as cousins. You are members of the great family that forms a clan. You offer each other food and hospitality. Although a child belongs to the clan of his father, it may be useful to remember the details of your mother's bloodline, too, in case you travel and need a stranger's help.

So, though the sweat pearled down our backs on those long afternoons, my big brother, Mahad, and I learned to chant, in unison, the names of both our lineages. Later, my grandmother began teaching my little sister, Haweya, to do the same, but she never got as far with her. Haweya was quick and bright, but she sat still even less often than Mahad and I.

The truth is that this ancestral knowledge seemed pointless to us modern children, brought up in concrete houses, with hard roofs, behind fixed, fenced walls. Mostly we pranced off, dodging the sharp smacks my grandmother aimed at our legs with the switches that she broke off our tree. We would rather climb the tree and play in its branches.

Above all, we loved listening to my grandmother's stories while my mother cooked over a charcoal brazier and we lay, on a mat, under our tree. These stories never came when we begged for them. They arrived by surprise. My grandmother would be weaving a mat, muttering to herself, and suddenly we would realize that the muttering had turned into a fairy tale.

"There was once a young nomad who married a beautiful wife, and they had a son," my grandmother would begin. The three of us knew to settle down instantly and pretend to be occupied with something; the slightest interruption could break her mood, and she would growl at us and go back to weaving the thin strips of dried grass that she sewed night and day into large, elaborate matting.

"The rains didn't come, so the nomad set out to walk across the desert, looking for pasture where he could settle with his family. Almost as soon as he began walking he came upon a patch of green young grass. On it was a hut made of strong branches, covered with freshly woven mats and swept clean.

"The hut was empty. The man went back to his wife and told her that after just one day of walking, he had found the perfect place. But two days later, when he returned to the pasture with his wife and baby, they found a stranger standing in the doorway of the hut. This stranger was not tall, but he was thickly built, and he had very white teeth and smooth skin."

Haweya would shiver with pleasure, and I with fear.

"The stranger said, 'You have a wife and child. Take the house, you're welcome to it,' and he smiled. The young nomad thought this stranger was remarkably friendly, and thanked him; he invited the stranger to visit any time. But the wife felt uncomfortable around the stranger. The baby, too, cried as soon as he cast eyes on this man.

"That night an animal sneaked into their hut and stole the baby out of his bed. The man had eaten well and slept heavily; he heard nothing. Such misfortune. The stranger visited the nomad and his wife to tell them of his sorrow. But when he spoke, the wife noticed that there were tiny pieces of red meat between his teeth, and one of those strong white teeth was just a little bit broken.

"The man stayed on with the couple in the house. For a whole year, the grass stayed green and the rains came, so there was no reason to move on. The wife had another baby in that hut, another beautiful son. But again, when the child was barely one season old, an animal came in the night and grabbed the baby in its jaws. This time the child's father ran after the creature, but he was too slow to catch up.

"The third time, the nomad caught up with the creature, and struggled with it, but the animal overpowered him. Again, it ate the baby! Finally, after her third baby was eaten, the wife told the nomad she would leave him. So now that stupid nomad had lost everything!

"So what have you learned?" my grandmother would shout at us. We knew the answer. That nomad had been lazy. He had taken the first pasture he found, even though there had to be something wrong with it. He had been stupid: he had failed to read the signs, the signals, which the baby and the woman had instinctively felt. The stranger was really He Who Rubs Himself with a Stick, the monstrous being who transforms himself into a hyena and devours children. We had spotted it. The nomad had been slow of mind, slow of limb, weak in strength and valor. He deserved to lose everything.

My grandmother's stories could be chilling. There were stories about an ugly old witch woman whose name was People Slayer or People Butcher, who had the power to transform herself, to adopt the face of someone you liked and respected, and who at the last minute lunged at you, laughing in your face, HAHAHAHAHA, before she slaughtered you with a long sharp knife that she had been hiding under the folds of her robe all along and then ate you up. My grandmother told us tales from when she was young, of the bands of fighters who raided the desert, stealing animals and women, burning settlements. She told us about all the unrecorded disasters of her life and her parents' lives: the pandemics of plague and malaria and drought that left whole regions barren of life.

She told us also about her life. The good times, when the rains came and made everything green, when streams of water suddenly raced through the dried riverbeds and there was milk and meat in abundance. She tried to teach us how that led to decadence: how when the grass grows green, herders become lazy and children grow fat. How men and women mix, in singing and drumming at twilight, and how that erodes their watchfulness, so that they fail to spot danger. Such mingling, she warned us, leads to competition, conflict, disaster.

Sometimes in my grandmother's stories there were brave women— mothers, like my mother—who used their cunning and their courage to save their children from danger. This made us feel safe, in a way. My grandmother, and my mother, too, were brave and clever: they would surely be able to save us when our time came to face the monsters.

In Somalia, little children learn quickly to be alert to betrayal. Things are not always what they seem; even a small slip can be fatal. The moral of every one of my grandmother's stories rested on our honor. We must be strong, clever, suspicious; we must obey the rules of the clan.

Suspicion is good, especially if you are a girl. For girls can be taken, or they may yield. And if a girl's virginity is despoiled, she not only obliterates her own honor, she also damages the honor of her father, uncles, brothers, male cousins. There is nothing worse than to be the agent of such catastrophe.

Even though we loved her stories, mostly we ignored my grandmother. She herded us around, much as she did the goats that she would tether to our tree, but we were more unruly. Stories and squabbles were our pastimes; I don't think I even saw a toy till I was eight and we had moved to Saudi Arabia. We pestered each other. Haweya and Mahad ganged up on me, or Haweya and I ganged up on Mahad. But my brother and I never did anything as a team. We hated each other. My grandmother always said this was because I was born just one year after Mahad: I stole Ma's lap from him.

We had no father, because our father was in prison.
I had no memory of him at all.

Most of the adults I knew grew up in the deserts of Somalia. The eastern-most country in Africa and one of the poorest, Somalia juts into the Indian Ocean, cradling the tip of the Arabian peninsula like a protective hand before dropping down the coast to Kenya. My family were nomads who moved constantly through the northern and northeastern deserts to find pasture for their herds. They would settle sometimes, for a season or two; when there was no longer enough water and pasture, or if the rains failed, they picked up their hut and stacked their mats onto camels and walked, trying to find somewhere better, to keep their herds alive.

My grandmother learned to weave dried grass so tight you could carry water for miles in one of her pitchers. She could make her own small domed house out of bent boughs and woven mats, then dismantle it and load it onto a nasty-tempered transport camel.

When my grandmother was about ten years old, her father, an Isaq herder, died. Her mother married her uncle. (This is a common practice. It saves a dowry and trouble.) When my grandmother was about thirteen, that uncle received a proposal for my grandmother's hand from a wealthy nomad named Artan, who was about forty years old. Artan was a Dhulbahante, which was a good bloodline of the Darod. He was widely respected, skilled with animals, and a good navigator: he could read his environment so well that he always knew when to move and where to go to find rain. Other clan members came to him to arbitrate their disputes.

Artan was already married, but he and his wife had only one child, a daughter who was a little younger than my grandmother. When he decided to take another wife, Artan first chose the father of the bride: he must be a man from a good clan, with a decent reputation. The girl must be hardworking, strong, young, and pure. My grandmother, Ibaado, was all that. Artan paid a bride price for her.

A few days after Artan married her and took her away, my grandmother bolted. She managed to walk almost all the way back to her mother's camp before Artan caught up with her. He agreed to let her rest for a bit with her mother, to recover. Then, after a week, her stepfather took her to Artan's camp and told her, "This is your destiny."

For the rest of her life, my grandmother was irreproachable in every way. She raised eight girls and one boy, and never was there a whisper of gossip about their virtue or their work. She instilled willpower and obedience and a sense of honor in her children. She grazed animals, fetched firewood, built fences of sticks laced with thorn branches. She had hard hands and a hard head, and when her husband hosted clan meetings in his role as a clan arbiter, she kept her girls safely apart from the men and the singing and the drums. They could listen only from afar to the poetry competitions and watch as the men traded goods and tales. My grandmother showed no jealousy toward her older co-wife, though she stayed out of her way; when the older wife died, my grandmother tolerated the presence of her haughty stepdaughter, Khadija, the girl who was almost her own age.

Artan had nine daughters and a young wife. Guarding the honor of his women was of paramount importance. He kept them well away from any other nomads, roaming for weeks to find a place with pasture and no young men. They navigated endlessly through the remotest deserts. As we sat under the talal tree outside our house in Mogadishu, my grandmother often told us about the beautiful emptiness of sitting in front of a hut she had built with her own hands, staring into the vast, neverending space.

In a sense, my grandmother was living in the Iron Age. There was no system of writing among the nomads. Metal artifacts were rare and precious. The British and Italians claimed to be ruling Somalia, but this would have meant nothing to my grandmother. To her there were only the clans: the great nomad clans of the Isaq and the Darod, the lesser Hawiye farmers, and, lower still, the inferior Sab. The first time she saw a white person my grandmother was in her thirties: she thought this person's skin had burned off.

My mother, Asha, was born sometime in the early 1940s, along with her identical twin sister, Halimo. My grandmother gave birth to them alone, under a tree. They were her third and fourth children; she was about eighteen, leading her goats and sheep to pasture when she felt the pains. She lay down and bore forth; then she cut the umbilical cords with her knife. A few hours later, she gathered together the goats and sheep and managed to bring the herd home safely before dark, carrying her newborn twins. Nobody was impressed by the exploit: she was only bringing home two more girls.

To my grandmother, feelings were a foolish self-indulgence. Pride was important, though—pride in your work, and your strength—and self-reliance. If you were weak, people would speak ill of you. If your thorn fences were not strong enough, your animals would be raided by lions, hyenas, and foxes, your husband would marry another, your daughters' virginity would be stolen, and your sons seen as worthless.

In her eyes, we were useless children. Bred in a cement-block house with a hard roof, we had no skills of value. We walked on roadways; the road in front of our house wasn't paved, but still, it was a marked passage in the dirt. We had water from a tap. We could never have found our way home after herding animals through the desert; we couldn't even milk a goat without getting kicked over.

My grandmother reserved particular scorn for me. I was terrified of insects, so in her eyes I was a truly stupid child. By the time her daughters were five or six, my grandmother had already taught them every major skill they would need to survive. I lacked all of them.

My mother told us stories, too. She had learned to care for her family's animals, and herded them through the desert to places that were safe. The goats were easy prey for a predator; so was a young girl. If my mother or her sisters were attacked by men out in the desert it would be their own fault: they should have fled at the first sight of an unknown camel. If they were ever captured they were to say, three times, "Allah be my witness, I want no conflict with you. Please leave me alone." To be raped would be far worse than dying, because it would tarnish the honor of everyone in their family.

If the invocation to Allah had no effect, my grandmother taught her daughters to run around behind a man, squat down, reach between his legs under his sarong, and yank his testicles hard. They were not to let go. He might hit or kick, but they were to tuck in their heads and take the blows on their backs and hope to hang on long enough to cause the attacker to faint. This move is called *Qworegoys,* and the women of my grandmother's family taught it to their daughters just as they taught them to make thorn-bush fences to protect the hut from hyenas.

I remember one afternoon when Haweya and I were small children, watching my grandmother rubbing sheep fat into a long coil of woven rope before she steeped it in the plant dye that would make it hard and black.

"A woman alone is like a piece of sheep fat in the sun," she told us. "Everything will come and feed on that fat. Before you know it, the ants and insects are crawling all over it, until there is nothing left but a smear of grease." My grandmother pointed to a gobbet of fat melting in the sun, just beyond the talal tree's shadow. It was black with ants and gnats. For years, this image inhabited my nightmares.

When my mother was a child, she was always dutiful, always obedient. But as she grew up, the world began changing. The old traditions of the nomads were shifting as modern life lured them to villages and cities. And so, when she was about fifteen years old, my mother walked out of the desert. She left her parents and her older sisters and even her twin sister behind her, and began walking. Then she got on a truck and went to the port city of Berbera, and she took a ship across the Red Sea, to Arabia.

Khadija had preceded her. Khadija was her older stepsister, the child of her father's first wife. Another of my mother's older sisters made the trip, too. I don't know what led them to do it; my mother rarely confided her private emotions. But it was the 1950s, and modern life was jabbing its sharp elbows into the farthest parts of the world. My mother was young, after all, and I think perhaps she simply didn't want to be left behind in the desert when all the young people had left for the city.

My mother went to Aden, where Khadija had already settled: a big city, a center of Britain's colonial rule over the Middle East. She got a job cleaning house for a British woman. She learned about forks and chairs and bathtubs and cleaning brushes. She loved the strict rituals—cleaning, folding, ironing—and the elaborate paraphernalia of settled life. My mother became even more scrupulously attentive about such matters than the woman she worked for.

Although she was alone in Aden, without parental supervision, my mother was supremely virtuous. She was determined that nobody would ever have grounds to gossip that she, Asha Artan, had behaved improperly. She never took a taxi or a bus for fear of being seated beside a strange man. She shunned the Somali men who chewed *qat* and the girls who brewed tea for them and joked around as the buzzy euphoria of the short, fat little leaves got them talking and laughing. Instead, in Aden, my mother learned to pray in the proper Islamic manner.

Living in the desert, my grandmother had never really had the time to pray. Among the nomads, women weren't expected to. It was men who spread their prayer mats on the sand five times a day and faced Mecca, chanting the Quran. But now, on the Arabian peninsula, where the Prophet Muhammad received Allah's revelation, my mother learned the ritual ablutions. She learned to cover herself with a plain cloth and pray—

standing, sitting, prostrating, turning right and left: the ballet of submission to Allah.

In the desert, nomad women were not covered. They *worked,* and it is hard to work under a long veil. While my grandmother herded and cooked, she draped herself in a roughly woven long cloth, the *goh,* leaving her arms, hair, and neck bare. In my grandmother's day, men were commonly present while women breast-fed their children; if there was anything arousing about seeing a few inches of female flesh, the men never showed it.

My mother had no protector in Aden—no father, no brother. Men leered and bothered her on the street. She began wearing a veil, like the Arab women who robed when they left their houses in a long black cloth that left only a slit for their eyes. The veil protected her from those leering men, and from the feeling of vileness it gave her to be looked at that way. Her veil was an emblem of her belief. To be beloved of God, you had to be modest, and Asha Artan wanted to be the most proper, most virtuous woman in the city.

One day my grandfather Artan came to Aden. He told my mother that he had received a request for her hand in marriage and had accepted. My mother was about eighteen; she could not defy her father. So she stayed silent. A virgin's silence is the proper answer to a marriage proposal; it signifies a dignified consent.

So my mother married this man, whose name was Ahmed, although she disliked him on sight: he was too short and too dark, and he smoked, which to her was as bad as chewing *qat.* Ahmed was a Darod, as she was, and of the Harti, too, like her; but instead of being a nomad Dhulbahante, like my mother, he was a trader, a Wersengeli. My mother therefore looked down on this man, although he was wealthy.

This Wersengeli man moved my mother to Kuwait, where she was mistress of a big house with a tile floor, hot running water, and electricity. The first thing my mother did was fire all the maids: nobody could clean the house well enough for Asha Artan. She set about creating an exemplary household. She had a son and called him Muhammad, after the Prophet, the proper name for an oldest boy.

Then her father, who was an old man now, died, and my mother did something extremely surprising: she told her husband that she wanted a divorce.

Of course, my mother had no right to a divorce under Muslim law. The only way she could have claimed one was if her husband had been impotent or left her completely indigent. All the members of her clan in Kuwait told her she was being ridiculous. Her husband was wealthy, and although he could have afforded several wives, he came home to her every night. What more could she want? If she divorced, my mother would be used goods—no longer a virgin. And besides, they argued, she would get a reputation that she was not *baarri*.

A woman who is *baarri* is like a pious slave. She honors her husband's family and feeds them without question or complaint. She never whines or makes demands of any kind. She is strong in service, but her head is bowed. If her husband is cruel, if he rapes her and then taunts her about it, if he decides to take another wife, or beats her, she lowers her gaze and hides her tears. And she works hard, faultlessly. She is a devoted, welcoming, well-trained work animal. This is *baarri*.

If you are a Somali woman you must learn to tell yourself that God is just and all-knowing and will reward you in the Hereafter. Meanwhile, everyone who knows about your patience and endurance will applaud your father and mother on the excellence of your upbringing. Your brothers will be grateful to you for preserving their honor. They will boast to other families about your heroic submission. And perhaps, eventually, your husband's family will appreciate your obedience, and your husband may one day treat you as a fellow human being.

If in the process of being *baarri* you feel grief, humiliation, fatigue, or a sense of everlasting exploitation, you hide it. If you long for love and comfort, you pray in silence to Allah to make your husband more bearable. Prayer is your strength. Nomadic mothers must try to give their daughters this skill and strength called *baarri*.

For years, my ma had been perfect. Her virtue had been legendary, her work habits impeccable. Partly it was her nature: my mother found strength and comfort in clear-cut rules and the dead certainty that if she were good, she would go to Paradise. I think, though, that she also feared her father might curse her if she disobeyed. A father's curse is the worst thing that can happen to you, a ticket straight to Hell.

But after her father died, my mother defied her husband. She turned away from him with the full force of the scorn she had stored up for so long. She refused even to speak to him. Finally, he agreed not to contest her claim for a divorce. The Kuwaiti judge granted her seven more years with her son. When he was ten, Muhammad would return to live with his father; till then, my mother was permitted to bring up her son alone.

When my mother was growing up, Somalia didn't exist. Although all the clans spoke the same language, albeit different dialects, they mostly lived in separate territories and saw themselves as distinct. The territory that is now Somalia was divided between the British and the Italians, who occupied the country as colonizers, splitting it in two. In 1960 the colonists left, leaving behind them a brand-new, independent state. A unified nation was born.

This new country, Somalia, had a democracy, a president, a flag, an army, even its own currency: sepia banknotes with dignified portraits of farm animals and people working in fields, like no scene my mother had ever witnessed. People who had always lived deep in the rural areas began streaming to the country's new capital, which the colonizers called Mogadishu. They thrilled to the idea of building one nation, great and powerful. So many hopes would be dashed in the coming years by the clan infighting, the corruption and violence into which the country, like so much of Africa, fell. But my mother couldn't have guessed what would happen, so, like so many others, she packed her bags, took her son and the dowry her husband had given her when she married him, and returned to Somalia, to Mogadishu, the capital, where she had never been.

For the rest of her life my grandmother berated my mother for this decision. Mogadishu was not Darod land. It was not even Isaq. It was deep in Hawiye territory, where my mother didn't belong. My grandmother always said that my mother's ex-husband must have cursed her, causing this foolhardy choice. Or maybe a djinn was let loose by my mother's bare-faced defiance of the marriage made for her by her father. My grandmother hated the hard cement houses, the narrow streets, the lack of a horizon in Mogadishu, and she hated knowing that her family was no longer safe in the Darod lands in the north. But once again, my mother departed from the traditions of her parents. And once again, she was following her half-sister, Khadija Artan, who had settled in Mogadishu with her husband.

Khadija was a striking woman, as tall as my mother and just as lean. She had taut, angular features, hawklike eyes, and a domineering manner. Her voice was powerful and her gestures dignified and elaborate. My grandmother loathed her. Khadija was bold; she wore long Western dresses that went down to her ankles but were held slim against her body with zips and buttons. She also draped cloth of the rural *goh* and the urban *dirha* around her. But Khadija's *goh*s and *dirha*s were made of the choicest fabrics, expensive silks and chiffon instead of the basic cottons, and the way she wore them made other women seem clumsy and inadequate. Khadija held her hair high in a turban of cloth. She was modern. She was ecstatic about independence, the politics, and nightly discussions on the street. She positively bustled with self-importance through the new capital city.

Although she was married (and well married, too), Khadija was barren: a terrible destiny. Some people said it was because she was a witch and strong-willed. My grandmother muttered that it was a curse for disobedience and waywardness. If there was a curse, Khadija managed to ignore it.

Khadija counseled my mother to buy a plot of land opposite a trucking business owned by her husband's oldest son by a previous wife. It was a new neighborhood, and now that Mogadishu had become the capital, Darod had begun moving in there. This area, Hoden, was cleaner and healthier than the center of town, where the graceful old Italian buildings were surrounded by filthy, densely packed streets. The roads were unpaved in our neighborhood, and not many houses had electricity; our house never did. But Ma bought the land. She moved into Khadija's place and began planning to build her own house.

My mother's idea of a house emerged in fits and starts, as materials became available. There were just two big rooms, with whitewashed cinder-block walls and a cement floor. The area in front of the main door was also cement; the rest was sand. Building this house took a long time. Everything was painted white, except the doors and shutters, which were green, the color my mother felt was appropriate for a proper Muslim door. The cooking fire was outside, under an awning, beside a tall talal tree, where a man might spread his mat in the shade on a hot afternoon.

Khadija was a busybody, always directing other people's destinies and arranging marriages. My mother was young, and she didn't have much to do; it would not have been proper for her to work. Khadija suggested that she leave little Muhammad with her and go out, perhaps attend a literacy class. A young man called Hirsi Magan had just returned from a university in America, and he was teaching ordinary people in Mogadishu to read and write.

That young man, Hirsi Magan, would become my father. When I was little, he was like a hero in a fable to me, only a little more real than my grandmother's werewolves. My father's older sister, Aunt Hawo Magan, used to come to our house and tell us stories about him, how he grew up in the northern desert. Their father, Magan, had been a legendary warrior. His name meant "The Protector"—or more specifically, "The Protector of those he conquered". Magan was an Osman Mahamud, from the Darod subclan that always claimed the right to conquer and rule over other peoples. Magan had fought for King Boqor, who ruled the Macherten lands near the sea, and then around 1890 he switched allegiance to Boqor's rival, Kenaidiid, who was a younger man and more eager to wage war and lead raids. (Boqor, Magan, and Kenaidiid were all cousins.)

Kenaidiid and Magan led their warriors through the southern lands of Senag and Mudug, which were occupied by smaller clans, including many Hawiye. The Hawiye were passive people, mostly farmers, and they had no army. Magan despised them. There is a story that he once had Hawiye villagers gather stones into a circle and then herded them inside it to be killed. Then he commanded his warriors to take the women and settle there, on Hawiye land, north of Mogadishu. According to my grandmother, the Hawiye in the Mudug region never forgot the name of Magan.

My father grew up in the northern desert, the son of Magan's last and youngest wife. She was twelve or thirteen when she married the old warrior, who was close to seventy. My father was Magan's youngest son, and the old man doted on him. When Magan died, my father was raised by his older brothers, some so old they already had grandchildren. They took him riding across the desert almost before he could walk.

Magan's sons were rich and powerful traders and warriors. My father grew up well cared for—bright, self-assured, pampered. He became friends with an older man, Osman Yusuf Kenaidiid, the grandson of the Kenaidiid whom his father had served. Magan had always mocked this man; he was quiet and covered his mouth with a cloth, because words are not something you should waste; they should come out of deep prior reflection.

Eloquence, the use of fine language, is admired in Somalia; the work of great poets is praised and memorized for miles around their villages, sometimes for generations. But few poets or people had ever written down any Somali words. The schools the colonizers had left behind were simply too few to educate a nation that now consisted of millions of people.

Osman Yusuf Kenaidiid was learned. He had invented a script to write down the sounds of the Somali language for the first time. People called it Osmaniya. It was slanted and curly and ingenious, and my father set about learning it.

Osman was a good tutor, and he had many connections with the Italian colonists who ruled southern Somalia. My father, his protégé, began attending a school in Mogadishu, the Italians' colonial capital. He joined the Somali Youth League and had heated discussions about the future, when the colonial powers who ruled over the great Somali nation could be cast off and one country formed, to dazzle Africa. He learned Italian, and even went to study in Rome for a period: this was a rare opportunity for a Somali, but Magan's descendents were wealthy. He married a woman, Maryan Farah, from the Marehan subclan of the Darod.

Then my father decided to attend college in the United States: Columbia University, in New York. He was inspired by America. He used to say, "If they can achieve what they have after only two hundred years, then we Somalis, with our endurance and our resilience—we can make America in Africa." My father insisted that his wife, Maryan, join him, and she began studying there, too. Their infant daughter, Arro, born in 1965, was left behind in Somalia with her grandmother.

When he graduated from Columbia with a degree in anthropology, he returned to Somalia, like many other privileged young men, to help shape the future of their nation. Maryan had failed her course; he required that she stay in America until she completed it. It seemed only natural to him to proceed to the new nation's capital, Mogadishu.

My father thought that if a bold new nation were to be established, then the people must become literate. He started a campaign to teach people to read and write. To set an example, he himself went to teach in one of the classes.

In Somalia, language is precious. It is all that binds the warring clans into what passes for a single nation. People flocked to Hirsi Magan's literacy class in Mogadishu. He was dark-skinned, long-nosed, with a high forehead; my father had the charm of a rather intellectual crooner. Though he was not tall, he had a presence. People loved to be around him; all his life, they listened to him with respect.

My mother was a graceful, clever poet in her own right, and became one of his best students. She learned quickly. One day she even dared to contest the way her teacher pronounced a Somali word, flicking back her shawl with haughty disdain. It was daring of her, and surprising. She was beautiful, too, slim and tall, with a back as straight as a young tree.

My father was attracted to my mother's clever tongue and her inflexible opinions. The attraction was mutual, and, of course, Khadija encouraged them.

My parents married in 1966. My mother knew that my father was still married to his first wife, Maryan. But Maryan was in New York, and my father did not inform her of his new bride. Maryan learned of it when she returned to Somalia, of course. I don't know precisely when that was.

There was always a strong electricity between my father and mother. They teased each other, challenged each other. In a culture that disapproved of choosing your own partner, they chose each other: their bond was strong.

In October 1968 my brother, Mahad, was born. My parents finished building the house on the land my mother had bought in Mogadishu, and moved in, bringing with them my older stepbrother, Muhammad, who was six. My mother quickly became pregnant again, with me, and my grandmother came to Mogadishu from the desert to help her through the last few months of pregnancy.

My father was bold, learned, popular, born to rule. He ran for Parliament from the northern town of Qardho but lost the election. He spent vast amounts of his own money funding literacy campaigns and invested in a sugar factory. He was involved in a project to build a dam in the north so people could have water all year round, instead of watching the river drain away into cracks in the sand.

On October 21, 1969, the government was overthrown in a coup. Twenty-three days later I was born, on November 13, six weeks too early and weighing a little more than three pounds. Perhaps my parents were happy. My father must have dandled me on his knee from time to time; I don't remember. Mahad says he can remember our father from those days, but they are only glancing recollections: Father was so often out of the house.

My sister, Haweya, was born in May 1971. A few months after that, my father's first wife, Maryan Farah, gave birth to my stepsister, Ijaabo. There was some sort of dispute, and my father and Maryan divorced. And then, in April 1972, when I was two years old, my father was taken away. He was put in the worst place in Mogadishu: the old Italian prison they called The Hole.

CHAPTER 2

Under the Talal Tree

I used to try to imagine my father when I was little. My mother, when I asked her, only told me that we had never met. *Afwayne,* who was a real monster, not like the kind in grandmother's stories, had put my father in jail. *Afwayne,* Big Mouth, was what everyone called the president, Siad Barré. There were huge portraits of him in every shop and every public space in Mogadishu; he had a huge mouth, with big, long teeth. Sometimes *Afwayne*'s special police burst into houses and took people away. They tortured them into admitting something terrible, then they killed them. Even I knew that. The adults in my house all went suddenly still when we heard the executioner's rifle in Tribunka Square.

Siad Barré had become the vice commander of Somalia's army at the time of Independence, in 1960, and later became an advocate of Marxism after training with Soviet officers. He was a Marehan, a small subclan of the Darod, and of very humble background. The exact circumstances of the coup are not very well known; it's not clear whether Barré ordered the assassination of the president, or whether he simply took power in the aftermath of the president's assassination. His regime was a classic Soviet client state, with a single party, single trade union, a women's organization, and young pioneer groups. A great deal of money was spent on weaponry rather than on development, but still, there was a conscious investment in schools, whether to educate children to adore the regime or simply to educate them.

Every night till I was six, as my mother stood over the charcoal brazier, we children knelt in a semicircle and begged Allah to free our father. At the time, this didn't make an enormous amount of sense. My mother never took the time to really tell us about God; he just *was,* and he minded the prayers of little children most of all. But although I tried my best to pray hard, it didn't seem to be working. When I asked Ma why Allah hadn't set my father free yet, she just urged us to pray more.

Our mother could visit our father in prison, but only my brother, Mahad, was allowed to go with her. Haweya and I had to stay at home with Grandma. We were too little to go out with my mother, and we were girls; Mahad, in every way, came first. Our brother was always angry when he came back from these visits, and my mother made him promise not to tell us anything about them: we might stupidly let some information out, and the secret police might hear.

Once, as he was walking out of the jail with my mother, Mahad attacked the huge cardboard portrait of *Afwayne* hung at the entrance. He must have been about six. "He was throwing stones at it and yelling," Ma told my grandmother when she came home that night. "Thank Allah, the prison guard was from our clan." Ma sounded as if she couldn't help admiring Mahad's warrior spirit. But the guard could have accused her of teaching her son to oppose the government, to be an "anti." I knew that were it not for Allah and the protection of the clan, Haweya and I could have been sitting alone under the tree that night with my grandmother, begging Allah to free our mother and brother from prison, too.

Allah was a mystery to me. One of my first memories, from when I was perhaps three years old, is of watching my grandmother engaged in an inexplicable performance. She was crouching facedown on a mat in her bedroom with her nose on the floor. I thought that she was playing some kind of game with me, so I pranced around and made faces at her, poking. She ignored me, and continued bending up and down, muttering things that sounded maddeningly strange. I couldn't understand it. Finally, when she had finished, she turned around to me with a very scary look on her face. "Bastard child!" she cursed, hitting me and biting my arms. "Let Almighty Allah take you away! May you never even *smell* Paradise!"

My cousin Sanyar, the thirteen-year-old daughter of my mother's twin, extricated me from my grandmother's fierce grasp and took me outside. Sanyar helped my grandmother look after us when Ma was out. She was kind and explained that I had disturbed my grandmother in prayer, which was like talking to God, the most important moment of an adult's life.

I was startled: I knew for sure there had been nobody but Grandma and me in that room. But Sanyar said I was too little to understand. When I grew up, I would feel Allah's presence.

*   *   *

My grandmother's vision of the universe was complex. A whole cosmology of magical entities existed alongside the one God, Allah. Djinns, who could be male or female, lived in an intermediate sphere adjoining ours and could be counted on to bring misfortune and disease. The souls of wise men and dead ancestors could also intercede with God on your behalf.

Another afternoon, when we were a little older, Haweya and I were fooling around under the talal tree when we heard Grandma talking. She had taken to her bed, suffering from some bout of pain, and we knew better than to disturb her. We crept over to the door of the room to listen.

"Dear forefathers, let me go," Grandma said in a choking voice.

There was no reply. Then came a thump.

"Abokor, let me go." Thump.

"Hassan, let me go." Thump.

"Dear forefathers, let me go."

Haweya and I were consumed with curiosity. We wanted to see these people. We opened the door, slowly. Grandma was lying on her back dressed in beautiful glittering clothes, as if it were the Ied festival. The room was full of the scent of smoldering frankincense, and she was hitting her chest with her hands, following each blow with the choked pleading. "Dear forefathers, let me go," she gasped, as if she were being strangled.

Puzzled, we looked about. There was no one in the room, nothing that remotely resembled a forefather—not that we had ever seen one. I pushed Haweya back and shut the door as silently as I could, but we were mystified. A few days later, we began to act out the scene. We lay next to one another in bed and begged our imagined forefathers to let us go, in choking voices. Grandma burst into the room, followed by Ma.

"May you burn in Hell!" Grandma screeched at us. "May the devil snatch you!" She chased us around the room and threatened to pack her bags and leave. Ma had to punish us. She needed Grandma. My mother was always out of the house—and this, too, was because of *Afwayne*.

Siad Barré introduced a police state in Somalia and also tried to set up a pretend economy. He allied with the Soviet Union, so Somalia had to become a communist country. In practice, for ordinary families, this meant they had to wait in a series of long lines, for hours, under the merciless rays of the Mogadishu sun to receive limited amounts of basic food: flour, sugar, oil, sorghum, rice, and beans. There was no meat, no eggs or fruit, no vegetables, and no olive oil or butter. Any extras had to be smuggled on the black market.

Ma never told us when she was leaving on a trip. She was there, and suddenly she was gone, sometimes for weeks at a time. I discovered that there was a kind of pattern to her movements. My distant but somehow dependable mother would become miserable. "What should I do now, O Allah?" she would wail. "Alone with three children and an old woman. Do I deserve to be punished like this?" My Ma would cry, and my Grandma would speak to her comfortingly; I would climb onto her lap and pat her, which only made her cry more. Then she would disappear for a while to some far-off village, often traveling with one of her father's cousins, a trader who had long ago sold his camels, bought a truck, and now transported food to the city.

Sometimes I would see her coming home on the back of a truck, just after sunset. Men dragged in sacks of food: rice, flour, sugar, and aluminum jars filled with tiny pieces of camel meat soaked in lard with dates and garlic. These unloadings were quick and secretive and were practically the only times we came into contact with any men at all. We were told to say nothing about the food, which was stored under the beds—otherwise our mother, and her cousin, too, could go to jail.

One time soldiers from the feared Guulwade brigade came to the house. Ma was out. They were *Afwayne*'s special guards—worse even than the police. A young man in a green uniform, with a gun, walked into our compound. Grandma was sitting under the talal tree. Startled and angry, she stood up. She was only a little taller than I was, but imperious. "You of lower birth!" she began declaiming. "Your gun won't give you back your missing honor!" Grandma hated the government. "You're only good for bullying old women, and children whose father your craven master has imprisoned!"

I ran inside the house, frightened. I could see there were at least three other uniformed men standing near our fence. The soldier made a move toward the house, and Grandma tried to block him off. She was much shorter than he was, but she had a fierce look about her; she stuck her neck out at him and jabbed with the long, sharp needle she used for weaving mats and baskets held tightly in her fist.

The soldier commanded her to get out of his way. "Coward," Grandma jeered at him. Then he pushed her. She fell back and then ran at him with her needle. "Coward! Coward!" she hissed. For a moment he hesitated. He looked at his colleagues in the distance. I thought he might go. Then he pushed Grandma with force. She fell on the ground, on her back. He and the others came in and turned everything upside down.

Then they left. Grandma shouted after them, "Sons of prostitutes!

Allah will burn you in Hell!" She looked exhausted, and the look on her face scared me enough to save my questions for some other time.

Much later that evening, Ma returned from her visit to my father in jail. She went there often. She cooked special food for him, choosing the most delicate parts of the animal, cutting the meat into tiny pieces the size of a thumbnail, marinating them and stewing them for days.

My baby sister, Quman, was born when I was three, but the only thing I remember about her is her death. There's a picture in my mind of a tall man standing in the doorway, holding a bundled infant in his arms. Everyone was whispering *Innaa Lillaahi wa innaa Illaahi raaji'uun*— " 'From Allah we come and to Allah we return.' " I remember pulling Ma's shawl and telling her that this man was trying to take away my sister; I remember my mother just chanting the same words over and over again, along with everyone else. Then, in my memory, the man leaves with Quman, who is screaming, and Ma follows him, her face blank with pain.

Years later, when I became old enough to understand what death was, I asked my mother why baby Quman had been screaming if she was dead. My mother said I had been the one doing the screaming. It had gone on for hours, as if I couldn't stop.

There were so many funerals in my childhood. Aunt Khadija's husband, our Uncle Ied, died when I was four. Never again would he drive up in his black car and bounce us on his lap, joking. Then Aunt Hawo Magan, my father's sister, became ill. She was very affectionate, and if we chanted our lineage correctly she gave us candy and boiled eggs. Haweya and I were allowed to go with my mother to the hospital. When she died, I wailed inconsolably. "She's gone. There's nothing to be done about it," my mother told me. "Stop crying. It's the way things are. Being born means we have to die some day. There is a Paradise, and good people like Aunt Hawo find peace there."

My mother's oldest sister, who was also named Hawo, came to stay with us when she fell ill. She had something inside her breast that meant she had to lie down on a mat on the floor all day. I will never forget the endless, muffled groans of pain coming through Aunt Hawo's gritted teeth as she lay there day in and day out. Grandma, Ma, and Ma's twin sister, Aunt Halimo, took turns smearing *malmal* herbs on her chest. When this Aunt Hawo died, there was a great gathering of women at our house. They built several fires, and lots of women cooked and talked. Some of the women swayed and waved their arms over their heads, and screamed, in cadence:

Allah ba'eyey,	O God, I am eliminated
Allah hoogayeey	O God, I am devastated
Allah Jabayoo dha'ayeey	O God, I am broken and fallen
Nafta, nafta, nafta	The soul, the soul, the soul.

When they reached the third line the women fell to their knees in theatrical hysterics. Then they got up and clutched their throats and cried out in shrill tones *"Nafta, nafta, nafta"*—" 'The soul, the soul, the soul!'"

My mother was appalled, I could see that. "Such disrespect for the dead!" she hissed. "Isaq women! They have no sense of honor or manners! How can they abandon themselves so shamelessly!" Ma was mourning quietly, in a corner, as is proper among her own Dhulbahante, a subclan of the Darod. She was so engrossed in her grief for Hawo, and her mounting anger at the Isaq women, that she hardly noticed that Haweya and I were watching the whole scene in awe.

About a fortnight later my mother and grandmother caught us beating our chests and shouting, "O, Allah, I am eliminated! O, Allah, I am devastated!" all over the yard, and throwing ourselves on the sand. We cried, "The soul, the soul!" and burst into wild giggles.

My grandmother was outraged beyond all reason. She thought we were tempting fate, possibly even awakening the unseen djinns who were always present, waiting for just such a call to unleash their devastation. To make matters even worse, she felt insulted by my mother's Darod snobbery about the Isaq. Those women were my grandmother's clan mates.

When Ma was home with us, we had schedules. Breakfast and lunch, both nonnegotiable; a nap in the afternoon; then, while my mother cooked the evening meal, prayers to Allah to persuade our bad government to release our father and to show mercy to the dead. Then we were forced to eat and forced to have a bath, and finally we were forced to go to bed. When Grandma and Sanyar were in charge, we didn't eat if we didn't want to. We were largely ignored and behaved abominably.

I was fascinated by the radio, a square box with a handle. Voices came out of a circle of black holes. I imagined that there were little people in the radio and I wanted to prod them out with my fingers. So I pushed a finger into every little hole. When no people came out, I rubbed the radio against my ear and tried to persuade them to come. I asked Allah to help me. Nothing happened, so I filled the holes with sand. Then I stood up and let the radio fall onto the ground, hoping that it would burst open.

That radio meant a lot to my grandmother. The first time she had seen one, she, too, had thought it was magic. In Somalia, the man who read the news on the Somali service of the BBC every evening was called He Who Scares the Old People. It was the one piece of modern life my grandmother knew how to control. So of course when I broke it she beat me.

One morning, when I was four or five years old, a truck came to our house, and instead of unloading food from it, my mother herded us children onto it. One of Ma's cousins lifted us high into the air and dropped us into the flatbed with the sheep and goats. No one had told us we were going anywhere; no one thought to explain anything to us children. But after suitcases and pots and pans were loaded on with us, the truck started moving. I think possibly our Grandma had persuaded my mother that we would behave better if we were exposed to the beneficent atmosphere of the countryside. Or perhaps there was some trouble about my mother's dealings on the black market.

The drive was noisy and bumpy. The adults complained and the animals bleated in horror. But it was an extremely exciting experience for us kids, and we loved every bit of it. After some hours, we fell asleep.

I woke up in a strange place, inside a house with walls made of grass mixed with mud and manure and smoothed onto a wooden frame. Mats covered the beaten-earth floor, and it was dark inside, without electricity. I went to look for Ma and found some strange women instead. The ground in front of the house was red dust and there was nothing around us except empty land with a few trees and a sprinkling of huts that looked like the one I had just woken up in.

We were in Matabaan, Ma told me when I found her, a village about eighty kilometers from Mogadishu, not far from the Shabelle River. Herders from the Hawiye clan lived there, and there was enough water to support at least some farmland on the sandy soil. My mother's cousin, the trader, must have had contacts in this village, and I suppose Ma thought that here we would be safe and well-fed. At any rate, she told us that she was tired of Mogadishu, of smuggling food, and keeping secrets. Here, she said, we needn't whisper any more, or hide from the government. She said, "Look how big this land is. We have everything we need, and you can run around as much as you like. Allah is going to take care of us."

The longer we stayed in Matabaan, the more pleasant it seemed. Haweya and I went for long walks with Grandma, herding goats and sheep. But I was frightened of everything that moved—every insect, every animal. My grandmother would sometimes try to reason with me. "A wild horse that bolts at every moving thing stumbles and breaks its leg," she told me. "As you run from your small insect you may fall onto this bush and die, because it is poisonous. You may fall onto this mound and die because it hides a snake. You must learn what to fear and what not to fear."

When you're on your own in the desert, you are completely on your own. Fear is sensible. In Matabaan my grandmother tried to teach us the rules of survival. With certain animals, she told us, it is best to run and hide—hyenas, for example, and snakes, and also some monkeys who don't like to stray far from their families. With other animals, you must quickly climb a tree, choosing branches cleverly so they cannot follow you. If you encounter a lion, you must squat and avoid eye contact. Most times, she told us, a lion won't come after a human being: only in extreme drought do they eat human meat. But lions will take your sheep or a goat, and if they do, you will be punished or left without food. Remember: most animals will not attack you unless they sense that you are afraid of them or that you wish to attack them first.

But my grandmother's world wasn't our world. Her lectures only frightened me even more. Lions? Hyenas? I had never seen such creatures. We were city children, which, to her nomad values, made us more inept than lowly farmers or the ignoble blacksmith clans.

Because I was entirely useless at manual crafts and herding, my only function in Matabaan was to fetch water from the large lake that lay about a mile from our hut. I went there every day with the neighbors' children. We collected henna leaves along the way; we chewed them and used them to stain our hands with clumsy orange designs. In my pail, the lake water was brown with dirt, but once I brought it home, Ma would put a special tablet in it that fizzed. Afterward, you could see the bottom of the pail right through the water.

People washed their clothes in the lake and boys swam in it. Ma was always afraid that the Hawiye boys would drown Mahad, who couldn't swim. Free to roam because he was a boy, our brother was now constantly away from the house. Ma never let Haweya and me stray in this way. Anyway, Mahad would not have taken us with him; he didn't want his friends to know that he played with his sisters.

Mahad was increasingly conscious of his honor as a male. Grandma encouraged him: she used to tell him he was the man of the house. Mahad never asked permission to leave the house; sometimes he'd return long after nightfall, and Ma would get so angry she would close the fence. He'd sit by that fence, howling, and she would shout coldly, "Think of your honor. Men don't cry."

My brother was rapidly becoming the bane of my existence. Once, it was time for the Ied festival that celebrates the end of the fasting month of Ramadan. Animals had been killed for a huge feast, and we had new clothes. I had a shiny new dress with a big blue bow, stiff with lace where it swirled about my knees, and frilly socks and new black patent leather shoes. I pranced about proudly, avoiding the dust. I was second to be bathed and dressed; now it was Haweya's turn to be scrubbed, and Mahad called me from outside.

"Ayaan, come and see," he yelled.

I ran to him. "What?"

Mahad was at the entrance of the toilet. "Look," he said, stretching out his hand to help me up onto the steps.

In Matabaan the toilet walls were just twigs strung together. In the middle of the beaten-earth floor there was a wide hole with two stone steps on either side. You were supposed to put your legs on these steps and pee or empty your bowels before an audience of large and hostile flies. Haweya and I were too frightened of the hole to manage this performance; besides, our legs weren't long enough to stretch. So, under supervision from Ma or Grandma, we did our business in the bushes nearby.

Now, though, I climbed up and looked down the deep, dark hole of the latrine. The smell was vile, and large flies zoomed about. Suddenly Mahad ran behind me and pushed me in. I screamed as I never had before. The latrine was truly disgusting and also really deep, almost level with my shoulders. When Ma fished me out, I was in an unspeakable condition, and so were my new clothes. She began cursing Mahad loudly.

"May the Almighty Allah take you away from me! May you rot in a hole! May you die in the fire! What can I ever expect of you? You communist! You Jew! You're a snake, not my son!" Ma had completely lost her temper. In a frenzy of rage, she grabbed Mahad and threw him down into the loathsome latrine.

Now Grandma had to fish out Mahad, and a good part of the festive morning was spent restoring the two of us to cleanliness. I had to part with my dress and shoes. My hands were chafed and my foot hurt. It was decreed that I should not leave Ma's side in case Mahad got hold of me. So later that morning, as Ma and Grandma cleaned the slaughtered meat together, I was sitting near them on the red earth.

"Mahad has no sense of honor whatsoever," Ma said, in tones of profound disgust.

"He's only a child," said Grandma. "How can he learn about honor, when the only men he sees are the stupid Hawiye farmers?"

"He'll kill Ayaan one of these days," Ma said.

"It is her fault, Ayaan is *doqon,* as dumb as a date palm."

"I am not dumb," I retorted.

"You show respect for your grandma," snapped my mother.

"Ma, he invited me to come and look, that's all," I wailed.

Grandma grinned. "So you went and looked?"

"Yes, *Ayeeyo,*" I replied, with the polite and respectful term and tone required when addressing Grandma.

Grandma cackled maliciously. "You see? She's dumb, and only Allah can help her. Any child who's lived five seasons should know better, Asha. You can curse the boy as much as you like, but Ayaan is stupid, and she'll bring you nothing but trouble."

Mahad had done wrong, but I had been unforgivably trusting, which meant I was fatally dense. I had failed to be suspicious. I deserved my grandma's scorn. I was not allowed to talk back to Grandma, and Ma said nothing to defend me. I could only sob, and seethe.

We returned to Mogadishu, as inexplicably and suddenly as we had left. Adults never explained anything. They saw children as akin to small animals, creatures who had to be tugged and beaten into adulthood before they were worthy of information and discussion. In a way, my mother's silence was understandable. The less we knew, the less we could betray to the Guulwade.

In Mogadishu, our days were once more long and empty, animated only by occasional visits from members of my mother's family. Aunts and cousins and the cousins of aunts would come—women from the desert who came to Mogadishu to be married, or men in search of jobs. But in a town environment, they were completely inept. They didn't understand traffic or even the toilet; Ma had to teach them not to empty their bowels on the floor. They were hicks, wore embarrassing clothes, and put any kind of glittery thing in their hair. Ma lectured them constantly: how to sit on chairs, wipe tables with a sponge, not eat like savages, and cover their shoulders instead of striding about in the country *goh,* a wide band of cloth that desert women wrapped over their body and slung over one shoulder, leaving their neck and much of their shoulders bare.

Like all city people, Ma felt superior to these hicks from the *miyé*. She knew they would have to accept that her way was better than theirs, because she had made the move to the city herself. But like all country people, her *miyé* relatives resented being spoken down to. If Ma was too sharp with them, they became indignant and moved out.

Mahad began primary school and I began my own little war on Grandma. Sometimes I climbed the talal tree as she sat underneath it, and then spat down. Not *on* Grandma, for I wasn't allowed to do that, but *next* to her, on the sand. Grandma would complain to Ma; then an endless discussion followed on whether the spitting was *on* Grandma or *near* her. This resulted in a general forbidding of all spitting. This kind of futile bickering was our pastime.

Ignored by the grown-ups, Haweya and I made up games precisely to annoy them. If they drove us out of the house, we played Guulwade. One of us would act aggressive and tyrannical, pretending she had a weapon, pushing and shoving in the air and demanding to see what lay under the beds. The other would do everything *Afwayne* forbade, such as hiding food or bidding our imaginary children to beg Allah for people to be released.

We also begged, quite loudly, for the destruction of *Afwayne* and his regime. Sometimes I would climb the talal tree and shout down to Haweya, "Ha ha, I am Darod, Harti, Macherten, Osman Mahamud, and the daughter of Hirsi Magan!" *Afwayne* had banned the clan system, and people were no longer permitted to ask who others were from. We were now supposed to be just Somalis, one glorious, clanless nation, united in worship of Siad Barré. Speaking of your clan made you an "anti"—an opponent of the regime—and could earn you prison and torture. Our loud breaches of orthodoxy made the adults witless with nerves, particularly Aunt Khadija, who was the only family member who actually supported *Afwayne*. After such outbreaks she and others would quickly herd us into the house to play.

Our bedroom was large and almost completely empty, its walls so high there was an echo. We developed the game of competing with the echo, making stranger and louder noises with it. This made such a phenomenal racket that Grandma would drive us back out of the house.

Aunt Khadija provided a solution for our apparently boundless energy. Khadija thoroughly approved of all things modern, including the brand-new local school. "Ayaan needs school in the morning and Quran school after lunch," she pronounced. Ma was reluctant to send her daughters out of the house, where we were protected from both harm and sin. In school I would be in danger of both. Still, Mahad was already in school, and my father, consulted on the subject, probably told her to do it. Finally, against her better judgment, she agreed.

So, at five years old, I received a crisp new uniform. I was to become a grown-up and go out on my own in the world. Ma warned me that in school I would be told to sing hymns of loyalty to Siad Barré, but I wasn't to do it. "Move your lips or just say the first verse of the Quran," she said. "You may not sing praises to *Afwayne*. Just learn to read and write, and don't talk to the other children—they could betray us. Keep to yourself." She repeated this every morning.

The first day, my class teacher hit me on the head when I wouldn't open my mouth to sing the songs. The hitting hurt, so I repeated her words. It felt awful: I was betraying both my father and my mother. Each morning, in line with other kids, I would try just to move my lips, and the same teacher would pull me out and beat me. She told my class by way of introduction that I was the daughter of an "anti" and that I there-fore was an "anti," too, because all we learned in school was to chant praises to Siad Barré and communism, and I refused to join in. I had no friends after that.

Quran school was a shed down the road. The other pupils were from the neighborhood. At first I liked it. I learned to mix ink from charcoal, water, and a little milk, and to write the Arabic alphabet on long wooden boards. I began learning the Quran, line by line, by heart. It was uplifting to be engaged in such an adult task.

But the kids at madrassah were tough. They fought. One girl, who was about eight years old, they called *kintirleey,* "she with the clitoris." I had no idea what a clitoris was, but the kids didn't even want to be seen with this girl. They spat on her and pinched her; they rubbed sand in her eyes, and once they caught her and tried to bury her in the sand behind the school. The madrassah teacher didn't help. Once in a while he called her *dammin,* dunce, and *kintirleey,* too.

My teenage cousin Sanyar used to pick me up after madrassah. One day she arrived just as a girl hit me in the face. Sanyar took me home and told the story. "Ayaan didn't even defend herself," she said in horror. "Coward!" my family jeered.

The next day Sanyar waited for me outside the madrassah with another teenager, the older sister of the girl who had hit me the day before. They caught hold of the two of us and tugged us over to an open space, then ordered us to fight. "Scratch her eyes out. Bite her," Sanyar hissed at me. "Come on, coward, think of your honor."

The other girl got the same encouragement. We flew at each other, fists tight, hitting, wrestling, pulling each other's hair, biting. "Ayaan, never cry!" Sanyar called out. The other children cheered us on. When they let us stop, our dresses were torn and my lip was bleeding, but Sanyar was delighted. "I don't want you to ever let another child hit you or make you cry," she said. "Fight. If you don't fight for your honor, you're a slave."

Then, as we walked away, the other girl shouted after me, *"Kintirleey!"*

Sanyar winced. I looked at her, horror dawning on me. I was like that other girl? I, too, had that filthy thing, a *kintir*?

In Somalia, like many countries across Africa and the Middle East, little girls are made "pure" by having their genitals cut out. There is no other way to describe this procedure, which typically occurs around the age of five. After the child's clitoris and labia are carved out, scraped off, or, in more compassionate areas, merely cut or pricked, the whole area is often sewn up, so that a thick band of tissue forms a chastity belt made of the girl's own scarred flesh. A small hole is carefully situated to permit a thin flow of pee. Only great force can tear the scar tissue wider, for sex.

Female genital mutilation predates Islam. Not all Muslims do this, and a few of the peoples who do are not Islamic. But in Somalia, where virtually every girl is excised, the practice is always justified in the name of Islam. Uncircumcised girls will be possessed by devils, fall into vice and perdition, and become whores. Imams never discourage the practice: it keeps girls pure.

Many girls die during or after their excision, from infection. Other complications cause enormous, more or less lifelong pain. My father was a modern man and considered the practice barbaric. He had always insisted that his daughters be left uncut. In this he was quite extraordinarily forward-thinking. Though I don't think it was for the same reason, Mahad, who was six, had also not yet been circumcised.

Not long after that first fight of mine at the madrassah, Grandma decided that the time was right for us to undergo the necessary and proper dignity of purification. My father was in jail and my mother was away for long periods, but Grandma would ensure that the old traditions would be respected in the old ways.

After she made the arrangements, Grandma was cheerful and friendly all week long. A special table was prepared in her bedroom, and various aunts, known and unknown, gathered in the house. When the day itself came I was not frightened, just curious. I had no idea what was going to happen, except that there was a festive atmosphere in the house and we—all three of us—were going to be cleansed. I wouldn't be called *kintirleey* anymore.

Mahad went first. I was driven out of the room, but after a while I stole back to the door and watched. Mahad was on the floor, with his head and arms on Grandma's lap. Two women were holding down his spread-eagled legs, and a strange man was bending down between them.

The room was warm and I could smell a mixture of sweat and frankincense. Grandma was whispering in Mahad's ears, "Don't cry, don't stain your mother's honor. These women will talk about what they have seen. Grit your teeth." Mahad wasn't making a sound, but tears rolled down his face as he bit into Grandma's shawl. His face was clenched and twisted in pain.

I couldn't see what the stranger was doing, but I could see blood. This frightened me.

I was next. Grandma swung her hand from side to side and said, "Once this long *kintir* is removed you and your sister will be pure." From Grandma's words and gestures I gathered that this hideous *kintir,* my clitoris, would one day grow so long that it would swing sideways between my legs. She caught hold of me and gripped my upper body in the same position as she had put Mahad. Two other women held my legs apart. The man, who was probably an itinerant traditional circumciser from the blacksmith clan, picked up a pair of scissors. With the other hand, he caught hold of the place between my legs and started tweaking it, like Grandma milking a goat. "There it is, there is the *kintir,*" one of the women said.

Then the scissors went down between my legs and the man cut off my inner labia and clitoris. I heard it, like a butcher snipping the fat off a piece of meat. A piercing pain shot up between my legs, indescribable, and I howled. Then came the sewing: the long, blunt needle clumsily pushed into my bleeding outer labia, my loud and anguished protests, Grandma's words of comfort and encouragement. "It's just this once in your life, Ayaan. Be brave, he's almost finished." When the sewing was finished, the man cut the thread off with his teeth.

That is all I can recall of it.

But I do remember Haweya's bloodcurdling howls. Though she was the youngest—she was four, I five, Mahad six—Haweya must have struggled much more than Mahad and I did, or perhaps the women were exhausted after fighting us, and slipped, because the man made some bad cuts on Haweya's thighs. She carried the scars of them her whole life.

I must have fallen asleep, for it wasn't until much later that day that I realized that my legs had been tied together, to prevent me from moving to facilitate the formation of a scar. It was dark and my bladder was bursting, but it hurt too much to pee. The sharp pain was still there, and my legs were covered in blood. I was sweating and shivering. It wasn't until the next day that my Grandma could persuade me to pee even a little. By then everything hurt. When I just lay still the pain throbbed miserably, but when I urinated the flash of pain was as sharp as when I had been cut.

It took about two weeks for us to recover. Grandma tended to us constantly, suddenly gentle and affectionate. She responded to each anguished howl or whimper, even in the night. After every tortured urination she washed our wounds carefully with warm water and dabbed them with purple liquid. Then she tied our legs again and reminded us to stay completely still or we would tear, and then the man would have to be called again to sew us back up.

After a week the man came and inspected us. He thought that Mahad and I were doing well, but said Haweya needed to be resewn. She had torn her wound while urinating and struggling with Grandma. We heard it happening; it was agony for her. The entire procedure was torture for all of us, but undoubtedly the one who suffered the most was Haweya.

Mahad was already up and about, quite healed, when the man returned to remove the thread he had used to sew me shut. This was again very painful. He used a pair of tweezers to dig out the threads, tugging on them sharply. Again, Grandma and two other women held me down. But after that, even though I had a thick, bumpy scar between my legs that hurt if I moved too much, at least my legs didn't have to be tied together anymore, and I no longer had to lie down without moving all day.

It took Haweya another week to reach the stage of thread removal, and four women had to hold her down. I was in the room when this happened. I will never forget the panic in her face and voice as she screamed with everything in her and struggled to keep her legs closed.

Haweya was never the same afterward. She became ill with a fever for several weeks and lost a lot of weight. She had horrible nightmares, and during the day began stomping off to be alone. My once cheerful, playful little sister changed. Sometimes she just stared vacantly at nothing for hours. We all started wetting our beds after the circumcision. In Mahad's case, it lasted a long time.

When Ma came back from her trip this time, she was furious. "Who asked you to circumcise them?" she yelled, more angry with her mother than I had ever seen her. "You know their father doesn't want it done! Allah knows, I have never in my life been so betrayed as by you. What possessed you?"

Grandma turned on my mother in fury. She yelled that she had done Ma a huge favor. "Imagine your daughters ten years from now—who would marry them with long *kintir*s dangling halfway down their legs? Do you think they'll remain children forever? You're ungrateful and dis-respectful, and if you don't want me in your house I'm going to leave." This time she really meant it.

Ma didn't want Grandma to leave, so she sent for her twin sister, Hal-imo, Sanyar's mother. Aunt Halimo and Ma looked exactly alike. Both of them were tall, thin, and dark-skinned, with hair that wasn't kinky like mine but waved gracefully around their faces and nestled into buns at the back of their necks. All the Artan women had long, thin limbs and hands and perfect posture, but despite their identical features, Aunt Halimo was much milder than my mother. They sat and talked for hours, waiting for Grandma to cool off. Then everyone, including Mahad, began begging Grandma to stay.

After that, the circumcision was not discussed at all. It was just some-thing that had happened—had *had* to happen. Everyone was cut.

There followed a period of intense whispering in our household. Some-thing had happened to our father. It seemed to be good. After several months of this Ma left us again, and when she came back it was with presents, not flour and vegetables. The ritual of praying for my father's freedom under the talal tree every evening suddenly stopped. Ma seemed less desperate, too, and less miserable and weary.

I didn't know it at the time, but my father had escaped from jail.

Apparently it was the director of the prison himself who helped my father to escape. Abdi Aynab was an Osman Mahamud, like my father, and what he did was truly noble. Despite the danger of betrayal, Abdi Aynab managed to get my father out of jail, and even went on to accom-pany him partway to the Ethiopian border, hidden along the way by members of the clan.

When Abdi Aynab returned to his job and family in Mogadishu, he was betrayed by an underling. He was executed by a firing squad on Tribunka Square. By that time, my father was already out of the country, helped from village to settlement and finally across into Ethiopia by his clansmen, although the border was bristling with soldiers. It was sometime in 1975, I believe; Ethiopia and Somalia were on the brink of war.

Somehow, my father got to the Ethiopian capital, Addis Ababa. Together with others he formed a political movement of Somali exiles opposed to Siad Barré's rule over Somalia. They called it the Somali Salvation Democratic Front, the SSDF.

The Ogaden War was brewing. Somalia and Ethiopia, the ancient enemies—nomads and mountain people, Muslims and Christians—locked into yet another hideous bout of violence. My father's group of exiles began receiving assistance from the Ethiopian government. President Mengistu was a dictator every bit as cruel as Siad Barré, but he was glad to fund Siad Barré's enemies. Weapons were purchased, and a base of fighters was set up in Dirirdawa, near the border.

I was told this story in bits and pieces as I grew up. It was not a child's place to know such things. All I knew then was that at five o'clock every day, my mother would secretly put on the radio, very quietly. All the adults would creep over to my grandmother's bed to listen to the BBC Somali Service and news of the SSDF advances. Stray aunts would be there, people from the *miyé*—anyone but Khadija, who still supported Siad Barré's regime. We children would be pushed outside, with Sanyar there to look after us and keep watch for the Guulwade brigades.

It was months before Mahad and I could gather any kind of concrete idea of what had happened to our father. Ma was determined to keep us safe by keeping us ignorant. In fact, I don't know how much she herself actually knew about where my father was. When Siad Barré's soldiers came to the door to demand information, she did a convincing job of yelling back that the last she had seen of her husband was in their custody: they owed *her* that information, not she them. But she also left for much longer trips after that, and we knew that these were trips we absolutely must not speak of or ask any questions about.

My mother was meeting my father clandestinely, in Saudi Arabia.

CHAPTER 3

Playing Tag in Allah's Palace

By this time, Somalia and Ethiopia were engaged in a crippling conflict. The war to come would kill thousands of citizens in both countries, ripping out the thin roots of two economic systems that had only just started to function. No travel between Mogadishu and Addis Ababa was permitted. It was obvious that my parents would have to meet somewhere else if they were going to see each other again.

Somali Airways didn't fly to very many places. One of them was Jeddah, in Saudi Arabia. Sending each other messages through the clan network, my parents agreed to meet there. The clan also produced a fake passport for my mother. She claimed to be an ordinary Dhulbahante woman on a pilgrimage to Mecca. I like to imagine them: my father and mother, young and happy, meeting in Jeddah, yearning to live once more as one family.

My mother didn't want to move to Ethiopia, because Ethiopians were Christians: unbelievers. Saudi Arabia was God's country, the homeland of the Prophet Muhammad. A truly Muslim country, it was resonant with Allah, the most suitable place to bring up children. My mother had learned Arabic in Aden; more important, she also imbibed a vision that Islam was purer, deeper, closer to God in the countries of the Arabian peninsula. Saudi Arabian law came straight from the Quran: it was the law of Allah. Inevitably, the life of our family, reunited in Saudi Arabia, would be predictable, certain, and *good*.

Somehow she convinced our father of this plan. He found a job in Saudi Arabia, at one of the government ministries. I remember his job as deciphering Morse code for some government office. He moved to Riyadh and lived at a clan mate's house while he waited for the preparations for our flight to be completed.

My mother was heroic. She managed to get another false passport, in which the names and dates of birth of her three children were listed so we could leave Somalia with her. She packed, in secret. She arranged for us to be driven discreetly to the airport. One morning in April 1978—I was eight years old—Grandma woke us up early, the gray light barely beginning to filter into the room. She dressed us in good dresses instead of school uniforms. Khadija's oldest stepson, who owned a garage opposite our house, arrived in his black car and bundled us in rapidly; Grandma stayed home. When we spilled out of the car, miles later, Ma pointed to a huge metal tube with flat wings poking out of it that was standing nearby. "That is an airplane," she announced. "We are going to fly on it."

We had never seen an airplane close up before, just the far-off machines that celebrated *Afwayne*'s rule by belching smoke across the city once a year on National Day. We shrieked and raced about, flapping our arms; the prospect of flight was so exciting, we imagined she might even mean we would fly like birds. With a fake passport and a grueling interrogation by the airport officials ahead of her, my mother didn't need the extra trouble. She swung her hard, flat hand at our heads and cuffed us into silence.

We couldn't stay good for long. We kids had almost never gone anywhere—we were never taken out on excursions—and here, at long last, was an utterly thrilling adventure. Herded into the aircraft, we wriggled out of our seat belts and fought for the window seat, biting and scratching and climbing over total strangers. As the plane rose into the sky my mother glared at us. "Let this plane crash, Allah," she called out. "Take them away. I don't want this life. Let us all die!" This was worse than being hit, the worst thing I had ever heard.

Our ears throbbed from the altitude and we screamed the entire flight. We were hated by every person on that plane. Then, just before we landed, along with all the other women passengers on the airplane, our mother covered herself with a huge black cloth, showing only her face. That silenced us. We followed her into the airport terminal in Jeddah, where, amid a completely astounding number of people with all kinds of garments and skin colors, Ma discovered that our father had not come to pick us up. We were completely on our own, abandoned in the airport in Jeddah.

I am not quite sure if this is exactly true, but this is my understanding of what happened. My father was expecting us to arrive, though he may not have known the precise date. Then a sudden call came for him from Addis Ababa.

The day we left Somalia there was an attempted coup against *Afwayne*.
Somalia's airspace was closed, and there was fighting. (After the coup leaders were executed, there was a period of much more intensive surveillance. If we hadn't left when we did, who knows when we would have
been able to get out.) For reasons that cannot have been unrelated to the
attempted coup, my father had rushed back to Ethiopia. In his haste, he
must have neglected to arrange for someone to meet the next Somali Airways flight to Jeddah, the flight that we had managed to get on.

Again and again, in years to come, Ma flung this scene at my father, in
accusation. For now we were well and truly stuck. This was Saudi Arabia,
where Islam originated, governed strictly according to the scriptures
and example of the Prophet Muhammad. And by law, all women in
Saudi Arabia must be in the care of a man.

My mother argued loudly with the Saudi immigration official, but he
merely repeated in an ever louder voice that she could not leave the airport without a man in charge. He never looked straight at her, only
somewhere just above her head.

We spent hours in that strange airport. We played tag. Mahad got lost.
I vomited. Ma said the devil was in us and cursed us to Hell and back. She
looked different, drained; she didn't seem to have anything under control.
She cried and said unkind things about Father, things I had never heard
her say. My mother must have felt betrayed. She had been so competent,
managing the clandestine departure, the false passports. And now she was
abandoned.

Just before nightfall a Somali man came up and asked my mother what
the matter was. He was a Dhulbahante, like her, so he offered to help. My
mother asked him to just take her into Jeddah, to the home of a Dhulbahante family she knew of, where we could stay. All she needed was his
help through the immigration desk and into the taxi; without a man in
charge, no taxi driver would accept her in his car.

We woke up in the house of this unknown family, in Jeddah. The bedroom was small and intensely hot, but my mother was fierce: we must
behave. That meant staying in the room, on the bed. If we talked louder
than a whisper we were hit, and if we walked around we were hit, too. We
could look out of the window, into a big courtyard where a half dozen
Somali women of all ages were cooking and talking.

One of them, a young woman, offered to take us out for a walk. Outdoors was a completely different world. The roads were paved; the traffic was astounding. And all the women in this country were covered in

black. They were humanlike shapes. The front of them was black and the back of them was black, too. You could see which way they were looking only by the direction their shoes pointed. We could tell they were women because the lady who was holding our hands tightly to prevent us from wandering off was covered in black, too. You could see her face, because she was Somali. Saudi women had no faces.

We pulled away and ran over to the black shapes. We stared up at them, trying to make out where their eyes could be. One raised her hand, gloved in black, and we shrieked, "They have hands!" We pulled faces at her. We were truly awful, but what we were seeing was so alien, so sinister, that we were trying to tame it, make it less awful. And what these Saudi women saw, of course, was little black kids acting like baboons.

After two or three days, two men of the Osman Mahamud clan arrived at the house with word from our father. He was in Ethiopia and might have to remain there for months. They asked my mother where she wanted to live while waiting for him to return. That night, something inside her seemed to snap. She cried and cursed and hit at us in a kind of frenzy. She threw shoes at whoever opened his or her mouth. We were all scared of her now, even Mahad, her favorite.

When the men came back the next day my mother told them, "Mecca." She must have felt that her life was going so wrong that if she clambered into Allah's embrace, He would make it better. Mecca, the home of the Prophet Muhammad, was the closest you could get to Allah. A week later all our stuff was loaded into a car.

We arrived at the foot of a tall building. Garbage was strewn all over the streets, heaps of rubbish covered in fat, buzzing flies. The stench in the stairwell was overpowering. The cockroaches were so contented they didn't even bother to scuttle away. Father had sent money to these guardians of ours to rent a flat, but Mecca was expensive: the only place they could find for us was a small apartment in a building occupied by Egyptian construction workers.

We had never been inside an apartment building before. As we climbed the stairwell, Ma told Haweya and me, "If you come out here on your own, the men who live behind these doors on the stairs will snatch you up and cut you into pieces and eat you." That was effective: never once did we venture outdoors alone.

She opened a door onto a two-room apartment. We were going to have electricity! There were switches on the wall that turned on light bulbs and—something we had never seen—a ceiling fan. When Ma's back was turned we began playing with the fan. We threw clothes and small objects at it just to watch them whirl. The fan broke.

That first week, the apartment was like a charcoal oven. We were so hot that Haweya's back broke out in fat little blisters, and for a week she was one big painful never-ending scream.

The uncles had already paid five months' rent up front; there was nothing to be done about the flat. All they could do was take us to the bazaar to buy essentials. Here we were too transfixed to misbehave. There were lights and glitter and toys—toys everywhere—and stalls pungent with blood and spices, the cackle of animals, and the plump promises of pastries. We had rarely been to a Somali market, and this huge array of stalls and shops was the most glorious thing we had ever seen. The uncles held our hands very firmly as we walked through this magical place and bought mattresses, bedsheets, pillows, a small fan. The next day we returned for some food, prayer mats, cutlery, cooking pots, a metal basin for washing clothes, a scrubbing brush, hard soap, and a pail.

Then our mother was alone with us—virtually the first time this had ever happened. With our grandmother staying behind in Somalia, my mother had nobody with whom to share tasks and plans. She could do nothing on her own. She wasn't supposed to go out on the street without these new guardians of ours, our uncles, and neither were we. To phone them she had to scuttle down to the corner grocer, with my ten-year-old brother in tow acting as her protective male.

All day long we would wait in the apartment for the uncles to do us favors, and all day long my mother cursed our father. "May Allah never bring him back," I remember her shouting. "May Allah make him barren. May he get a painful disease. May he never see Paradise." Worst of all, "May *Afwayne* catch him and torture him. May he be cut off from the bloodline and die alone."

Realistically, we could do nothing but wait. Mother set about reestablishing discipline in her household. We children had grown wild in the months she had left us alone with our grandma. Ma saw us pretty much as camels: to tame us, she yelled and hit a lot. If we ran around, she yelled "Sit. SIT!" and we would shrink to the floor; then she would flick us with the radio cable on our legs and arms. When we cried, she would yell "QUIET!" and hit us again.

This wasn't pleasant, but the hitting was not wanton, and though it hurt, it was controlled. To my mother, corporal punishment was a reasonable and necessary part of bringing up a child. In those days, as we learned to behave better, she hit us less.

When the mosques in Mecca cried for prayer, they created a kind of synchronized chain we heard every day: first our neighborhood mosque and then the next one, and the next, calling across the whole city and the country and the world. We developed a game of rushing from one window to another, testing who could remember best which direction the next call would come from.

In Somalia we had been Muslims, but our Islam was diluted, relaxed about regular praying, mixed up with more ancient beliefs. Now our mother began insisting that we pray when the mosques called, five times each day. Before every prayer we had to wash and robe ourselves, and then we had to line up and follow her instruction. After the evening prayer we had to go to bed.

My mother also enrolled us in a local Quran school, although we spoke practically no Arabic. In Somalia, both school and Quran school had been mixed (boys and girls); here, everything was segregated. Mahad had to go a madrassah for boys, and Haweya and I to one for girls. All the girls at madrassah were white; I thought of them as white, and myself, for the first time, as black. They called Haweya and I *Abid,* which meant slaves. Being called a slave—the racial prejudice this term conveyed—was a big part of what I hated in Saudi Arabia. The teacher didn't teach us to write, just recited to us from the Quran. We had to learn it, verse by verse, by heart.

We had already learned part of the Quran by heart in Mogadishu, although of course we had never understood more than a word or two of it, because it was in Arabic. But the teacher in Mecca said we recited it disrespectfully: we raced it, to show off. So now we had to learn it all by heart again, but this time with reverent pauses. We still didn't understand more than the bare gist of it. Apparently, understanding wasn't the point.

Everything in Saudi Arabia was about sin. You weren't naughty; you were sinful. You weren't clean; you were pure. The word *haram,* forbidden, was something we heard every day. Taking a bus with men was *haram.* Boys and girls playing together was *haram.* When we played with the other girls in the courtyard of the Quran school, if our white headscarves shook loose, that was *haram,* too, even if there were no boys around.

Ma decided to take us to the Grand Mosque, which was a welcome break from being cooped up. The air shimmered with heat; it was another punishingly, blindingly hot afternoon, the heat in Mecca like nothing I had ever known. And we walked into a place that was utterly beautiful: white, cool, dim, vast. A breeze flowed inside this building. It felt like being let out of jail. As my mother followed the solemn ritual, pacing slowly seven times around the sacred stone, we sprinted all over the place and skidded around on the floor, shrieking for joy.

The people in this place were almost as varied as at the airport, many even blacker than we were, and some who were so much whiter than the Saudis that they looked bleached. And because this was God's house, all these people were kind. When we ran into a grown-up he took our hands gently and led us back to Ma. She was furious, and I knew that we had shamed her, so I knelt down in front of her and performed the begging prayer that I had learned in the madrassah, cupping my hands before her and asking for her forgiveness. To my astonishment, it worked: she smiled.

My mother found comfort in the vastness and beauty of the Grand Mosque, and it seemed to give her hope and a sense of peace. We all liked going there; we even got ice cream afterward. Gradually, the rituals and stories centered on this place began to mean something to me. People were patient with each other in the Grand Mosque, and communal— everyone washing his or her feet in the same fountain, with no shoving or prejudice. We were all Muslims in God's house, and it was beautiful. It had a quality of timelessness. I think this is one reason Muslims believe that Islam means peace: because in a large, cool place full of kindness you do feel peaceful.

But as soon as we left the mosque, Saudi Arabia meant intense heat and filth and cruelty. People had their heads cut off in public squares. Adults spoke of it. It was a normal, routine thing: after the Friday noon prayer you could go home for lunch, or you could go and watch the executions. Hands were cut off. Men were flogged. Women were stoned. In the late 1970s, Saudi Arabia was booming, but though the price of oil was tugging the country's economy into the modern world, its society seemed fixed in the Middle Ages.

When the month of pilgrimage came, Ma said we couldn't go to the Grand Mosque any more. We couldn't even leave the house, for fear of stampedes by the huge crowds of pilgrims. We could only watch the crowds of people robed in white walking down the street and listen from our windows to the constant prayer.

One evening during the pilgrimage month, just after bedtime, there was a knock at the door. We heard one of the uncles shout, "Here is your father!" We rushed out of bed. Mahad hurled himself at one of the men who walked in. Rather sheepishly at first, Haweya and I did the same, clutching at this stranger, pulling him down to the floor.

I had fantasized a father who would understand me, know that I was trying to be good. Now here was that man. We clambered over him and crammed in close to him, just touching him. Ma wanted to put us back to bed, but our father said no, we should stay up. I fell asleep on the mat, arm outstretched, watching my father eat.

My Abeh was lean. He had high cheekbones like mine, and a round forehead; he had a strong neck and broad shoulders that were slightly stooped. His eyes were creased, which I thought was because he read a lot of books and worried a great deal about the future of our country. His hairline was high, which made him look distinguished. His voice was low and seemed always to have a smile in it. And unlike all the other adults in our lives, he thought we children were wonderful.

The next morning Abeh woke us up for prayer. The mats were spread out already, with Mahad's next to his, and Ma's and Haweya's and mine behind. We began to wrap ourselves in long white cloths for prayer, as Ma had begun insisting we do, but Abeh stopped us. "You don't have to do that until you're grown up," he said. And when Ma protested, my wonderful Abeh told her, "Asha, you know, it's not the rules, it's the spirit."

After that, Haweya and I squirreled in between him and Mahad for the prayer. He didn't push us away. When Ma protested "It's forbidden," Abeh shushed her.

We did that and over: at every prayer throughout the day we stuck by my father's side. By the evening prayer Abeh must have realized it wasn't going to stop by itself, and besides, Ma was right: it was forbidden. Men do not pray alongside women. Women pray behind, because though they cover themselves for prayer, that cloth could shift and uncover a piece of clothing, or skin, which could distract the men and lead them into sin. But my Abeh didn't explain it like that. He said, "You must stand behind now, because you are big girls."

We, of course, asked, "Why?"

"Allah wills it."

"But why does Allah will it? He made me, too, but he always prefers Mahad."

Abeh made us move back behind him because that was the way things were. But I loved my Abeh, and it wasn't fair, so while he was kneeling on the mat I crawled forward anyway, until by the end of the prayer Haweya and I were just about level with him and Mahad. To my mother's horror, we did this again and again. After about a week my father was irritated and my mother was sort of pleased, because it proved she had been right: he should never have let us move forward in the first place. In any case, Ma said, women do not pray with men. From the very first day Abeh should have been praying in one room with Mahad, and she with us in a separate room. But Abeh said no, "We pray together as a family. This is how God wants it."

After Abeh returned to us, all the rules relaxed a bit. He said that although we must do the ritual ablution before the morning prayer, we need not wash before the other prayers unless we had passed wind or gone to the bathroom. Washing at every prayer even if we were clean was a waste of water, Abeh said, and Allah wouldn't want that.

For a while, before every prayer, when Ma asked, "Have you washed?" we would all chant, "I am pure." Ma would say "Pure! You're filthy!" and we would say, "But, Ma, dust is not impure." Before the next prayer, again, "We are pure!" and again, until my Ma would blow up and say, "We are going to put a stop to this nonsense right now," and drag us off to the bathroom and douse us.

After my father arrived back in my life, I opened up the way a cactus blooms after rain. He showered me with attention, swept me up in the air, told me I was clever and pretty. Sometimes in the evenings he gathered all three of us children together and talked to us about the importance of God, and of good behavior. He encouraged us to ask questions; my father hated what he called stupid learning—learning by rote. The question "Why?" drove my mother mad, but my father loved it: it could set off a river of lecturing, even if nine-tenths of it was way above our heads.

Ma taught us to tell the truth because otherwise we would be punished and go to Hell. Our father taught us to be honest because truth is good in itself. I loved his evening lectures, and although we all soaked up the attention he gave us, from the beginning I was Abeh's favorite.

If we kids behaved badly, I always took the lead in owning up. I would say, "You won't punish us if I confess something, will you? Because if I do tell the truth and you do punish me, you'll be forcing me to lie to you next time." My father would burst out laughing and say, "Tell the truth then," and I would tell him: we had broken something, or annoyed the neighbors. He never hit us, just made us promise not to let it happen again.

My mother was spartan. She provided no more than the necessary attention and affection to anyone except Mahad. And even with him, her benevolence was relative: she simply didn't hit him as much as she hit Haweya and me. My mother was not a warm, cuddly woman to begin with, and life hardened her. She was worried all the time, and when she laid down rules, she meant it. But after a few weeks with Abeh we had learned to chant, "It's not the rules, it's the spirit." It drove Ma crazy.

Whatever my father's job really was, it paid well. But even though his Saudi work permit stipulated that he must not continue with his political activities, my father continued to work with the SSDF in secret. He thought the Saudis were crude and stupid and he didn't believe they would manage to find out that he was still part of the leadership of a political movement in exile.

When the five months' paid rent was up on our flat, my father insisted we move to Riyadh, where he worked. Ma didn't want to leave Mecca, but we children hated that apartment building, and I think even Ma was secretly relieved when Abeh found us a larger, much cooler house in Riyadh. It had sections, the woman's house and the men's (although we didn't live that way), with a hallway and a closed door between the two. Men came and went by the front gate, an imposing metal grille with lamps on either side. We were never allowed to venture out unaccompanied. But a little doorway led from the courtyard in the women's section to the courtyard of the women's house next door, so that women and children could circulate between them without ever going outdoors.

Haweya and I obtained permission to visit the neighbors via this little doorway. We used to watch TV. There were reruns of an endless TV series about the life of the Prophet and the battles he fought to establish Islam and bring stray polytheists to the straight path of the one true God; his face was never shown, because he was holy and nobody could act his role. We learned the clapping games of the little girls in the neighborhood. While their fathers were out and their lethargic, almost inert mothers slept away the afternoons, the girls who lived next door used to congregate together and play music. There were five or six of them—I suppose from several mothers—from about ten to fifteen years old. They tied cloths around their hips and swayed at each other, rotating their hips and shoulders and wrists with meaningful glances. I was eight years old, and to me these girls, even the ten-year-olds, exuded a torrid, and completely unfamiliar, eroticism.

I had never seen this kind of dancing, only the ritual ceremonies that rainmakers sometimes staged in their neighborhood in Mogadishu: a jerky magical ceremony rather than a dance. When Haweya and I play-acted this new kind of dancing at home, my mother went mad with rage. She had brought us to Saudi Arabia to become pure and live the narrow path of Islam alongside the Saudis, and now Saudi women were leading us astray.

Some of the Saudi women in our neighborhood were regularly beaten by their husbands. You could hear them at night. Their screams resounded across the courtyards: "No! Please! By Allah!" This appalled my father. He saw this horrible, casual violence as a prime example of the crudeness of the Saudis, and when he caught sight of the men who did it—all the neighborhood could identify who it was, from the voices—he would mutter, "Stupid bully, like all the Saudis." He never lifted a hand to my mother in this way; he thought it was unspeakably low.

Still, we had to be allowed to leave the house *sometimes,* and my mother couldn't ban us from going to the neighbors'; it would have been rude. Their families were very different from ours. For one thing, their mothers were idle; they had servants. And the little boys simply ran rampant. All the children ran around as much as they liked—Arabs are very tolerant of small children—but the boys were in charge. They would turn off their mother's TV program and order their older sisters off their chair.

In Saudi Arabia, everything bad was the fault of the Jews. When the air conditioner broke or suddenly the tap stopped running, the Saudi women next door used to say the Jews did it. The children next door were taught to pray for the health of their parents and the destruction of the Jews. Later, when we went to school, our teachers lamented at length all the evil things Jews had done and planned to do against Muslims. When they were gossiping, the women next door used to say, "She's ugly, she's disobedient, she's a whore—she's sleeping with a Jew." Jews were like djinns, I decided. I had never met a Jew. (Neither had these Saudis.)

Yet these same neighbors could be very caring. They came around to ask if everything was going well, and brought us sweets and sticky pastries. Sometimes they invited my mother to weddings. Even though she didn't approve of these women, she felt she couldn't refuse, and would go—which meant she took us along, too. Weddings meant three evenings of festivities, all attended only by women, who seemed to come to life on these occasions, dressed up in their finery. On the first evening the bride was covered to protect her from the evil eye; you could see only her ankles, decorated with spiral henna designs. The next day she glittered in Arab dress and jewels. On the last evening, which is called the Night of Defloration, she wore a long white dress in lace and satin and looked frightened.

On that evening the man she would marry was there, the only man ever allowed in the presence of women not from his family. He would be sweaty, ordinary looking, sometimes much older, wearing the long Saudi robe. The women would all hush as he came in. To Haweya and me, men were not from another planet, but to the Saudi women in the room, the bridegroom's arrival was hugely significant. Every wedding was like this: all the women falling silent, breathless with anticipation, and the figure who appeared, entirely banal.

Things were not going well at home. My parents' once strong bond was breaking down. Each had very different expectations of life. My mother felt that my father was not attentive enough to his family. It often fell to my mother to accompany us to school and back—different schools, because Mahad was a boy—returning alone. She hated having to go out without a man, hated being hissed at by men on the street, stared at with insolence. All the Somalis told stories about women who had been accosted on the street, driven away, dumped on the roadside hours later, or simply never seen again. To be a woman out on her own was bad enough. To be a foreigner, and moreover a black foreigner, meant you were barely human, unprotected: fair game.

When my mother went shopping without a male driver or spouse to act as guardian, grocers wouldn't attend to her. Even when she took Mahad along, some shop assistants wouldn't speak to her. She would collect tomatoes and fruit and spices and ask loudly, "How much?" When she received no reply she'd put the money down and say "Take it or leave it" and walk out. The next day she would have to go back to the same grocer. Mahad saw it all and couldn't really help her; he was only ten.

My mother never saw her tribulations as in any way the fault of the Saudis. She just wanted my father to do the shopping and the outdoor work, like all the Saudi men did. None of the Saudi women we knew went out in the street alone. They couldn't: their husbands locked their front doors when they left their houses. All the neighborhood women pitied my mother, having to walk on her own. It was humiliating; it was low.

My mother felt my father had failed her in many ways. He made her take on responsibilities she felt should rightly have been his. Somali culture didn't make it any easier. To my father, it was natural to waltz in with an extra eight or ten men he'd invited for lunch. He never told her where he was going or when he'd be back. If the atmosphere became less than congenial at home, he would go to the mosque in the morning and turn up a day or two later. My mother had to wash every little sock and headscarf by hand. She was alone.

I think there were times when she was happy: cooking in the evenings, her family around her. But how many of those evenings did she have? Sometimes, at night, I would hear my parents talking, my mother listing all the ways my father had failed her, her voice tense with rage. Abeh would tell her, "Asha, I am working to give us a future in our own country." Or he would say, "These things wouldn't happen if we were living in a normal country." Abeh never liked Saudi Arabia and always wanted us to move to Ethiopia with him. But my mother wouldn't do it: Ethiopians were unbelievers.

A few months after our move, my grandmother arrived to help my mother with the household. She didn't like the way Ma talked about Abeh either. "When you're born a woman, you must live as a woman," she used to say, quoting a proverb. "The quicker you understand that, the easier it will be to accept."

Some time after we moved to Riyadh we started school, real school, in the morning, with Quran school in the afternoon. But real school in Saudi Arabia was just like madrassah. We studied only Arabic, math, and the Quran, and the Quran must have taken up four-fifths of our time. Quran study was divided into a reciting class, a class on meaning, a class on the *hadith,* which are the holy verses written after the Quran, a class on the *sirat,* the traditional biographies of the Prophet Muhammad, and a class on *fiqh,* Islamic law. We learned to recite the ninety-nine names of Allah, and we learned how good Muslim girls should behave: what to say when we sneezed; on which side we should begin to sleep, and to what position it was permissible to move during sleep; with which foot to step into the toilet, and in what posture to sit. The teacher was an Egyptian woman, and she used to beat me. I was sure she picked on me because I was the only black child. When she hit me with a ruler she called me *Aswad Abda:* black slave-girl. I hated Saudi Arabia.

Not all Saudis were like this. One morning, while I was in school, a sudden wind blew in, so strong it almost pushed me over. With it came the heady smell of rain, which made me homesick. (The smell of rain is per-

haps the most poignant scent I remember from my short life in Somalia.)
Storm clouds began to gather and parents drove up to collect their children; because of the storm, school was closing early, but my mother must
not have realized that. It began to rain: first big drops that hit me hard,
then huge drifts like solid sheets of water thundering down. The streets
were flooding fast. When I was the last child waiting at the school gate I
ran in the direction I thought must lead me home. The water was more
than halfway up my shins. I fell down, crying.

A big arm folded over my chest from behind and hauled me out of the
water. I thought a Saudi had come to take me away, rape me, cut me to
pieces, and bury me in the desert, as in my mother's stories. I started
screaming, "Whatever you do to me Allah will see you!" But this man
wordlessly carried me into his house and dropped me on his wife's lap.
She gave me dry clothes to wear and calmed me down with warm milk
while her husband went back out to my school and found my mother
and Haweya. Then, when the rain stopped, he drove us all home.

We told our father we didn't want to be girls. It wasn't fair that we
weren't allowed to go out with him and do all the things that Mahad
could. Abeh would always protest, and quote the Quran: "Paradise is at
the feet of your mother!" But when we looked down at them, our
mother's bare feet were cracked from washing the floor every day, and
Abeh's were clad in expensive Italian leather shoes. We burst out laughing every time, because in every sense of the word, Paradise was not at her
feet but at his. He was important, he was saving Somalia, he had lovely
clothes, he went outside when he wanted to. And we, and she, were not
allowed to do as we wished.

The separation was etched into every detail of every day. If we wanted
to go somewhere as a family, we had to take separate buses: my father and
Mahad in the men's bus, Ma and Haweya and I in the women's. My
father would mutter with rage at the stupidity of it all when we finally
met up together, at the bazaar or the gold market. "This isn't Muslim at
all!" he would rage. "This is from the time of Ignorance! The Saudis are
as stupid as livestock!" In practice, the rule of separate buses applied only
to foreign workers. All the Saudis seemed to be rich, and Saudi women
were driven around by drivers in their husband's car.

When I told people I wanted to grow up to be like my Abeh, he
would glow and say "You see! The children will save the country!" and
hoist me up in his arms. Then the visitors—Somali men who waited def-

erentially for my father to come home and spoke to him with respect—all looked at me and chuckled and said I looked just like my father, with my round forehead and sharp cheekbones. Later on, he would hug me and say I was his only son. It made Mahad hate me even more.

Often my mother, too, received visitors—other Somali women, Dhulbahante, like my mother, who almost all worked as maids for Saudi households. One of them was called Obah. She was young and pretty, always nicely dressed. Her nails were always hennaed, and when she talked she waved her hands about in the air, leaving, to my mother's disgust, a trail of cigarette smoke. One day Obah had to leave the people she worked for, for fear of being dishonored; or perhaps she had been dishonored, and that was why she had to leave.

My mother disapproved of Obah's feminine flourishes and her cigarettes. She saw all this frivolity as sin. Still, she agreed to shelter her; Obah was a clan mate, and it is expected.

We children liked having Obah in the house. She laughed and waved her smoke around and wore her headscarf so loose you could see her gold earrings. She used a yellow powder and water to keep her skin soft and smooth. She was nothing like my austere, demanding mother.

One day Mahad and I stole some of Obah's cigarettes. We smoked them, and vomited. My mother told her she had to go. I don't know where she went after that, but a few months later we heard through the Dhulbahante network that Obah had been arrested and charged with prostitution. We were told she was jailed, then flogged in public, and that she had been deported to Somalia.

To the Saudis, the very fact that Obah was in the country alone would have been enough to establish that she was a prostitute; no further proof was required. And to Siad Barré's regime in Somalia, the very fact of having left her country and sought employment abroad would be enough to establish that she was a dangerous "anti."

When my father heard what had happened to Obah he was enraged. "This is not Islam—this is the Saudis, perverting Islam," he roared. My father was Muslim, but he hated Saudi judges and Saudi law; he thought it was all barbaric, all Arab desert culture. Whenever we heard of an execution or a stoning, my mother always said, "It is God's law and God's will, and who are we to judge it?" But we also knew that no Somali could ever win if a Saudi decided to take him to court.

My father's scorn for the Saudis was all-embracing. On September 16, 1978, there was an eclipse of the moon in Riyadh. Late one afternoon it became visible: a dark shadow moving slowly across the face of the pale moon in the darkening blue sky. There was a frantic knocking on the door. When I opened it, our neighbor asked if we were safe. He said it was the Day of Judgment, when the Quran says the sun will rise from the west and the seas will flood, when all the dead will rise and Allah's angels will weigh our sins and virtue, expediting the good to Paradise and the bad to Hell.

Though it was barely twilight, the muezzin suddenly called for prayer—not one mosque calling carefully after the other, as they usually did, but all the mosques clamoring all at once, all over the city. There was shouting across the neighborhood. When I looked outside I saw people praying in the street. Ma called us indoors and said, "Everybody is praying. We should pray."

The sky grew dark. It was a sign! Now more neighbors came knocking, asking us to pardon past misdeeds. They told us children to pray for them, because children's prayers are answered most. The gates of Hell yawned open before us. We were panicked. Finally, Abeh came home, well after nightfall. "Abeh!" We ran to him. "It's the Day of Judgment. You must ask Ma to forgive you!"

My father bent down till he was level with us and he hugged us. He said, slowly, "If you go to a Saudi and do this"—and he clapped loudly in our faces—"it will cause the Day of Judgment, for the Saudis. They are sheep."

"So it's not the Day of Judgment?"

"A shadow has fallen over the moon," he explained. "It is normal. It will pass."

Abeh was right. On the Day of Judgment, the sun will rise in the west, but the next morning, the sun was safely in its usual place, fat and implacable, and the world wasn't ending after all.

Our house in Riyadh had a balcony on the upper floor of the women's section, where we slept. It was covered with a curtain and an intricate grille. We could sit there and look out into the street without being seen, and Ma sometimes did this for hours. One afternoon she was sitting there when she caught sight of two Somali men who were making their way to our house. When she recognized them, she made a strangled noise. Something was wrong.

The men knocked at the door and Ma said, "I know it's bad news. Is it my son?" They said yes. My stepbrother, Muhammad, had been run over by a truck in Kuwait, and he was dead.

I had no memory of this older brother of mine, the product of the mystifying union of my mother with some other, alternate husband whom she hadn't liked. My mother had told me stories about Muhammad. He had killed a scorpion that bit me when I was little: surely I remembered the scorpion, and Muhammad carrying me into the house? I didn't. Muhammad had left Mogadishu when I was two or three years old, to live with his father in Kuwait.

But to Ma, Muhammad was to have been her savior. She would always say, "When I grow old Muhammad will come and rescue me from this life." After she learned of Muhammad's death, my mother went to her room, and a cloud of darkness and sadness fell over the house. Dhulbahante women came and attended to her and cooked for us, because Ma was frozen. It was as if she were in a coma, not crying, not shouting at us. She just lay there with a broken heart. All the adults told us, "Just this once be quiet and nice," and for once we were. When my father came back from Ethiopia he, too, was as good as a house cat. He was affectionate to my mother, and called her Asha, and held her hand until finally she rose from her bed.

Abeh decided he should stage his political meetings at our house; that way, he could spend more time at home. Anywhere between five and twenty men would come to these meetings, and they would eat and talk until three or four in the morning. Sometimes their wives would come, too, and help my mother in the kitchen, but they were always far too sloppy for her. She needed help hosting all these people, and by now I was almost nine—old enough to work in the house.

These meetings happened almost every week. I had to clean and help prepare the food all afternoon, while Mahad, because he was a boy, played with the neighbors, and Haweya, because she was too little to do chores, pestered me. That was bad enough, but what I really hated was washing up after dinner, late at night, the dirty glasses and plates stacked across every surface. I had to stand on a little box so I'd be tall enough to wash the huge cooking pots; one of them was so deep I could climb inside it to scrub it. I remember how resentful I felt, and how sleepy.

One night I couldn't bear it. I was so tired that I piled up all the dishes and stacked them inside the fridge—I just hid them. Then I quickly cleaned enough so that the kitchen looked nice. At dawn the next morning, when my father woke up for prayer, he opened the fridge to get a glass of cold water, and a stack of dishes crashed to the floor. The noise was enormous—it woke the whole household—and my mother raged into my bedroom. She hauled me out of bed to wash the dishes before school.

I cried and said it wasn't fair. My father came in as I was finishing, and told me, "It isn't fair, but it's not a good idea to put the dirty dishes in the fridge. Just tell your ma, 'I'm tired, I'll do them in the morning.'" My father was kind, but sometimes he seemed entirely uncomprehending of my mother's determination to instill responsibility and obedience into me, her eldest daughter.

One day in 1979 my father came home early and said we had been deported. We had twenty-four hours to leave the country. I never learned the reason.

Instead of going to school, we had to pack, while my Ma raged at my father with horrible anger. "It's your fault," she told him. "If you cared enough about your family this wouldn't have happened. You trust everyone with your secrets."

We went to the airport. My father said we had to get on the first flight out or the Saudi policemen would come to take us away. There was a plane leaving for Ethiopia, but Ma insisted we could not go to a non-Muslim country. The only other flight was to Sudan. Through the whole flight my Ma stared blackly at the sky.

When we landed in Sudan we weren't allowed in the country. We spent four days at the airport in Khartoum. Finally we got on another plane, and this time it was indeed to Ethiopia. The evil unbelievers lived there, but we had no choice.

CHAPTER 4

Weeping Orphans
and Widowed Wives

The first place we stayed in Ethiopia was an old mansion in the heart of the capital. It had chairs, which felt peculiar after a life of sitting on the floor. There were wooden floors and a Persian carpet and, intimidatingly, even servants to cook and clean. I think it was the first time I had ever seen a garden, with hedges and flowers and a little pond, and a gardener.

I suppose this mansion must have belonged to the Ethiopian government and was used to house visiting dignitaries. For in this country, my father was an important man. An official car came to drive him away to places. Meetings constantly took place downstairs; large, dark men smoked a lot and shouted at each other, sitting on gilt chairs in the formal dining room.

According to these men, all of them Somali exiles, the situation at home in Somalia was boiling over. My father's opposition movement, the SSDF, was attracting huge waves of volunteers. People who made it across the border now were not coming to escape, but to prepare to fight. They were ready to die to take revenge on *Afwayne*. They still called him that. Siad Barré, The Big Mouth, the huge maw that crushed people.

In 1974, a revolution had overturned the Ethiopian monarch, Emperor Haile Selassie. A committee of low-ranking officers and enlisted soldiers known as the Derg took over, among them the brutal Mengistu Haile Mariam, who became Ethiopia's next ruler. Siad Barré seized that moment to invade the Ogaden region, which Ethiopia claimed as its own but which was mostly occupied by Somali speakers, the Ogaden subclan of the Darod. The Ethiopian revolutionary leadership called for Soviet help, and the Soviets, abandoning Siad Barré, sent massive reinforcements to the Ethiopians. Siad Barré's army was forced to retreat. Naturally, Ethiopia gave aid and shelter to the forces of Siad Barré's opposition, my father's SSDF among them.

In 1978, on the day that we left Somalia for Saudi Arabia, the attempted coup against Siad Barré's government had been led by army officers who were all Macherten, like my father. To punish them, Siad Barré sent his army to destroy the Macherten lands. The troops burned settlements, raped women, and smashed the reservoirs that nomads had constructed to store rainfall. Thousands of people died of hunger and thirst. The government stole Macherten property and called it communism. With every new attack by Siad Barré, more volunteers poured across the border to Ethiopia, seeking to join forces with the SSDF and wreak vengeance.

By the time our family arrived in Ethiopia, the SSDF was an army, with a base of fighters on the border, at a place called Dirirdawa. Headquarters was a mansion just outside Addis Ababa, the capital city, behind a long high wall topped with broken glass and barbed wire, with a guard at the gate.

Abeh enrolled all three of us in school, which was taught in Amharic. We spoke only Somali and Arabic, so everything was completely foreign again for a little while. It wasn't until I could communicate that I came to a startling realization: the little girls in school with me were not Muslims. They said they were *Kiristaan,* Christian, which in Saudi Arabia had been a hideous playground insult, meaning *impure.* I went bewildered to my mother, who confirmed it. Ethiopians were *kufr;* the very sound of the word was scornful. They drank alcohol and they didn't wash properly. They were despicable.

You could see the differences in the street. Ethiopian women wore skirts only to their knees, and even trousers. They smoked cigarettes and laughed in public and looked men in the face. Children were allowed to run around wherever they wanted.

Ethiopians were also much poorer than any kind of people I had ever seen, much poorer even than people had been in Mogadishu. Whole families of lepers—some of them children, with flies on their gummy eyes and stubs for limbs—implored us for money on the way to school. It was painful to walk past them. The worst, though, was the frighteningly empty, creamy gray eyes of the blind beggar down the road. I shuddered when I had to approach his corner.

Once, a woman who was walking ahead of us down a street in Addis

Ababa simply spread her legs, squatted slightly, and pissed under her long skirt, right on the side of the road. My mother's face contorted with disgust. She despised Ethiopia. But despite the beggars and the dirt, I adored it. The people were kind. The teachers didn't punish anyone much. I had friends, for the first time. We never had to wear headscarves or long robes; we could run, and did run, for the first time in years. And I never had to wash the clothes or the dishes. It felt like being free.

After a few months, we moved across the city to the SSDF headquarters behind high walls. I don't remember any kind of announcement: one afternoon we were simply brought there after school by Abeh's driver. This building must have once been a palatial hotel, with its marble staircase and balustrade and seemingly endless carpeted corridors. We were housed in two bedrooms at the end of a corridor on the ground floor, and had a bathroom and a kitchenette.

At first our food was brought to us from the big kitchens by the Ethiopian cook. When my father was home the cook had to taste the food in front of us, to make sure it hadn't been poisoned. We could go to the kitchen and run around the grounds, but if we were caught in the offices my father used to implore my mother to control us better.

Ma tried to make us stay indoors, but she couldn't keep us there for long. The whole compound swiftly became ours to explore. To us, this was high adventure. Addis is green and lush—it rains often—and the grounds of the complex seemed huge. If we pestered the guard at the gate too much he used to dump us into the cracked old stone fountain near the entrance, which was so deep we couldn't clamber out on our own.

Dozens of men in green uniforms came and went. When they were headed to the border, they carried guns. Most of them, though, were convalescents; they had been evacuated from the front, to the hospital, and now they were recovering from wounds and amputations. Some of the wounded men were friendly and played with us in the dirt.

After a few weeks Ma took out her charcoal brazier and began cooking our meals on the ground outside our rooms. Soldiers drifted by. Some of them would settle down to wait for my father to finish his evening broadcast for Radio Kulmis; these programs made his voice instantly recognizable to a whole generation of Somali exiles. We had evenings of poetry, which reminded us all of our Somali roots. Ma would cook *chapattis* and meat stewed with herbs, and the men would declaim lines they had memorized and compose apt replies. One of them was a great modern poet whose work Ma knew by heart, Khalif Sheikh Mohamoud.

It may be the Lord's will that the Macherten be consumed like
     honey.
Like the wild berries in the plain of Do'aan, the Macherten have
     been devoured.
Hungry men yearn to bite the flesh of the prostrate corpses.
Weeping orphans, widowed wives are despoiled and stripped of
     their herds.
Humans must accept they are mortal, for Allah decrees it.
But it is hard to accept the gloating of the oppressor over the scat-
     tered bodies . . .

In Somali, the rhymes wail; they are hauntingly sad. After such
evenings Ma would visibly soften. She told us stories of when she was little: watching great poets compete beside the fire in the desert, reciting
more and more majestically until all concurred that a new, truly great poet
had been found.

Most of these limbless, wounded men in Ethiopia knew they were not
great poets, however, and felt their lives were over. There was a smell of
failure about them, something not quite washed, stale with cigarette
smoke and not enough sleep, and bitterness. The atmosphere was always
thick with muttering. Everybody complained about Abdellahi Yusuf,
the SSDF leader. He picked favorites, they said, stocking high places only
with relatives from his subclan. Almost all the men who were not
Macherten were leaving because of Abdellahi Yusuf. Those who
remained grumbled about him.

Abdellahi Yusuf was an Omar Mahamud. My mother told us that the
Omar Mahamud always think they should be in charge, but they always
mess it up. Of course, my mother was married to an Osman Mahamud,
so she would think that. With Somalis, everything is about your family:
Osman Mahamud are arrogant. Dhulbahante are inflexible. The Isaq
chew *qat*.

This is how it works. I am an Osman Mahamud, because thirteen
generations ago, I had a forefather named Mahamud who had a son
called Osman. In fact, Mahamud had three sons—perhaps more, but
three were powerful enough to found subclans. Osman, the oldest
brother, was a natural warrior, born to lead, which is why Osman
Mahamuds are so arrogant—they feel an inborn right to rule. Isse, the
youngest son, was a herder and a poet, and Isse Mahamuds, like my
paternal grandmother, still do those things. Omar was the middle son, a

perpetual malcontent, which is why the Omar Mahamuds never could manage anything.

So went the muttering. Because the wrong men were in charge of the SSDF's logistics, there weren't sufficient weapons. Ammunition didn't arrive on time. Men we knew were killed: friendly soldiers who the week before had squatted down and played with us were pointlessly mowed down. There were massacres in which hundreds were killed or maimed. These were the kinds of conversations that my mother listened to as she cooked. My father had always presented his struggle as heroic; but to my mother, listening in, the reality seemed to be death and mayhem, the dream of an independent, free Somalia falling apart miserably as she watched.

There were hardly any Somali women on this compound. We were the only children. All the other leaders of the exiles' army kept their families in Kenya, seven hundred miles to the south, where a huge community of Somalis lived. So my mother had to bring us up surrounded by only men. She hated that.

Some of the men expected her to make tea for them. Many of them chewed *qat* and left the old stalks around the place afterward. Once she caught Haweya and me drinking make-believe tea out of empty cups, waving cigarette butts in the air, and chewing old *qat* leaves. She flared up. "You can't bring up young girls in a place like this!" she yelled at my father. "Do you think they'll be children forever? How can girls grow up in a barracks, among men? What are you doing to your family?"

My sister and I thought it was a pity to spoil the little time we had with Abeh with these rows. I hated to hear my parents fighting. Although he never, so far as I know, lifted a hand to my mother, Abeh could get very angry. One afternoon we saw an ambulance arrive, and my father thundered into our rooms in a fury. Some man had raised his arm to hit him in an argument, he told us, and he had knocked the man down and broken his leg.

My mother became pregnant. She lost the baby, a little boy, who was stillborn. For several weeks, she was hospitalized and returned silent, bitter, unpredictably hostile.

After we had lived in Ethiopia for about a year, my father finally decided that my mother was right: we needed to be around other families. He would move us to Kenya, where most of the other exiled families lived. Ma didn't want to go to Kenya; she wanted to move to a Muslim country. Kenya, too, was an infidel country. But the decision was Abeh's to make.

*   *   *

That is how, by the time I turned ten, I had lived through three different political systems, all of them failures. The police state in Mogadishu rationed people into hunger and bombed them into obedience. Islamic law in Saudi Arabia treated half its citizens like animals, with no rights or recourse, disposing of women without regard. And the old Somali rule of the clan, which saved you when you needed refuge, so easily broke down into suspicion, conspiracy, and revenge. In the years to come, clan warfare would sharpen and splinter and finally tear the whole of Somalia to pieces in one of the most destructive civil wars in Africa.

Of course, I didn't see it that way then.

CHAPTER 5

Secret Rendezvous, Sex, and the Scent of Sukumawiki

We flew to Nairobi in July 1980. My mother loathed the idea; not only were Kenyans unbelievers, just like Ethiopians, but they looked different from us. To my mother, they were barely human. Ma told us that Kenyans were filthy and would infect us with hideous diseases. She said they were cannibals. She called them *abid,* which means slave, and *dhagah,* which means stones, and *gaalo,* another ugly word for infidel. My grandmother, who could navigate through the desert by the smell of fresh rain; whose nose could detect if a woman was pregnant; who would sniff the air and glance away scornfully and say someone was *in heat*—my grandmother said Kenyans stank. Throughout the ten years they lived in Kenya, the two of them treated Kenyans almost exactly as the Saudis had behaved toward us.

But my father chose Kenya because it was practical, a relatively wealthy country in those distant days; people said it was the safest place in Africa. In Kenya, my father had official refugee status: we could receive an education grant and living allowance from the United Nations High Commission for Refugees. He also knew that he could leave us there for part of the year, in the care of prominent members of the Osman Mahamud clan. There were many men who lived there who chose not to join the struggle as fighters, but who contributed funds and protected the families of men who did.

Abeh planned to live with us as much as he could; that's what he told my mother. But my mother didn't want to live alone in this foreign place. She didn't want to live off charity and the borrowed kindness of other women's men. She felt that my father had already given enough of his life, his money, and his family to the SSDF. She told him the SSDF was no better than *Afwayne:* it was corrupt, and inept, and rotten with clan backbiting. If we had to live in Nairobi, she wanted him to be there, too, providing for us. Perhaps he could set up a business of his own for a change, and let some other fighter's family live off *our* charity.

To my father, the idea of giving up the fight against Siad Barré was anathema. Somalia's destiny as a free nation—that's what meant most to him. Throughout his life, our mother told us, we, his family, never came first.

Initially, we lived in a hotel run by Somalis in Eastleigh, a packed, noisy neighborhood where most of the Somalis in Nairobi lived. Then we found a flat near Juja Road, on the edge of Eastleigh, where fewer Somalis lived. The main difference between Eastleigh and Juja Road was that the two neighborhoods smelled different. Eastleigh carried odors with which we were familiar: delicious foods spiced with coriander and ginger, tea laced with cardamom and cloves; women who walked past us in *dirha,* flowing Somali robes, left behind a whiff of frankincense and strong perfume. Once in a while, a repugnant stench from the open sewer would drift over to mingle with these sweet fragrances.

In contrast, the Juja Road neighborhood was inhabited mainly by native Kenyans, who ate *ugali,* powdered maize boiled in water to become a hard ball. *Ugali* was eaten with *sukumawiki,* a vegetable with large green leaves that were cut into tiny pieces and boiled for hours, similar to collard greens. *Sukumawiki* carried a pungent, terrible smell that pervaded the entire neighborhood from midmorning to late at night.

Our apartment was three flights up a newly slapped-together cinderblock building, across the road from an empty field. My grandmother bought a sheep in the market and trained it to hop up and down the stairs. She grazed it in the field and let it sleep in the bathroom. It was a pet, really; we never ate it. Looking after that sheep made her feel less estranged and gave her something familiar to do.

My father enrolled us in an English-language school. Soon after, my mother coldly informed him that young girls would be safer and better cared for in their own home than out in some *gaalo* school among the unbelievers in the filthy country he had brought them to. My father exploded. He yelled that he would curse her straight to Hell if she took us out of school without his permission. Then, a few days later, he left for Ethiopia.

It was my father who took us to school on our first day. Each of us children had a different school uniform; mine was a gray pinafore with a white shirt underneath and a gray sweater. Once again, school was totally foreign. Our lessons were in English, but everything that went on in the playground was in Swahili. Again, I spoke neither. The first few weeks were a nightmare of loneliness and bullying, but I never told Ma. I feared she'd take us out of school altogether, and I wanted more than anything to be with other children, out of the house.

The bullying faded, in any case, as I learned Swahili. Haweya suffered from bullying far more than I did. She seemed to close up and become more ferocious under the constant teasing. She came home bruised and angry. It was easier for me to adjust to school; I just tried to become as invisible as possible.

Juja Road Primary School was clearly modeled on British colonial schools. We had assembly every morning, saluting the flag and chanting the Kenyan national pledge instead of singing "God Save the Queen." Prefects checked our nails and school uniforms. The schoolwork was difficult, and if we didn't understand, we were made to kneel in the sun outside our classroom. There was no taking us aside to explain something again. The math teacher, Mrs. Nziani, used to hit us for every mistake, with a black plastic pipe she called her black mamba. I would get hit again and again until my hand swelled. Finally I realized that I could take some of the ropes that my grandmother wove from the long grass in the field outside our house and trade them with a girl named Angela, to use for skipping rope; in return, Angela let me copy her math homework.

Numbers were a mystery to me. I was so far behind. It was only in Nairobi, at age ten, that I figured out anything at all about the way time is calculated: minutes, hours, years. In Saudi Arabia the calendar had been Islamic, based on lunar months; Ethiopia maintained an ancient solar calendar. The year was written 1399 in Saudi Arabia, 1972 in Ethiopia, and 1980 in Kenya and everywhere else. In Ethiopia we even had a different clock: sunrise was called one o'clock and noon was called six. (Even within Kenya, people used two systems for telling time, the British and the Swahili.) The months, the days—everything was conceived differently. Only in Juja Road Primary School did I begin to figure out what people meant when they referred to precise dates and times. Grandma never learned to tell time at all. All her life, noon was when shadows were short, and your age was measured by rainy seasons. She got by perfectly well with her system.

Once I had learned to read English, I discovered the school library. If we were good, we were allowed to take books home. I remember the *Best-*

Loved Tales of the Brothers Grimm and a collection of Hans Christian Andersen. Most seductive of all were the ragged paperbacks the other girls passed each other. Haweya and I devoured these books in corners, shared them with each other, hid them behind schoolbooks, read them in a single night. We began with the Nancy Drew adventures, stories of pluck and independence. There was Enid Blighton, the Secret Seven, the Famous Five: tales of freedom, adventure, of equality between girls and boys, trust, and friendship. These were not like my grandmother's stark tales of the clan, with their messages of danger and suspicion. These stories were fun, they seemed real, and they spoke to me as the old legends never had.

Sometimes after school Haweya and I would sneak over to Juja Road Square, where an Indian shop sold ice cream, exercise books, ballpoint pens, and *pan,* a spicy coconut mixture that stained our lips red. But mostly Ma made us stay at home. She and Grandma were far from reconciled to letting us go to school. They didn't trust the Kenyans to teach us anything; they rejected Kenya in every detail. But Haweya and I were like sponges, eager to absorb everything around us.

One time, I informed my mother that people had walked on the moon. Ma said it was nonsense. "The *Kiristaan* are so fanciful they could take an airplane to a mountain and think it's the moon," she told me. The day I came home and told her humans had descended from apes, she told me, "That's the end of your school fees. Kenyans may have come from apes, yes. But not Muslims."

Still, my mother kept us in school. My father had threatened to curse her, and having escaped one husband, she wasn't willing to risk eternal punishment once again.

When my father returned from Ethiopia my parents fought all the time. Ma tried involving the clan, hoping some friendly man would influence Abeh to look after his wife and children properly; but of course no man would interfere in the private decisions of Hirsi Magan. Ma stopped eating and fell ill, moaning and swearing she would die. Abeh took her to the hospital, where they diagnosed anemia and prescribed vitamins.

After several months, Abeh found us a larger, nicer place to live, a house on Racecourse Road, in a neighborhood called Kariokor. But Ma had never wanted to be in Kenya in the first place; she wanted us all to go back to Mecca.

I don't know what their final fight was about, but I overheard the last of it. He was on his way to the airport again. Ma told Abeh, "If you leave now, don't come back."

He didn't—not for a very long time.

We moved into the new house in Kariokor without Abeh. At first my father used to call us occasionally, using the phone at Jinni Boqor's apartment nearby. Jinni Boqor was an Osman Mahamud businessman who was supposed to keep an eye on us. He would send someone over to tell us our father had called and would phone again in an hour, and we would rush over there and stiffly shout at each other in Jinni Boqor's living room. Abeh wrote us letters in the curly Osmaniya script he loved, but we could no longer read Osmaniya. I drew up the courage to write, in English, and tell him so. After that my father's letters became fewer and fewer. One day, they stopped arriving altogether.

It was a miserable time. Every month my mother used to walk to Dayib Haji's office to pick up three thousand shillings. In the beginning that was a lot of money; later, inflation reduced it to very little. Every month a truck would arrive from the storehouse of another Somali businessman, Farah Gouré, with sacks of flour and rice and oil. The clan was providing for her, but she was all alone.

Ma never told us that our father wasn't coming back, but if I woke up in the middle of the night I often heard her crying. One night I walked in and put my hand on her cheek. Ma began to scream at me for sneaking up on her, and she hit me, yelling that I should go back to bed. After that I would just crouch at the door of her room, listening, wishing that in some way I could take away her pain.

As the years went by we all gave up pretending to each other that our father would return.

After barely a year in Nairobi, Mahad managed to win a place at one of the best secondary schools in Kenya. Starehe Boys' Center was a remarkable establishment that gave a number of full scholarships every year to street children and to children whose parents could not hope to pay the fees. Only two hundred children were accepted every year. Mahad made it in because after only a year of speaking English, his grades were in the top ten of the Kenyan national exams. When he was accepted, my mother for once beamed with unadulterated joy. To show off, all Mahad had to do was walk around our neighborhood in his uniform, and all we had to do was walk proudly beside him. All the kids on our street wanted to go to Starehe, but nobody else had ever managed.

Mr. Griffin, Mahad's headmaster, was the incarnation of benevolent authority, and his school was heaven, with sports facilities and a library.

Mahad had a lot of trouble getting out of bed, however, so, to instill some discipline into him, Mr. Griffin agreed to accept him as a boarder. For a while there was a truce between us kids. Mahad came home only on weekends, which was fine by me, and he didn't bully us as much.

When I turned fourteen my mother enrolled me in Muslim Girls' Secondary School on Park Road. It was not a wealthy neighborhood, and this school stood out, clean and white, with a big metal gate and beautifully kept grass that we girls weren't allowed to walk on. The first day, a Somali girl came up to me and introduced herself; she said her name was Amina. Out of mischief and a desire to find a protector in this new place, I said that was my name, too. For my next four years in school, everyone called me Amina: Amina Hirsi Magan.

I made another friend, Halwa, a Yemeni girl who lived near us. Halwa's mother and her aunt each had nine children and lived next door to each other. I took to spending afternoons over there. It was like a tiny village, with lots of women relatives coming and going. Many of these relatives were staying for weeks or months; often, a mother from Halwa's family village in the remote Hadramut in Yemen would arrive with daughters to marry, or simply for a visit. Again I saw the odd, bossy and indignant interaction between the rural *miyé* people coming to the *magalo*—rural visitors from the old world, with their old ways, suddenly crammed into the modern environment of town folk like Halwa's mother and aunt.

Halwa wasn't allowed out of her mother's sight except to go to school, but once she was home she was free to do as she liked. She did no housework: there were women enough around the place. She had no bedtime. We swapped homework—I was becoming good at English, Halwa did my math—and watched TV a lot. Halwa's mother invited me to go along on picnics to the Arboretum, a botanical park. Whenever I could, I went over to her house.

Walking back home from Halwa's house in the late afternoons I would sometimes be overtaken by a swarm of street children heading to the center of town before it grew dark. They were utterly ragged and filthy, the older children all tugging or carrying a younger, even more gummy-eyed child. They traveled in flocks that could number several dozen; perhaps this was safer for them.

These kids lived off garbage heaps like the one at the end of our street. They were engulfed in the disgusting odor of rotting food and dead rats. I sometimes stopped and watched them picking out food and things to sell. They covered themselves in plastic bags when it rained and sniffed shoe polish out of paper bags until a film of black polish coated their faces. Thinking about these children's lives made me feel both pained and incredibly lucky. I had a roof over my head and a mother, and when I got home there would be something to eat. Compared to these kids, I had nothing to complain about.

Still, the atmosphere at our house was heavy with reproach. My grandmother squatted balefully on her bed, miserable in our new environment. Again and again she told my mother the source of their troubles: a curse that had taken form when Ma left her first husband, long ago, in Aden. This deepened my mother's moodiness. She developed great whirlwinds of sudden, random anger. She smashed furniture and plates. She broke two charcoal braziers because they wouldn't light. Where she had been merely distant, and occasionally even kind, she began to beat us for the slightest misdemeanor, grabbing our hair, hitting us until she couldn't lift her hand any more. She was tyrannical, unreasonable; she screamed a lifetime of frustration in our faces.

I knew it was not hatred for us but because she was so unhappy, and I pitied her. Our mother had been abandoned in a foreign country that she scorned, with three children to guide and no man to act as her anchor. Her daily life in no way resembled the life to which she aspired and that she felt she deserved. My mother saw herself as a victim. Once upon a time she had shaped her future and made decisions—she had left Somalia for Aden, divorced her first husband and chosen my father—but at some point, it seemed, she lost hope.

Many Somali women in her position would have worked, would have taken control of their lives, but my mother, having absorbed the Arab attitude that pious women should not work outside the home, felt that this would not be proper. It never occurred to her to go out and create a new life for herself, although she can't have been older than thirty-five or forty when my father left. Instead, she remained completely dependent. She nursed grievances; she was resentful; she was often violent; and she was always depressed.

Even though my new school was called Muslim Girls', many of the girls weren't Muslim. Almost half the class were Kenyans, who were mostly Christians, although the Kikuyu also had another, pagan god. Kenyans were divided into tribes, which were very different from the clans in Somalia; the tribes looked different, spoke different languages, and had different beliefs, whereas all the Somali clans spoke the same language and believed in Islam.

Still, there were similarities. The Kikuyu saw themselves as warriors; having fought for independence, they felt their tribe had a right to rule. The Kamba earned a lot of money—they were traders—but the other girls said they were stingy; they had a saying, "If you marry a Kamba, you'll starve to death." The Luo considered themselves smarter than the others, and it was true that they worked hard and always did well at school.

Almost all the girls at my primary school had been Kenyans, so I was already more or less familiar with these differences. What was new to me at Muslim Girls' Secondary was that more than half of my classmates were from the Arabian peninsula and South Asia. With these children, too, it seemed every ethnic group was clearly distinct and splintered along lines of class and tribe. The Indians had an inaccessibly complicated system of social classes, all of them unbelievers to Muslim eyes. The Pakistanis were Muslims, but they, too, had castes. The Untouchable girls, both Indian and Pakistani, were darker-skinned. The others wouldn't play with them because they were Untouchable. We thought that was funny—because of course they were touchable: we touched them, see?—but also horrifying, to think of yourself as untouchable, despicable to the human race.

The Somalis divided into clans and subclans, but there was also a new distinction between recent Somali exiles, who were the families of warriors, and older immigrants who had grown up in Kenya and whose grasp of the Somali language was poor. Some of the Arab girls had clans, as we did. If you were a Yemeni called Sharif then you were superior to a Yemeni called Zubaydi. Any kind of Arab girl considered herself superior to everyone else: she was born closer to the Prophet Muhammad.

On the school playground, the Somalis and Yemenis were close, and the Indians and Pakistanis were close. The Yemenis, Somalis, Indians, and Pakistanis played with each other and interacted, but in the hierarchy of Muslim Girls' Secondary School, the Kenyans were the lowest.

These sharp fragmentations of the student body extended even to our lunch boxes. At lunch break we sat in the school garden, which was like a park with benches shaded by trees where we could eat. The Pakistani and Indian girls' corner smelled of curry and *bhajias*. The Yemeni and Somali girls' food had fragrances of coriander and ginger. The Kenyan girls carried *ugali* and ate it with *sukumawiki,* the food with the strongest smell of all.

If we got pocket money, the lunch boxes remained closed because we bought fish and chips served on a newspaper at the school canteen. Sometimes we bought cassava with chili and lemon, and green mangoes sold at the gate of the school. It was a strange scene, with all the girls extending money through the bars of the locked gate and the large, Kenyan mama on the other side enduring our yelling and serving each girl with a smile.

My mother was appalled by our contact with all these children. Perhaps worst of all, for her, was the specter of the Somali kids who had lost their language, who spoke only what to her was the Kenyans' mongrel Swahili. My mother had her clan's love of words. She insisted that we speak perfect Somali at home, mocking us mercilessly for the slightest slip. She began teaching us to memorize poetry, old chants of war and death, raids, herding, green pastures, herds of many camels.

There is little romance in Somali poetry. Even the lesser, women's poems do not mention love. Love is considered synonymous with desire, and sexual desire is seen as low—literally unspeakable. To Haweya and me, these poems lacked the seductive power of the stories our classmates lent us.

At Muslim Girls', a dainty Luo woman called Mrs. Kataka taught us literature. We read *1984*, *Huckleberry Finn*, *The Thirty-Nine Steps*. Later, we read English translations of Russian novels, with their strange patronymics and snowy vistas. We imagined the British moors in *Wuthering Heights* and the fight for racial equality in South Africa in *Cry, the Beloved Country*. An entire world of Western ideas began to take shape.

Haweya and I read all the time. Mahad used to read, too; if we did him favors, he would pass us the Robert Ludlum thrillers he picked up from his friends. Later on there were sexy books: *Valley of the Dolls*, Barbara Cartland, Danielle Steele. All these books, even the trashy ones, carried with them ideas—races were equal, women were equal to men—and concepts of freedom, struggle, and adventure that were new to me. Even our plain old biology and science textbooks seemed to follow a powerful narrative: you went out with knowledge and sought to advance humanity.

After school, Ma began insisting that I do all the housework. At first we were all supposed to share the chores, but Mahad only sneered when Ma told him to clean his room, and Haweya point-blank refused. It was my job anyway: I was the eldest daughter. That was my destiny.

The floors had to be washed by hand, the clothes—even Mahad's filthy socks—scrubbed perfectly and hung out to dry. Every night I had to knead the *chapattis* for the next morning's breakfast . I had to accompany Ma on constant errands to act as her translator: whenever she went to the doctor for her headaches, her psoriasis, a mysterious pain in her womb, or when she had to pay the electric bills or pick up the mail. Every time, we had to walk, because Ma said the rattling Kenyan buses stank, and also because she simply didn't know how to navigate them.

Haweya pitied me. She always said, "Just refuse." But I couldn't—I wasn't like my sister. When we were disobedient, we were beaten. My mother would catch me, pull my hair, fix my hands behind my back with rope, and put me down on the floor, on my belly. She tied my hands to my ankles, and then with a stick or a wire she would beat me until I begged for mercy and swore I would never do it again. I couldn't stand the pain of Ma's beatings, and for as long as I could remember, a sense of responsibility had been drilled into me. I *should* be helping my mother.

Other children were punished, too. All the children I knew were sometimes beaten by their parents. But not everyone got tied up, and it didn't happen to them every week, as it sometimes did with me. I was punished far more often than Mahad. But Haweya was punished most of all.

Yet Haweya seemed immune to pain. She took the worst beatings my mother could hand out but refused to relent. Haweya simply would not do the housework—the cleaning, the washing of all the clothes and sheets by hand, wringing them out and hanging them straight in the sun. Haweya would just yell and yell, a ball of fury twice as strong as my mother. As time went by, it became too much trouble to beat her.

We had report cards every term. Haweya's and Mahad's reports glowed, but when Ma looked at mine, she always said, "I have three children and one of them is retarded." It wasn't fair. It was true that I was slower than Mahad and Haweya, but I had so much housework to do that I often didn't have time for homework. I knew, though, that if I complained, Ma might take me out of school altogether.

Mahad was the man of the house now. Strangely, I think that Mahad was actually relieved when my father left. Abeh always disapproved of his laziness and the way he bullied and bossed us. If we didn't do what Mahad wanted, he hurt us so much that even brave Haweya did his bidding. Ma never interfered with this; if anything, she encouraged Mahad's authority.

Mahad was about fifteen, and as a boy he didn't have to mind my mother as much as we did. He used to walk home from Starehe Boys'

School on Friday afternoons, and sometimes he didn't turn up until long after nightfall. He had discovered the lure of the streets. If Ma yelled at him, he simply ignored her. If she hit him, he walked out of the house. After my mother bought padlocks, Mahad climbed the high fence around the gate to escape. He slicked his hair with gel until he looked like Lionel Ritchie. He listened to Michael Jackson on a battered tape deck he had somehow laid his hands on; my mother called it "devil music" and threw the tape out of the window. Mahad hung out on corners with Kenyan boys, and when he came home he stank of cigarettes and cologne.

On such evenings, Ma would drag me around the neighborhood to look for my brother. Ma complained about the choking odors of *suku-mawiki* and beer, but we tramped from one family's house to the next. The Kenyan parents of Mahad's friends had big glass mugs of beer on their tables, and they always offered a glass to Ma. She would huff, "I am a Muslim!" indignantly, and lecture them. The jovial Kenyan fathers used to laugh at her and say things like "Leave your boy to walk around, he will work things out." Ma would stomp out, and I would cringe at her rudeness.

These evenings were long and mostly fruitless: looking for Mahad was like combing the whole desert for one lost camel. But if I refused to go out looking with her, if I said "My homework is more important," I would be punished.

When I was fourteen I got my period, without even knowing menstruation existed. I had no older sister, and my mother never discussed anything to do with sex. In one class, when I was twelve, all the girls got the assignment to go home and ask our parents what the moon meant. Probably the moon meant menstruation to some Kenyan tribe, and when they went home with this question, presumably they received some kind of explanation. But when I told Ma of our school assignment and asked her what the moon meant, she pointed at the sky and said, "There it is. And if the slaves don't know that, then why am I sending you to their school?"

So I was mystified. The next day the teacher, who was male, wrote up a bunch of diagrams and some words on the blackboard, and there was a lot of giggling. Perhaps menstruation was one of the words, but I couldn't tell you. I had not the first idea of what the whole thing was about.

Two years after that episode, I woke up on a Thursday morning with blood running down my legs. There was no cut on my thighs, and I couldn't figure out why I should bleed. It continued all day, enough to fill my underpants, and I didn't have that many underpants; so I washed them out and hid them behind the boiler to dry. I kept bleeding all the next day, too, and by now there were four or five underpants balled up behind the boiler and the pants I was wearing were wet. I was worried— I thought there was a cut inside my belly, that I might die—but I didn't tell my mother. I knew that what was happening to me was shameful, though I didn't know why.

Then Haweya, who used to sneak around and spy on me, found the stash of stained underwear. She came into the living room waving them. My mother howled and screamed at me, "Filthy prostitute! May you be barren! May you get cancer!" She started to hit me with the ball of her fist. I ran for refuge to the bedroom that Haweya and I shared.

Then Mahad came in. I will always be grateful to Mahad for this; he told me, "Listen, Ayaan, this is normal. It will happen to you every month. It is because you are a woman and you can get pregnant." He gave me ten shillings and said, "This is all the money I have, but if you go to the grocery store it will buy you three packages of Stayfree. It is a little padded paper towel that you put inside your underpants to catch the blood."

I asked him, "When did this happen to you, and where is your Stayfree?" But Mahad told me, "I don't have this happen to me because I am a man." It was the first time in years that Mahad had acted toward me as a friend and confidant rather than a bully.

A few days later my mother simmered down; perhaps my grandmother calmed her. She sat me down and told me that this was my burden as a woman, and that from now on I would have to sew rags into cloth towels and wash them out. I didn't care; I had my Stayfree.

There was no further discussion. In our household, the whole subject of what was between your legs was taboo. I knew what I needed to know about sex, and my mother knew that I knew it. I was a Somali woman, and therefore my sexuality belonged to the owner of my family: my father or my uncles. It was obvious that I absolutely had to be a virgin at marriage, because to do otherwise would damage the honor of my father and his whole clan—uncles, brothers, male cousins—forever and irretrievably. The place between my legs was sewn up to prevent it. It would be broken only by my husband. I don't remember my mother ever telling me these things, but I knew them.

In the months after I first got my period, I educated myself. I read through the chapter on human reproduction in our biology book that Mrs. Karim had carefully skipped. I attended the optional class on "grooming" that the district nurse gave every year. She told us we could now get pregnant and taught us about contraception and the basic biology of wombs and embryos. She did not explain how the sperm got to the egg; there was just this sperm. It didn't help me much.

I did know that sex was bad. Sometimes in the evenings, when I tramped with Ma through the neighborhood searching for Mahad, listening to her never-ending complaints about the foul odor of *sukumawiki,* we came across people making out in alleyways. The nights were dark in the side streets; we could barely see these couples before we were practically on top of them. When this happened Ma would grab me by the hair and yank me down the alley and beat me, as if I had been the one engaged in sex, and scream, "Tell me you didn't look at anything!"

Haweya and I were entering the danger zone, the time of our lives when we should not be permitted out of the house without supervision. About a month after my first period, Ma decided we girls should stop attending Quran school. We had been attending a Somali-style Quran school, with boys and girls mixed, fifty kids of every age crammed into a room with one *ma'alim,* teacher. The *ma'alim* really didn't notice who was learning and who was just moving their lips, and he never seemed to notice, either, that a lot of meaningful eye contact was going on there every Saturday. I could see it out of the corner of my eye.

In addition, Haweya and I got up to an unforgivable amount of mischief on the way to Quran school. One afternoon we developed a game with two other Somali girls. We'd talk to some random small child on the street, take his hand, and walk a few blocks, then deposit the child in front of a house, ring the doorbell like crazy, and run away. When the people opened the door they'd look out, mystified, at adult height, find no one, and then catch sight of an unknown small child who was far too little to reach the doorbell. They'd be so bewildered, and there'd be such a ruckus of women looking for their children and the baby screaming. It doesn't seem funny to me now, but at the time this game made us all weak with laughter.

One day those fat, screaming mothers followed us to Quran school and told the *ma'alim* "It was that one, and THAT one." That night we were punished beyond endurance. And from then on, Ma hired an itinerant preacher to come to our house every Saturday to teach us the Quran.

This itinerant *ma'alim* was young and ragged, straight from the most rural depths of Somalia. He taught us the Quran the old way. You opened chapter one of the Quran, got your long wooden board, wrote it down in Arabic, learned it by heart in Arabic, recited it by heart, washed the board with reverence because it was now holy, and did it again. You did this for two hours, and every mistake earned you a rap on your hands or legs with a thin, sharp stick. There was no discussion about meaning. Often we had no idea what the words meant: we were learning a text in a language that I only barely remembered, and most other children didn't even begin to understand.

It was boring and tiresome. I already had so much to do on Saturday. I had homework. I had to deal with my hair: hours of shampoo and coconut oil and braiding by my mother into ten or eleven tight rows so it would lie flat another week. Then I would have to wash my school uniforms, and because my mother begged me, I would wash Haweya's and Mahad's as well. I also had to clean my part of the house. And then, because this new *ma'alim* did everything the old Somali way, I had to make ink before every lesson, scraping a piece of charcoal into powder with a broken piece of rough stone roofing tile, carefully dribbling milk and water onto the powder in a jam jar.

One Saturday Ma beat me because I didn't finish the washing or cleaning and hadn't washed my hair; I had done only my homework. Also, I was being argumentative and talked back to her. When the time came to make the ink I was already furious with the injustice of it all. I told Haweya, "You know what? I'm not going to do this anymore. Bring a book and we'll lock ourselves in the bathroom. You just stay quiet, so you won't get beaten."

When the *ma'alim* arrived, there were no boards, no mats, no ink, and no children.

My mother came to the bathroom door and cursed us. The *ma'alim* tried to make us come out, too, but we said no. We were insolent. "People stopped writing on wooden boards five hundred years ago," we told him. "You're primitive. You don't teach us religion properly. You are not our relative and you should not be in our house without our father's permission, and according to the Quran you should leave."

Finally, my mother told the *ma'alim* she had to go out, so he couldn't stay in the house. She paid him for the month and told him not to come back. He said, "Your children need discipline, and I can help you. But if you wish, we will leave it in the hands of Allah," and he left. My mother left, and then my grandmother went out to visit some of her Isaq relatives. And she left the gate unlocked.

Haweya and I slowly emerged as we heard the others leave. We watched the *ma'alim* walking down Juja Road toward Eastleigh. We realized we were free to go, and Haweya zipped out to a friend's. I was feeling guilty, and also worried about the scale of the punishment that would inevitably ensue, and so I began cleaning the house, doing the chores I hadn't done that morning. Then I remembered that the gate was still open; I ran out in the yard to close it.

Just as I was closing the gate, a hand came down on my wrist. The *ma'alim* was back, with another man. He must have walked all the way to Eastleigh and brought this man back with him, because he could not be alone with girls in a strange house. They dragged me inside and the *ma'alim* blindfolded me with a cloth and started to hit me with all his strength with a sharp stick, to teach me a lesson.

Because I had been washing the floor I was wearing only an undershirt and skirt; my arms and lower legs were bare, and the lashes were really painful. Suddenly I felt a surge of rage. I tore off the blindfold and glared at the *ma'alim*. I really wanted to stand up to this man. He grabbed my braided hair and pulled my head back, and then he shoved it against the wall. I distinctly heard a cracking noise. Then he stopped. There was this uneasy quiet, like something had gone wrong. And then the *ma'alim* picked up his things and left, along with the stranger he had brought with him.

My whole body was burning and swollen from the lashes and my nose had begun to bleed. For a little while I just held my head. Finally I went to close the gate and took a cold shower to make it hurt less. I felt so giddy that although I wanted to make the fire and cook, I just couldn't. I just lay down in my bed, and nobody woke me.

The next thing I knew it was Sunday morning, and when I went downstairs my mother said, "There's something about your face." I told her I didn't care. She began listing my chores—do the washing, this and that—and I refused. I answered back. I was impossible. By the end of the day she had lost her temper completely: she was going to tie me down and teach me a lesson.

Normally she would grab me and then tell me to lie down on my belly on the floor and hold my ankles, so that she could tie me up for my beating. My mother used to beat us only on our arms and legs. But now I refused to lie down and hold my ankles as I should. She pulled my hair—on the side where I was hurt—but I didn't care any more. I wouldn't do it. She bit me and pinched me and called my grandmother to help her—and everything, by this time, was hurting—but I wouldn't get down. I didn't cry: I looked at her, full of hate, and told her, "I'm not going to take this anymore."

Ma demanded that Mahad help her get me down. I told him, in English so she wouldn't understand, "Please don't do it. Yesterday she beat me and I was beaten by the *ma'alim*. Now they are beating me the same way. I do all the work here and it isn't fair."

Mahad said, "I'll have no part in this," and he left. Now Ma was even more angry, because she felt betrayed. At around midnight she and Grandma finally managed to get me down. They tied me up, and I said to my mother, just like Haweya always did, "Go on. Get it over with—kill me. And if you don't do it now, I'll do it myself when you've let me go." My mother beat me—really beat me—and then she said, "I'm not going to untie you. You can sleep on the floor tonight."

Around three in the morning Ma came back in from her bedroom and released me, and I fell asleep. At eight it was time to go to school. I was blurry and off balance, and just before lunchtime I fainted. Someone brought me home, and I slept some more, and then my mother went out. I went into her bedroom and opened the drawer that was full of all kinds of medicine. I took a huge mug of water and started swallowing pills. I probably took forty or fifty of them.

Later, the doctor said they were mostly vitamin pills, but at the time I didn't know that—I wanted to die. I was in pain, physically, mentally, and socially. Our life seemed to have unraveled. Everyone was unhappy. My mother gave us no sense of security or direction; she was using me to vent all her anger and pain, and I had to face facts: my father was never going to come back.

But I didn't die, and the next day I had to go to school again. One of my eyes had burst a blood vessel, either from the *ma'alim* beating me, or my mother. I just told the other girls to leave me alone.

That Tuesday, Aunt Jim'o Musse came to visit my mother. Aunt Jim'o was the sister of Abshir Musse, one of the other prominent men in the SSDF. My father and Abshir and Jim'o felt close because their mothers were Isse Mahamud. When I came home from school Aunt Jim'o looked at me, and her voice changed. "Ayaan, what is it?" she asked. "Are you all right?" I said, "I have a headache, and I have this swelling, here." When Jim'o Musse touched the left side of my head she looked worried. "Who has done this to you?" she said. "We have to get you to the hospital." There was a lump like an overripe tomato, and she thought that if she pressed it with her finger she might go right through the skull, it was so soft.

My mother ran in and said, "What's wrong? Who hit your head?" By then I was utterly drained. I said, "On Saturday, when you left, the *ma'alim* came back, and he hit me, and on Sunday you finished the job." My mother began crying and wailing, "Now there's this, on top of everything else—what have I done to deserve it all, Allah?"

Aunt Jim'o Musse was a top-flight Osman Mahamud, so she mobilized the clan. "Hirsi Magan's daughter is probably going to die," she told them. "She has a huge wound on her head, and we have to get her to the hospital." The next morning men came and drove me to Nairobi Hospital, which was absolutely the finest hospital in Nairobi but very expensive. An Italian doctor ordered X rays. My skull was fractured, and a huge amount of blood had collected between my head skin and my skull; it was compressing the brain, and I needed an immediate operation. They shaved off my hair, which was horrible; I had an enormous scar and had to stay in the hospital for twelve days. The clan paid.

It was while I was in the hospital that I saw for the first time that my mother did, truly, love me, deep in her heart, and that all the abuse wasn't really directed at me, but at the world, which had taken her rightful life away. I confessed to her that I had taken the pills, and every time she visited she would cling to me and tell me she loved me and cry. I had never seen her so vulnerable.

After that, she didn't beat me again for several years.

When I went back to school, things were different. Girls I used to know had left; when I asked about it, people shrugged and said they had probably gone to be married. This had happened before, from time to time; even in primary school, one girl left because she was betrothed. Somehow, though, I had never really noticed it before.

Now I saw that Latifa, one of the Arab girls from the coast, had suddenly disappeared from our classroom. According to Halwa, one Saturday afternoon Latifa's father told her that she was never going back to school; the time had come for her to prepare to become a woman. A classmate had been invited to Latifa's wedding, and she talked about it. The groom was older, from Mombasa; there had been lots of presents. Latifa had looked frightened; she had cried, and her tears stained the dress she wore, which had been stiff and white.

One after another, girls began announcing that they were leaving school to get married. Mostly they told the teachers about it, too. It was perfectly respectable. It wouldn't have occurred to anyone in authority to prevent these children from being taken out of school to marry total strangers, even though most of the girls were reluctant and some were petrified. One girl was forced to marry her uncle's son, her cousin. A fifteen-year-old Yemeni classmate told us she had just been betrothed to a much older man; she wasn't happy about it, but, she added, "At least it's not as bad as for my sister—she was twelve."

Zainab, a talkative Yemeni girl with round cheeks pockmarked with acne, never came back from the Christmas vacation of 1985. I met her a year later at a festival at the Muslim community center, next to school. She was pregnant, dressed in black, suddenly ugly and fat, with someone else's toddlers in tow. Zainab said she almost never left the house without her mother-in-law. She pleaded for news of school. There seemed to be nothing left of her jokiness, the spark and mischief of the girl who used to fool around with us in the corridors.

I was invited to the joint wedding of Halwa's sisters Siham and Nasrien, who were seventeen and nineteen and had finished school. Women from both sides of the match came to Nairobi from all over Kenya, from Yemen, from Uganda. Before the ceremonies began, all of these women had to inspect the brides. We all filed past Siham and Nasrien, who were lying stiffly on cushions on the floor, with their faces and torsos covered in a green cloth but their arms and legs bare. Every woman gasped at the beauty and ingenuity of the girls' henna designs, though in reality, of course, they were inspecting the merchandise.

The next day the women congregated in a rented hall and feasted and danced—women only. The brides sat on a sofa in pink lace dresses, with makeup like a magazine photo, motionless, like perfect little dolls.

On the final night the feast was in another large hall, and men were present; they ate and talked on the other side of a long, high partition that divided the room, leaving only a raised dais visible to everyone. On the women's side were tables with thousands of pastries and different dishes. I remember thinking I had never eaten food so delicious. After the feasting, the women began ululating, and the brides arrived, in Western dresses, with their faces covered. The two grooms walked up to the dais and lifted their brides' veils, then sat down stiffly. They seemed awkward, straight from Yemen. It was like a scene from Saudi Arabia.

Nasrien had met her husband-to-be briefly, during the preparations. She seemed less nervous, resigned to the whole thing. But Siham, who hadn't met the man she was marrying, was pale, and trembled. They left a little later, with the closest members of the family. I knew from Halwa that there would be bloody sheets, and more celebrating.

"What if you don't bleed?" I asked Halwa. "That would mean you're not a virgin," she whispered. We looked away from each other quickly. Such a thing was unthinkable.

Halwa herself had been betrothed when she was about nine to a cousin she had never met. She didn't want to marry him, but she knew that one day it would happen. Your parents decided these things for you. If your father was kind—and rich—then maybe he would find a husband for you who was also kind and rich. If not, well, that was your destiny.

Love marriages were a stupid mistake and always ended badly, in poverty and divorce; we knew this. If you married outside the rules, you didn't have your clan's protection when your husband left you. Your father's relatives wouldn't intercede on your behalf or help you with money. You sank into a hideous destiny of impurity, godlessness, and disease. People like my grandmother pointed at you and spat at you on the street. It was the worst thing you could do to your family's honor: you damaged your parents, sisters, brothers, and cousins.

But the allure of romance called to us from the pages of books. In school we read good books, Charlotte Brontë, Jane Austen, and Daphne du Maurier; out of school, Halwa's sisters kept us supplied with cheap Harlequins. These were trashy soap opera–like novels, but they were exciting—sexually exciting. And buried in all of these books was a message: women had a choice. Heroines fell in love, they fought off family obstacles and questions of wealth and status, and they married the man they chose.

Most of my Muslim classmates were steeped in these cheap paperbacks, and they made us all unhappy. We, too, wanted to fall in love, with men we imagined in our bed at night. Nobody *wanted* to get married to a stranger chosen by her father. But we knew that the best we could do was simply stave off the inevitable. Halwa's father allowed all his daughters to finish school before marrying them off. Halwa used to beg her father to let her off the hook even after she had finished school. She used to tell me sometimes that I was lucky: with my father away, no one would make me get married before I finished my first round of exams, at least.

I turned sixteen, and a new teacher arrived to teach Islamic education. Religious education was a compulsory subject at Muslim Girls', and it was divided into two sections: Islamic and Christian. The Islamic class, which we naturally attended, was dry and dull, the least spiritual class you could imagine. There was no analysis, no ethical discussion, just basic, neutral historical information; we learned lists of battles and revelations by the Prophet, following a curriculum for the national exams.

But Sister Aziza was different from any other teacher we had ever had. For one thing, she wanted to be called by her first name, Sister Aziza, rather than Miss Said. For another, she was veiled. Not just with a head-scarf, which many teachers wore; Sister Aziza cloaked herself in full *hid-jab*. Thick black cloth fell from the top of her head to the tips of her gloves and the very limit of her toes. It was spectacular. Her pale, heart-shaped face stood out against a sea of black. Sister Aziza was young and beauti-ful—light-skinned and fine-nosed—and she had a smile in her eyes. She never shouted the way other teachers did.

The first thing Sister Aziza asked was, "How many of you are Mus-lims?" The whole class put their hands up, of course. We were clearly Muslims, had been since birth. But Sister Aziza shook her head sadly, and said, "I don't think you are Muslims."

We were startled. Not Muslims? What could she possibly mean? She pointed at me. "When was the last time you prayed?" I quaked inwardly. It had been over a year since I had ritually washed myself and put on the white cloth and prostrated myself for the long ritual submission to God. "I don't remember," I mumbled. Sister Aziza pointed to other girls in the class. And you? And you?" All but a few said they couldn't remember either.

We were not true Muslims, Sister Aziza sadly informed the abashed and suddenly silent classroom. Allah did not look on us with delight. He could see into our hearts, and He knew we were not dedicated to Him. The goal of prayer was awareness—constant awareness of the presence of God and the angels—and an inward submission to God's will that per-meated every thought and action, every day.

Sister Aziza reminded us of the angels we had learned about in school in Saudi Arabia, who hovered above each of our shoulders. On the left and on the right, they recorded our thoughts, intentions, and ideas—bad and good. Even if we did cover ourselves and pray, that was not suffi-ciently meaningful for God. What counted was the *intention*. If your mind strayed—if you were doing it for the wrong reasons—God and the angels could look in your heart and/know.

We had heard all about Hell. That was what Quran school was mostly about: Hell and all the mistakes that could put us there. The Quran lists Hell's torments in vivid detail: sores, boiling water, peeling skin, burning flesh, dissolving bowels, the everlasting fire that burns you forever, for as your flesh chars and your juices boil, you form a new skin. These details overpower you, ensuring that you will obey. The *ma'alim* whose class Haweya and I now had to attend on Saturdays used to shriek out the taboos and restrictions, the rules to obey, spitting sometimes with the excitement of it: "You will go to Hell! And YOU will go to Hell! And YOU, and YOU—UNLESS! . . ."

Hell in the Quran has seven gates. The heat and pain of burning are endless. The thirst is intense and causes so much pain, so much more than any thirst does on earth, that you start wailing for water. The searing juices from your burning body are thrown into your mouth. You long for Heaven, and this longing goes on forever and ever. This intensely harsh, desertlike Hereafter was much more vivid to us than Heaven. In the Quran, Heaven was a cool climate, with breezes and delicious drinks; this was pleasant, but rather vague.

Sister Aziza believed in Hell, there was no question about that. But she didn't emphasize fear, as all the other preachers did. She told us it was our choice. We could choose to submit to God's pureness and light and earn a place in Heaven, or we could take the low road.

Her classes were compelling, but I didn't become an instant convert. And what was so great about Sister Aziza was that she didn't mind. She didn't mind if we didn't wear white trousers under our skirts to hide our legs. She didn't mind if we didn't pray five times a day. She told us God didn't want us to do anything—not even pray—without the inner intention. He wanted true, deep submission: this is the meaning of Islam. "This is how Allah and the Prophet want us to dress," she told us. "But you should do it only when you're ready, because if you do it earlier and you take the robe off again, you'll only be sinning more. When you're ready for it, you'll choose, and then you'll never take it off."

Often Mahad brought two of his best friends home with him on weekends. Both were Kenyans, but Mahad didn't want to tell Ma that he had only Kenyan friends; she wouldn't have let two Kenyan kids into the house. So Mahad cooked up a story that his best friend, who was in reality named Kennedy, was a Somali boy called Yusuf, from eastern Kenya, where they don't speak Somali anymore. My mother didn't mind that so much, and at least having a friend at home kept Mahad inside her four walls. (She tolerated the other friend, who was called Olulo. His features were so Kenyan that there was no way Mahad could pretend he was Somali.)

When the boys came in late in the evening I would often be busy preparing the dough for the next morning's breakfast, and I'd cook them up some dinner. Yusuf was cute, and kind to me, and those evenings were fun—making jokes, being teased. In the beginning Yusuf and I were never alone together, but gradually we began bumping into each other in the kitchen. He began coming over even if Mahad was out, claiming he was looking for him. He used to joke with me that his name wasn't really Yusuf, it was Kennedy, and he was Kenyan. I didn't believe him, of course. Yusuf was interested in me; I knew it, and liked it. There was no touching—nothing was said, or done—but every so often a meaningful stare made my knees tremble.

Sister Aziza never actually told us we should robe as she did, or not to go to the cinema or talk to boys. She just read through the verses in the Holy Quran, using an English-Arabic edition, so we could understand it. Then she talked about them. She said, "I'm not telling you to behave like this. I'm only telling you what God said: avoid sin."

I knew precisely what Sister Aziza meant when she talked about sinning. Sin was the feeling I had when I was with Yusuf. The sudden, tingling awareness, the inner excitement. At night I thought about how much I would like to marry Yusuf when I grew up. I tried to put it in a context where this feeling would not be sinful.

One evening Yusuf asked if I'd like to go to the movies with him. My heart pounding, because this was clearly forbidden, I said yes. We agreed to meet in Uhuru Park, the big park in downtown Nairobi; that way nobody from the neighborhood would see us. I wore a short dress—at least, it seemed short to me: knee-length. And I used deodorant for the first time. It felt wanton.

I took the *matatou,* the rattling Kenyan minibus, by myself. There he was, by the lake, where he said he'd be. We had an hour before the film would begin. As we walked around, talking, Yusuf fumbled for my hand. My heart thudded so hard when he touched me I thought people must have heard it.

We sat on the grass and talked about Yusuf's family, and Kisii, where his family lived, and his brother's house where he stayed on weekends in Nairobi. He asked me to call him Ken, which still seemed like a joke. I still didn't know he was really Kenyan, though it wouldn't have made any difference to me. I wouldn't have minded what he was. Ken asked, "How do you feel about me?" and I said, "I really like you." He said he really liked me, too, and we started to kiss.

It was my first kiss. It was wonderful, and went on for a long time. That's all we did: held hands, kissed, and then we went to the cinema and he took me to the bus stop and went away. And all the way home I felt I was floating.

Ken and I didn't see each other very often. I could escape my mother's surveillance only once in a while, and even when I did, I knew that any Somali person who walked past could report us, so we couldn't relax our guard very often. But the feeling of kissing was the best I had ever felt in my life. I told Ken, "You know I can't sleep with you," and he said, "I know. You're Somali and you have to remain a virgin. I love you very much and I will wait for you. We'll get married." It was completely mutual, completely innocent, and it felt so good.

But I also knew that it was evil. I was living on several levels in my brain. There was kissing Kennedy; there was clan honor; and there was Sister Aziza and God.

In the classroom, Sister Aziza listed the seductions of Satan: the desire to look beautiful and attract men; the thrill of having fun; and music and evil books. She knew about these things. Sister Aziza was an Arab Kenyan, from the coast, and after she left school she was a stewardess and a bank teller in Nairobi. For both jobs, she told us, she had to dress in pumps and Western dresses and fix her hair.

But that life had been too empty for her. She found that what she truly wanted was to become a good Muslim, so she went to study in Saudi Arabia, in Medina. Her faith had become deeper, straighter, more pure. She had cast aside ignorant practices, such as praying to saints. She had returned to the true faith at the source of Islam; this was why she had chosen to cover herself, to seek the deeper satisfaction of pleasing God.

As women, we were immensely powerful, Sister Aziza explained. The way Allah had created us, our hair, our nails, our heels, our neck, and ankles—every little curve in our body was arousing. If a woman aroused a man who was not her husband, she was sinning doubly in God's eyes, by leading the man into temptation and evil thoughts to match her own. Only the robe worn by the wives of the Prophet could prevent us from arousing men and leading society into *fitna,* uncontrollable confusion and social chaos.

She was strict about obedience and hygiene. Every month, Sister Aziza told us, we must shave our underarms and pubic hair to make ourselves pure. We must purify ourselves after our periods. Womanhood was both irresistibly desirable and essentially filthy, and all these interventions were necessary to earn Allah's pleasure.

Sister Aziza introduced us to the inner struggle. There were two kinds of struggle for Allah, and the first effort was the *jihad* within ourselves: submission of our will. We must *want* to obey our parents, and to behave in a manner that spreads kindness. We must want to be dutiful. We must think about Allah's will in every gesture of every day and choose to lay down ourselves before Him. She ignored the textbooks that were supposed to prepare us for the national exam in Islamic studies. Like our Quran teachers in Saudi Arabia, Sister Aziza was preparing us for a practice of faith, not prepping us in the history of Islam.

I began praying in the evenings sometimes. It is a long ritual. First you wash and cover yourself in the long white cloth, fixing your gaze to the floor, because Allah is present and you do not look God in the eye. You recite the opening chapter of the Quran, a short chapter made up of just seven verses. Then you prostrate yourself, with your palms open toward Mecca, the heartland of religion. You say *Praise be to Allah,* and stand up again; you say another verse of the Quran—you are free to choose which verse. You repeat the whole procedure, two, three, or four times, depending on what time of day it is. Each time you must recite the first chapter of the Quran and one other small chapter or some verses from a longer chapter of your choosing. Then you sit and end the prayer by looking sideways, first right and then left, and you cup your hands together and ask for God's blessing. You beg: *Allah make me wise, forgive my sins. Bless my parents and give them health, and please Allah, put my parents in Paradise. Please Allah, keep me on the safe path.*

Then you take your prayer beads, which are a multiple of thirty-three—or, as I did, for I had no beads, you use your finger bones. Each hand has fifteen bones in it, counting the base of your thumbs, so two hands, plus the three digits of one extra finger, are thirty-three. You say *Praise be to Allah* thirty-three times; *God forgive me* thirty-three times; *Allah is great* thirty-three times; and then, if you choose, you may also say *Gratitude to Allah.*

Prayer is a long procedure, and it is required five times a day. In the beginning I almost never managed to do all of it, but it felt good to be trying.

Sister Aziza told us about the Jews. She described them in such a way that I imagined them as physically monstrous: they had horns on their heads, and noses so large they stuck right out of their faces like great beaks. Devils and djinns literally flew out of their heads to mislead Muslims and spread evil. Everything that went wrong was the fault of the Jews. The Iraqi tyrant Saddam Hussein, who had attacked the Islamic Revolution in Iran, was a Jew. The Americans, who were giving money to Saddam, were controlled by the Jews. The Jews controlled the world, and that was why we had to be pure: to resist this evil influence. Islam was under attack, and we should step forward and fight the Jews, for only if all Jews were destroyed would peace come for Muslims.

I began to experiment with the headscarf. I wore it long, so the shape of my neck and shoulders could not be seen. I wore trousers under my school uniform, to hide my bare legs. I wanted to be like Sister Aziza. I wanted to be pure, and good, and serve Allah. I began to pray five times a day, fighting to collect my thoughts through the whole long process. I wanted to understand better how to live the life that Allah, who was infinitely just, wanted for me.

I asked my mother for money so Sister Aziza's tailor could make me a huge black cloak, with just three tight bands around my wrists and neck and a long zipper. It fell to my toes. I began wearing this robe to school, on top of the school uniform that hung off my scrawny frame, with a black scarf over my hair and shoulders.

It had a thrill to it, a sensuous feeling. It made me feel powerful: underneath this screen lay a previously unsuspected, but potentially lethal, femininity. I was unique: very few people walked about like that in those days in Nairobi. Weirdly, it made me feel like an individual. It sent out a message of superiority: I was the one true Muslim. All those other girls with their little white headscarves were children, hypocrites. I was a star of God. When I spread out my hands I felt like I could fly.

I was one of the first to robe in school. Some of the Yemeni girls, like Halwa, wore long buttoned coats, but these were tailored to fit the body; you could see a female shape inside. The *hidjab* I draped over my scrawny frame was overwhelmingly enveloping: there was simply nothing left to see except a small face and two hands.

When I arrived in school, I took off my robe and folded it up inside my desk. Then, at the end of the day, I modestly unfolded it and put it on—and suddenly I was interesting, mysterious, powerful. I could see it just by looking at my classmates. And the delight in my mother's eyes when she saw me in that garment! It was the silver lining to the long, dark cloud of her life. Finally I was doing something right.

Sister Aziza told us it was our duty to convert our Christian classmates. She told us it was the only way to spare our friends the pain of Hell. I tried my best to approach the other girls with the message of the true faith. They answered things like, "How would you feel if I tried to make you a Christian?" They said their parents had taught them about Jesus just as mine had taught me about the Prophet Muhammad, and I should respect their beliefs.

I had to admit I could see their point. Still, I really wanted to prevent these friends of mine from going to Hell. I remember telling Emily one day about the torments that lay in store for her in the afterlife. She said, "But I just don't believe in that. I am saved. Jesus has come for me, he died for me, and he will redeem me." The Christian girls talked about their Trinity: God, the Holy Spirit, and God's Son, all one. To me, this was first-class blasphemy. We'd bicker about theology till it swiftly got to the point where if we didn't leave the subject alone our friendships would have been over.

I went to Sister Aziza and said, "The other girls won't become Muslims. Their parents have taught them other religions. It isn't their fault, and I don't think it's fair that they'll burn in Hell." Sister Aziza told me I was wrong. Through me, Allah had given them a choice. If these girls rejected the true religion, then it was right that they should burn. It made me think that by even trying I was probably making things worse, so I stopped trying to convert my classmates.

Still, it bothered me. If we were created by Allah, and before our birth He had already determined whether we would come to rest in Heaven or Hell, then why would we take the trouble to try to convert these girls, who were also created the way they were by God? Sister Aziza had a very complex theological explanation for predestination. Besides the path that Allah had already determined for us in the womb, there was a further dimension, which was that we had free will, and if you bent your will to the service of God instead of Satan then you pleased God. It wasn't very convincing, but I thought it was my fault that I couldn't understand her.

Quite soon after Sister Aziza arrived, I noticed that a whole religious revival had begun in the school corridors. Just as I and a few other girls met in an unused classroom for Islamic prayer at noon, a group of

Kenyan girls prayed together, too, hollering "Hallelujah!" and singing Gospel songs. I don't know if it was a reaction to the revival of Islam, or some kind of common impulse that drove teenage Nairobi in that direction; but it seemed as though, at the same time that more young Muslims were flocking to a new kind of Islam, more and more Christians were going to church. And they, too, were heading for a purer faith, closer to the roots of their religion. A faith that was less passive, more engaged with personal study of holy texts.

The charismatic Christians were no less aggressive than the fundamentalist Muslims in those days. The whole country was beginning to fall apart; perhaps people were grabbing for certainties. Preachers of some sect or other were all over the place. Girls in school talked about Alice Lakwena, in neighboring Uganda, whose followers were immune to bullets. That was the most spectacular movement, but there were many other small bands of strange zealots. Shabby street-front churches began to sprout where once there were grocery stalls. Jehovah's Witnesses used to go from door to door. And, of course, at every street corner there were all kinds of old tribal soothsayers and magicians. Even in my class at Muslim Girls' Secondary, girls would buy love potions made of crushed fingernails and animal skin, or amulets to help them pass exams.

The state in Kenya was crumbling from within, buckling under the larceny and nepotism of the men in control. People were given jobs in ministries who couldn't spell the word minister. The mayor, who was supposed to look after the streets of Nairobi, was barely literate. The government was only there to take your money; its services were minimal. Citizens were no longer citizens—the people who had put such hope in the future of their own, independent nation so short a time ago weren't loyal to the nation any longer. More and more, Kenyan people saw themselves as members of their tribe above all. And any kind of interaction between the tribes was mediated through religion. Religion and a stronger awareness of tribe and clan belonging were replacing any shared national feeling.

The same thing was also happening in Somalia, though I didn't know it then. It was happening, in fact, almost everywhere in Africa and throughout the Islamic world. The more corrupt and unreliable the apparatus of government—the more it persecuted its people—the more those people headed back into their tribe, traditions, their church or mosque, and hunkered down, like among like.

A new kind of Islam was on the march. It was much deeper, much clearer and stronger—much closer to the source of the religion—than the old kind of Islam my grandmother believed in, along with her spirit ancestors and djinns. It was not like the Islam in the mosques, where imams mostly recited by memory old sermons written by long-dead scholars, in an Arabic that barely anyone could understand. It was not a passive, mostly ignorant, acceptance of the rules: *Insh'Allah,* "God wills it." It was about studying the Quran, really learning about it, getting to the heart of the nature of the Prophet's message. It was a huge evangelical sect backed massively by Saudi Arabian oil wealth and Iranian martyr propaganda. It was militant, and it was growing. And I was becoming a very small part of it.

CHAPTER 6

Doubt and Defiance

While I was taking the high road to God, Haweya was veering off the rails. My struggle to submit my will to Allah held no interest whatsoever for my little sister. She said Sister Aziza acted as if we all still rode camels. She called my black robe hideous. Haweya was tall and pretty, and she knew it. She had no intention of creeping around Nairobi covered in a tent, as she described my veil.

My mother may have beaten me a lot, but she also installed in me a sense of discipline. I struggled to do well in school, and I liked it there; I had a lot of friends. But Haweya hated Muslim Girls' Secondary. She made friends but always ended up fighting with them. She was far brighter than I: she let crowds of girls copy her homework in return for the paperback novels that she liked to read. But Haweya's classes were chaotic: In 1985 the Kenyan government decided to purge the secondary school system of aspects it deemed too colonial. This meant that textbooks were missing and teachers had no idea of the syllabus. My sister was bored stiff at school, and she was also tired of being cooped up in our house.

Haweya had always been headstrong and never bowed her will to Ma. She refused to do household chores unless Mahad was made to do them, too—knowing, of course, that that would never happen. When Ma did beat her, Haweya could just withdraw inside herself, as if she were immune to pain. My mother would hit her until her arm hurt, and when she'd finished Haweya would still be defiant. My sister had a will of steel. Sometimes she locked herself in the bathroom and cursed my mother—screaming, calling her hateful and cruel and selfish. But somehow Haweya avoided crying.

My mother had simply no idea of how to manage teenagers. It was as if she had never imagined we would grow up. Adolescence was another part of modern life that was completely foreign to her upbringing. In the desert, where my mother grew up, there is no meaningful space between childhood and becoming a woman.

Haweya was clear-minded and honest, and a fighter. Part of me admired her guts. But sometimes in those teenage years the house would almost explode with the rage it contained. The scenes were hideous. They made me want to crawl inside myself and hide there. Ma, Grandma, Haweya: all of them would scream until fat veins stood out on their foreheads. Any of them might at any time stand up suddenly and push the table over, yelling and cursing to Hell. The sheer volume of it shattered me.

One time Haweya went over to Jinni Boqor's house and asked if she could use his phone to call our father. She said she needed Abeh to send her money to groom herself. Jinni gave Haweya two hundred shillings, and she got her hair straightened and cut into curls around her face. Ma complained to Jinni, but he just winked and said, "The phone call would cost me almost as much. And anyway, she does look good!"

Haweya usually won her battles. She wore high-heeled sandals with straps round her toes, skirts above her knees, and she painted her nails. She looked like my mother's worst nightmare. When Haweya got her period, Ma just burst into tears.

Then Haweya met Sahra, an Isaq woman. Actually, it was my grandmother who met her first, while she was out grazing her sheep, and brought her home for tea—a kinswoman. Sahra dressed in trousers and blouses and wore huge sunglasses, and her hair was dyed red. Sahra was older than we were, about twenty-three or twenty-four. She'd been married at fourteen and had three children. She invited Haweya and me over to her house to watch TV. I had no time for Sahra, but Haweya liked it at her place and took to going there almost every afternoon. The two of them could talk and watch videos for hours. Sometimes Sahra would go out by herself, while Haweya looked after her children; she would buy Haweya books and lipsticks in return.

Gradually, Haweya and Sahra began going out together, to afternoon discos. Sahra used to tell me I, too, should go out and have fun; fun was something you couldn't do when you were older and married. These places were noisy and creepy and didn't appeal to me at all, but Haweya loved to dress up in Sahra's clothes and go dancing.

Sahra told Haweya how awful it was to be married. She said her husband, Abdallah, was repulsive. She told Haweya what it was like when Abdallah had first tried to penetrate her after they were married: pushing his way into her, trying to tear open the scar between her legs, how much it had hurt. She said Abdallah had wanted to cut her open with a knife, because she was sewn so tight that he couldn't push his penis inside. She described him holding the knife in his hand while she screamed and begged him not to—and I suppose he felt pity for that poor fourteen-year-old child, because he agreed to take her to the hospital to be cut.

Sahra's wedding didn't end with a celebration: there was no bloody sheet to show off to the applause and ululations of the wedding guests. There was only a murmur of disappointment and doubt, a suspicion about Sahra's virginity and a snickering about her husband's manhood, before she was taken to the hospital to be made ready for Abdallah the next night.

The story frightened me: a huge group of people, a bloodied sheet—a kind of rape, organized with the benediction of Sahra's family. It didn't in the least seem like something that could happen to Haweya, or to me. But this was marriage, to Sahra: physical assault, public humiliation.

Sahra told Haweya, "I never had a childhood. They took my life away from me." Abdallah was ten or fifteen years older than she; he was some kind of cousin. He didn't seem to beat her, but her hatred of him was implacable. Her revenge was that she did nothing for her kids. She called them his kids. She treated her nine-year-old daughter, Hasna, like a slave. Hasna did the groceries, cooked, and cleaned; Sahra constantly beat her, and spent all her husband's money on clothes and makeup. I thoroughly disapproved of Sahra.

Haweya wasn't the only member of the family straying off the hard and narrow path our mother had in mind for us. Mahad dropped out of school the year he turned sixteen. He just stopped attending. After a few months, Mr. Griffin, his headmaster, told Ma there was nothing more he could do: Mahad couldn't be allowed back. Ma was outraged when Mahad was expelled, but he just sneered, looking down at her, far too tall and strong now for her to hit.

Mahad had no father to guide him through adolescence. He had only his friends, some of whom smoked hashish and drank beer in bars, acting cool. Mahad had always been close to my mother—she colluded with him, cooking special meals for him when he snuck out of school—but sometime after we got to Kenya, as he became bigger and stronger and just plain smarter than she was, he stopped feeling that he had to obey her and so he disregarded her authority. Ma's restrictive Somali traditions seemed completely pointless from the viewpoint of a normal boy who spent much of his life in the streets of Nairobi. Islam, at the time, had no appeal for him.

He had never worked at his studies but couldn't tolerate getting lower grades than other boys whom he'd once outshone. Mahad lost his way.

My mother had no idea what to do about Mahad's future. And he wasn't her only worry. The house that we rented in Kariokor had been sold to another owner and Ma couldn't stave off our eviction for long. But rents had gone up, and she had no money, only what my father's Osman Mahamud relatives gave her to live on. Month after month she had to walk to the house of Farah Gouré, one of the big Osman Mahamud businessmen in Nairobi, and pretend not to be begging when she haughtily informed him that the cost of living had gone up again. Ma didn't want to live in some cramped, noisy apartment building in Eastleigh, like most of the other Somalis in Nairobi. She wanted a nice house, somewhere clean.

Farah Gouré was a good man, but his pockets were not bottomless. He finally told Ma point-blank that she would have to move to a flat. We were not the only SSDF family without a father, and he wasn't prepared to pay for us to live in an even more expensive house. It was a standoff.

The whole household was miserable and in an unsettled state when my mother's older brother, Uncle Muhammad, arrived like a breath of fresh air from Mogadishu in December 1985. Uncle Muhammad was tall and vigorous; it was a good feeling to have a man like him in the house. He looked just like my mother, although he was much taller and far more playful. He used to sit on a mat on the floor, wearing a sarong, with a shawl over his shoulders, and joke with us that we were women now, cooing and teasing us that we should be getting married soon, and that he had fine, rich, young husbands for us back home in Somalia.

Uncle Muhammad brought with him news of my father, and of the SSDF. Key leaders of the movement were defecting, he said. They were taking up jobs in Siad Barré's government. A lot of muttering went on downstairs between the adults. Late one night Haweya, who had been eavesdropping, came into our bedroom with huge, startled eyes and hissed, "Ayaan, we have a sister. Abeh has married somebody else. He has another family."

I crept halfway down the red staircase and listened. It was true. Uncle Muhammad was talking about a woman our father had married. He was living in Ethiopia with this new wife of his, and they had a child.

The next morning I demanded more information. "Does Abeh have another wife?" I asked Ma. But it was Grandma who answered, very snooty and superior. "We won't discuss your father's wives," she said.

"We know that men marry. It will not be said of my daughters and granddaughters that they are jealous."

In our clan, jealousy is considered demeaning. It is unspeakable, a feeling so low that you may not admit it. So I knew I must not ask more about Abeh's new wife, but I did ask, "Do we have a sister, then? How old is she?" Again, it was my grandmother who answered, in the same strained but airy voice: "Oh, she must be nine years old now." Then my mother turned around and said in a strangled tone, "No, I think three or four." And in the silence that followed, all of us did the math. Our father must have married right after he left us behind, in 1981—perhaps just a few months later.

I thought about my father's succession of wives and children: how he had abandoned his first children, and then us, and now had made another daughter, whom, I thought, he would surely abandon, too. I felt a sudden wave of compassion for Ma, with all her worries: trying to find us a decent house to live in, having to take charity from my father's clan, dealing with Mahad dropping out, and worrying about my wayward sister, Haweya. If my father had been with us, none of this would have happened.

I was also crushed. I felt as if all the hope had suddenly drained out of my bones. I almost never admitted it to myself, but in those days I still imagined in the back of my mind that Abeh would come home one day and make us a proper family again, re-create that sphere of closeness and warmth. To learn he had another child—this was a betrayal, as if he'd slapped me hard in the face.

In the next days and weeks, I told myself that I would never let this happen to me. I would never be dependent on anyone in this way. My mother had so little control over her own life that she hadn't even known when her husband had gotten married again. I raged internally when I thought about it. I raged for her. Life seemed to be so unfair to Ma. She could be cruel, but she was loyal to my father and she was always there for us children. She didn't deserve any of this.

I was beginning to rebel internally against women's traditional subjugation. In those days, I was still wearing a *hidjab*. I thought a lot about God, how to be good in His eyes, and about the beauty of obedience and submission. I tried to still my mind so it would become a simple vessel for the will of Allah and the words of the Quran. But my mind seemed bent on being distracted from the Straight Path.

Something inside me always resisted the moral values behind Sister Aziza's lectures: a small spark of independence. Perhaps it was a reaction to the stark gap between the behavior demanded by the Holy Writings and the realities of actual daily life, with all its twists and turns. Even as a child, I could never comprehend the downright unfairness of the rules, especially for women. How could a just God—a God so just that almost every page of the Quran praises His fairness—desire that women be treated so unfairly? When the *ma'alim* told us that a woman's testimony is worth half of a man's, I would think, *Why?* If God was merciful, why did He demand that His creatures be hanged in public? If He was compassionate, why did unbelievers have to go to Hell? If Allah was almighty and powerful, why didn't He just make believers out of the unbelievers and have them all go to Paradise?

Inwardly, I resisted the teachings, and secretly I transgressed them. Like many of the other girls in my class, I continued to read sensual romance novels and trashy thrillers, even though I knew that doing so was resisting Islam in the most basic way. Reading novels that aroused me was indulging in the one thing a Muslim woman must never feel: sexual desire outside of marriage.

A Muslim woman must not feel wild, or free, or any of the other emotions and longings I felt when I read those books. A Muslim girl does not make her own decisions or seek control. She is trained to be docile. If you are a Muslim girl, you disappear, until there is almost no you inside you. In Islam, becoming an individual is not a necessary development; many people, especially women, never develop a clear individual will. You submit: that is the literal meaning of the word *islam*: submission. The goal is to become quiet inside, so that you never raise your eyes, not even inside your mind.

But the spark of will inside me grew even as I studied and practiced to submit. It was fanned by the free-spirited novels, the absence of my father, and the frustration of watching my mother's helplessness living in a non-Muslim country. Most of all, I think it was the novels that saved me from submission. I was young, but the first tiny, meek beginnings of my rebellion had already clicked into place.

Our family had never been very united, but it seemed to fall apart completely after that December. Uncle Muhammad went back to Somalia and Mahad went with him, to find his way and become a man. I was glad to see him go—he was a bully—but I was also envious. Mahad could travel and have adventures. Nothing like that could ever happen to me, because I was a girl.

A month after Mahad's departure, the eviction police arrived and our household was flung into crisis. After years of clawing a few months' more delay out of the owners, Ma had still not found us a place to live. It was Grandma who finally found a practical solution—through the clan network, as usual—and we moved to temporary lodging in the house of an Isaq man in the neighborhood.

This man, whose name was Abdillahi Ahmed, was a recent widower. His wife had died a few months before, and Grandma had spent a few weeks at his house, helping; these are the sorts of things you do for people in your clan. When he heard about our plight, Abdillahi Ahmed naturally offered to take us in.

Abdillahi Ahmed had many children, but he had moved the younger ones to his farm out of town. Only his two oldest daughters, Fardawsa and Amina, lived with him now in his house in Nairobi. Abdillahi Ahmed was a businessman and a Somali, so he had no idea how to bring up teenage girls. An older woman, Hanan, who was a relative, lived with them and was supposed to take care of that.

We lived in one bedroom: my grandmother in one bed, Haweya and me in bunks, and my mother on a mattress on the floor. Our stuff was stored under our grandmother's bed or in various houses in the neighborhood. We shared the kitchen. Mostly Fardawsa or Amina would cook for their family, and I would cook for us.

Fardawsa and Amina had grown up in Kenya, and both their Somali and their English were poor. We spoke to each other in Swahili, though this disgusted my mother. After dinner we used to joke around in the kitchen, making the dough for the next morning's *angello,* the traditional Somali pancake. Amina, the older girl, was outgoing and Haweya liked her; I preferred Fardawsa, who was mild and sweet.

But my mother and Hanan stalked each other like a pair of scorpions. Hanan chewed *qat.* My mother couldn't believe she had to live in the house of a woman who stooped to something so low. Although *qat*-chewing is prevalent in Somalia, Muslim doctrine opposes any kind of intoxication, and Ma saw it as particularly horrifying in a woman. Whenever Hanan chewed *qat,* Ma would stare at her with her eyes narrowed and stomp off to our room.

In the morning, when Hanan was hungover from her *qat* habit, she could be vicious. But after a few hours' chewing after lunch, the *qat* made Hanan patient and pleasant to be around. Her supervision was far more lax than my mother's at the best of times. Amina and Haweya began sneaking out of the house in the afternoons. Amina had a boyfriend, Farah Gouré's youngest son, the prince of the estate. He was cool and drove his own car. She was Isaq and he was Osman Mahamud; it was terribly romantic, like Romeo and Juliet. As for Haweya, I think she mostly went to the movies.

Fardawsa and I began sneaking out sometimes, too. We would go to movies with Hawo, Jim'o Musse's older daughter, who lived in the house directly opposite Abdillahi Ahmed's house. Hawo thought my *hidjab* was absolutely a joke; when she saw me coming home from school in my black robe she'd howl with laughter. Then she'd pull me to the Odeon to see some improbable Bollywood epic.

One day Kennedy caught sight of Haweya at an afternoon disco and asked her for news of Mahad and me—especially me. The two of us had barely seen each other since Mahad had dropped out of Starehe Boys School, which Kennedy was still attending, in the equivalent of grade 13. (In the British system, secondary school begins in grade 8; you take O levels at the end of year 11, usually called fourth form, and A levels in year 13, called sixth form.) Kennedy gave Haweya a note for me with his phone number.

When I saw that note my legs shook, and of course I called him. When we spoke, I stammered, and all my nerve endings seemed to come alive with excitement. My black *hidjab* didn't shield me from the effect Ken had on me. We agreed to meet in the house of one of his relatives; in a cinema or a park, someone might see us.

I went robed from head to toe. I told myself I would tell Kennedy about Allah. I would tell him that if Allah had willed us to fall in love, then we should get married one day—it was meant to be.

When I rang the bell, Ken was startled to see me cloaked in black. He said, "What's happened to you? Are you mad?" I said, "No, I'm not mad. I'm taking my religion seriously. You should, too." He took my hand and smiled. He was so nice, such a very nice person. Then he took me into the house, and I took off my robe and folded it, pretending there was nothing at all unusual about being alone in a house with a grown man.

Underneath the robe I was dressed in a long skirt and a blouse buttoned up to my neck. I sat on the edge of the sofa, and Ken and I made small talk for a little while. Then he kissed me. And again, it was as if a switch had clicked shut in my mind. I knew the angels were watching me, but I kissed him back.

When it got dark Ken prepared dinner. I had never been served by a man. It was fun; Ken was thoughtful and kind and interesting; he indulged me—he was completely unlike my brother. After dinner, as we sat together, I asked him, "Tell me, really: your name is Yusuf, right?" Here I was, risking my soul, coming to see him. I thought I had a right to know his real name and his people.

He said, "No, I told you, my name is Kennedy."

I thought he was still joking, because I had convinced myself that the whole Ken thing was some kind of gag, another way for him and Mahad to tease me for being so gullible and protected from the outside world. But Ken said, "The truth is that my name is Kennedy Okioga and I'm from the Kisii tribe. I'm not Somali. Mahad invented that so your mother would accept me, because your ma is new in this country. I'm Kenyan."

I was stunned. I said, "So you're not a Muslim?" and he said, "No. I'm not." "But you will have to become a Muslim!" I burst out, and Kennedy began laughing. "Of course I won't become a Muslim," he said. "Then I would have to look like you."

I got all earnest and told him, "But men don't have to wear these clothes." And Kennedy said, "I know that, but I'm not going to become a Muslim."

Then he told me he was an atheist, that he didn't believe in any God. I was horrified. I couldn't believe such an evil thing was possible, coming from someone so kind and so handsome. I burst out, "But you will burn!" Kennedy said, "There is no Hell, you know. It's all nonsense."

There was a horrible silence. I realized that we must never see each other again. It didn't matter how much I liked him, I could never marry a non-Muslim. It wasn't just because of the rule that a Muslim woman must never marry an unbeliever. It was my clan's Somali bigotry, as well. Ayaan Hirsi Magan could never marry a Kenyan. The clan simply would not stand for it. If I married Ken, he might even be killed.

If Ken had been willing to convert to Islam, I could have tried to argue that we are all equal under Allah, no matter the clan or tribe. Perhaps the Osman Mahamud one day could have accepted that, though all of them would certainly have sneered at me my whole life. But at age seventeen, even I could not conceive of marrying an unbeliever.

So everything had to be over. It was horribly painful. When I left, I told him, "I really think the two of us is impossible." Ken answered, "I know about the Somalis, but love is stronger than anything—let's give it a try." It was sweet, but futile; that kind of childish wishing was behind us. I just looked down and mumbled, "Please, can I think about it?" He knew—both of us knew—that we were saying good-bye.

* * *

It was not a good time for anyone in our family. A few weeks later, just before she turned sixteen, Haweya announced that she was dropping out of school. She told me about it the night before she told Ma. I begged her not to do it. She had only two more years to go before her O-level exams and she had always been so effortlessly clever. I had to work far harder than she did, for worse grades. I told her, "If you don't get a diploma, you'll be nothing—you'll be like Ma." But Haweya was adamant. School was stupid. She wanted to go to Somalia, like Mahad. She wanted to live anywhere but in the one bedroom we shared with Grandma and Ma.

The morning after she told me about her decision, Haweya went over to Farah Gouré's house, where Ma used to stride every month, head high, to *accept* her allowance. It was a huge courtyard, always full of Somali men, and Haweya just walked in, wearing her usual clothes: her school skirt, no headscarf. She announced, "I have come for a consultation with Farah Gouré."

Everyone laughed at her and told her to come back with her mother. A young girl can't just talk directly to an older man with no intermediary. But when Farah Gouré emerged from his house, Haweya walked up to him and said, "I am the daughter of Hirsi Magan and I have come to ask you a favor. You can hear it, and say yes or no. Or you can tell me, right now, 'Go home, you are not welcome,' and I won't come back."

Farah Gouré started to laugh. He asked Haweya if she wanted a cup of tea and she said, "No, I want to go to Somalia." Just like that. She said, "My brother is in Mogadishu, my family is in Mogadishu, and my father will be in Somalia soon, when Siad Barré is finally defeated. I don't want to be in Kenya any more. I have dreamt of Somalia since I was a little girl, and I know you go there twice a month, so please take me."

Farah Gouré asked, "Does your mother know this?" and Haweya said, "Yes, she does. If you agree to take me she will let me go." Which wasn't true, of course.

Farah Gouré was quite a character. He was small and round, an Osman Mahamud; we shared the ninth grandfather, I think. In 1987 he must have been about sixty, and though he couldn't read or write he owned a whole fleet of trucks that traveled all over eastern and southern Africa. But although Farah Gouré had made his wealth from his own initiative and efforts, it wasn't his in the way that a Westerner's wealth belongs to him alone. Farah Gouré believed in the clan and in the SSDF.

By taking care of the SSDF families in Kenya, he believed he freed his countrymen to fight. It was the sort of thing the Osman Mahamud have always done. Farah Gouré shared his money and good fortune with the clan and the cause: his house was open to almost any Osman Mahamud who wanted to be there.

Much later, we heard the story of how he met Fadumo, his wife. When Farah Gouré was fifteen, he left his parents to make his fortune. That is the tradition in Bari, where he was born: a man must prove himself, alone. So Farah Gouré left Bari and went to Kismayo, in the south. He was young, he didn't understand the people or the accent in Kismayo, and there was nobody looking after him or doing his laundry. His money ran out very quickly and his clothes were a mess, but he couldn't go home a failure: the shame of it would have been intolerable.

One day, walking through the market, Farah Gouré saw a young woman about his age making *angello,* cooking the pancakes on a charcoal brazier on the ground, rolling them up with sugar and butter, and selling them to passersby. He walked up and down smelling the *angello* and she called to him, "So, you look hungry," and he laughed with relief, because her accent was from Bari.

Farah Gouré and this young woman started listing their ancestry, as Somalis always do. Both of them were Osman Mahamud, so they could call each other brother and sister. He asked what she was doing in Kismayo, and this woman, whose name was Fadumo, said, "I told my parents I would leave to make my fortune and this is what I did. I have an *angello* stall but one day I will buy a truck. You can start an *angello* stall, too." Farah Gouré said, "Of course I can't, I'm a man."

Fadumo made him an *angello,* and when he said he couldn't pay for it she offered to let him earn his pancake. She said, "I'll make sure that you have breakfast every morning, and you can go and find out how the truck business works. I have to be here with the *angello*s and I'm a woman, so it's not as easy for me to look into it as it will be for you." That's how Farah Gouré apprenticed himself to a transporter. He and Fadumo talked every day about her dream to have trucks working all over Somalia. He offered to marry her and she said, "Of course not. I'm not going to marry a man who can't even earn his own breakfast."

They did marry in the end, of course. And after a year or so of making *angello*s and renting trucks and trading between Kismayo and Mogadishu, Fadumo and Farah Gouré bought their first truck. Then they bought another, and a real *angello* stand, with employees. It was the women of the *tolka,* the closest of our Osman Mahamud relatives, who told and retold the story to us, and each time it became more romantic, Fadumo braver and wittier and Farah even more enchanted by her. When this lovely story was told in the presence of Fadumo herself she would listen silently, with a small smile on her face, saying nothing. She was a big, happy woman with a huge houseful of children and guests, just down the road from Abdillahi Ahmed's house.

When Fadumo was pregnant with their seventh child, Farah Gouré married another woman, and then a third. But Fadumo never flinched. She told the other wives, "You're welcome here. But you earn your own money. The money he married you with is mine."

I don't know how much of that story was true, but the moral lesson was clear: as a woman you are better off in life earning your own money. You couldn't prevent your husband from leaving you or taking another wife, but you could save some of your dignity if you didn't have to beg him for financial support.

I suppose that's why Farah Gouré decided to help Haweya: he liked strong, bold women. He agreed to pay for her trip to Mogadishu and made all the arrangements.

Grandma was proud of Haweya. She was doing what a Darod woman should do, returning to her land to learn the ancestral traditions. But Ma was angry that Haweya had arranged all this behind her back. She knew the Osman Mahamud women would gossip: for a daughter to leave her mother in this way reflected very badly on her upbringing. Still, Ma knew she could not stand in the way of Haweya going to Somalia to visit her father's relatives—that would look even worse.

Ma had several long, flowing *dirha* made for Haweya, and pleaded with her to obey her elders and not damage her parents' honor. When the day came for her to leave, Ma and I walked her over to Farah Gouré's house with her suitcase. She was excited; I cried. Mainly I felt sorry for myself, left behind to share a bedroom with Grandma and Ma and finish school alone. Father had left years ago, then Mahad, and now Haweya was going, too. Grandma talked endlessly of how much better she would feel if she were back home in Somalia again with the rest of her daughters and son. Our family was disintegrating.

When she got to Mogadishu, Haweya would have to stay with our father's first wife, Maryan Farah, our closest relative in Somalia. Not to stay with her would have been rude and would have sent a message of jealousy and spite. We were above all that.

We had never met Maryan Farah, but we knew about her and her children, whom we called our sisters. Arro was much older than I; Ijaabo was close to Haweya's age. Maryan was a small, proud woman, and had not remarried after my father divorced her. She worked in Mogadishu in some important job for the government. Maryan was Marehan—from the same small subclan as the dictator Siad Barré.

There was a constant tug of clan the whole time Haweya was in Somalia. In Kenya, clans had never mattered much to us, but in Somalia they were omnipresent. The Osman Mahamud understood that Haweya had to live with her stepmother, even though Maryan was of another clan, because that is how these things are always done. But they wanted to keep an eye on her. They sneered at the Marehan, the clan of the upstart *Afwayne.* They didn't want a Marehan woman saying she had to support an Osman Mahamud child, so they gave Haweya pocket money.

As soon as Haweya would return to Maryan's house from a visit with our father's relatives, our stepsisters would fall on her. Arro and Ijaabo would plead and beg and even demand that she share the cash. They took her stuff without asking, things like shampoo and soap. They jeered at her for not knowing the proper codes and for reading all the time. Haweya didn't like them.

Haweya found more congenial company at the house of Ibado Dhadey Magan, an older sister of my father's who had taught herself to read and write, earned a nursing certificate, and had risen to become director of the Digfeer Hospital, where I was born. Ibado Dhadey was in her late forties or early fifties, but she was modern. She was married, but she had no children, and she liked my sister's pluck.

Ibado told Haweya she was lucky to have gone to school at all, and that she needed to study so she could work for her living. She showed Haweya around her house, with its tiled verandah and lush garden, and told her, "Nobody gave me any of this. I worked for it. Go out and get yourself a qualification, and work."

When Haweya used the money Ibado gave her to buy trousers, blouses, and skirts, Maryan's household was outraged. Food was another difficult issue. In our house in Nairobi we never ate from one plate, as Somalis do. Ma had long ago adopted the Western manner, using individual plates, though we did mostly eat with spoons or our hands. But in Maryan's house, like almost everywhere in Mogadishu, all the men ate out of one plate in one part of the courtyard, and all the women and small children squatted and ate at another corner of the courtyard from another dish.

Haweya disliked it; she thought it was unhygienic. It killed her appetite. She had gotten into the habit at home of eating alone, after all of us, while reading a book. It made her miserable to eat without reading, and she lost weight, which Maryan took as a personal insult.

Haweya began going to restaurants with the money Ibado gave her. A young woman, on her own, in a restaurant: this was absolutely unheard of. She would order lunch, and then, in front of everyone, she would eat it, slowly, while reading a novel. Waiters and male clients would badger her, but she just told them off. This was hugely deviant behavior.

Maryan's relatives began focusing on Haweya, the poor little daughter of Hirsi Magan who had been allowed to grow up a barbarian in Kenya. They sought to influence her. They talked about her, they talked to her—all of them got involved in what she ate, when she ate, how she dressed, why was she reading novels and not the Quran. Haweya wrote me that she had gone to Somalia to be free of our mother, but was being suffocated by an entire cabal.

I was seventeen, and I was miserable with Haweya away. My friend Fardawsa Abdillahi Ahmed had left Nairobi, too, to live with her younger brothers and sisters in the countryside until she was married off. In school the only subject that interested me was Islamic education. The prospect of taking my O-level exams didn't interest me one bit. I needed to get to the core of what I believed in. All the other girls were content to accept the rules of our religion at face value, but I felt compelled to try to understand them. I needed my belief system to be logical and consistent. Essentially, I needed to be convinced that Islam was *true.* And it was beginning to dawn on me that although many wonderful people were sure it was true, there seemed to be breakdowns in its consistency.

If God were merciful, then why did Muslims have to shun non-Muslims—even attack them, to establish a state based on Allah's laws? If He was just, then why were women so downtrodden? I began collecting together all the verses in the Quran that said God was wise, God was omnipotent, God was just—and there were many. I pondered them. Clearly, in real life, Muslim women were not "different but equal," as Sister Aziza maintained. The Quran said "Men rule over women." In the eyes of the law and in every detail of daily life, we were clearly worth less than men.

I was also still attending Quran classes, alongside Muslim Girls' Secondary. My *ma'alim* was a young man whom people called Boqol Sawm,

He Who Fasts for a Hundred Days. Grandma used to say his belly touched his spine, he was so thin. Boqol Sawm was a fanatic, even by a zealot's standard. He wore a Saudi robe, cut short so we could see his scrawny ankles. He used to walk around Eastleigh knocking on doors and lecturing people. He told Farah Gouré, "All your daughters are uncovered! All of you will writhe in Hell!" Farah Gouré threw him out of the house.

But in time Boqol Sawm acquired a large following. Most of them were women, and among them was my mother. When he came to the door, women accepted the audiocassettes of sermons that he handed out, and they exchanged them with each other. They turned their living rooms over to Quran study, filling them with women listening eagerly to his sermons on tape or even to Boqol Sawn in person, with an opaque curtain separating him from the women, just as the Prophet had ordained.

Boqol Sawm became the most sought-after lecturer in the community, and as time passed, the effect of his sermons became visible in the streets of the Somali neighborhoods. Women who used to wear colorful *dirhas* with seductive petticoats underneath and Italian sandals that showed off pedicured toes painted in nail varnish or henna began to cloak in the *burka*. They shrouded themselves in dark brown, black, and dark blue cloth of the roughest cotton fabric possible, with only a little bit of their faces visible. Some even began to cover their faces. There are so many variations in exactly how you must cover yourself; the form of veil that now spread among the Somali fundamentalists was called a *jilbab,* a thick cloth covering everything from the head to below the knees and another thick skirt underneath. All of a sudden, my black cloak seemed too thin and revealing.

My mother was drawn to Boqol Sawm's certitude. She encouraged me to listen to his sermons on tape and attend his lectures when he preached at homes in our neighborhood.

With Sister Aziza, there was an atmosphere of trust and intimacy: she let us draw our own conclusions. But to Boqol Sawm, teaching the Quran meant shouting it, loud, in a mishmash of Arabic and Somali, and then yelling out the rules: what was forbidden, what was permitted. He didn't translate the text properly, or explain its underlying intention.

One day when I was seventeen, Boqol Sawm turned to the verses on how women were supposed to behave with their husbands. We owed our husbands absolute obedience, he told the mothers and teenage girls who had gathered to listen to him. If we disobeyed them, they could beat us. We must be sexually available at any time outside our periods, "even on the saddle of a camel," as the *hadith* says. This wasn't any kind of loving partnership, or mutual giving; it didn't even sound possible. But Boqol Sawm yelled, "TOTAL OBEDIENCE: this is the rule in Islam." It enraged me, and I stood up behind the curtain. In a shaky voice I asked, "Must our husbands obey us, too?"

There is nothing wrong with that question, but Boqol Sawm's voice rose, hard and dry. "Certainly not!"

I dug my nails into my hand to stop myself from shaking and went on, "Men and women are then not equal."

Boqol Sawm said, "They are equal."

"But they're *not,*" I told him. "I'm supposed to totally obey my husband, but he is not totally obedient to me, and therefore we are not equal. The Quran says on almost every page that Allah is just, but this is not just."

Boqol Sawm's voice rose to a shout. "You may not question Allah's word! His mind is hidden. Satan is speaking to you, girl! Sit down instantly!"

I sat down, but as I did I hissed "Stupid" under my breath. It alarmed the other women in the room; they thought I truly must have lost my mind to a demon. But I knew I had genuinely sought the truth, and Boqol Sawm had shut me up because he didn't know it. The flaw could not be in the Quran, because that was God's word. It must lie with the stupid *ma'alim,* with the whole inept cohort of *ma'alims* that it had been my unhappy lot to encounter.

I thought that perhaps Boqol Sawm was translating the Quran poorly: Surely Allah could not have said that men should beat their wives when they were disobedient? Surely a woman's statement in court should be worth the same as a man's? I told myself, "None of these people understands that the real Quran is about true equality. The Quran is higher and better than these men."

I bought my own English edition of the Quran and read it so I could understand it better. But I found that everything Boqol Sawm had said was in there. Women should obey their husbands. Women were worth half a man. Infidels should be killed.

I talked to Sister Aziza, and she confirmed it. Women are emotionally stronger than men, she said. They can endure more, so they are tested more. Husbands may punish their wives—not for small infractions, like being late, but for major infractions, like being provocative to other men. This is just, because of the overwhelming sexual power of women. I asked, "What if the man provokes other women?" Sister Aziza said, "In an Islamic society, that's impossible."

Furthermore, she told me, I was not permitted for one second to imagine that perhaps the Quran's words could be adapted to a modern era. The Quran had been written by God, not by men. "The Quran is the word of Allah and it is forbidden to refute it," Sister Aziza told me.

You obey, and you serve Allah—that is the test. If you submit to God's will on earth, you will attain bliss in the Hereafter. The rule is strict and pure. My doubts severely diminished my chances for eternal bliss, but I found that I couldn't ignore them. I had to resolve this.

As Boqol Sawm's following grew, his sermons caused a lot of quarrels between spouses. At first, the Somali fathers and husbands were amused and teased their wives, predicting that after a week the silly, bored women would find some other pastime. After a while, however, irritations arose. The living room, usually well furnished, is the domain of the man. Somali men bring their male friends home and sit with them in the living room having men-talk (honor, money, politics, and whether to take a second or third wife) as they drink scented sweet tea and chew *qat*. The evenings and Friday afternoons are their preferred times, and Boqol Sawm chose to give his lectures especially at those times.

When Boqol Sawm was visiting a house, the men were relegated to the women's quarters: the kitchen, backyard, and, in some of the bigger houses, the smaller and uglier living rooms usually occupied by the women. And after their wives converted to the True Islam of the Muslim Brotherhood believers, they began saying that chewing *qat,* smoking, and skipping prayers were forbidden. They actually sent their husbands off, calling them unbelievers. When the men shouted about disobedience, the women replied that in the hierarchy of submission, we must follow Allah even before husband and father: Allah and the Prophet decreed that wives should obey only husbands who themselves obey Allah.

The Muslim Brotherhood believed that there was a pure, original Islam to which we all should return. Traditional ways of practicing Islam had become corrupted, diluted with ancient beliefs that should no longer have currency. The movement was founded in the 1920s in Egypt as an Islamic revivalist movement, then caught on and spread—slowly at first, but much faster in the 1970s, as waves of funding flooded in from the suddenly massively rich Saudis. By 1987 the Muslim Brotherhood's ideas had reached the Somali housewives of Eastleigh in the gaunt and angry shape of Boqol Sawm.

Within months the first divorces were occurring, and secular Somali men were threatening Boqol Sawm for breaking up their families. Boqol Sawm was chased away by angry husbands from the living room sessions and from the Somali mosques, but copies of his tapes continued to spread even as he was in hiding.

In the tapes, when he wasn't warning about hellfire and the enemies of Islam, Boqol Sawm was issuing detailed prescriptions on the rituals permitted in Islam and the ceremonies of birth, lovemaking, marriage, divorce, and so on. Celebrating the birthday of the Prophet was forbidden because it resembled Christmas, when Christians celebrate the birthday of Jesus, and Muslims should never imitate unbelievers in any way. Wearing amulets as my grandmother did and asking favors of dead forefathers was blasphemous, as it associated Allah with lesser gods, and for that you could burn forever. Refusing to sleep with your husband if he didn't observe the obligations of prayer and fasting was permitted. When entering a bathroom to use the toilet, start with the left foot, and when coming out, put the right leg out first. The only greeting permitted among Muslims is *Assalamu-Allaikum Warahmatullahi Wabarakaatuhu,* "Peace be to you and the mercy of Allah and His blessings." If you are greeted in any other way you must not answer.

Boqol Sawm wasn't the only preacher who had come to our neighborhood to guide the lost back to Allah's Straight Path after a stint in Medina or Cairo. More and more young men of the Muslim Brotherhood, dressed in ankle-length white robes and red-and-white checked shawls, were striding through the streets. People who converted to their cause started to collect money from family; some women gave their dowries, and all kinds of donations came in. By 1987 the first Muslim Brotherhood mosque was built in Eastleigh, and Boqol Sawm came out of hiding to preach there every Friday, screaming at the top of his lungs through the loudspeakers behind the white minaret topped with a green crescent and a single star.

Boqol Sawm shouted that the men who rejected their wives' call to Islam would burn. The rich who spent their money on earthly things would burn. The Muslims who abandoned their fellow Muslims—the Palestinians—were not true Muslims, and they would burn, too. Islam was under threat and its enemies—the Jews and the Americans—would burn forever. Those Muslim families who sent their children to universities in the United States, Britain, and other lands of the infidels would burn. Life on earth is temporary, Boqol Sawm yelled; it was meant by Allah to test people. The hypocrites who were too weak to resist the

worldly temptations would burn. If you did not break off your friendships with non-Muslims, you would burn.

I had questions about Boqol Sawm, but at age seventeen, I mostly
believed in the Brotherhood's values. And, as the movement swelled,
there were two clear benefits. Fewer young men were getting addicted to
qat and other drugs. At the time, AIDS was just starting to kill people;
many Muslim families thought the best answer was abstinence, and
abstinence was exactly what the religious zealots of every stripe were
preaching.

Another benefit was a curbing of corruption. In Muslim Brotherhood
enterprises there was virtually no corruption. Medical centers and char-
ities managed by the Brotherhood were reliable and trustworthy. If non-
Muslim Kenyans converted, they, too, could benefit from these facilities,
and in the slums many Kenyans began converting to Islam.

A brand-new mosque was built in Majengo with money contributed
by a rich Saudi man. One Friday evening I went there to pray with classmates because Sister Aziza said it was important to visit poor neighborhoods. It was after the evening prayer, and the street near the mosque was
crowded with Kenyan women clumsy in their new *jilbab*s. At the entrance
of the mosque a Kenyan woman carrying a baby had just sat down on the
stone steps. She lifted her *jilbab* and opened the buttons of the dress she
was wearing underneath, then directed a completely naked and volup-
tuous breast into her baby's mouth as if it was the most common act in the
world. In front of her was a mountain of men's shoes, and behind her
men—strange men—were engaged in prayer, but this young woman
seemed shockingly oblivious to these surroundings.

All the girls from Sister Aziza's class shrieked in unison, and we transported this young woman to a hall in the women's section. An older
woman of Swahili origin, covered from head to toe in black, started to
instruct her in the Islamic way of breast-feeding. First you say *Bismillah*
before you put the nipple into the mouth. As the baby is feeding, beg
Allah to protect your child from illness, earthly temptations, and the evil
ways of the Jews. Of course, no strange man must *ever* be present: better
that the baby go hungry.

I was never one of Boqol Sawm's great admirers. I thought his sermons
were crude; they didn't seem to answer my questions. But I was drawn
to a discussion group of young Muslims that took place in the community center near my school. These were young people who were dissat-

isfied with the intellectual level of the teaching at the madrassahs and who, like me, sought deeper religious learning, true understanding of the example of the Prophet Muhammad, the better to walk in his footsteps. They felt Islam should not be something you nodded at a few times a week. They wanted to immerse themselves in it as a minutely detailed way of life, a passion, a constant internal pursuit.

A group of Somali and Pakistani young men had begun organizing weekly Islamic debates in English to discuss these matters. Going there was not like attending the mosque, where sermons were often just a recitation of old texts in Arabic. The speakers at our youth debates talked about relationships between men and women, Muslims and non-Muslims, Islam and Christianity. The talks were lively, and often clever, as well as much more relevant to our lives than the mosque.

The audience was mostly very bright, deeply committed older students, and they were there voluntarily—unlike Quran school, which parents obliged their kids to attend. A speaker stood on a dais. The boys, in front, wore mainly Western clothes, and the girls behind them wore large headscarves. The segregation was voluntary, and the atmosphere was harmonious: we were all good Muslims, striving for perfection.

We were not like the passive old school, for whom Islam meant a few rules and more or less devoutly observed rituals, and who interlaced their Quran with tribal customs and magical beliefs in amulets and spirits. We were God's shock troops. The Islam that we were imbibing stemmed from the hard, essentialist beliefs of thinkers seeking to revive the original Islam of the Prophet Muhammad and His disciples in the seventh century. The intention was to live according to the ancient ways in every detail of our lives. We weren't just learning a text by heart: we were discussing its meaning and how it applied to us every day.

We read Hasan al-Banna, who set up the Society of Muslim Brothers to oppose the rise of Western ideas in the lands of Islam and promote a return to the Islam of the Prophet. We read Sayyid Qutb, another Egyptian, who said preaching was not enough, that we must stage a catastrophic revolution to establish the kingdom of God on Earth. We thrilled to new movements called *Akhwan* (Brotherhood) and *Tawheed* (the Straight Path); they were small groups of true believers, as we felt ourselves to be. This was the True Islam, this harking back to the purity of the Prophet.

Everyone was convinced that there was an evil worldwide crusade aimed at eradicating Islam, directed by the Jews and by the whole Godless West. We needed to defend Islam. We wanted to be involved in the *jihad,* a word that may have multiple meanings. It may mean that the faith needs financial support, or that an effort should be made to convert new believers. Or it may mean violence; violent *jihad* is a historical constant in Islam.

As much as I wanted to be a devout Muslim, I always found it uncomfortable to be opposed to the West. For me, Britain and America were the countries in my books where there was decency and individual choice. The West to me meant all those ideas, in addition to pop music and cinema and the completely silly pen-pal relationships we'd had at Muslim Girls' Secondary School with girls from Finland and Canada who thought we lived in trees in the jungle. In my own personal experience of the West—which was, admittedly, minimal—it really didn't seem to be terribly evil. But I stared long and hard at the photos of dead Muslims that were passed around: we had to give meaning to these deaths, and we were told that the West had caused them. We were taught that, as Muslims, we should oppose the West.

Our goal was a global Islamic government, for everyone.

How would we fight? Some said the most important goal was preaching: to spread Islam among non-Muslims and to awaken passive Muslims to the call of the true, pure belief. Several young men left the group to go to Egypt, to become members of the original Muslim Brotherhood there. Others received scholarships from various Saudi-funded groups to go to Quran schools in Medina, in Saudi Arabia.

Sister Aziza became a Shia when she married a Shia man. She was enthralled by the Islamic Revolution in Iran, which by 1987 was eight years old. She talked to us about the saintliness of the Ayatollah Khomeini; finally, a voice was standing up to the perversions and guiles of the Western Crusaders. She showed us photos of dead Iranian boys, their lifeless heads still wearing the green cloth bands of martyrdom, who had given their lives to uphold the Iranian Revolution. She took us to the Iranian Embassy in Nairobi. We talked about going to Iran, to do what we could for the Ayatollah, but when my mother found out we had been to the embassy, she was angry. Ma would never let me go to Iran, among the Shia.

At the debating center we had long discussions about how to behave in daily life. There were so many rules, with minutely detailed prescriptions, and so many authorities had pronounced on them all. Truly Muslim women should cover their bodies even in front of a blind man, even in their own houses. They had no right to walk down the middle of the street. They should not move out of their father's house without permission.

I found it remarkable how many esteemed Muslim thinkers had philosophized at such length about precisely how much female skin could be bared without causing chaos to break out across the landscape. Of course, almost all these thinkers agreed that once a girl reaches puberty, every part of her body except her face and her hands must be covered when in the company of any men who are not immediate family, and at all times outside the home. This was because her bare skin would involuntarily cause men to feel an uncontrollable frenzy of sexual arousal. But not all thinkers agreed on exactly which parts of a woman's face and hands were so beguiling that they must be covered.

Some scholars held that the eyes of women were the strongest source of sexual provocation: when the Quran said women should lower their gaze, it actually meant they should hide their eyes. Another school of thought held that the very sight of a woman's lips, especially full ones that were firm and young, could bring a man into a sexual state that could cause his downfall. Yet other thinkers spent pages and pages on the sensual curve of the chin, a pretty nose, or long, slender fingers and the tendency of some women to move their hands in a way that attracted attention to their temptations. For every limitation the Prophet was quoted.

Even when all women had been covered completely from head to toe, another line of thought was opened. For this was not enough. High heels tapped and could trigger in men the image of a woman's legs; to avoid sin, women must wear flat shoes that make no noise. Next came perfume: using any kind of pleasant fragrance, even perfumed soap and shampoo, would distract the minds of men from Allah's worship and cause them to fantasize about sinning. The safest way to cause no harm to anyone seemed to be to avoid contact with any man at all times and just stay in the house. A man's sinful erotic thoughts were always the fault of the woman who incited them.

One day, I finally stood up and asked, "What about the men? Shouldn't they cover? Don't women also have desire for male bodies? Couldn't they be tempted by the sight of men's skin?" It seemed logical to me, but the whole room fell about laughing. There was no way I could go on with my objections.

I was lonely without Haweya and Fardawsa, and many of my school friends were avoiding me, uncomfortable with a religious freak in a black tent. I took to spending afternoons after school at Farah Gouré's house. A whole gaggle of young women—his teenage daughters and girls from the Osman Mahamud clan who had just arrived from Somalia—lived there, under the keen but benevolent eye of his wife Fadumo. Several of the Somali girls at Fadumo's house were fresh from the Somali countryside or the provinces and were properly betrothed to good men of the clan. My mother thought they would be a fine influence on me, so she let me go to Farah Gouré's house as much as I liked. And I did like.

It was my first contact with Somali girls from Somalia. One of these girls was Jawahir, who was quick, pretty, rather excitable. She was about twenty-five and had come to Nairobi to marry one of Farah Gouré's truck drivers. She was waiting at Farah Gouré's place for her husband-to-be to return to Nairobi from a five-month trip through southern Africa. Ali was a dependable employee, and Fadumo needed Jawahir to feel happy in Nairobi; if Jawahir were miserable she might persuade Ali to return to Somalia with her. So Fadumo asked me to show Jawahir around town and keep her company.

Jawahir was tiny but exuberant, all airs and graces; she rolled her eyes and flounced her arms around, telling stories in her shrill voice. She inflected everything with so much drama. Jawahir reminded me of the Isaq women who mourned at the funeral of my aunt in Mogadishu, under the talal tree; in fact, along with her Isaq manner, she had even picked up an Isaq accent from living near Hargeisa, where her parents settled for a while. Jawahir didn't read books—she was illiterate—but she was really amusing.

A whole group of us met for long, giggly girls' conversations in the afternoons, while the older people napped with the children. The talk centered on Jawahir's impending marriage and the various prospects for other people's marriages. And of course we talked about circumcision. All these girls knew they would be married soon; it was inevitable that we talk about our excisions. This was what we had been sewn up for.

The talk was mostly boasting. All the girls said how tightly closed they were; this made them even more pure, doubly virginal. Jawahir was particularly proud of her circumcision. She used to say, "See the palm of your hand? I am like that. Flat. Closed."

One afternoon, gossiping about another girl, Jawahir said, "If you're walking past the toilet when she's in there, you can *hear* that she isn't a virgin. She doesn't drip. She pees loudly, like a man."

We discussed our periods, too, the essence of what made us filthy and unworthy of prayer. When we were menstruating, we weren't allowed even to pray or to touch the Quran. All the girls felt guilty for bleeding every month. It was proof that we were less worthy than men.

We never actually talked about sex itself, the act that would take place on the marriage night, the reason why we had been sewn. Somalis almost never talk about sexuality directly. The subject is shameful and dirty. Sometimes, though, as Jawahir and I walked around the neighborhood, we would come across people—Kenyans—making out, in broad daylight. Dainty little Jawahir would recoil: this was a nasty country.

On other afternoons Jawahir used to ask me to read to her out loud from the books I carried everywhere. She had never gone to school, and books were strange to her. These books were mostly thrillers and mushy love stories, but all of them had sex scenes. I would read them to her, and she would sniff and say, "It's not like that for Muslims. We are pure."

Jawahir's wedding took place at Farah Gouré's house. All the women had elaborate curlicues hennaed on their hands and were wearing gauze *dirha* gowns. We danced together to a woman drummer. I don't think the men danced or had music. We had a huge meal—several sheep and goats were slaughtered—and in the evening little Jawahir appeared, in a white Western dress, with her hair piled up in a beehive. She was enjoying the attention: she loved to perform.

For a week after the wedding Ma wouldn't let me go to see Jawahir: she said it wouldn't be proper. So it wasn't until the next weekend that I visited her. Jawahir sat on the sofa, gingerly shifting her weight from one side of her bottom to the other. Finally I asked her what it had been like, having sex.

She evaded the question. I was holding one of Halwa's Harlequin paperbacks and she grabbed it and asked, "What is this filthy book you're reading?" I said, "Come on, you know all about it now, tell me what it's like." Jawahir said, "Not until you read this book to me."

It was a mild enough book, about a man, a woman, a doomed romance, one or two sexy bits. But when the man and woman kissed, he put his hand on the woman's breast, and he then put his mouth to her nipple. Jawahir was horrified. "These Christians are filthy!" she squeaked. "This is forbidden! For Muslims it's not like that at all!"

Now Jawahir really had to tell me what sex was like. She said it was awful. After the wedding ceremony, they went into the bedroom of the flat that Ali had rented for them. Ali turned off the lights. Jawahir lay down on the bed, fully dressed. He groped under her dress, opened her legs, took off her underpants, and tried to push his penis inside her. He didn't cut her with a knife, just with his penis. It took a long time, and hurt. This resembled the stories that Sahra had told me.

Every night it was almost as painful, and always the same: Ali would push inside, move up and down inside her, and then ejaculate. That was it. Then he would stand up and take a shower to purify himself; she would get up and shower, also to purify herself, and apply Dettol to the parts that were bleeding. That was Jawahir's sex life.

This was nothing at all like the scenes I used to linger on in books. I was about to turn eighteen. I had reared myself on Harlequins and kissed Kennedy. What Jawahir described fell far short of the thrilling sex I had imagined. I was crestfallen, and told her I would never get married.

Jawahir laughed, and said, "Wait until your father comes back one day— you'll see then." She seemed perfectly resigned to her life. Ali appeared to be a kind man, not violent or mean, and a decent provider. Jawahir seemed convinced that good women were forbidden by God to feel desire.

I already knew what Sister Aziza would say about sex and marriage. She counseled many young married couples. Women often told her how horrible it was for them to have sex. Sister Aziza used to respond that they were complaining only because they had read licentious, un-Islamic descriptions of sexual experiences in Western books. We Muslim women were not to copy the behavior of unbelievers. We shouldn't dress like them, or make love like them, or behave like them in any way. We should not read their books, for they would lead us off the straight, true path to Allah.

A woman couldn't break a marriage because it was awful or boring: that was utterly forbidden, and the way of Satan. "If your husband hurts you," Sister Aziza would tell these women, "you must tell him that, and ask him to do it differently. If you cooperate it will always be less painful. And if he's not hurting you, then count yourself among the lucky ones."

At Abdillahi Ahmed's house, relations between Ma and Hanan were deteriorating. They had had a couple of spats early on, but Ma restrained herself: she knew if there was a big quarrel we would have to leave the house. Then, in early 1988, we heard that once again open warfare had broken out in Somalia. In May, Siad Barré's forces began bombing Isaq territory. Hanan turned into a witch. She was Isaq, and she yelled that she didn't want a Darod woman in her house.

We had certainly never considered Siad Barré a kinsman. Siad Barré was a Darod, but he was from the Marehan, nothing close to my father's Osman Mahamud family or my mother's subclan, the Dhulbahante. My mother tried to reason with Hanan. What Siad Barré was doing to the Isaq in 1988, he had already done to my father's people ten years before. "All of us are victims of Siad Barré," Ma said. "That's why we left our home, that's why I'm a beggar in this country, with my children."

But to make matters worse, as he was attacking the Isaq, Siad Barré offered an amnesty to the Macherten fighters of the SSDF. Several prominent SSDF members took up the offer, some of them my own Osman Mahamud relatives. Jim'o Musse's brother capitulated and became Siad Barré's Minister for Telecommunications. Hanan became impossible.

Every day at five o'clock, just as I got home from school, the Somali service of the BBC would be turned up loud in the kitchen, announcing to Hanan how many Isaq had died and how many were fleeing. In our bedroom my mother and grandmother would be listening to the same thing. Hanan would start screaming—cursing the Dhulbahante, the Macherten, and all Darod to Hell and high places—and sometimes my mother would lose her cool and step out of our bedroom to confront her. These two wrinkled women would shout at each other among the pots and pans, my mother spitting out a poem she'd invented on the spot, accusing Hanan of cowardice, and Hanan howling that my mother was a far worse coward, because she'd left Somalia so much longer ago. My grandmother would be in the kitchen, too, pleading with them to stop it. And I would just creep out of the house to get away from the whole howling mess.

Jawahir had been pleading with me to move in with her, to keep her company while Ali was away on long hauls and to help her in the house. Fadumo knew about the situation at home—nothing any Somali does is a secret—and interceded on my behalf. She told Ma that a young Somali matron like Jawahir would be the perfect companion for a growing girl; even Ma could see how difficult it was for me to study at Abdillahi Ahmed's house. So I moved in with Jawahir, just for a few months, to prepare for my exams.

I felt grown up. The house was in Eastleigh, the Somali neighborhood, so I remained under the watchful eye of the clan. Still, it was freer and calmer than the murderous atmosphere around Hanan and Ma. When her husband was home, Jawahir fluttered around putting on pretty clothes and perfuming herself with frankincense. Ali never seemed to notice, but he was at least respectful and kind.

While I was staying at Jawahir's house, two of Ali's coworkers proposed to me. It came as a surprise—the first time, Jawahir exploded with laughter at how taken aback I was—but it was all very proper and respectful. First these men went to Ali, one after the other, and then Ali came to me to present their case. Each time he went into detail about the man: what a hard worker he was, and a decent provider, reliable, Osman Mahamud, of course; how I could move into a house nearby and this man would take care of me. It was all about money and security. There was no idea of love as described in the novels I had read. Even Bollywood movies contained more romance than this.

One of these suitors was very persistent. He was in his late twenties, a staunch Muslim, but thick, I thought, as well as ugly and completely unschooled. He pleaded. He told me how motivated he was to protect me; that was his highest card. If I said yes, he told me, he would travel to Somalia to look for my father, or at least my brother, and obtain their approval, which was, obviously, the only permission that actually counted. There was no discussion of attraction or compatibility.

Privately, I thought it was surreal. This wasn't my idea of wooing. I wanted excitement, someone dashing and gorgeous, deeply learned, with dark eyes and a sense of humor. I wanted to be swept off my feet. I dreaded becoming a married woman. I didn't want to settle down to Jawahir's life. I didn't want to grow fat and old like my schoolmate Zainab. I didn't want to turn into my mother and have the kind of sex that Sahra and Jawahir did.

I said no, each time, very politely. I told Ali that I wanted to finish school before I could even consider such a thing. Thankfully Ma backed me up. She told Ali that I couldn't be betrothed in the absence of my father and brother. It wouldn't be right; it wouldn't be following the rules. It would look furtive, she told him. Privately, I'm sure, she considered such marriages beneath me.

When Halwa's parents moved to a new house they had constructed in one of the expensive estates that were springing up around the city, they offered to rent my mother an apartment in the small building they had just left on Park Road. Just before we moved in, Haweya returned from Mogadishu, with a suitcase full of short skirts and a new glint in her eye. When she saw her, Ma covered her eyes and exclaimed, "Allah! What now!" My mother had hoped that Somalia would tame Haweya, but she returned even more willful than when she'd left, with a completely adult determination about her.

Haweya had seen a different side to Somalia than my mother had expected. Somali women do seek to be *baarri,* the ideal behavior for a woman, to serve well. Almost all of them are genitally excised, which the Arabs mostly don't do. But traditionally, Somali women work, which makes them unlike Arab women, and perhaps freer. Islam was never as forceful in Somalia as it has always been in Saudi Arabia, the country of its origin, and some Somali women of my father's generation were very modern in their outlook. Our aunt, Ibado Dhadey Magan—and even, to some extent, our stepmother, Maryan Farah—were examples to Haweya. They were very different from my mother, who had become frozen in passive, bitter resentment since the day my father left.

Haweya came home full of plans to go out and work. She said she had decided to come back to Kenya because the education was better: Ibado Dhadey had convinced her that she needed qualifications. Haweya didn't want to return to high school and study for her O-level exams; she thought she was much too old for that. She would go to secretarial school, since she didn't need O-levels to get in.

A few months after Haweya came back, I took my O-level exams and barely passed. There was no way I could go on to do A-levels with such grades, and I was too proud to even think of going back a year and trying again. Haweya and I decided that we would go to secretarial school together. We knew it wouldn't be easy to persuade Ma, who wanted me to go and stay in an Islamic boardinghouse for girls down the road, to learn to cook and clean and read the Quran. I told her I was already cooking and cleaning and reading the Quran, and that secretarial school would be just like secondary school really.

Haweya and I carefully avoided stating the obvious, which was that secretarial school would make us qualified to work in offices—that we planned, in fact, to earn our own living. We told Ma that Ibado would pay Haweya's fees. The United Nations refugee agency would pay part of mine, because I was a refugee and had completed high school, and this was vocational training. Finally, grudgingly, Ma agreed to pay the rest.

Early in 1988, Mahad sent Ma a letter from Somalia. He wrote that he had met Abdellahi Abdi Aynab, the eldest son of the prison director who had been executed for helping my father escape from jail. Abdellahi lived in Aden, Mahad said. He had his own business, was only twenty-four years old, worked hard, and was devout. And Abdellahi Abdi Aynab respectfully requested my hand in marriage.

My mother sat me down. This was a beautiful match, she told me.

There was a symmetry to it. My father would certainly approve. She did her best to persuade me to say yes to Mahad's plan. But the whole idea chilled me. I honored this man's father, of course; he was a saint to us. Still, could Mahad really expect me to say yes, to marry someone I hadn't even met, and live in a country I had never been?

I wrote the most perfect letter back to Mahad. I told him, "My dearest brother, I am only eighteen, and marriage remains far from my mind. I must experience a period of adulthood before I jump from being a child to my husband's house." It was polite and respectful, but clear.

Then Mahad wrote to me directly to tell me to think about it. And a few days later a letter arrived from Abdellahi Abdi Aynab himself. It was a beautiful letter, in elegant Somali—he was from a very cultivated family—introducing himself, talking about his views of life, and including two photographs of him in Aden. It was a little like a pen-pal letter, minus the smiley faces. I still didn't feel drawn to the idea of marrying this man, but in terms of wedding proposals to a complete stranger, he did his best, I thought.

My mother was swept off her feet by the photographs of Aden, the city where her adult life had begun. She told me this marriage was my destiny. I wasn't ready to make this decision and felt trapped just thinking about it. Still, my mother and my brother more or less settled between themselves that when it came time for me to marry, it would be to this man.

I didn't think it was much of a threat. Abdellahi Abdi Aynab was in Aden; Mahad was in Somalia. It wasn't as if there were any kind of immediate plan. I wrote back to him saying that I wasn't rejecting him as a person—that I couldn't, since I had never met him—but marriage was simply not on my horizon right now. And this was fine. Nothing was signed. Nobody forced me.

I had begun to skip the Islamic debates on Thursday nights. As the months went on I found them more predictable and less inspiring. I kept seeing inconsistencies in the arguments, and my questions were getting no real answers. There was nothing new. The speakers were making us aware of the old fundamentals of Islam, and the need to adhere to and practice that faith much more actively, but there was no progress in the lessons, no change, and any interpretation seemed to be for the sake of convenience rather than logic.

It was as if my head had somehow divided in two. When in Sister Aziza's world, I was devout, meek, and respectful of the many, many bar-

riers that restricted me to a very narrow role. The rest of the time I read
novels and lived in the world of my imagination, filled with daring. As a
reader, I could put on someone else's shoes and live through his adventures, borrow his individuality and make choices that I didn't have at
home.

The moral dilemmas I found in books were so interesting they kept
me awake. The answers to them were unexpected and difficult, but they
had an internal logic you could understand. Reading *Dr. Jekyll and Mr.
Hyde,* I understood that the two characters were just one person, that
both evil and good live in each of us at one time. This was more exciting
than rereading the *hadith.*

I began sneaking out from time to time to go to the cinema with
Haweya or some of the other Somali girls. It didn't feel like sinning; it
felt like friendship. When I prayed these days, I skipped a lot of the
prayers. It was rare, now, for me to pray five times every day.

In February 1989, the BBC ran the news that the Ayatollah Khomeini
had issued an order to kill a man called Salman Rushdie, who had written a book about the wives of the Prophet Muhammad titled *The Satanic
Verses.* There had been riots across the Muslim world about this evil
book. The Ayatollah said Rushdie, who was born Muslim, was guilty of
blasphemy and the crime of apostasy—seeking to renounce the faith—
which is punishable by execution. He sentenced him to death and set a
price on Rushdie's head.

One evening a few weeks later, Sister Aziza and her husband stopped
by our flat to ask me to take a walk with them over to the Muslim community center beside the school where our debates took place. A small
crowd had gathered in the parking lot. Some young men drove up in a
car and made a show of burning small flags: the Israeli flag, the American
flag. Then they tied Rushdie's book onto a stick and doused it with
kerosene and held a cigarette lighter to it, cheering as it smoldered piti-
fully in the drizzle.

Sister Aziza was cheering and chanting beside me. I felt estranged,
somehow very uncomfortable. I wondered if it wasn't a little silly to have
bought even one copy of this book to burn it; after all, the money would
still go to its author. It didn't even occur to me to question that Salman
Rushdie should be killed: if Rushdie had insulted the Prophet, then he
deserved to die. Evidently Rushdie had written something so horrible
that I didn't even know what it was. But burning a book seemed like
something that the apartheid government in South Africa would do. I

couldn't articulate why I was uneasy, but I left early. I think that may have been the last time I went to the debate center.

Haweya and I started classes at a secretarial college downtown. It was rubbish. Fifty or sixty girls were crammed into a big room above a shop, with not even enough typewriters to go round. Lesson one was "Left hand, first finger. Type ffff. Right hand, first finger. Type jjj." We learned nothing, so at the end of the day we demanded that our fees be refunded. It was an extraordinary feeling to stand alongside Haweya and demand something from a total stranger. Together, I found, we could both be strong.

We looked around for a better education. We asked girls we knew, who worked, where the best secretaries came from. They recommended Valley Secretarial College, which had fifteen students per class and taught shorthand and had real computers. It was in Kilimani, two bus rides across the sprawl of outer Nairobi, and it was expensive, but we registered.

Secretarial school wasn't intellectually stimulating, but it meant we were out in the world. For the first time I really saw the streets of Nairobi as we rattled back and forth in the *matatou* bus every day. One time, as I was walking to the *matatou,* I heard a shriek of "THIEF!" A crowd of people caught a man who was running down the road, a Kenyan boy, about my age, wearing just a pair of shorts. As I walked by, I saw him, cringing on the ground in the middle of a circle of people who were throwing big stones at him.

The crowd got bigger and more determined, some of them dressed in tatters and others wearing suits. Young girls were cheering as if the Kenyan team had won the World Cup. There were stones, shrieks, kicks, more stones. People were shouting *MWIZI, MWIZI,* "Thief, Thief." The kid was severely wounded. Blood was streaming from his head. Every blow made him bleed more. His eyes were so swollen you couldn't see them anymore. Then someone kicked him hard, in the mouth, and he just lay there, on the ground, twitching.

I thought I would throw up. I slipped back; I couldn't watch anymore. This was the most disgusting sight I had ever seen. I felt guilty just having watched, as though I had participated. The boy probably died. As long as we had lived in Nairobi we had heard about lynchings: thieves killed on the streets by vengeful mobs. But this was the first time I had ever seen one.

The atmosphere at secretarial college was also far more lurid than at Muslim Girls'. In school, some of the Kenyan girls had giggled about sex;

to them, it was natural to go out and attract boys. Still, almost all of them were practicing Christians and devoted to the ideals of Christian marriage. But at Valley College Secretarial School our classmates were openly unchaste. They freely admitted to having sex with men. They lived the lives my mother banned us from living, which made them both deeply shocking to me and also fascinating.

Lucy, for example, was chatty and friendly and loved to talk. She wore clothes so tight you could see every roll in her thighs. She said, "A man likes something to hold on to." Lucy went to discos every weekend to drink beer and meet men, and when she was fed up with one man after a few weeks, she found another. She just laughed when we commented, and told us with friendly scorn, "You can't eat the same meal every day."

Lucy talked about sex all the time. To her, a virgin was either too ugly and stuck up for boys to want her, or a religious fanatic. Virginity was ridiculous. "Why would I promise myself to one man when I can get them all?" she asked me once. "What is this cage you're in, girl?"

Lucy considered religion in general boring and Islam in particular creepy, and she made no secret of it. She didn't aspire to marriage, she aspired to fun; and to Lucy, sex was fun. Sometimes men gave you money, which was good, and sometimes they could dance well, which was terrific, but that wasn't the point. Lucy liked having sex, and when she stopped liking it with one man, she just found another man to be with.

After we had known her for a few months Lucy announced that she was pregnant. She said she had done it on purpose, because this man was just too good-looking and she wanted a pretty baby. Her life seemed almost otherworldly to me; at the time, I was still putting on my robe every evening to take the *matatou* home. We asked Lucy if her parents would not punish her severely for this, but she laughed that no, her parents would take care of the baby; they would even be pleased with her if it was particularly cute.

I still missed my father. I was staggered by Lucy's irresponsibility about her baby, and I confess I lectured her. We ended up falling out. But whether it was Lucy's influence or not, I did begin to relax a bit about my huge black robe. It was dawning on me that I wouldn't be able to keep wearing it for long if I was planning to work in an office in Nairobi. I almost certainly wouldn't be allowed to wear my *hidjab* at work.

The robe had begun to seem cumbersome, too, and also rather stupid. What counted, surely, was my intention to behave modestly. I began wearing a long, tailored coat, like Halwa did. I also began avoiding Sister Aziza. I knew she wouldn't approve.

We received our grades in September 1989. Lucy, by now visibly pregnant, failed. Haweya and I both graduated with first-class certificates as Valley College secretaries. We came home elated and told Ma she needn't worry any more about all the rent we owed. Now that we could work, we would be able to support her.

Ma got up from the stool she used to sit on by the brazier with a face like thunder. We would not work. She was adamant. To our mother, for a young, unmarried girl to work in an office was second cousin to prostitution. Grandma was behind her all the way. "Money earned by a woman has never made anyone rich," she said, quoting yet another from her endless supply of anachronistic proverbs.

I turned to Haweya grimly and said, in English, "Then we'll move out." I knew now that there were such things as hostels; we could rent a room, somewhere decent, and live our own lives.

Perhaps Ma understood more English than I thought. When we stomped into our room, she slipped out and bought a huge stock of food and three padlocks. When Haweya and I headed out that evening for a walk, we found all the doors barred. "You're not going anywhere," Ma said. "You have food—cook it if you're hungry."

Haweya went insane. She pulled off her headscarf and coat and yelled, "It's my ambition in life to become a prostitute! I know everything about how to get pregnant! Look at my breasts and buttocks. I will call a man to the window and tell him to give me his sperm and I will GET PREGNANT!" Her screaming went on for hours. I could see that in a way Ma was enjoying Haweya's sharp, biting language, but that didn't make her any less angry.

Days of rage and tedium went by, behind bars. I found an outrage inside myself I hadn't known I possessed. We passed notes through the window to people who lived in our building and asked them to take them to Halwa and Sahra. Halwa's mother came over to try to persuade Ma that she couldn't keep us locked up until we died there. It simply wasn't a solution. We were clever girls and had no father, and after all, our mother didn't have any other means of support. She told Ma we could find a decent, Muslim company to work for, one that would at least permit us to wear a headscarf.

Ma went to the Osman Mahamud again, to Farah Gouré and the

other men. Farah Gouré agreed that Ma had a perfect right to prevent us from working, if that was best for us in her judgment. But we could not be married, because our father was not available to approve the match. And padlocking us into the house was simply not a long-term solution. Farah Gouré said the only thing to do was to send us both back to Somalia, a good Muslim country. We could perhaps work there; in any case, it was obvious we could benefit from living among Somalis.

Ma had no choice but to agree. When we heard we would be going to Somalia, I was thrilled. Haweya told me, "Ayaan, put both your legs back on the ground. You won't like it." She knew what I was expecting: I was expecting to be recognized, and loved. I thought Somalia would be full of only decent people, all behaving toward one another as they should. Somehow the Somalis in Somalia would be different from all the Somalis I knew in Kenya. Jawahir had told me there was no crime or violence there. The weather would be warm all the time, not cold and misty as it often was in Nairobi. When I was growing up I was always told that every little thing that went wrong in my mother's life was the fault of the Kenyans; Somalia meant trust and justice and fairness. In Somalia, everything would fall into place, and make sense.

I had also heard the news that the SSDF forces had advanced across the north of the country, all the way to Bari. My father had already visited Somalia once, but he had refused to renounce the struggle and return to the wide smile of Siad Barré, as some of the other exiles had. Siad Barré's rule really did seem to be crumbling. One day soon, peace would come, and all Somali exiles would be able to go home.

When we left, in March 1990, I was twenty years old. I wasn't frightened of going to Mogadishu. I was glad to be leaving my mother and Nairobi, and to be heading back to my true home and my roots.

CHAPTER 7

Disillusion and Deceit

As soon we came out of the plane in Mogadishu the heat hit us. I loved it. I was so excited that Farah Gouré's assistant, who was traveling with us, burst out laughing at me. But I was taken aback by the chaos. The airstrip was a path swept in the sand. Passengers scrabbled and tugged at a huge heap of battered suitcases that were dumped, unceremoniously, under the plane. Outside the airport, a swarm of men descended on us, urging us to ride with them into town. There was no order, no systems in place at all.

It didn't matter; this was just the airport. I was prepared to forgive almost anything from the place where I would at last be at home.

Mogadishu was beautiful at dusk. In those days, the city was not the scabbed, burned-out ruin that it is today, devastated by the violence of the clans. It was gentle and pleasant. As we rode to Maryan Farah's house in a taxi, the streets looked deeply familiar. Downtown, the Italian buildings were stately, and the streets were fine white sand. All the people looked like me. They walked high and tall, the women striding down the street in long patterned *dirhas*. I fancied that I was truly coming home.

We went to Maryan Farah, my father's first wife, who lived in a big white villa in the Casa Populare neighborhood, right near Tribunka Square. I'm not sure what I was expecting, but it wasn't this: a prosperous, self-confident stepmother with a government job.

I met my two stepsisters, who were as different as two girls could be. Arro, who was twenty-five, and who I had actually met briefly in 1984 when her mother brought her to Nairobi for medical treatment, looked like our father—like me—with a round forehead and high cheekbones. She was delicate and small, in a pale green and mauve gauze *dirha* so transparent you could see her lace bra strap, with a pale green underskirt and mauve high heels. Arro was a medical student. Her younger sister, Ijaabo, had just left school; she was dumpier, and dressed in a thick, dirt-brown Islamic robe.

Mahad was living in Mogadishu, and he came to welcome us that evening. I hardly recognized my own brother. Mahad had never been fat, but in Kenya there was always something soft about him. Now he had grown taller and more muscled, and the sun had burned his skin dark. He had spent two years in Mogadishu, studying at an international college, but he had also been to Bari. And he had seen our father.

Our father was in Somalia! He was just a few miles away, and Mahad had stayed with him! My heart leapt.

Abeh was in a place called Ayl, on the coast, quite near Bari. He had entered the country with the SSDF forces, which had gained control of most of the old Isse Mahamud territory. There had been a lot of fighting, and our father was establishing a new administration on what was now "free" Somali soil.

The situation in Ayl was stable, but the road there from Mogadishu was extremely dangerous, so Mahad couldn't take us there yet. We would have to wait until an air connection could be opened. Bandits were roaming unchecked across the disputed territory; the army checkpoints alone were dangerous to pass. In the rainy season, a four-wheel-drive vehicle could be stuck for days in the mud. People were robbed and raped on the road. Mahad couldn't risk delivering dead bodies to our father. But Abeh was well. We would have to be patient.

That first evening we went to one of the neighborhoods near the ocean, where the cool breeze filters in from the sea in the evenings. I filled my lungs with the smells: garlic, frankincense, and the salt sea. We bought lamb wrapped in hot pita bread. Walking through the streets, I remembered playing on sand just like this as a little girl, and I took off my shoes and walked barefoot.

It was such a pleasure to feel the fine, dry white grains of sand on my feet. In Nairobi it was dusty, and when it rained, which was often, the ground was mud, so you never felt clean. And in Nairobi everyone went to bed early. In Mogadishu, everyone came alive at night. All the shops were open, and the only pools of light in the darkness came from the shopkeepers' bare lightbulbs; there were no street lamps in this neighborhood. Groups of people strolled around, young families with children.

As we walked past the tailors' stalls, however, the electricity failed, so that the shops went dark and the whole street was suddenly plunged into complete darkness. Gradually, candles were lit, and lanterns, and a generator coughed to life. Somalia was clearly a lot poorer than Kenya. This hadn't occurred to me before.

Mahad told us we would have to stay at Maryan's house; leaving her would make our family look bad. People would say there was jealousy in Hirsi Magan's family. He didn't issue an order, but he had a much more authoritative air about him now. It was a request, but it was also more than that. Haweya couldn't stand living in Maryan's house, even though she liked and respected Maryan. She may have hated Ma sometimes, but she felt a fierce loyalty to her, and liking Maryan made her feel guilty. After a short while Haweya moved out. But Mahad asked me to stay, for the good of the family.

It was an awkward situation. I always felt a tension when Maryan Farah was around. It wasn't her fault—she was gracious, perfectly observant of all the proper behavior—but I always felt there was a crosscurrent of something we were not supposed to feel, let alone voice.

The house had an uncomfortable amount of static in the air, anyway. Our older sister, Arro, could be spiteful, and she squabbled constantly with Ijaabo. Ijaabo wore a headscarf even inside the house and dressed in drab grays and browns. Outside the house she wore the full *jilbab,* which covered the eyes with a separate thin black cloth. She eyed my *hidjab* with approval, but there was something insufferably cloying about her. Both sisters clearly had mixed feelings about Haweya; they seemed to envy her defiance but didn't seem to like her.

Arro and Ijaabo treated us both as if we were in some way retarded. They sneered at our weirdness; we were tarnished by having grown up far away. Yet Arro, in particular, coveted every Western item that we owned. Neither of our new sisters read for pleasure; it was quite difficult to find books in Somalia, and no one seemed to read novels, which were common in Nairobi. Instead, they watched endless Indian movies and Arab soaps on TV, which we found mystifying, because the stories were fatuous and Arro and Ijaabo spoke even less Arabic and Hindi than we did.

Arro was out of the house a lot, at the university. Ijaabo, however, was still in high school. She was a completely devout believer in the Muslim Brotherhood. Maryan thought Ijaabo's devotions were probably just a phase, but she allowed her to study with a *ma'alim,* who came every week to instruct Ijaabo in the Quran.

Ijaabo invited me to join her Quran study a few times, but never again after I told her that I thought her *ma'alim* wasn't really teaching her anything, just reading the Quran in Arabic while she nodded. Ijaabo was indignant. Who did I think I was, I who spoke English, the language of infidels? How could I dare say this man, who had studied in Medina, was wrong?

When Mahad visited it was a relief to get out of the house. He often came over, usually with his friend Abshir, the younger son of the prison director who was executed for helping my father and the brother of Abdellahi Abdi Aynab, the young man who had asked me to marry him. It felt natural for all of us to go out together, with Haweya and Ijaabo, in a pack. We went to see other family members.

It felt good to belong. This is what the bloodline was: this self-evident feeling of not having to justify your existence or explain anything. We joked around. We had fun. Mahad was always gallant and pleasant, even to Ijaabo. His friend Abshir was dark-skinned and handsome, very polite and civilized, and bright. He was an imam in the Muslim Brotherhood movement, which was rapidly capturing the imagination of young people in the city. Abshir was intensely devout. He had put his mind to learning how to be a good Muslim, an example to others. I admired this in him and also that, like me, Abshir sought explanations. Whenever we were alone together we would have deep discussions of religion, in Somali and English, which he had taught himself to speak and read. He was nothing at all like any imam I had ever met.

In Somalia the Muslim Brotherhood was cool. Siad Barré's dictatorship was anticlan and secular. The generation that grew up under his rule wasn't driven so much by clan: they wanted religion. They wanted Islamic law. The Brotherhood was above politics—and clan; it was fighting for God's justice. And it had money. Funds were pouring in from the oil-rich Arab countries to support and promote the pure, true Islam.

By the time I arrived, little congregations had formed all over Mogadishu. People called them the Assalam-Alaikums, the Blessed-be's. That was how they greeted you on the street, in Arabic, which in a Somali context was like someone suddenly spouting liturgical Latin. The most fanatical Brotherhood members, who were usually in their teens and twenties, spoke only to other Brotherhood people, and they attended their own mosques and Quran schools, in houses. They sneered at the big official mosques that older people attended, where the imams reported to the government. A Muslim Brotherhood mosque was a place of inquiry and conspiracy, where people muttered against Siad Barré and shouted doctrine at each other in corners.

As Abshir took Mahad to places like that, Mahad was becoming more of a believer, too. I liked Abshir's influence on my brother. As the weeks went by, and we spent almost every evening all together, I found myself telling Abshir about Kenya, about myself. He liked me, too, and sought me out. One twilight, as we sat on the verandah at Maryan Farah's house, he said to me, "I wish I could meet a girl like you." I looked up at him and answered, "And I wish I could meet a man like you." He took my hand and very poetically expressed his desire.

After that, our legs and hands seemed often to brush against each other. We happened to find each other alone. We held hands. After a few weeks, I decided to tell Mahad and Haweya that I was having some kind of relationship with Abshir; that way, Mahad could untangle matters with Abshir's older brother.

It made Mahad very angry to have to write a letter to Aden to explain that I would not, in fact, be marrying Abdellahi. I told him he was wrong to have promised such a thing anyway. He yelled at me, only this time, it wasn't the old Mahad, twisting my arm. He lectured me on honor, and the clan, and the impact of my decisions on our kinsmen. Certain decisions, he informed me, were better made by the men of the family.

Ijaabo and the others were also scandalized by my announcement. Many kids had relationships—they kissed and touched in corners—but you weren't supposed to admit it. It was shocking, un-Islamic, un-Somali to fall in love. You were supposed to hide such a thing. Of course, someone would have noticed and gossiped; but you were supposed to wait until the boy's family asked your father, and then you were supposed to cry. I was violating all the codes. Gossip was rampant.

In Mogadishu I felt the tension between the new wave of Brotherhood Islam and those who thought of religion as important but not all-pervading. The older generation was bothered by the mixing of the sexes but had learned to accept it, as part of the modern culture of life in the city, the *magalo;* in fact, some modern older women wore Western skirts, too. And not all young people in Somalia were traditional. Many wanted to fall in love and date just like Westerners. But the younger generation was split into two blocs: those who looked to the West for inspiration, and especially entertainment, and those who subscribed to the sermons of men from the Muslim Brotherhood like Boqol Sawm.

On my visits to Arro's campus, where she was studying medicine, I saw crowds of young students strolling on the grounds; beautiful girls dressed in the latest Italian designs actually held hands with their boyfriends. Arro had to pinch me and hiss in my ears not to stare. In

Arro's crowd, staring was considered something that only bumpkins from the *miyé* would do, and Arro had been boasting that her sisters had come to visit from abroad. Among her friends, having relatives abroad enhanced your status and proved how worldly your family was.

At the university Ijaabo attended, Lafoole, the students seemed to be divided almost equally between the West and the Muslim Brotherhood, characterized by their choice of dress. Some girls wore Western skirts and high heels; when they passed they left a trail of Dior, Chanel, or Anaïs Anaïs, not frankincense. The boys who hung around them had fitted shirts that they tucked into their trousers and drove cars.

The girls in the other group wore the *jilbab* or were shrouded in the nine-yard-long cloth that my grandmother once wore as a *guntiino*. The boys they associated with wore white robes; if they did wear trousers they never tucked in their shirts, and the trousers, like their robes, stopped short of their ankles. They looked peculiar, with wispy beards and scrawny lower legs, but this was a way of showing how strong you were in your belief. They had as much confidence as the kids in the cool cars.

When I visited Arro's university, she demanded I come dressed like Iman, the famous Somali model. When I visited Ijaabo she demanded I wear the *jilbab*. Living in the same house with Arro and Ijaabo when they were both present—on Fridays and Saturdays and throughout the long holiday in July and August—was like being in the middle of a religious war. Arro derided Ijaabo's clothes, friends, and way of life, and Ijaabo made it a sacred aim of her life to persuade Arro to pray and return to the Straight Path of Allah.

Nobody told the "adults" about me and Abshir, and because Mahad, Haweya, Ijaabo, and the rest of the family respected Abshir, they began to leave the two of us alone more often. Abshir and I talked constantly about the Prophet. Abshir thought of himself as a pure, true believer. He persuaded me to get another robe, even thicker than the zippered *hidjab* I already wore, with material so stiff it showed not one curve of my body. I confessed to him that I found it difficult to keep up the five daily prayers and steer my mind from sinful thoughts.

I was having more and more sinful thoughts. When we were alone Abshir would kiss me, and he could really kiss. It was long and gentle and thrilling and therefore sinful. Afterward I would tell him how bad I felt in the eyes of Allah, how much that bothered me. And Abshir would say, "If we were married, then it wouldn't be sinful. We must exercise

willpower and not do it anymore." So for a day or so we would steel ourselves and refrain, and then the next day we would look at each other and
just kiss again. He would say, "I'm too weak. I think of you all day long."

Our attraction was definitely mutual. But it was beginning to seem as
if we were taking God for a ride. Abshir would tell me, "We must
repent," so we did, and tried to steel ourselves; but then we would kiss
again, sometimes even before the next evening's prayer.

From Sister Aziza and from my own reading, I knew that what mattered was not just the act, but the intention. It was not only the kissing
that was forbidden—or even breaking your promise to God—it was
wanting to break that promise. I enjoyed those kisses, longed for them,
thought about them constantly, wanted more. I fought these thoughts,
but they seemed uncontrollable. I wanted Abshir; he wanted me. And
that was evil.

Ramadan began, the Holy Month of fasting, when everyone must
behave in the holiest possible way. Somalia is an entirely Muslim country, and Ramadan is also a month of family togetherness, the great festive
event of the year. Mahad came over to see us almost every day; when we
heard the call to prayer at twilight, we would all break the day's fast
together, with three dates and a glass of water. We would pray three
rakhas and then eat out of a big communal dish, laughing, happy, all the
young people sitting together around our own dish, separate from the
adults.

At 8 p.m., when the call would come for the last prayer of the day, all
of us young people walked together to the mosque. Although Abshir was
an imam at his own mosque, he sometimes asked a friend to replace him
in leading prayers so he could accompany us. All the shops were lit; there
were people laughing in the street and huge crowds heading to the grand
central mosque. Inside, the large, carpeted men's area was ornate. The
women's area behind it was much less showy—just a white hall with sisal
mats—but even so, there was an architectural sense of awe in a space so
large, so charged with meaning.

After the evening service, some of the older women would go home,
but Ijaabo and I always continued to pray, as did Mahad and his friends.
Every night of that Ramadan we prayed the whole *Taraweh,* the long,
optional Ramadan prayer, an intensive stream of chanting and bowing
that could go on until eleven o'clock. Tucked in the back, we women
didn't face an imam, just a loudspeaker. But the mosque was full: there
was a feeling of oneness and union, a huge sense of community from

everyone involved in a small space doing just one thing, and doing it voluntarily.

When you pray, you are supposed to feel the force of God and know that you are in His presence. But though I tried hard to open my mind to that force, I never seemed to feel it. To be honest, I prayed because I knew I should, but I never felt very much during prayer, only the discomfort of the grass mat pressing against my feet and the unpleasant odors of some of the bodies around me as the imam droned, monotonously, for hours. I never felt as exalted by prayer as Ijaabo said she did. Ijaabo had a mystical, beatific look on her face during *Taraweh*. Afterward she would talk about how wonderful it was, how she had seen the light of Allah and felt the presence of the angels, how she had traveled in her mind to a place that resembled Paradise. I never reached a transcendental state; there was no inner light.

One evening, just as Ramadan was ending, we went to see Abshir preaching in his little mosque. It was just a storefront really, in a house in Wardhiigley, a formerly poor neighborhood where people were beginning to build fancy houses. Abshir had a beautiful voice; he had learned the whole Quran by heart, and the way he led prayer was compelling. When he commented on the Quran, he really seemed to understand it.

Abshir had a following. Although many of them were older than he was, they were still young people, all of them Muslim Brotherhood. The boys wore their sarongs or kaftans short and had wispy beards. The girls, behind a partition, were silent. Standing in that women's room, I heard Abshir preaching, through a loudspeaker. He preached that intimacy before marriage is forbidden. He talked about purity—purity in deed and thought—and said the remedy for forbidden thoughts is more prayer.

Afterward, he tried to kiss me.

It was Ramadan, which made it triply worse. I was repelled. My reaction was completely physical: my skin crawled. I found I couldn't bear him to touch me any more. There was something creepy about it. I detached myself from Abshir—he saw how shocked I was—and asked him to take us home.

In hindsight I don't think of Abshir as a creep at all. He was just as trapped in a mental cage as I was. Abshir and I and all the other young people who joined the Muslim Brotherhood movement wanted to live as much as possible like our beloved Prophet, but the rules of the last Messenger of Allah were too strict, and their very strictness led us to hypocrisy. At the time, though, I could see only that either Abshir or Islam was thoroughly flawed, and of course I assumed it was Abshir.

I told Mahad I wanted to end things with Abshir. My brother was exasperated with me; he thought I was typically female, incapable of knowing my own mind. I wrote Abshir a letter. He pleaded and begged; it was as if he had lost his mind. He took to hanging out at Maryan's house, lamenting to Ijaabo. The whole family—the whole Osman Mahamud clan—began looking after him.

Most of the family, including the women, explained my sudden change of heart as the result of female indecision. They said women were in the grip of invisible forces that played with their minds and made them switch from one extreme mood to another. That was why Allah had ordained that the testimony of two women is equal to that of one man, and also why women should not be allowed to govern or accept public offices, for leadership requires mindful contemplation and judgments reached after careful thought. Women lacked all these by nature. We were flighty and irrational, and it was much better for us if our fathers and other male guardians decided who we should spend the rest of our lives with.

Only Haweya understood me. She liked Abshir, but she hadn't liked seeing the way I was with him: didn't like the robe he had me wearing, and my recent Brotherhood behavior. Somehow in that period she managed to lay her hands on some books and passed them to me. Even the bad ones came as a cool stream to a dry riverbed. They provided me with an escape.

I was loath to admit it to her, but I was disappointed with Somalia. I had expected a country where everything made sense to me—a country where I would belong, where I could be accepted, where I could root and discover myself as a person. But even though I loved the heat, the wind, the smells, I didn't fit in. There was a sense of belonging in Somalia: I could take for granted who I was, and enjoyed the easy acceptance of my family and clan. But even though Haweya had warned me, I was not prepared for the limitations and the price I had to pay for that sense of belonging. Everyone was involved in everyone else's business. The complete lack of privacy, of individual space, and the social control were suffocating.

Conforming to my allotted role in Somali society—in a clan, in a subclan, in Islam—might have brought me peace of mind: a fixed destiny and a secure place in Heaven. I had less trouble with obedience than

Haweya did. But still, I wanted more than to marry Abshir and bear his children, a destiny just like my mother's. I wanted a challenge, something daring. I felt, suddenly, that the price of my sense of belonging in Somalia would be my sense of self.

Religion gave me a sense of peace only from its assurance of a life after death. It was fairly easy to follow most of the rules: good behavior, politeness, avoiding gossip and pork and usury and alcohol. But I had found that I couldn't follow the deeper rules of Islam that control sexuality and the mind. I didn't want to follow them. I wanted to be someone, to stand on my own. If I stayed in Somalia and married Abshir, I would become a faceless unit. That prospect seized me with a sudden panic. I was in a state of moral confusion—a crisis of faith.

I spoke to Mahad about my doubts and fears, and he comforted me. He said it was all normal, just part of growing up, that the questions, the feelings of confusion, and the sense of moral crisis were part of the transition into adulthood. He said, "Just remain sincere, and you'll see, everything will be fine."

I took to going to the mosque more often in that period as I searched for answers. I began to attend the Friday noon prayers at the central mosque, to listen to the imam's sermons in Somali. Again, though, I found myself having mental debates with him.

You're not supposed to argue with an imam. You are definitely not supposed to argue with the word of Allah. Islam is submission. You submit, on earth, in order to earn your place in Heaven. Life on earth is a test and I was failing it, even though I was trying as hard as I knew how to. I was failing as a Muslim. When I prayed, I felt that the angel on my left shoulder was growing weary of writing down all my sins. I imagined arriving in Heaven with a slim book of good deeds and a volume of sins as vast as the unabridged *Oxford Dictionary*. I wanted to feel a renewed sense of being a Muslim, a sense of the meaning of Allah. But I felt nothing. I told myself it meant that Allah didn't want me. I wasn't worthy.

Haweya moved out of Maryan's house—she couldn't stand Ijaabo's disapproval and Arro's constant sniping—and moved in with Ibado Dhadey Magan, our aunt. As the director of Digfeer Hospital, Ibado had contacts with the UN and got Haweya a job.

Then she found me a job, too, with a small office that the United Nations Development Program had set up to establish phone lines into rural Somalia. The work was not inspiring. I was supposed to be a secretary, but I often ended up translating for my boss, a rather bewildered Englishman. He would meet with a delegation from the provinces, and I would try to explain why he wouldn't just give them the cash to set up a phone line. He would also try to explain why they shouldn't tear up and resell the cables he'd just laid, while they ignored him and talked among themselves. He had no authority over his staff, but this was a so-called multilateral project, so he was under orders to respect their views and their way of doing things even if they had neither views nor methodology.

While I was working in that office I began to realize just how much fighting was going on in the country. More and more UN offices were closing and leaving the rural areas because they were unsafe. The Hawiye clan had formed their own political movement, called the United Somali Congress, led by Ali Mahdi and General Muhammad Farah Aideed. Although Mogadishu itself was peaceful, with Siad Barré still in control, the Hawiye were now in rebellion against the dictator in the south and the Darod and the Isaq in the north.

Working also gave me a close-up look at the Somali bureaucracy. Almost every civil servant I encountered seemed abysmally ignorant. Their scorn for all things *gaalo,* including my boss, was profound. (*Gaalo* usually means "white unbeliever," but not always. Ma used this word for the Kenyans, too.) They were completely uninterested in doing their jobs, and spent their time scheming about how to "transfer" government funds, a euphemism for stealing them.

In Somalia, to have a stake in government was to have a family member in the place where tax money and money from kickbacks was distributed. No more, no less. I saw what that does to a nation: it destroys public trust.

In the face of such widespread corruption, no wonder people were susceptible to the lure of preachers who said all the answers were to be found in the Holy Writings. Organizations set up by Brotherhood sympathizers were not corrupt. Many Somalis had ceased to trust the banking system and carried out financial transactions in shops and warehouses that were owned by Brotherhood people. The Brotherhood also gave free health care to the needy. They set up Quran schools for the unemployed youths who roamed the city. On Fridays they distributed grain and meat outside the mosque. Their ranks were swelling, as was their influence.

A UN car took me to and from work, and I wore a headscarf in the office, where I worked from eight until two. It was a comfortable routine, but my job was tedious. My boss was polite, but we had no personal interaction, no conversation or teaching. When work ended, I went back to Maryan's house and talked to the maid.

Maryan's house was filling up with more and more of her Marehan relatives from the countryside. They came in dribs and drabs, to escape the troubles in the provinces. Ijaabo and Maryan tried to enforce house rules and teach these country cousins to flush the toilet and sit on chairs, but if Ijaabo or Arro spoke to them sharply, the visitors responded angrily and accused the girls of having turned away from "our culture."

There were reports that crime was rising in the neighborhood. One of Maryan's recently arrived uncles bought a gun.

Haweya and I received constant invitations from people on my father's side of the family. We went to my cousin Aflao's house and spent time with his wife, Shukri, his sisters, Amran and Idil, and his cousin Ainanshie, who lived with them all and worked at Aflao's espresso bar downtown. They were a clamorous, friendly family, full of gossip about Maryan's side of the family. Ainanshie, in particular, hated anyone from Siad Barré's clan, the Marehan, and he had a grudge against Maryan.

Aflao's sister Amran took us strolling along the beach, where the Arabs lived in houses enclosed by high walls the color of the sand. Once in a while a woman completely covered in black would scuttle along the walls, heading in. These women walked barefoot, because of the sand, and all you could see of them was their feet. Even though these shapeless black heaps were moving forward, they might just as well have been inanimate; you couldn't talk to them. Amran called them the Confined; she said, "Pay no attention to them," with disdain. It reminded me of Saudi Arabia.

Soon after I broke it off with Abshir I stopped wearing the stiff, horribly hot cloak that the Brotherhood girls wore and reverted to my black robe from Nairobi; it was cooler. But on top of a long dress and long sleeves, even that robe came to seem excessive. It stood out a lot on the street. Nobody in Somalia wears *black*. I began dressing in a light-colored *dirha,* like most people: a long tunic with a flap on the side, and a cotton shawl draped on my head.

Far fewer women dressed in Western clothes in Mogadishu in 1990 than they had just ten or twenty years before. They had always been a minority, but now the tide had visibly shifted against them. Ainanshie used to say, "Before the Brotherhood came, you could see everyone's arms and legs. We never used to notice. But now that women are covering so much, all I can think about is those round calves and silky arms and the hair, smelling of coconut. I never used to think about a neck before, but ooh, a neck is so sexy now."

Ijaabo's schoolmates and Ainanshie's pals from downtown would laugh at the Brotherhood's gibberish and sneer that it was all Arab cultural dominance, but a few weeks later some of them, too, would be wearing robes and spouting Arabic. The movement wasn't only about religion. Its members were hardworking and clever. They probably received money from Saudi Arabia, but there were also lots of successful businesses run by Brotherhood followers, especially in transportation and money transfers. They helped swell the Brotherhood's coffers.

One afternoon, Ainanshie was walking us back to Aunt Maryan's neighborhood after lunch, as he always did. Because he hated Maryan and all the Marehan, he used to leave us about a hundred yards from her house. Just before we reached the corner where we usually bade him good-bye, a hand gripped my neck, hard, and I felt the sharp blade of a knife pressed against my throat. I looked at Haweya: a scrawny man with huge, red-rimmed dark eyes was pointing a knife at her, too. I assumed this was the end. I remember thinking, "Well, we made it to age eighteen and twenty." I knew Ainanshie was armed—he always had a little pistol on him—but under these circumstances, that wasn't going to be much use.

"The gold!" said the man who gripped Haweya. I croaked, "We're not wearing any." The man holding me started feeling my ears and neck under my shawl, keeping the sharp knife pointed into my throat. He sneered, "Where do these tall beautiful girls come from, and who is this little shit they're standing on the street with?"

The man was Isaq; I could tell from his accent. Mogadishu was filled with Isaq refugees, displaced from the north by the fighting. I thought perhaps he would let us go if we were Isaq, too, so I quickly began reciting my grandmother's clan, just as she taught me. Ainanshie caught on; he was very calm. He didn't pull his gun out; if he had, my throat would have been slit in a minute. "See? These girls are your Isaq sisters," he told the muggers. "And I am married to another of their sisters. I am escorting them home."

Just as quickly as they appeared, the men melted away.

After that, Haweya and I realized that it wasn't safe to walk on the streets of Mogadishu alone anymore. Every day there were reports of killings, rapes, and houses burned by armed robbers. Homeless refugees lived all over the place. Displaced people, like the Isaq men who attacked us, had moved to the city with nothing to lose, armed and filled with rage. Army soldiers also roamed about with their weapons. Although we didn't yet know this, large sections of the army had defected and were joining the various clan-led factions all over Somalia who could not wait to get their teeth into Siad Barré's throat.

In contrast to the clan warfare, the Brotherhood seemed to have a more universal character because it included people of every clan. Of these groups, the Brotherhood seemed to many to be the most reliable. As its following grew, the movement became more self-assured. Brotherhood imams began operating in larger mosques, no longer restricting themselves to semiclandestine houses. We heard more and more gossip about openly political sermons announcing that the government's days were over and the time for Islamic law had come.

Siad Barré began sending troops to mosques, to disperse large gatherings; they would shoot their machine guns overhead, as a signal of who was in power, and people were often killed in the ensuing stampedes. After every such action, the Brotherhood's support in the city would grow. The movement had become a power to reckon with in businesses, hospitals, schools, and universities. Ijaabo's university, Lafoole, on the outskirts of Mogadishu, was pretty much a Brotherhood enclave now.

In mid-1990, a group of politicians—elders representing virtually every clan—published a manifesto calling for Siad Barré to resign. They told him that the country was in chaos and he should relinquish power so elections could be held. Siad Barré had some of these men thrown in jail. A stable peace in the country seemed remote.

Maryan's country relatives bought several small machine guns and began sitting at her gate, day and night, with coils of ammunition across their bellies. The same happened at other relatives' homes. Guards armed to the teeth, often clan members from the countryside, took up positions in front of the doors of their urban relatives to protect their lives and property.

I fell out with Arro and moved in to Ibado Dhadey's house. One particularly lugubrious Saturday, I decided to visit my Aunt Khadija, my mother's much older half-sister. Khadija was grand and imperious, almost as old as my grandmother but taller, more regal, and even sharper-tongued. I groaned inwardly as I thought about the tongue-lashing she was bound to inflict on me for having visited her so little in the months I'd been in Mogadishu.

I was careful to be impeccably clean and ironed my clothes, and I made sure I had a present for her. Khadija was a hawk about etiquette. She pounced on every infelicity of diction. You had to wait for her to greet you, and then greet her poetically back, standing perfectly upright.

I acquitted myself acceptably at the doorway; we swept into the dining room for tea. I marveled at the room and its antique European chairs and knives and forks. Khadija must have been the only woman in Mogadishu to live this way. I was so astonished that, despite my wary pledge to myself to put on my best manners, I made the mistake of flopping on a chair.

Khadija was at me in a minute. "Didn't poor Asha even teach you how to sit? Are you a little monkey?" Her tongue-lashing went on and on, comparing me to a host of little animals of which no manners could be expected, and constantly tossing out half-veiled insults at my mother, who hadn't trained me right. It was really a bravura performance, and although part of me was insulted, I also marveled at the play of language—this beautiful, haughty, dry prose, delivered by an old woman sitting ramrod straight, with the steadiest gaze I had ever seen.

You couldn't rebel, or cry, or protest when Khadija scolded you. If you did, you'd get another lecture on how weak your character was, how you would never learn anything, and die as shabbily as you were born. You were required to look her in the eye, nodding to show you were taking it in, and I did that. I could see my stoicism pleased my august aunt.

When she was finished, Khadija commenced serving tea. I turned toward the door and was startled to see a young man standing in the doorway. He was strikingly good-looking, and he was grinning broadly at my predicament. Clearly he had witnessed the whole scene.

Khadija introduced us. This was my cousin Mahmud, the son of my mother's brother, Uncle Muhammad. Mahmud lived with Khadija when he was home from the army. His mother had died; he didn't care for his stepmother, and so, when he was still a teenager, he had become a soldier. Khadija had no children—she was barren—so she had looked through the family's children and selected Mahmud.

I politely gave Mahmud news of my mother, trying hard to hold my gaze against the obviously sexual interest in his eyes. This man was looking at me as a woman, quite openly; it was almost carnivorous.

Then Khadija asked me about Abshir. She had heard the talk, of course. I had no idea what to say, and blurted out, "I had feelings for him in that way, but now I don't want to spend my life with him." Which was at least the truth, although the truth about these things always somehow seemed to be impolite in Somalia.

Khadija's manner abruptly shifted. She leaned over the table, her eyes glinting, and cooed, "But my dear, I have just the person for you!" Then she swept her arm over to the end of the table, where Mahmud was sitting. As he smiled, he seemed to be evaluating me, quite deliberately, from head to toe. Was I disciplined enough? Resilient enough? Proud enough? Or was I a weakling, chaotic, one who gives in easily and allows herself to be defeated by the harsh side of life? I felt undressed. But more than that, I felt exposed.

I passed muster. Khadija invited me over the following Thursday for dinner, and once again Mahmud was there. Halfway through the meal Khadija announced she was going to pray, left the room, and never reappeared. The meal went on, scrupulously politely, with both of us pretending nothing unusual was going on. Mahmud asked if I had ever been outside Mogadishu and offered to take me. I parried by inviting Haweya along, too. We called each other "cousin": "my dear cousin," "my very dear cousin," "my lovely cousin."

The next day Mahmud arrived in a car to take us to the country. Haweya had met him before—she had told me how handsome our cousin Mahmud was—and now her eyes widened when she looked at the way his shoulders filled his white shirt. "So, is he going to be your boyfriend?" she asked me in English, and again in English I answered, "Don't be silly. That would be incest."

Mahmud told Haweya to translate, and she did. He smiled again, showing his white teeth, and answered, "Not at all, my lovely cousin. Maternal cousins are perfect mates, I've been told." Haweya almost licked her lips.

Mahmud was utterly gorgeous, the malest man I'd ever seen, and I fell in love with him. He was used to taking charge. Not refined; not a tortured intellectual, like Abshir. Mahmud quoted old fables and roared with laughter, and he flirted with me mercilessly.

When Mahmud looked at me I felt as if I were on fire. But he never made a sexual move, and he obeyed all the conventions. He absolutely exuded the impression that his loins were burning for mine, but he never once touched me. I was his cousin. Family honor was involved.

Although I don't know when it was taken, I love this photo of my father. The determination in those eyes! Even today I carry it with me in my wallet.

My father had asked me to accompany Osman to the airport. By then I had known him for only two weeks. The man on the left is one of his friends who came along as a chaperon. I remember feeling lost and numb. All my dreams of freedom and love had been taken from me. I was condemned to a predictable fate, that of being a subservient wife to a stranger.

In the Name of Allah Most Gracious Most Merciful.

Ayan Hirsi Maga
A.Z.C. Lunteren
Hessenweg 83
6741 JP Lunteren
HOLLAND.

27 January 1993

Hirsi Magan Isse
P.O. Box 51087
NAIROBI

Remarks:
As I shall not open your letters, never attempt to write.

Dearest father
After very warm greetings, I will just get to the point and tell you that I have become a disappointment to you and I have decided to divorce Osman Musse Isse. No amount of apologies or beggings for forgiveness will make you feel any better, but I will just beg you to understand and I am very sorry. Of course I don't expect you to feel understandable towards me but that is that.

Osman telephoned you and followed your advice to bring the matter to the attention of the man relations (TOLKA) and we have met and reached an agreement peacefully and honourably (if the can be anything honourable in such a situation) The agreement was that the DIVORCE goes through.

This is the letter that I sent to my father after the *tolka* meeting in Hasna's caravan. A couple of days later I received the letter back with my father's harsh response written in red.

I am very sorry Father but that is that I shall come back to Kenya as soon I work enough money to pay for my tick and as soon as I get a visa back Right now I go to school.

Father I feel your unhappiness tou me but please reply and try, when your an over to understand me and forgive me. Ma is too much to ask but I also need your bless.

Love

Dear deceitful Mary Fox,

your loving daugh with reference to your under line above statement, you do not need me, and I do not need you. Just invoked Allah to disgrace you as you disgraced me & Ar

This is the last message you w have received from me as you Hev was the last message I wiu to accept for you. Go to Hell and Devil Be with you.

May ALLAH PUNISH YOU FOR YOUR DECEPTION. AM YOU IS, THE

Feb. 5, 199-3

This photo was taken in 1993 by some friends in Veluwe in the Netherlands. My greatest nightmare at the time was that my family would see me looking this way. My short hair would have shocked them.

When Haweya asked me for photos of myself in 1993, I put on this embroidered loose dress, a *thaub,* and a headscarf to make my family happy.

This photo was taken while Haweya was working for the United Nations in Kenya. The only real farmer in the photo was the man on the right. I laugh when looking at this. Haweya is looking at the field and hoping that her smile will entice the maize to grow by itself, just as she used to look at the dirty dishes at home, hoping they would miraculously wash themselves.

I think this photo was taken at the office of the refugee center. It must have been in the fall of 1994. Haweya had arrived in January of that year. Even today I can see the sorrow in her eyes.

This is the photo that Haweya brought me of Mahad. It was taken in Nairobi in 1992. The building behind them is a national landmark in Kenya, and you can also see a formidable statue of President Jomo Kenyatta after whom the building was named. I don't know who the man on the right is.

This was my first holiday ever! In 1994, Ellen and I went to London for three days. The trip was a lot of fun although slightly chaotic. We realized that we had forgotten to write down the name of our hotel and so were lost in the city for hours! What a child I was then.

This photo was taken in 1996. It was the first time I met Mirjam's parents. Her father has a collection of hats and here we are trying them on! I got the police cap.

This photo was taken when I was visiting my father at my cousin Sa'diyo's house in Düsseldorf in June 2000. I was being accused of succumbing to Western cultural imperialism in my ideas as well as my choice of clothing. My rebuttal was that wearing the veil and headscarf was succumbing to Arab cultural imperialism. Sa'diyo rushed into her room and came back with this piece of vintage Somali clothing. I put on the *guntina* (nine meters of cloth that you wrap around yourself), thus demonstrating why the Somalis could never achieve cultural imperialism!

Any kind of sexual contact between us would have been deeply improper—unthinkable. I thought about it constantly myself, but I couldn't possibly make the first move.

We took to meeting every weekend at Aunt Khadija's house. She peppered me with pronouncements on the horror of marrying men from strange families and the advisability of marrying a cousin: the family will always look after you; you are so close; you understand each other. She also told me it was a mistake to marry Osman Mahamud men like Abshir. They were too political, she told me, and too self-involved, and they marry second wives without even informing you. She never once mentioned my father, but I knew what she meant. And I was glad she did not mention him: for all the authority Khadija exuded, I wouldn't accept any criticism of my father.

Aunt Khadija was still haughty, but far warmer to me now that I was caught in the web she'd woven. She hadn't changed since the days when she married my father and mother: it was impossible to resist her wiles.

Mahmud had no more future in the Somali army; in fact, very soon there was going to be no Somali army at all. He told us that large groups in the army were defecting to the militia of their clans, smuggling weapons and stocks of ammunition along with them.

Alone among our close family, Khadija had supported Siad Barré all her life. The overthrow of his brand of communism was looming, and she saw this as the betrayal of Somalia's only hope for a bright future. To Aunt Khadija, only communism could overcome the bitter divisions of Somalis by clan, and to reject it was only more evidence of the barbaric and narrow self-interest inherent in our clan system.

I kept to myself my own memories of communism: the long queues in the burning sun, the whispering in our house, the imprisonment of my father, the way I was beaten in school to sing songs in praise of Siad Barré. Instead, I asked her about the Brotherhood, to which I was still very sympathetic.

Khadija compared the Brotherhood to cancer, the sickness that my Aunt Hawo died of when I was small. She said the Brotherhood did not represent true Islam and had no knowledge of our Prophet, but though they were small, they would swell like the tumor in my aunt's breast and eat our country from the inside until they finally destroyed us all. She told me to stay away from them.

Then Mahmud told us he had been given a prestigious award to study in Russia and would be leaving the country in a few days, perhaps for a long time. Before he left, Aunt Khadija informed us both that it was high time to make things formal. There was no big proposal scene, as in the West, with suitor on bended knee: Khadija handled the whole thing. She talked, I agreed.

In spite of our mutual attraction, Mahmud and I weren't compatible in any way. Our conversations were never inspiring the way my talks with Abshir had been, or close and deep as they had been with Kennedy. I'm not even sure we liked each other much. I certainly hadn't evaluated his suitability as a partner for the rest of my life. I was simply consumed with lust for him. That's what it amounted to: a storm of hormones. I agreed to marry him just to be able to have sex.

Excision doesn't remove your desire or ability to enjoy sexual pleasure. The excision of women is cruel on many levels. It is physically cruel and painful; it sets girls up for a lifetime of suffering. And it is not even effective in its intent to remove their desire. Even though I had been infatuated with Kennedy and Abshir, I was completely unprepared to deal with the force of my desire for Mahmud.

Mahmud wanted us to marry quickly, before he left. It would be like staking a claim: no other man could come near me. My brother would never agree to a quick wedding, though. Because I was Hirsi Magan's daughter, by rights my marriage should be a big clan event. Mahad would insist that my father approve the match, and that could take months.

We would have to be married in secret, Mahmud said. He made the arrangements. The ceremony would take place the night before he left Somalia. A mutual cousin of ours, Ali Wersengeli, agreed to stand in as my guardian. I knew that wasn't right—it should be my father or brother—but Mahmud said it would be all right. Khadija would smooth matters over with my mother's family. As for my father's family, they wouldn't like it, but nobody could really oppose a marriage between maternal cousins. Even if we eloped without the proper authorization, it was clearly an acceptable match, and nobody could undo it.

Today, I know that we were risking all sorts of genetic abnormalities in our offspring, but we had absolutely no idea of such a thing. In Somalia, as in much of the Middle East and Africa, marriages between cousins are often seen as the safest unions possible: they keep the family wealth together, and any possible conflict will be quickly resolved by the couple's relatives.

The night we were to be married, our *nikah,* the excitement of it caught me by the throat. I was twenty years old, and I was getting married in secret to the man I desired. I hadn't even told Haweya; only Khadija knew. I spent the day drawing henna designs on my hands and feet. When Mahmud came to pick me up at Khadija's house I was wearing a long red dress and high heels, the kind of clothes I had never even thought of wearing before, and perfume. When I looked in the mirror, a grown woman looked back.

We went to a photo studio to be immortalized. Then we drove to the house of the *qali* who would perform the marriage ceremony. It was dark on the roads—once again, the electricity had been cut—so we parked and made our way by lantern down an alley. The sheikh was waiting for us outside the door of his house, in a white robe and white skullcap that shone out in the total blackness of the alleyway. My distant cousin Ali Wersengeli and another man I didn't know were already there. It began to dawn on me that I was getting into something very serious, but it was too late to opt out now. My ankles were shaking as I stumbled down the alley in the darkness.

The *qali* nodded at us, then began asking the required questions.

"Are you Mahmud Muhammad Artan?"

"Yes."

"Are you Ayaan Hirsi Magan? You are not required to answer, your presence is enough."

I simply sat.

The *qali* recited Mahmud's names and our respective ages. Then the *qali* turned to me and said, "Are you a virgin?" I kept silent, which was the appropriate answer, and he filled in "virgin" on the marriage certificate.

The *qali* pronounced that we were married according to the law of Islam, and then he asked us, "And the bride price is?"

We looked at each other—we hadn't thought of it—and Mahmud said, "One Holy Quran," the symbolic response. There was no one to pay a bride price to: I was a secret bride. Mahmud signed the document and asked for a copy, but the *qali* said no, it would have to be stamped and given to the authorities first. Ali would have to pick it up the following week.

There were grateful male handshakes and both the witnesses disappeared. I was now alone in a Land Cruiser with my cousin—my husband. I felt stunned by the enormity of what I had done, and stole a glance at him. He didn't even look over at me. There was no touching now, either, not even one kiss. I knew what would be coming, though: it was my wedding night.

Mahmud swerved into the parking lot of the Hotel Arubo, the fanciest hotel in town. He hadn't made a reservation, but he wanted to pay for a room with his wife. The reception clerk asked him for a marriage certificate; this was the growing Muslim Brotherhood influence. But Mahmud didn't have one. He returned to the car, fuming, and cursing the Brotherhood. "I don't know what is happening to this country," he said. "Who are these people?"

It happened again at the next hotel, and then another. I ventured to wonder whether perhaps I should go in, and he yelled, "Have you lost your senses? Next morning there will be a poster of you calling you a prostitute: a woman with a man and no marriage certificate. Think of your name!"

The hotel he finally took me to must have been one of the cheapest places in Mogadishu, the kind of place where they didn't check marriage certificates. The electricity still wasn't working. We had to take a lantern to the room. A cockroach scuttled under the bed when the door opened. Mahmud handed me the lantern and looked into my face for the first time the entire evening. He said I could go into the bathroom and get ready.

I washed, mechanically, in the bathroom, which was filthy. Then I lay down on the bed, fully clothed: I didn't know what else to do. I wanted everything to be wildly erotic, with me in the role of Marilyn Monroe or Lady Chatterley, but I didn't even know how to undress. When Mahmud came back into the room he said, "Oh, you want to play coy?"

Coy was the last thing I wanted to play. I said, "What do you want me to do?"

"Take your clothes off, of course."

So I did, awkwardly, woodenly. Nothing was happening as I had dreamed. I made an attempt at foreplay, like I'd read about in books, and Mahmud looked at me quizzically. "Hey, have you done this before?" he asked me.

I mumbled no, and let him get on with it. If I had lied and told Mahmud I had sexual experience, then perhaps we would have had foreplay; but then, of course, he would probably have divorced me. Because I admitted to being a virgin, there was no pleasure at all. Jawahir, Sahra, and all the other girls were right, I thought. Good girls are virgins who feel nothing at all.

It wasn't rape. I wanted to have sex with Mahmud—just not this way. He gasped and shoved and sweated with the effort of forcing open my scar. It was horribly painful and took so long. I gritted my teeth and endured the pain until I became numb. Afterward Mahmud fell heavily asleep, and I went and washed again in the hideous bathroom. In every respect my wedding night had turned out exactly as Jawahir had described hers, a year before in Kenya.

Very early the next morning, Mahmud drove me back to Ibado Dhadey's house. He was leaving for Russia that afternoon; I wouldn't see him again. We bade each other adieu. I was on some kind of mental autopilot, but it must have seemed as though I were acting perfectly normally. Perhaps I was a little timid, but that may have seemed natural under the circumstances.

Ibado was frantic when I came in. I told her I had spent the night at Aunt Khadija's, then went upstairs and washed, applying disinfectant to the cuts, just as Jawahir had done. I knew I never wanted to see Mahmud again. My scar hurt so much I could barely stand up, and I told Ibado I was ill. When Haweya came in, her face showed so much concern that I broke down and told her everything. I felt too bad about myself to carry the guilt alone. I had behaved abominably: I had given in to temptation, betrayed my family, and now I would be trapped forever by this man, by my own fault.

Haweya was perfect. She didn't judge me; she seemed awed by the romance of the whole thing. When I told her how much I was hurting she cared for me. She told me she didn't think the ceremony was legitimate. Ali Wersengeli couldn't simply step in to act as my official guardian when my brother and father were both in the country. We both prayed to Allah not to let me become pregnant.

Ali Wersengeli came to the house a few days later to deliver a copy of the marriage certificate; he told me he had already sent the other copy to Mahmud in Russia. I put it away without reading it. By then I could sit up and walk, though the cuts were still painful. Two weeks later I got my period, and Allah's benevolence was confirmed.

Inside the city, violence was quickly becoming so normal that people weren't even very interested in reports of attacks unless they knew the person concerned. The soldiers were the worst: there was no money to pay them, and bands of soldiers would raid houses, preying on ordinary people. Occasionally there would be an outburst of gunfire, and children would run out into the street, responding to the sound of the bullets as if they were fireworks.

In the countryside, the rebellion against Siad Barré was becoming intense. The Macherten and the Isaq were fighting his army in the east and north; now the Hawiye revolt in the south was turning into open warfare, too. People openly sneered at Siad Barré and his weakened army. They said the Hawiye fighters had the city almost encircled; instead of *Afwayne,* they now called him the Mayor of Mogadishu because that was all the territory Siad Barré still held.

Halfway through October 1990, the telecom agency I worked at was closed down. It was becoming too unsafe for foreigners to stay in the country, and nonessential personnel of the UN were repatriated. One of them was my British boss. Listening to the radio in Kenya, Ma was becoming frantic. She insisted that Haweya and I come back to Nairobi.

A flood of nostalgia for Kenya washed over me. I missed the movies and books, I missed Halwa, and I missed my mother; it sounds odd, but I missed her moral honesty. I missed her clear sense of correct behavior, which I had expected to find in Somalia, and hadn't. Instead, I had screwed up my life and my relationship with God. I felt ugly and confused, and when Ma summoned us home to Nairobi, I was relieved.

CHAPTER 8

Refugees

Haweya and I left Mogadishu in mid-November 1990, crammed onto wooden benches with about thirty others in the back of a pickup. We were accompanied by Qubqac, Ibado's nephew and our second cousin once removed, who had some family over the border in Kenya. It was going to be a very long detour. The road to Kismayo on the coast of Somalia was already in the hands of the Hawiye rebels; it was far too dangerous to traverse. The only way for us Darod to make it safely out to Kenya was the long road up north to Baidoa, in the hills, and then west, across the desert. Even on this road, there might be bandits or stray members of the rebel armies, looking for adventure and crazy with *qat*.

A few hours' drive out of town, we got to Afgoye, one of the main market towns of southern Somalia. The landscape became suddenly green. Along the river were fields of rice and orchards: papayas and guavas and plantations of bananas and mangos. The street stalls overflowed with food, and the meat was wonderful.

The people in Afgoye looked different, more like Kenyans. These were the descendants of slaves and peasants, the outcast Sab. They lived in the arable land that feeds the rest of Somalia, and yet these people were supposed to be inferior to us. They stepped off the pavement to let us by. One highborn Darod man from our pickup actually pushed aside an old Sab woman who didn't move out of his way fast enough. It made me glad I was leaving. The open bigotry was one of the things I hated about Somalia. I had thought that belonging to a higher clan signified a higher morality. I didn't see it as a justification for mistreating people on the basis of their physical characteristics and the quality of their blood. Yet whenever I protested about the blatant prejudice against people of the Sab clans I was called a communist.

When I thought about it, the attitude of the Sab themselves also exas-

perated me. In places like Afgoye and Baidoa they were in the majority:
Why did they obey like this? What were they waiting for? Did they fear
the airplanes of the higher clans, and the bombs? Or was it that they were
dependent on the northern Somalis for money? Could they have truly
internalized this idea of their own inferiority, this daily humiliation?
Why didn't they rise up?

We spent the first night in Baidoa, a hot, dusty market town about 150
miles northwest of Mogadishu and about two hundred miles from the
Kenyan border, where we arrived just after nightfall. Then we got on
another ramshackle bus to drive to Luuq, an old trading post on the Juba
River. As we left Baidoa, the countryside emptied out: there was only
sand, scrub brush, thorn trees, and one or two baobabs. This was the kind
of land in which my grandmother had grown up. Occasionally we'd pass
a young boy herding camels, who would squint at us in the sun, or a
woman with a cloth tied around one shoulder and a baby tied to her back,
walking into the distance with a stack of firewood tied to her belly.

In Luuq, the people were thin. Refugees were sleeping in the streets,
and the houses were pockmarked with bullet holes. The hotel's tiny
rooms were as hot as ovens, so everyone slept outside, the women all on
mats laid out in the inner courtyard, the men in the outer yard. There was
no running water or electricity. Everyone washed out of a jug and mocked
Haweya and me for using the foreigner's instrument, a toothbrush,
instead of rubbing an acacia twig against our teeth. Breakfast was goat liver
with garlic and onion; I couldn't face it so early, but the others tried to
induce me to eat it before we entered the hungry places. There would be
less food farther down the road.

The pickup droned through the sand in the fierce sun, probably following some kind of path that we couldn't see. We had no shade; we simply sat on wooden benches.

We spent the next night in Bulo Haawo, a small village on the Somali
side of the Kenyan border, with a few thatch-and-stick huts and a shop
that had a cupboard with some ice in it. But just a few hundred yards past
that shanty village we crossed the border, and there we found the Kenyan
town of Mandera, with buildings made of concrete, a paved road, and
electricity. Electricity had become a rarity in Mogadishu; we were startled
to see it here. We went through an official checkpoint, where people were
openly bribing the uniformed officials. (Since Qubqac had a Kenyan ID,
and Haweya and I spoke perfect Swahili, we could get into the country
without having to pay any bribes.)

Once in Mandera, Qubqac took us to the home of his stepmother and stepsisters, to pay our respects; they had electricity and running water. Mandera had shops and a school, even a district council office and a police station. In every way this little town in Kenya, a country Somalis considered inferior, functioned far better than almost anything in Somalia, just a few miles behind us.

Mandera is inhabited by Sejui Somalis (otherwise known as Kenyan-Somalis), who speak in singsong voices and mix Swahili words into their Somali. The only "native" Kenyans were the police who kept order and the army who manned the border. Events in Somalia had a way of spilling over into Kenya, however. There were frequent cross-border raids on property and cattle, and smugglers brought *qat* and all sorts of goods and people across the border.

We spent two nights in Mandera before Qubqac agreed to get back on the road. We took a country bus to Garissa, a large town 350 miles farther south, which had asphalt roads, hotels, a bus station, traffic lights, a mosque. There, we bought bus tickets to Nairobi. We were almost home.

As we finally drove into Nairobi, about a week after our departure from Mogadishu, and made our way through the smells and colors of Eastleigh, everything looked exactly as we had left it. Even the pungent odor of *sukumawiki* was welcome: it meant home to me now. I was looking forward to seeing my mother again, but as we neared our neighborhood, I found I was also dreading the fights and emotional scenes that we would inevitably endure.

A few days after we arrived in Nairobi, at the end of November, open warfare broke out around Mogadishu. Siad Barré's army still held the center of town, but the outskirts were completely encircled by the Hawiye rebel forces. Gunmen rode around in pickups, high on *qat*, shooting at whatever they felt like and burning down farms and orchards.

To split the opposition against him, Siad Barré had been playing on the clan hostility that is always latent in Somalia. His forces staged attacks on the Darod as if the attackers were Hawiye: they left their scenes of murder daubed with slogans like "Cleanse the Darod from Hawiye land," and "USC," the initials of one of the Hawiye militias. They did the same to the Hawiye, with slogans like "The Hawiye are inferior and deserve to be wiped out."

So, as Siad Barré went down, he took the country with him: the fight to oust him became a full-fledged civil war. The Hawiye were no longer just demanding Siad Barré's head: they wanted ethnic cleansing. The Darod were caught by surprise. They had expected that the Hawiye would seek revenge from Siad Barré's subclan, but not that they would attack all of the different clans of the Darod. Mogadishu fell into chaos, with looting, wanton killing, and destruction of property. Fighters suddenly swept into neighborhoods and burned houses; children were left behind as their parents fled. Any Darod who could escape drove, walked, or crawled as far as Afgoye, Baidoa, to Kismayo on the coast, and to towns and villages all the way to the borders of Kenya and Ethiopia.

Some of the Darod fought back, and in these battles both the Darod and the Hawiye died in large numbers. Siad Barré's army had shrunk to the soldiers who guarded his presidential palace. On January 27, 1991, in the midst of this mayhem, Ma, Haweya, and I learned from the BBC Somali Service that Barré had been flown out to safety—to Nairobi.

One evening, as we listened anxiously to the radio in our apartment on Park Road, there was a knock on the door. I was startled to see Abdellahi Yasin, one of Mahad's best friends in Mogadishu, on our doorstep. Accompanying him was the son of his older sister, a young man whom he introduced to us as Osman Abdihalin Osman Yusuf Kenaidiid, a grandson of Osman, the man who had taught my father to read and write, and a great-grandson of the king whom my grandfather Magan had served. We were simply awed. It was an honor to take this man into our home.

Abdellahi and Osman told us that Mogadishu was virtually paralyzed. Only armed cars were on the streets. In areas that the Hawiye already controlled, gunmen were going door to door rounding up Darod men. Mahad left the city before them, heading for Bari, which was now solidly under the control of the SSDF. My mother became almost hysterical with fear, and Haweya and I were terribly anxious.

Abdellahi and Osman moved into our living room, and they were sleeping on mattresses there two weeks later when Mahad arrived at our door. Ma, Haweya, and I were weak with relief to see him. He had wanted to go to Bari, but the clan had insisted he return to safety in Kenya. He took the same route out of the city as we had, and only just in time: the day after he passed through Afgoye, the town fell to the Hawiye rebels.

Mahad was accompanied by our cousin Warsame, the son of Ma's twin sister, and by two of Warsame's half-brothers. We now had six men, all of them more or less family members, sleeping on mattresses in the living room. Next to arrive was Osman's older brother, Mahamuud. Again, it was a great honor to offer him hospitality, but Ma's face crumbled in terror when Mahamuud told us that Mogadishu had all but fallen when he left the city. The Hawiye had Siad Barré's palace under siege, and there was rape and looting everywhere. Hawiye gunmen dragged Darod women and children into the street and murdered them, he said; they even burned down houses with people still inside. Water was scarce, and people were already so weak from the lack of food that they could not fight or flee. Later we would learn that our Aunt Khadija had made it out to Kismayo, where she fell ill. Eventually we received word that she had died there.

Ibabo Dhadey Magan, whose mother was Hawiye, gathered a number of kinsmen into her compound to keep them safe. But the Darod were beginning to move out of the city, in vehicles or on foot, fleeing the disaster. They were making their way down to the coast along with people running from the burning farmland south of Afgoye. There were now hundreds of thousands of people on the move. The massive exodus from Somalia to Kenya, Ethiopia, and beyond had begun.

Mahamuud told us he had left his wife and children in Kismayo with family members; he had made the journey to the Kenyan port of Mombasa in a boat crammed with other refugees, in order to find a safe place for his family to stay in Nairobi. Now he needed to return to the border and bring them to Nairobi. He calculated that they had enough gas to make it roughly to the Kenyan border, to a place that refugees were gathering, about a hundred miles into the desert. Everyone called it Dhobley, the Muddy Place.

Every day for a whole week, Mahamuud pleaded with Mahad, who had a proper Kenyan ID and spoke Swahili and English, to go with him to the border to fetch his family. The border was chaos, and the Kenyan government was trying to stop more refugees from crossing into Kenya; Mahamuud would need help.

But Mahad procrastinated. Every day he waved Mahamuud aside: tomorrow they would begin the trip to the border. We could all feel Mahamuud's anxiety. Finally, one night, at dinner, he announced that he would leave, alone, the next day. I couldn't stand it anymore and said, "I also speak Swahili and English, and Haweya and I have just traveled from the border, so I know what to do. I'll go with you."

My mother said no, a young girl should not be allowed to go to a war zone. But I told her I would stay on the Kenyan side: How bad could it be? The conversation lasted for several days. Everyone took sides. Mahad kept promising to leave, then he would head out the door saying he was going to the mosque and stay out until nightfall. It was clear that Mahamuud would have to go with me or go alone.

Finally, at the end of January, we left. I had been home two months.

After a night or two on the road, we arrived at the Kenyan border town of Liboye. Mahamuud was so nervous he could barely speak. He had a leather pouch under his shirt, full of U.S. dollars to use as bribes, but it would be up to me to negotiate with the police at the border post. I had never tried to bribe anyone before; I didn't even know what a dollar might be worth so far away from the capital.

At the border, soldiers in green uniforms were everywhere, with machine guns and ammunition belts slung across their shoulders. We found an army officer who said he was the commander. I took a deep breath and told him, in Swahili, "This man is looking for his family. They just went on holiday to Somalia and they've been trapped there. All we need to do is cross the border and get them."

The officer looked me over and asked, "How many people will you bring in?" I answered, "One woman with four tiny children. Just one woman, really, because the kids are so small they hardly count."

He looked at me quizzically, and I reckoned that now was the proper time to give him money. I turned to Mahamuud and said, "Do you have something like five hundred shillings?" I was guessing wildly. It was about a week's rent on our flat in Nairobi. Mahamuud pushed a banknote into my hand and I handed it to the officer. He looked down and told me "Two more." We gave it to him and he said, "So, go." ·

I asked the officer for his name. He said, "Mwaura, " which is a common Kikuyu name. But I didn't think this officer was Kikuyu: he was too tall. I told Mahamuud that I didn't trust this man. We had absolutely no guarantees. Even if we found Mahamuud's wife and children, there was no way to be sure that we would find this officer again, or that he would really let us all back into Kenya. We hadn't received a piece of paper or even a handshake. All we had was this dubious name Mwaura and my Swahili, but we had no choice.

We headed into the border zone alone, walking down an empty hill. It was a scene of utter desperation, with refugee tents and ragged shelters strung out as far as the eye could see. It looked as though the entire population of Somalia was camped there. Somewhere beyond this desolate zone was the settlement of Dhobley, erected suddenly by the refugees; and somewhere in Dhobley, Mahamuud hoped to find his wife and children.

It was very dusty, and there were absolutely no trees, no shade at all. The United Nations refugee agency had set up camp on the Kenyan side of the border, at the bottom of the hill. Dozens of bright blue plastic tarps clustered near a large, well-made tarpaulin tent where people were lining up in the sun to register. We passed a health center—really just a place where you could report the dead—around which were thousands and thousands of tents.

The farther we walked, the shabbier the tents became. At first, most of them were blue tarpaulins strung onto branches and twigs, with whole families sheltering under them. A little farther on, the tarpaulins ran out and thin branches and twigs were just shoved into the soil, with cloths arranged over them, women's shawls or a shirt, so the children could sit in the shade. The tents were clumped around little waterholes in the sand, some of them no more than muddy puddles. The smell of recent rain was still in the air, but the puddles were already evaporating in the heat.

We walked on until we got to a huge parking area where there were a number of pickup trucks and Land Cruisers. Everyone here was Darod—Macherten or Marehan or Wersengeli or Ogaden, but all of them Darod—so we felt comfortable around them. Though there was tension between the subclans, there would not be a massacre here. Mahamuud explained that we needed to drive to Dhobley, which was eighteen kilometers (about twelve miles) away. He negotiated the price for a little while and found a Macherten driver who agreed to take us, but we had to wait for him to fill his car with more passengers.

It was about four in the afternoon when we arrived in Dhobley. There were people everywhere we looked. Under every high thorn tree a family squatted, most on mats, a few just on the dry white sand. Sometimes they had tents, but these were even more shabby and decrepit than the ones closer to the border; they were made of cloths, twigs, and rags.

As we left the car we walked past two men who were arguing about a jerry can of water. One of them lost his temper and pulled a gun, and my heart thudded. Suddenly all the men around us had guns—pistols or rifles. My eye caught a series of spent bullets on the ground, nestled in the sand. Three or four older men walked up to the man with the gun with their arms out and said, "Take the water. It's yours—go," and gave it to him. He sat down on the sand and put his hands over his head and cried. His clothes were torn; his toes poked out of his broken shoes; he looked wretched.

The older men tried to take his gun away, but they couldn't get him to give it up. They gave the other man another can of water. Everyone badly wanted everything to stay calm—suddenly everyone was an expert in conflict prevention. I crept up to Mahamuud and said, "These people are dangerous." He looked at me and said, "They are dangerous. They are hungry and thirsty. They have been walking for a long time. They have nothing left to lose. They feel like they are dead already."

He was right. The people all around us looked like ghosts. They were gaunt. They had been moving away from their homes for weeks, and had lost everything along the way. Babies had died; there were listless children in almost every mother's arms. They had been attacked by bandits, and they had crossed all kinds of battlefronts. When I looked into people's eyes, it was disorienting. They looked as if they had been to Hell and back.

I felt totally helpless. I had come to help one man find his family, and there was a sea of desperate people around me. Among them I stood out as the only one who seemed rested and well-fed. I looked like almost the last hope of every woman, every family, under every tree. Many people came up to me begging, "Will you talk to the border guards, can you take me there? I have family." And I had to say "No. No I can't, there is nothing I can do." I was there with Mahamuud, and he had only one aim, which was to find his family.

We pushed on, asking everyone if they had seen a woman named Si'eedo Mahmud Osman Yusuf Kenaidiid; Mahamuud's wife was his cousin, so they shared the same grandfather names. As we walked on, people asked our names, of course, and it was natural to answer with the long version: "I am Ayaan Hirsi Magan Isse." It was like a massive clan gathering: your name was your identity card.

Someone said, "Under that tree, over there, are some Jama Magans," and when I walked over I saw them: Ainanshie and Aflao, and Amran and Idil, from Mogadishu. When I had last seen them—the day I left Mogadishu myself, barely ten weeks before—they were rich people, with fat, powerful legs and arms. Now they were gaunt figures in clothes that hung loose and huge on their bony frames. Their faces were familiar, but these weren't the same people at all. They were so thin. With them was Abdiwahab, another second cousin of mine, who worked in Aflao's espresso bar. Abdiwahab had been enormously fat and tall; now he was like a skeleton, and appeared even taller. His eyes bulged out of deep sockets, and his cheeks had caved in so that his head resembled a skull, with skin that seemed only barely to stretch across his bones. It was like looking at a zombie.

They came up to me and hugged me and started to cry—we all cried—and the two girls, Amran and Idil, began pleading, "Please don't leave us here, take us with you," and I knew I couldn't.

I had no money of my own. Mahamuud had only enough to save his own family. I had told the border official we would have only one woman with us, and we hadn't even found her yet. All I could do was tell them that I would go back to Nairobi and we would raise the money for Mahad to return to the border and somehow get them out.

They started to cry desperately. Amran and Idil were only about seventeen and eighteen years old. They said, "You're here with this man to save *his* family, and we are your family, but you won't save us—we thought you came for us." They were hysterical. Haweya had once called Amran and Idil the Barrels, they were so fat; now they were malnourished, frightened, and desperate.

Aflao's wife had miscarried a baby on the road, and Ainanshie had had to leave his wife and their tiny baby behind in Mogadishu, because she was Hawiye, from the clan of the enemy, and she would have been killed on the road by the other Darod refugees. Ainanshie told me that he had fought with the Darod against the Hawiye in Mogadishu, and had killed people. He said it felt good to do it, to take revenge for all the slaughter. "There was one man with a knife. I shot him and cut his throat from ear to ear," he said with something like satisfaction. I started to shake—the whole thing was impossible, it was a kind of hallucination of horror. I remember thinking, "This is Hell: this is the beginning, the first gate of Hell."

Mahamuud was pressing me to move on, to find his family before nightfall. I promised to return on our way back to the border, and painfully detached from Ainanshie and his family. We walked on, inquiring under every tree. Under the tallest trees were the families with men who had guns. Women who were alone were trying to shelter their children under bushes that were barely more than scrub. Mahamuud began meeting people whom he knew—business partners, neighbors—and they kept telling him, "Farther back. They are back there."

Mahamuud spotted Fadumo, the wife of his older brother, Mahamed. Fadumo was also the sister of Mahamuud's wife. She grabbed Mahamuud's arm as if she would never let go. Her husband came running, barefoot. He still had his mustache and bushy eyebrows, but the rest of him had shrunk into cavities of bone. He looked like a corpse running. Mahamed and Fadumo had four children with them, who looked up at me as though an angel had just come to them from heaven.

Mahamed told us that Mahamuud's wife was just a short distance away, and their children were well. He grabbed his brother's arm and we started walking. Mahamuud's wife caught sight of him from far off and began running to greet him. When she threw herself at him she began to sob.

It was the first time I had ever seen a Somali couple display affection to each other like that. They were clinging to each other and stroking each other's faces, both of them crying and not letting go. The children came running and clung to the two of them—there was a moment of pure joy and tears which was very private, and Mahamed and I turned away out of respect.

Still grasping Mahamuud's arm, his wife, Si'eedo, took us under the tree where she was camped. Sitting there was Mahamuud's younger sister, Marian, and her two children. Marian's three-year-old daughter was the most beautiful child I had ever seen. But when I looked at Marian's baby, it seemed almost as though there was no baby in there—just a tiny, crumpled-up human form, a few days old, clinging to the dry breast of his starving mother. A malnourished baby has horrifying physical proportions, his head seemingly bigger than the rest of his body. I thought it was the most terrifying thing I could ever see.

At the same time, I saw in the child a sudden pull of life. It was being extinguished, but it was there. I said to Marian, "We have to save this baby. It's alive—we must get it across the border." She looked at me and said, "Allah has given me this child, and if He wills it, Allah will take him away." She was one of the real Brotherhood people and seemed completely passive. She felt that she was being tested by Allah; she had to accept that the child would die if Allah wanted it to be that way. To show bitterness, or despair, would be to fail the test of faith. In fact, everybody seemed to be patiently waiting for this baby to die in her lap. And why not—after all, other babies were dying. Mahamuud's youngest child, who was about a year and a half old, was sick, too; his little bottom was flaccid and wrinkled from dehydration.

I said, "We have to leave tomorrow. We have to save this baby." Everybody thought I was being sentimental, that I was dazed, that this was my way of dealing with death and the horror that was all around us. Perhaps

it was. There was no way this child was going to live. We boiled water for
tea, and I cooled some of the water and handed a glass to Marian to give
to the baby. When she held it to the baby's lips they started moving.

That night we slept on mats and thin cloths spread on the white sand,
all near each other. Si'eedo cooked a kind of watery sorghum porridge
with dirty water. There was no nutrition in it, not even any salt. Then we
fell asleep where we'd eaten, wrapped in shawls. It was comfortable in a
strange way; the sand was soft, and the wind smelled like Mogadishu. But
everyone had scabies and lice and warned me I would catch them, too.
The children had lice visibly trailing along their necks, and there I was
with my sporty little duffel bag, with a toothbrush and toothpaste and a
change of underwear and clean clothes. It was surreal.

The next day, as everyone was collecting their stuff, I decided to walk
back to the tree where Aflao and Ainanshie and their family were
camped. As I was headed there everyone asked me who I was. I answered,
"I'm Hirsi Magan's daughter," and someone asked, "Which wife?"

I said, "The Dhulbahante wife, Asha Artan." They told me to go over
under another tree, where I found another cousin, whom I had never
met: Zainab Muhammad Artan, the half-sister of Mahmud, whom I had
secretly married in Mogadishu just three months before. When I heard
who she was, I started. I felt as if that life had been eons ago.

Zainab told me she had taken the coastal road out of Mogadishu, to
Kismayo. When Hawiye fighters attacked Kismayo, she and her husband
left in panic, and they had had to bring another woman's children with
them—two boys who had been playing with Zainab's children when the
fighters came, and whose parents must now have no idea where they
were.

She pointed them out. I recognized them. They were Ahmed and
Aidarus, the two youngest sons of my mother's youngest sister. They
were about seven and five. One of the boys ran over and clutched my
right hand and the other my left, and they looked up at me. They didn't
even plead—they didn't have to. I had to take them. These children
were mine—my responsibility.

I took the boys back to Mahamuud and told him the story and he just
nodded. He, too, knew we had to take them.

We had to get back to the Kenyan border as quickly as we could
before our army officer, Mr. Mwaura, forgot about us. We looked around.
We had told him that we would return with one woman and four little
children, but now, in addition, we had Mahamuud's brother and his fam-

ily, his sister and her two children, and my two little boy cousins. On top of that, both the wives had young women relatives along with them. So now we were accompanied by one man, five women, and twelve children. Instead of being a party of seven, we were now a huddle of twenty human beings.

We decided to try to make it together, even though we knew that we might not have enough money to get everyone through into Kenya. Mahamuud paid for a pickup to transport all of us back to the parking lot near the border. It cleaned out all his Somali money. Now he had only U.S. dollars on him, and if he showed those here, with all the guns around, he would be killed. When the truck dropped us off, we were in the no-man's-land between countries. There was a sea of people between us and the riverbed where the UN High Commission for Refugees had its tent, even more people than there had been the day before. We settled down in the sun to wait for Mahamuud to arrange matters.

It was late when Mahamuud returned to us, and he was being carried by four men, who dumped him on the sand by our mat. He had been stung by a scorpion and was nearly paralyzed with the pain. We lay him down on a *guntino* cloth and tried to make him comfortable; there was nothing else to do. His leg was swollen and black.

Now it was up to me to walk back into Kenya, to talk to the border guards, and to try to find some food for us all while we waited here on the Somali side for Mahamuud to recover enough to move. If he were to die, which can happen from a scorpion bite, our situation would be even more desperate.

The guards let me into Liboye with my ID, and I managed to buy some milk; my grandmother always said camel's milk counteracts scorpion venom, but cow's milk was all I could find. When I returned, I saved some of it for the little baby, though the others grumbled that it was a waste, and I gave Marian some to help start up her own breast milk. But when I told her to give the baby a name she refused; she didn't want to get attached to the child because she had prepared herself for him to die.

We waited for days in the shadeless zone full of tarpaulins and desperate people. Mahamuud developed a fever. When it rained we gathered water from a pothole that was coated green with algae. We crushed maize flour into the water and I gave some of it to the baby.

All the children cried all the time, a constant moaning wail. The youngest of my cousins had some kind of respiratory infection. Everyone had diarrhea. The baby was so small and bony and vulnerable that I was too frightened to hold him. Marian kept the child tight to her chest, wrapped in a cloth.

The UN began to distribute food; basically they handed rations to people who claimed to be clan leaders, and these people either kept it for their own families or sold it. You could get rations only if you registered at the main tent, but hundreds of people were lined up there. There was a water tank, but I never managed to get close to it: water was the scarcest commodity of all, and there were constant fights over it. People were dying all around us. The UN had hired Kenyan and Somali guards to help bury the bodies.

The place was crawling with scorpions and snakes, all kinds of reptiles, and I had no idea which of them were dangerous. I tried desperately to recall my grandmother's lessons as I tried to figure out what we needed to do to keep us all alive. Everyone else had become so passive; it was as if they were stunned, just waiting to die. Everywhere I went, people looked at me as though I could somehow save them. In my shoes, with my toothbrush, walking to and from the border to buy maize flour and bananas, I looked like an emissary from another world—the world of normal life, which still existed somewhere.

One morning when I went to get water with all the throngs of other women I heard that a woman had been attacked in the night. She had arrived alone, and she was from a small subclan; she had no men to protect her. Kenyan soldiers had taken her out of her hut in the night and raped her.

I went to see her in the tiny rag hut she had made for herself. She was one big wound. Her face was swollen and covered in dried blood, her clothes were torn, there were marks all over her legs. She was shaking uncontrollably. I touched her hand and asked if I could help her but she didn't talk. All she could say was *Ya'Allah, Ya'Allah,* "Allah have mercy on me."

I went to get her more water, and all the people nearby told me, "You shouldn't be seen with that woman. She is impure. People will say you're the same." All I could see was a human being who had been abused, who was on the verge of death, but to them, she was an outcast.

I knew she would die soon. I walked all the way to the UNHCR tent and found a Sri Lankan woman and told her, in English, that there was a woman alone who had been raped. I explained that Somalis would leave this woman to die. She came to the tent with some guards and took her away. I told Mahamed and the others about it and they said, "Of course it is not the woman's fault, but you know, there are so many problems. You can't save everyone here." I did know that, but we could have taken care of each other. Two days later, again there was a story of another woman who had been raped. It began happening all the time: Kenyan soldiers came at night to rape Somali women who were alone without protectors. And then all these women would be shunned and left to die.

This is what my grandmother had meant when she warned me: if you are a Somali woman alone, you are like a piece of sheep fat in the sun. Ants and insects crawl all over you, and you cannot move or hide; you will be eaten and melted until nothing is left but a thin smear of grease. And she also warned us that if this happened, it would be our fault.

It was horrible. Everyone in that camp called themselves Muslims and yet nobody helped these women in the name of Allah. Everyone was praying—even the woman in that hut had been praying—but no one showed compassion.

Mahamuud's fever had already begun to abate when Mahad arrived in this no-man's-land, straight from Nairobi. He had Kenyan shillings with him; he had raised money from the Osman Mahamud to come and rescue as many people as he could. I told Mahad he must go to Dhobley and get Aflao and Ainanshie's family out to safety, and he said he would do it.

My brother was now acting as though he were commander in chief, though to me it seemed as though he had arrived after the battle. He loudly expressed concern for my well-being in this appalling place. He ordered me to head straight for Nairobi with Mahamuud's wife and children; he said he would return to pick up Mahamed's family, and Marian, with her two kids. But I knew Mahad: his intentions had a way of not corresponding with reality. So I told him I would stay. I couldn't leave these two families, especially the little baby with no name.

Mahad left for Dhobley. He was gone for two nights. Two days after he returned, together with Ainanshie and Aflao and everyone else, Mahamuud finally stood up. The fever had gone. Everyone was still alive, even the baby. The money that was supposed to pay for bribes and transport had severely diminished as I bought food in the Kenyan border village, and the people camped around us were beginning to eye our stocks hungrily. Now that Mahamuud was well enough to move, it was time to try to cross the border.

It was now Mahad and me, Mahamuud and his family, Mahamed's

family, Aflao and Ainanshie's family, Marian and her child and baby, and my two little cousins: fifteen adults and sixteen children.

We decided to separate. Mahad would wait for a day or so with Aflao and Ainanshie's family. I would leave now, with Mahamuud, with two men, three women, the two young girls traveling with them, and twelve very young children.

First we had to find Mwaura and renegotiate. I walked with Mahamuud along the path into Liboye. Every time soldiers stopped and questioned us, I spoke to them in Swahili. We finally tracked Mwaura down in the empty lot where hundreds of refugees were massing and trying to negotiate with Kenyan men with pickups and buses. Mwaura looked at me and said, "Ah, the girl who speaks Swahili." He was friendlier now. I bribed him several thousand extra shillings to let us all get through. It had become an easy transaction, adult to adult, eye to eye. He was not a bad man, and I later realized that I had vastly overpaid him. Mahad made the same trip after us for far less money.

But then it took several days for Mahamuud to negotiate our transportation from the border. Again and again he trudged back to the Somali side of the border, where we waited for him, and told us "Maybe tomorrow." There were simply too many of us, and the prices were too high. All the Somalis who still had money, as we did, were also bribing the police and offering huge sums to anyone who would drive them closer to Nairobi. Finally Mahamuud told us he had made a deal. He had found a bus driver who would take us—but he had agreed to pay him almost all our remaining money.

The bus took us to a place in the foothills of Garissa, where we spent the night. Then we took another bus to Garissa, and yet another one to Nairobi. By this time, the children were no longer even crying; they were almost motionless.

We walked into my mother's house at 10:30 in the morning at the end of February 1992. I had been gone for three weeks. She had been so desperate about us—she, too, looked thin and haggard. She was stunned to see me walk in, filthy and crawling with lice, with a huge crowd of starving people.

We ate and drank clean water; then, before we even washed, I put Marian in a taxi with me and told the driver to go to Nairobi Hospital. We had no money left and I knew Nairobi Hospital was expensive; it was where I had been operated on when the *ma'alim* broke my skull. But I also knew that there they would help us first and ask us to pay later. Saving the baby's life had become the only thing that mattered to me.

At the reception desk I announced, "This baby is going to die," and the nurse's eyes went wide with horror. She took him and put a drip in his arm, and very slowly, this tiny shape seemed to uncrumple slightly. After a little while, his eyes opened.

The nurse said, "The child will live," and told us to deal with the bill at the cash desk. I asked her who her director was, and found him, and told this middle-aged Indian doctor the whole story. I said I couldn't pay the bill. He took it and tore it up. He said it didn't matter. Then he told me how to look after the baby, and where to get rehydration salts, and we took a taxi home.

Ma paid for the taxi and looked at me, her eyes round with respect. "Well done," she said. It was a rare compliment.

In the next few days the baby began filling out, growing from a crumpled horror-movie image into a real baby, watchful, alive. One evening at dinner I said, "Now we must give this baby a name." He must have been about six weeks old by then. Just as I said that, there was a knock at the door and yet another refugee arrived, the eighteen-year-old younger brother of Osman and Mahamuud and Mahamed. His name was Abbas Abdihalin. "Let him be named after me, after the great Abbas!" he crowed. So the child was named Abbas. He must be a teenager now.

Little Abbas was everyone's favorite. A child with no father and no future—a child who could so easily have died, but for the grace of Allah—he was a gem, winning and lively, cooed over and protected by us all. The house was full and everyone was jubilant just to be alive. The two cousins I had brought with me became my mother's children. She was gentle with them and cooked separate meals for them. Ma was oddly happy for a while with this huge tribe around her. Ramadan came—the time of families—and our flat was like a clan meeting of the Osman Mahamud.

People began sending us money from abroad. Somalis living all over the world, in Canada, in Europe, sent us money by *hawala*. The *hawala* system is a fine example of Somali ingenuity. You go to see a man in Toronto or Stockholm or Kuala Lumpur. You give him cash. He calls a grocery store in a Somali neighborhood in Nairobi, or Birmingham, or anywhere else, and arranges for your friend to pick up the money. There's a commission, but no paperwork. The whole thing takes a few phone calls and just a day or two; it's based entirely on trust within the clan, or within the Muslim Brotherhood, which runs the cheapest and most reliable systems of all. The same thing was happening for Somali families sheltering refugees all over Kenya: money was coming in from the clans.

But even though we had enough money for food, the apartment was still a madhouse. The noise alone was insane. Order was barely maintained by the men leaving the house all day. The scabies and lice drove us mad, too—scabies especially. We bought crates of lotion at a time at the clinic, but the lotion only works if everybody uses it at the same time and washes everything; in our apartment, people always forgot, or just didn't bother, and more people were constantly arriving. At one point there must have been thirty-five or forty of us. We were constantly reinfested; it was like a plague.

One afternoon Mahad came home with two Hawiye men he had known in Mogadishu, friends of his, who had nowhere to go. He couldn't leave them on the street in Nairobi, but our flat was full of Darod—full to bursting of Darod men who cursed the Hawiye butchers from day into night. Mahad walked into the house, stood straight in the doorway, and introduced these two men. He explained that they had nowhere to go and nothing to reproach themselves for, and told everyone, "We are not going to say anything negative about the Hawiye." Everyone was frozen with shock but obeyed. They stayed a week.

One morning in March, I received a letter, in English, from a woman in Finland. She said she was in love with Mahmud Muhammad Artan, and enclosed a picture of herself with him. He was standing, tall and handsome, in a white shirt, with his arm around a white-blonde woman against a backdrop of blue sea. The Finnish girl wrote that Mahmud had a framed photograph of the two of us, but he had told her that I was his cousin. Was I really just his cousin? the letter asked me. Because this Finnish girl planned to marry Mahmud.

It was like a gift. I had almost forgotten about Mahmud, and now this Finnish woman was proposing to take him off my hands. I wrote a polite reply. Of course I was Mahmud's cousin, I wrote, and of *course* I couldn't possibly be his wife: that would be incest. If he was implying that we might in any way be married, this was just teasing. Then I folded up her letter and the photograph, feeling like such an adult for solving my personal problems so neatly.

CHAPTER 9

Abeh

In April 1991, my father came to Nairobi. The Abdihalin brothers burst in with the news one night after the Ramadan dinner. They told us they had been at the house of Farah Gouré and they had heard that our father was in Nairobi. I jumped up screaming with excitement and began dancing for joy all over the place. Haweya was happy, too. Mahad was a bit quiet, and Ma had a look on her face that seemed to marvel at how forgiving we were.

I told her, "Ma, I'm going to look for Abeh and bring him home." She said, "Nothing of the sort. He can't stay here." But I told her, "We'll talk about that later," completely dismissing her emotions on the subject. She didn't make a scene about it because she couldn't. A mother is not permitted to separate children from their father: we belonged to him.

Haweya and I wrapped ourselves up in shawls and walked to Farah Gouré's house, which was also flooded with refugees, with people sleeping on every floor. We went from room to room until we found Fadumo and asked, "Where is Abeh?" She began smiling as if the sun had come out. He was in Nairobi, she told us. Everybody was at the mosque right then performing the *Taraweh;* they would be home later. Fadumo had tears in her eyes, she was so happy for us, but she said we had to understand that everybody was waiting to spend time with our father. He had arrived yesterday, and all these people had been waiting to see him. Still, we had a right to him—the most important right.

We sat and waited until almost midnight, when the doorway suddenly filled up with the shape of my father. We rushed and jumped at him, just as we had when he arrived years before in Mecca, even though we were now easily twice as tall. We took him down to the floor and he was laughing and shouting "My daughters, my daughters, my children!" and hugging us. He looked at us and said, "You're grown women now, but you still look exactly the same." There was so much affection in his eyes.

Fadumo invited us to sit in the living room, but we wanted to take our father home with us. Abeh stood up, smiled at her, and said, "There is a time to go and a time to stay, and this is not the time to stay." His hair was grayer, he was older, but he was still exactly the same person. He even smelled the same; I put my head in his neck and kept smelling him until he removed his shawl and gave it to me. We were gleeful, and everyone around us was beaming—among all the murder and mayhem and refugees and diseases and loss, there was this joy. They were so happy for us. They said, "Go with the children." So we tugged Abeh out of the house, and someone drove us home.

There in the dark, in the street in front of the house, stood Ma and Mahad. I realized Ma had not wanted to greet our father in front of everyone; she had been waiting for us on the sidewalk for hours. My father got out of the car and opened his arms wide and said "Ah, Asha!" in a clear voice; she turned her face away, and said, "No." My father embraced her anyway, but she was steel-cold rejection.

Then Mahad hugged my father—it was a quiet kind of greeting—and he put his arms around our mother and took her into the house.

Haweya and I followed with Abeh, and when they saw him, everyone in the house began shouting and greeting and telling stories. Ma stayed in the kitchen.

The first night he was there, Abeh slept in the living room with all the men. At 5:30 next morning he woke up, turned on all the lights, and began singing the call to prayer, *Allaahu Akbar,* like at the mosque. All the young men on the floor were startled awake, and they all more or less abashedly stood up and began to wash, to prepare themselves. In our bedroom, Ma woke us up, saying, "Your father is calling to pray." The whole house started praying.

Ma wondered loudly if people were praying to please Allah or Abeh, as few of these people had shown evidence of praying before his arrival. Mahad, Haweya, and I giggled at her apt analysis, but still, there was something very beautiful there for a moment. Everyone was tired, but everyone felt it.

Nothing seemed to make my Ma more tender toward Abeh. Every morning, he greeted her, "Asha, how are you this morning?" And every morning, she turned away. She never once spoke to our father or looked him in the face for the six months he lived with us. Yet she would wake me early every morning and insist I make a separate breakfast for my father, much better than everyone else's; and every night before bed she would set aside his plate, his glass, his fork, spoon, and knife, so that in this cramped kitchen there was one shelf that held the crockery and pans reserved for my father.

I admired my mother's sensitivity to the code of honor, and her dignity, but I didn't like the way she ignored Abeh, though I could see why she did it. She had been neglected, left alone to bring up his children and beg his family for money. She felt that she was no longer his wife. So she fed him; she insisted that everyone in the house respect his privacy and his need for peace; she observed all the proper behavior; but she extricated herself from the situation, went cold, and disappeared.

I cleaned out the pantry for Abeh to stay in, a small room with a very small high window. He slept there on a mattress on the floor, with his clothes in a little pile on a cowhide stool, his copy of the Quran, and a naked lightbulb to read by.

When Abeh was home there was a sense of order in our household. People were more dignified; they sat up straighter and listened—he did the talking. Before he was around, the young men had spent whole afternoons chewing qat and playing cards; they were careful to throw away the evidence before Ma walked in, but they did it. Now our flat was like a madrassah. It was clean: the men began folding their clothes and removing their shoes in the doorway. Bedtime changed drastically: we went to bed early and got up early. And we prayed.

Abeh was out most of the day, at the mosque, meeting with elders, various people from the clans, trying to sew things together, to come to some sort of peaceful arrangement. He was still completely caught up in his vision of a unified, ideal Somalia, but he now believed that only Islam could bind the warring clans together. The kind of violence that had been unleashed across the country could be pacified only by the rule of Allah. My father had given up on American-style democracy.

Abeh told me about his little daughter in Addis Ababa. Her name was Marian; she didn't speak Somali yet, but he would teach her. His new wife spoke only Ethiopian. We didn't talk about her much; speaking about a consort with the children of another wife is impolite. But Abeh sounded so tender when he spoke about their little girl, I forgave him.

Ramadan ended, and people began to realize they couldn't all stay in our apartment forever. I started tramping through Eastleigh with one or another of the men, trying to track down landlords and find places to rent. Quite quickly Mahamuud found an apartment for his family, Mahamed's family, and Marian and her children. Some of the other young men moved into a long-stay hotel on Ngara Road.

Still, there were a lot of us. My life became devoted to the management of the various problems of our suddenly expanded family: finding new flats, getting the utilities turned on, arranging money transfers, translating everything. I did the housework, which Ma considered my responsibility as the elder daughter, took children to the doctor, and went to the electricity company to pay the bill. I helped register people for resettlement programs in foreign countries, which were taking educated refugees from Somalia. I rushed to get them to the Somali Embassy to get proper passports, before the entire state apparatus of Somalia collapsed and all Somali diplomacy closed down, stranding them for who knows how long.

After several weeks, more young men arrived, friends of Mahad's. The more men there are, the less help women have around the house, and when Mahamuud left, he took away all the women who had been helping me with the housework. Now I was alone to do it all, and I protested. I told Ma that we must hire a maid, a Kenyan girl, to wash the clothes and keep the house clean; under these circumstances, this would not be a luxury.

Ma said no. I defied her, and said, "If you don't want a maid, you will have to do it yourself." I went to my father and said I needed three hundred shillings a month for a maid. We had money now that Abeh was here; he paid the rent. He was glad to pay for a maid to help me.

But after a few weeks Ma chased the girl away. She said having a maid was against her principles. I told her I couldn't do all the work myself—all the washing, by hand, and scrubbing, and cooking. She never helped with it. But now I refused to wash any clothes, and she beat me with a rolling pin for insolence.

Ma was depressed and becoming bitter and unreasonable again, closing in on herself and hitting me more often. She was unwelcoming; people were moving out of her house because of her. She felt everything was going wrong in her life, while in the wider world, people were slaughtering each other like animals.

After returning to Nairobi I didn't resume going to the Islamic youth debates, and I avoided seeing Sister Aziza. The idea that somehow everything would fall into place when the House of Islam was completed—that a beautiful caliphate would rise up, in which everyone would be compassionate, helpful, and live according to the rules, where everything would work right—seemed almost fatuous. When my father had us pray I simply went through the motions, thinking about breakfast, about my chores, and about the day that lay ahead.

A few months later, Maryan Farah, my father's first wife, arrived from Mogadishu with Arro and Ijaabo. Maryan didn't come live with us; that would have been too much to ask. She had some relatives in Eastleigh, and at first moved there with the girls. But this Eastleigh family was far too sinful for Ijaabo; she didn't want to live with people who chewed *qat* and watched Western movies. So although Arro stayed in Eastleigh, Ijaabo moved in with us, to be with Abeh. He was her father, too.

Ijaabo's stories about Mogadishu were horrific. She had watched dogs eating bodies on the street, and the stench of the corpses had been horrible. Ijaabo was alive only because her grandmother, Maryan's mother, had been from a Hawiye family of the same lineage as the forces that besieged Mogadishu. Maryan, although a Darod, was not snobbish, and had always treated her Hawiye relatives with respect. When the Collapse came, the Hawiye side of their family kept Maryan's house safe, even though the rest of the neighborhood was bathed in blood.

When Maryan and the girls finally left Mogadishu, the city was more than half empty: only the weakest and the Hawiye were left. It had become a place of unpredictable murder, Ijaabo told us. There was no authority—no one could enforce any kind of order.

My stepsister was thinner now, and even more devout. In a way, I could understand this. For Ijaabo, death had become very real: any one of us could die at any moment, and it was urgent to prepare to face God. But this also meant that Ijaabo behaved like some kind of robot, constantly hectoring everyone to be more observant. After a few weeks it irritated us all. More than once, Haweya snarled at her to stop it. Ijaabo would always wail in her teeny high-pitched voice, "I am your *sister* and I love you so *much* and I am not telling you to pray to bother you, but because I want you to go to *Heaven*. Allah said, verse *this*, verse *that*, 'Remember: those who do not pray, they shall be charcoal for the *fire*.' "

One afternoon, just after Ijaabo settled into our apartment, a young woman, Fawzia, knocked at our door, looking for Abdellahi Yasin. She told him she had nowhere to go. Fawzia had her three-year-old boy with her. The child was the son of someone Abdellahi knew, an Osman Mahamud, but he was *garac*, a bastard, born out of wedlock. Fawzia was alone, and she begged Abdellahi to ask if she could stay in our house.

Abdellahi Yasin was embarrassed, but he came and told Ma and me the story. Ma got a look on her face like something smelled bad. She couldn't have a prostitute in the house, she said. I recoiled. There was nothing at all to indicate that Fawzia was a prostitute. I saw in front of me the image of the woman in the rag hut, in the camp. I said to Ma, "If you don't let her stay, I'm leaving."

It was a long struggle, but Mahad and Haweya backed me, and we won. Finally, Ma said, "She can stay, but I don't want to see her." I found a clean sheet and a towel—those were the rarest things in our household—and this poor woman ended up staying with us for a few months with her little boy. By that time, there were so many of us that Haweya, Ijaabo, and I had to share a mattress.

To Ijaabo, Fawzia was the living face of shame, and she immediately embarked on a program to persuade her to repent her sinful ways and become a member of the Brotherhood. Ijaabo used to say, "The only way to wash off your shame is to pray, pray, pray and give your life to Allah, in search of forgiveness." One evening when she was getting at Fawzia again, I snapped and told her to shut up—she was utterly irritating. I said Allah wouldn't test us on whether we condemned somebody who became pregnant outside of marriage; He would test us on our hospitality and charity.

Ijaabo quoted the Quran for the six-hundredth time that day. "The man and the woman who commit adultery, flog each of them one hundred times," she said. I told her, "Okay, here's a stick. Since we don't have Islamic law in Kenya, do you want to do the flogging?" Abeh, who was in the room at the time, laughed and took my side. Ijaabo acted angry and insulted for weeks.

Mahad and Haweya knew I was Abeh's favorite, but they had also learned long ago not to complain about it. Jealousy is forbidden.

The Somalis all shunned Fawzia. When we went out to do the shopping, she was constantly molested on the street. Men would grab at her breast and stare at her lasciviously. They would never have dared to look at me that way: I was Hirsi Magan's daughter. But Fawzia was known to all as a harlot, and she had no clan protector. She was prey.

Fawzia was used to the verbal and physical abuse. She was conditioned to believe that she deserved it. She told me to ignore Ijaabo's remarks. Unlike Ijaabo, Fawzia used to help me with the cooking, cleaning, and shopping. After the early morning prayer, she didn't go back to bed like everyone else did, but instead helped me bake *angellos* for everyone's breakfast.

Fawzia told me clearly that she lived for only one thing: her son. He was prey, too. The other, bigger children treated the boy as an outcast. Aidarus and Ahmed, my young cousins, used to plague him. My family never stepped in to prevent the abuse. There was a stigma on him. It was the first time I had knowingly met the child of an unmarried woman.

Most unmarried Somali girls who got pregnant committed suicide. I knew of one girl in Mogadishu who poured a can of gasoline over herself in the living room, with everyone there, and burned herself alive. Of course, if she hadn't done this, her father and brothers would probably have killed her anyway.

A letter arrived from Switzerland for Mahamed Abdihalin's wife, Fadumo. Her sister, who was living in Europe, had managed to prepare all the papers to get Fadumo and her children a visa to Switzerland. We had only to go to the Swiss Embassy to pick up the visa and buy the tickets. The plan was this: Fadumo would travel to Europe with the children. But instead of going to Switzerland, which almost never gave refugee status to Somalis, she would stop over in Holland. Once she was at the Amsterdam airport, Fadumo would tear up her ticket and ask for asylum in the Netherlands, where it was much easier to qualify as a refugee, and then live there, receiving money from the state.

Mahamed stayed in Nairobi; he was trying to get a business going. If Fadumo got refugee status, he could travel to Europe, too. For Mahamed, sending his wife and family to Europe was like insurance: if things didn't work out in Nairobi, then as a last resort he could join them there.

A week after Fadumo left, she sent word that she was in a camp in Holland. It didn't sound that attractive, a *camp*. Months later, Mahamuud also left; he moved to Abu Dhabi with Si'eedo, to set up a business. These people had lost everything—relatives, property, businesses, social lives, plans for the future—but they were prepared to start from scratch in foreign countries. I didn't think of any part of this as cheating: I admired their resilience.

A few months after Maryan Farah came to Nairobi, Abeh decided to marry her again. He would move out of our Park Road apartment to live with Maryan, Ijaabo, and Arro. I suppose that when Maryan found out that Ma never said a word to him, she proposed the move; it made so much sense. When the decision was made, Abeh called Mahad, Haweya, and me together, and told us about it. He asked for our blessing, and we

gave it, though of course we declined to be present at the wedding ceremony. I know that Haweya and Mahad were resentful of his decision, but
although I was not exactly glad, I wanted Abeh to be happy.

Maryan and Abeh rented a small house in Buruburu. Abeh told me I
could visit them any time. He even proposed that I live with them. That
was nonsense, of course. I could never have abandoned my mother to
live with another of my father's consorts.

When my father moved out, Ma showed no emotion. She just said,
"Well, the storeroom's empty now," and we put the stuff back in it again.
She was dry and hard, but inside, I knew, it was killing her—all the
years of living alone, sleeping alone, the emotional abandonment, and
now, again, the public rejection.

Ma became hostile and spoke to me in the ugliest kind of way. She
began to beat me again. I think perhaps my mother went a little mad at
one point. She had once seized control of her life, in Aden, and then she
somehow lost it; now she found herself in a country where she didn't
want to be, with no self left at all. She was marooned. I think that was
what made her so angry.

One Friday afternoon at the end of January 1992, my father came straight
from the mosque to our flat. He never did that—never paid us a visit
these days—and when he arrived he was completely excited. "Ayaan, my
daughter, I have good news for you—the best news—my prayers are
answered!" he crowed. "Today in the mosque a blessed man came to me
with a proposal of marriage, and I offered him your hand!"

I remember letting him talk while I felt my heels sinking into the
ground. I cleared my throat and said no, but he didn't hear me. I said,
"I'm not going to marry a stranger!" and my father, bubbling with enthu-
siasm, answered, "But he's not a stranger! He's not a stranger at all!
He's your cousin! He's an Osman Mahamud!" He began chanting back
all of this man's names.

I said, "Not a stranger in that sense, Abeh," and he answered, "In what
sense, then?" "But I haven't even met him!" I wailed. My father told me,
"That's fine—you will meet him tomorrow."

My father had given me away to a man called Osman Moussa, a fine
young Somali man who had grown up in Canada. He had come to
Nairobi to find and rescue family members who had been stranded by the
civil war, and also to find a bride. He thought the Somali girls in Canada

were too Westernized, by which he meant that they dressed indecently, disobeyed their husbands, and mixed freely with men; they were not *baarri,* which made them unworthy of marriage. And the civil war meant that daughters of the best families in Somalia were available for practically nothing.

My father had met this young man in the mosque barely two hours before. He was tall, he told me, with strong bones and white teeth, well fed on milk and meat in North America. Osman Moussa must have approached him. I can imagine the scene, the respectful recitation of lineage, finally the request: "You are the father of daughters, and I seek a bride." My father must have felt so very happy.

Arro was older than I, so my father should really have offered her. But he didn't. My father chose me, his devout, dutiful, *deserving* daughter, Ayaan. He offered me to this good fortune, and Osman Moussa accepted me, and the two of them paraded around the mosque announcing their marvelous, God-given match to all the elders of the clan. It never even occurred to them to ask me what I thought.

There was no bride price. Because of the civil war, it would have been indecent to ask for one. But this was a strategic marriage; Osman Moussa could boast that he was married to a Magan, and we would now have relatives in Canada. There were all kinds of reasons for my father to be happy about this match.

I summoned the strength to say to my father "Abeh, what if I am already with some other person?" but he wasn't even listening. He said, "Allah has sent us the answer." He was overcome with his own cleverness.

After Abeh left, still bubbling with joy, I went and told Ma about it. She just said, "Oh, now we are father enough to take responsibility for our daughters' marriages, are we? Fine." Nothing more.

I was in a panic, but I wasn't crying. I rarely cried in those days. I could just see, very clearly and dispassionately, the bars closing in on me.

The next day, my father came to the house with Osman Moussa. The living room was clean, and everyone was excited except me. I just wore normal clothes, a loose dress and headscarf. I wasn't going to dress up for this.

This man came in. He wanted to shake my hand. He was very tall, and wore enormously long blue jeans; he looked like a basketball player, with a shaved head and a baseball cap. I was polite. I said, "Hello, come in. I am Ayaan," without looking him in the eye, and fetched my mother.

My father and mother both remained in the room with us—Ma and I sat on the bed—and this man talked about Canada, where he had lived since he was a small boy, and about the refugees and the war.

We didn't make eye contact. Osman Moussa was talking with my mother, trying to pass muster. When I could look up, I scrutinized him—the way he talked, his face—thinking, "Will I like this man?" I was supposed to make a home and a life with him; cook, bear his kids, respond to his whims. And what did I know of him? His Somali was poor, half-learned. He seemed earnest.

A good, believing Muslim would pray to Allah for guidance, wisdom, strength, but I didn't. I felt this was for me to sort out. I found myself thinking about the one night I had spent with Mahmud, and imagining this Osman Moussa in that light. Did I want to go to bed with this man? I couldn't ask Allah to do anything to help me decide about *that*.

Kennedy had been generous and tender. There was a spark of connection between us: we shared things. He had seen me scrubbing floors and washing socks, and in every situation he liked me and respected me. Even with Abshir, who was so cramped up about rules, there was an attraction between us. But this Osman Moussa was a total stranger. He neither repelled nor attracted me. I felt indifferent, completely without feeling. I didn't detect that he had any special interest in me, either.

The marriage was set for Saturday, six days away.

Our second meeting was more intimate. Osman Moussa and his sister came, and I asked Haweya and Mahad to be with me, to help me evaluate this man. Ma left us five young people alone. I asked about prayer; I wanted to find out how religious this Osman Moussa was. I felt I had to make some sort of decision fast, even though there seemed to be no way I could stop the arrangement from proceeding. He clearly had Brotherhood leanings but was not quite as devout as Ijaabo, judging by his clothes; he wore jeans and a baseball cap. But although he was less stalwart in his devotion, he seemed even more concerned than Ijaabo about policing the piety of others.

I asked, "What do you expect of a wife?" Osman's sister was mortified, and said, "Maybe we shouldn't be here if you're going to discuss such things!" But Osman Moussa belly-laughed and said, "You're going to give me six sons. We will be a home for all the Osman Mahamud."

He went on and on about how Somali girls who grew up in Canada, as he had, were all practically whores, drinking alcohol, going to discos, not covering themselves, and sleeping with white men. They were out of control; he would never choose one to be the mother of his children. For the mother of his six sons this man needed someone like me, who dressed like me, who was dutiful, irreproachable, and the daughter of such a devout man, the marvelous Hirsi Magan.

We grilled him subtly in the Somali epics we had learned from our mother, some of them composed by the Abdihalin brothers' great-grandfather, to our eternal wonder. He knew none of them. Worse still, instead of admitting his ignorance he pretended he knew what we were talking about, which made him seem small. We asked him Grandma's old riddles; he failed them.

We switched to English—we assumed this man's English must be better than his limping Somali—and Haweya asked him what kind of books he read. He said, "Hmya. I read, you know, stuff." I realized that his English was half-learned, too, and he clearly read nothing at all.

I summoned enough courage to ask him to take off his baseball cap, which he did. I thought perhaps I might fall in love with his head of hair or something. But though Osman was only twenty-seven years old, his head was already as bald as the bottom of baby Abbas. Baldness is associated with wisdom among Somalis, but this man had nothing to show for losing so much hair at such an early age.

Mahad brought up politics; all kinds of talk was going on about peace then. He asked, "So when we all go back to Somalia, what would you contribute?" Osman Moussa said, "I'll obviously have a place in government. I've lived outside the country, and I'm an Osman Mahamud. The only solution for Somalia is for the Osman Mahamud to rule. We are the only people with experience at governing."

The three of us didn't even have to discuss it: the man was an idiot. He thought the Osman Mahamud were the chosen people; he was dull, trite, and a bigot, a dyed-in-the-wool Brotherhood type. I remember thinking, "No, surely Abeh could not do this to me?"

When Osman Moussa finally left I tried to pull together the courage to take matters into my own hands. I put on my coat and went to Buruburu, where my father was living. When he opened the door I said, "Osman Moussa came to our house today and Haweya and Mahad and I tested him. We think he's a pea-brain. He's not eloquent, he's not brave enough to admit his shortcomings, and he's a bigot."

Just like that. That way my father couldn't ignore what I was saying, as he mostly did. He had me come and sit down and said, "Now tell me."

"I don't think this man and I are compatible," I said.

He said, smiling broadly, "On the basis of one afternoon?"

I told my father, "You thought on the basis of one minute that we would be compatible, so I may think on the basis of one afternoon that we are not."

But Abeh said, "No, I know more than that. He is the son of the son of the son of "—he quoted the lineage. "He has a good job in Canada, he doesn't chew *qat,* he is clean and a conscientious worker, he is strong. I am giving you to him to ensure your safety."

He went on, "The ceremony will be Saturday, at Farah Gouré's house. The sheep have been bought, the *qali* has been hired. Your saying you don't want this—it's not a question. We are living in bad times. Surely you won't reject my choice of a husband for you just because he doesn't read novels."

He reduced it to the smallest thing. Imagine how trivial my opposition would sound to Abeh if I added: but he has no hair!

Still, I sat up straight and told him, "I am not going to do it."

My father said, "I can't accept a no from you for something you haven't even tried."

I asked, "You mean I can't say no before I get married?"

He answered, "Of course not. Everything is all arranged."

Nobody tied me up. I was not shackled. I was not forced at gunpoint. But I had no realistic way out.

In Islam, the *nikah* ceremony is the moment when you become legally bound to your spouse. A marriage contract is signed, but it is not always followed immediately by consummation; the night of defloration usually follows a party that ends in the house that husband and wife will share. My father decided that my *nikah* on Saturday would not have to be followed immediately by a wedding party—or a wedding night. We could celebrate that with Osman Moussa's family in Canada.

He came to Ma's house the next day to tell me so. "The *nikah* will be on Saturday, but you can have another gathering in Canada for the wedding night. This way you'll have the whole of next week to get to know each other, before Osman leaves," he told me cheerfully. "And once he's gone you can write each other letters or you can talk on the phone. See? There's ample opportunity for the two of you to get to know each other."

I was cold to my father. I told him, "I'm not coming to the *nikah,*" and all he said was "You're not required." Legally, that is true.

By now, my father was the center of attention. What a match he had made, what a piece of good news in these hard times! He was impatient with what he saw as my bleating.

As if all this were not enough drama for our household, on the next afternoon—Tuesday—Ali Wersengeli, the cousin who had officiated as guardian at my wedding ceremony with Mahmud barely eighteen months ago, blew into our doorway in a righteous rage. He had heard about my coming nuptials with Osman Moussa and had come to assert Mahmud's property rights over my person.

When Ma came to the door, Ali told her I had married Uncle Muhammad's son Mahmud. He said Hirsi Magan must learn of it: the wedding must be stopped.

Luckily, Mahad was home, and he broke in. "What marriage is this?" he blustered. "This can't be true. Who was the guardian? I was not present, and neither was her father. There was no marriage."

My mother collected herself. She was completely composed, as she always was—in public. "Who was the guardian at this supposed ceremony?" she inquired haughtily.

"I was," Ali admitted.

"You had no right to act as guardian," Mahad interjected, his voice raised. "I was in Mogadishu. Did you call me? Did you call her father? You could have come and fetched me! Why didn't you?"

"It doesn't matter," Ali said. "The marriage took place."

"Do you have proof of any such ceremony? Do you have a paper?"

Ali had none. They talked. When Ali said he was leaving, my mother didn't beg him to stay, as required by etiquette. "There will be no gossiping about my children," she told him firmly.

Mahad turned on me as soon as Ali had left. "Where is the certificate?" he demanded. There was no point denying what had happened. I admitted to everything—or almost everything. I didn't mention the night in the hotel, but I said I had married Mahmud in Mogadishu the night before he left for Russia, and that he had later fallen for a Finnish girl whom he planned to marry. I went to get the photos she had sent me, and her letter. "So you see, Mahmud wants to forget about it, and I wrote that that was fine," I ended lamely. "It was a mistake."

I produced the paper from the *qali* that Ali Wersengeli had given me in Mogadishu.

Mahad grabbed it suspiciously. "This is not a legal document—it is rubbish," he announced. "There is no valid guardian."

He tore it up, scattering the pieces on the floor, and launched into a tirade about my irresponsibility. My mother barely said anything. I knew she was incensed, but above all, she was relieved that my marriage to Mahmud was invalid; in an immediate sense she was concerned only with figuring out a way to spare her family from scandal.

Mahad's goal in life now became preventing Ali Wersengeli from intervening before the *nikah*, which was four days away. First he went to my father and told him that a maternal cousin of ours had arrived in Nairobi, an evil-minded man who was spreading all sorts of groundless rumors about Ayaan out of sheer spite. Abeh, of course, was revolted that such terrible people could exist in this world.

Then Mahad found out where Ali Wersengeli was staying and went to see him. He told him my *nikah* was scheduled in ten days' time and promised to take him to consult with my father the following week.

By then it would be too late: I would be married.

The day of my wedding I did what I always did every day. I dressed normally and did my chores. I was in denial. I knew that over at Farah Gouré's house there was a *qali* registering my union with Osman Moussa before my father and Mahad and a crowd of other men. Afterward there would be a big lunch with roasted sheep, for men only. I would not be present. Neither my presence nor my signature was required for the Islamic ceremony.

I made lunch at home, and after lunch I went out with Haweya. We walked to the Arboretum and talked about the mess life had suddenly become in the past eight days.

After the *nikah,* my new husband and I had a week together to get to know each other. I went with him to Uhuru Park. I met his friends. He talked about his life when he was young, his dreams. It was all so nondescript, I've almost deleted it from my mind. We talked a lot about religion: Osman Moussa was very devoted to Islam, and to the good name of his family. He said Somalia was in a civil war because we had left the way of Allah. He talked again about Somali girls in Canada and their loose morals. He never made a carnal gesture toward me because he respected me as my father's daughter and his own distant cousin. We would wait for the wedding party in Canada.

When we were alone together, I felt completely frozen. I couldn't even imagine wanting to go to bed with this man, or waking up every morning beside him.

Not everything was traditional. No mother-in-law inspected my virginity. We were above that undignified procedure. It was all a show thing: I met his friends, and behaved properly, as the daughter of Hirsi Magan should, wearing my black *hidjab,* of which they thoroughly approved. We all made small talk about the war and current events. I concentrated on behaving properly: speaking softly, being polite, avoiding shame to my parents. I felt empty.

When Osman's friends got angry, it wasn't about people cheating or lying, but about women who didn't wear the headscarf or men who didn't pray often enough. I recognized the attitude from Ijaabo. It was beginning to irritate me more and more.

I accompanied Osman to the airport after six days, when he returned to Toronto. He would expedite the visa papers as soon as possible and I would fly to meet him there as soon as I could: that was the plan. At the airport, he gave me a hug and said, "Look forward to seeing you." I nodded solemnly, said, "Travel safely," and edged out of his embrace. I was aware of being cold, and I felt sorry for it, but I could do no better.

Ali Wersengeli did eventually go to see my father. Abeh closed the door in his face, then came to see me in Park Road. He was always popping by these days with papers to sign and visas to discuss, ebullient with his own cleverness and energized by the new task of preparing my journey. "I hear stories of you and Mahmud, the son of your mother's brother," he said to me. "What is the truth of this?" I told him, "Nothing." So my father went away again, singing. He was always happy these days.

Ali Wersengeli didn't have much of a story, it turned out. There was no proof of any wedding ceremony between me and Mahmud: Mahad had torn up my paper, and Mahmud himself conspicuously failed to assert his so-called conjugal claim over me. Most people swiftly concluded that it was all just as Mahad said: a spiteful rumor. Nobody wanted anything to go wrong for Ayaan Hirsi Magan. Amid all the depressing news and chaos of the civil war in Somalia, I was a symbol of hope: a pious, obedient girl who deserved the marvelous match that her father had made.

A *qali* is a recognized marriage official, and weeks after the *nikah,* my father took the marriage certificate drawn up by the *qali* and officially registered my wedding with the Kenyan marriage bureau. I knew this because one day in June he brought me home an official Kenyan government document written in English and Arabic, with a special box to indicate "Whether Virgin or Not" and the "Amount of Dowry." The boxes were all filled in for me—the answers were "Virgin" and "Ten books of Holy Quran"—and the document also indicated that I had been represented at my wedding in February by my father. My father told me I must now sign this Kenyan document.

I hesitated, but I was already married to Osman Moussa in the eyes of Islam and every Muslim I knew. What difference could it possibly make if I signed, I thought? So right under my father's signature, in Arabic, I signed it: A. H. Magan.

Abeh worked hard to get me travel documents from the UNHCR office. Within weeks he had my passport, then he went after a visa. Every few days he spoke on the phone with Osman Moussa about it. The Canadian Embassy in Nairobi was crowded with Somalis trying to emigrate, and it seemed impossible to get anything done in the corruption and chaos of the Kenyan bureaucracy. My father ended up enlisting the help of a relative living in Düsseldorf, whose name was Mursal, and together they decided I should go to Germany to wait for the final visa to come in. It would be quicker that way, and more practical.

My father began calling me to his house in Buruburu for what amounted to a series of extra lectures in Islam and how to be a good wife. We spent several mornings taking up chapters of the Quran on the duties of a wife and formally discussing them. For example, her duty to ask permission to leave the house. My father told me, "You can do the following: you can agree together, early on, that permission is permanently given. That is a form of trust, his trust in you, so you don't have to ask permission every time you go out for groceries."

There is a Quranic injunction to women to be sexually available to their husband at all times. My father didn't go into the details, but he read it: *"Your wives are your tillage, go in unto your tillage in what manner so ever you will."* He said, "You must always be there for your husband, in bed and outside it. Don't make your husband beg; don't refuse him; don't make him look elsewhere. This is also a kind of permission you give from the onset: you are always available. He can't abuse that because he is from a good family. Force and rape are not an issue because he is a believing Muslim and he is an Osman Mahamud."

We talked about living as a Muslim in the West. Having unbelievers as friends was a gray area, my father said; it's discouraged, but if you can make good, honest friendships with infidels, so long as you don't follow their ways, then such relationships are not forbidden.

We went into what you are supposed to teach children. There is one

God, no djinns, no saints, no magic, no intercession. Asking help from a spirit or djinn is forbidden; it puts other beings on a level with Allah. In everything you do, ask yourself, "What would the Prophet do?" Some things are clearly permitted and others clearly forbidden, but in gray areas, my father said, the Prophet was liberal: he would never make anything obligatory if it harmed you. "There is no coercion in Islam," my father said. "No human being has the right to punish another for not observing his religious duties. Only Allah can do that."

It was like Quran school, but more intelligent. We even talked about martyrdom. My father said that committing suicide for Holy War was acceptable only in the time of the Prophet—and then only because the unbelievers had attacked the Prophet first. Today there could not be a Holy War, he said, because only the Prophet Muhammad could call for a Holy War.

This was my father's Islam: a mostly nonviolent religion that was his own interpretation of the Prophet's words. It relied on one's own sense of right and wrong, at least to some degree. It was more intelligent than the Islam I had learned from the *ma'alim,* and it was also far more humane. Still, this version of Islam also left me with unanswered questions and a sense of injustice: Why was it that only women needed to ask permission from their husband to leave the house, and not the other way round?

My father's Islam was also clearly an *interpretation* of what the Prophet said. As such, it was not legitimate. You may not interpret the will of Allah and the words of the Quran: it says so, right there in the book. There is a read-only lock. It is forbidden to pick and choose: you may only obey. The Prophet said, *"I have left you with clear guidance; no one deviates from it after me, except that he shall be destroyed."* A fundamentalist would tell my father, "The sentence 'Only the Prophet can call a Holy War' is not in the Quran. You're putting it in there. That is blasphemy."

Osman Moussa paid for all my travel arrangements because I was now his. There are rules about these things: you pay for your wife. I did the rounds, bade good-bye to everyone: Halwa, and Ainanshie, and Farah Gouré's family. They were now my close cousins, because they were my husband's relatives, too.

I said good-bye to my father the night before I was due to leave. He embraced me, and said we might not see each other again for a very long time. "When we depart, we may intend to return," he told me, "but many things might prevent us from doing so." I eyed him skeptically; I knew that he was speaking from experience.

The day of my departure, Ma overheard Haweya and me talking about what to do. Haweya thought the best plan would be to divorce Osman Moussa as soon as possible once I was in Canada. Once I was divorced, I could travel to America, she said, and live my own life. She spun a whole romantic story for me.

Then Ma burst in and said we were immoral. She said I was a slut and a hypocrite who had destroyed her relationship with her own brother and would wreck the honor of her family and my father's. She said, "There are two conditions if you want me to say good-bye to you and wish you well. The first one is that you promise to stay married to Osman Moussa. You will be a good wife to him and pray to Allah, and be grateful for the destiny your father has made for you. And the second is that you go to your father and tell him everything."

I told myself that my mother was right. I should just go to Abeh and tell him everything; that way maybe he would find me a way out. So I put my headscarf on and went to see him again. I said, "Abeh, I have something to tell you," and he greeted me with his arms outstretched once again. "Ah! Ayaan! My beloved daughter has visited me again!"

I said, "I have something to confess, about mother's brother Muhammad, and his son Mahmud."

Abeh said loudly, "But we dealt with that, didn't we? It's all done, child. Are you worried about your dear old father? My darling, you should be off preparing your departure."

He kept overflowing with words, and my tongue stuck in my throat. I think he may have known that what I wanted to tell him was unwelcome. So I went back home, and I told my mother the whole scene. She ordered me to go right back to Buruburu and say it all anyway. I said, "I will miss the plane," and she said, "Then promise me in the name of Allah that you will stay with this man, your husband."

I said no. I told her I wouldn't promise that.

So my mother didn't bid me farewell. I said good-bye to her stiff back, then I left, in a taxi, for the airport.

PART II

My Freedom

CHAPTER 10

Running Away

When we landed at the Frankfurt airport, early in the morning, I was dazed by the scale of it. Everything around me was glass and steel, and all so *finished,* down to the last little fixture. That impressed me: where I came from, airports were chaos, constantly expanding, always half-built. And everyone around me seemed so sure of where they were headed. There were women as old as my mother, even my grandmother, with fashionable handbags, pushing trolleys full of matching suitcases with energy and purpose.

I was lost. I was looking for the ticket office. I knew I was supposed to be going to Düsseldorf, but my ticket said Munich, so I knew I must somehow get it changed. I went wandering about, navigating by asking people for help; I didn't even notice the signage. The airport was as big as a neighborhood, and all of it looked the same: I felt hapless, like a country yokel from the *miyé.*

My distant uncle, Mursal, had agreed to look after me in Germany while I was waiting for my visa. I had never met him. When I finally got to Düsseldorf, I changed some dollars to Deutschmarks, figured out which was the right coin, and phoned the number Mursal had given my father. Another man answered the phone. He was Omar, Mursal's associate. He said, "So you're Hirsi Magan's daughter. Can you write down an address and give it to the driver of a taxi?"

I said yes, took the address down, and stepped outside. Everything was so clean, it was like a movie. The roads, the pavement, the people—nothing in my life had ever looked like this, except perhaps Nairobi Hospital. It was so modern it seemed sterile. The landscape looked like geometry class, or physics, where everything was in straight lines and had to be perfect and precise. These buildings were cubes and triangles, and they gave me that same neutral, almost frightening feeling. The letters on the signs resembled English, but I couldn't understand them; it felt like trying to make sense of algebra.

My grandmother must have felt this way when she went to a city for the first time and saw a lightbulb, a radio, a whole road full of cars. I felt that foreign.

There was a line for taxis; the word was in English. But all the taxis were cream Mercedes. In Nairobi, such taxis would line up only at fancy hotels: they were the most luxurious option conceivable, really only for foreigners and government ministers. Before I got into such a car, I felt I must ask the driver how much money the ride would cost.

He said, "About twenty marks," which I could pay. I asked, "But will you drive me in *this* car?" and the driver laughed. He was nice, and spoke English. I sat in the front beside him and he told me all about Düsseldorf, and how good and kind the German people were.

The old city of Düsseldorf was indeed wonderful, its church spires and angled towers a bit like minarets. The streets were cobbled; they looked as if made for humans, unlike the scary, ultramodern airport.

The taxi dropped me off and I was met by Omar: a tall, easygoing man with a mustache, wearing a gray suit and no tie. He said I was amazing. Nobody ever made it all the way from the airport so easily, and to have changed planes in Frankfurt, too—I was a prodigy. "You'll be fine here," he told me. "Most Somalis call in the middle of night and say 'Please come and get me.' When I say 'Where are you?' they tell me 'I'm standing next to a tall building.' They're useless."

Omar wasn't troubled by the fact that my luggage hadn't arrived with me. He said that in Germany such things never got lost. My uncle was detained by business and would meet me later, so Omar took me to a hotel in the old city. He said he would be back at eight to take me to dinner.

Everything in the room was white, and pristine. I examined the duvet, vowing to tell Haweya about this amazing invention. The room was small, but all somehow cleverly planned to fit: the closets fit into the wall, the TV inside a cabinet. How cool, I thought.

The bathroom was another revelation. We had a shower in Park Road, but it never had hot water, so we boiled water and used a pail and a scoop. Here was hot water, tons of it, in different jets from above and from the sides. I washed. It was still light outside, so I decided to go out. I had to see more of this place.

I wrote down the name of the hotel—I knew I would get lost—pulled on my headscarf and long coat, and walked into the street. I had never seen so many white people. The women were bare—they seemed *naked*—their legs, their whole arms, their faces and hair and shoulders were all completely uncovered. Kenyan women were often more uncovered than we Somalis, but somehow the whiteness of these women's skin drew my eye more. Men and women were sitting together, not at bars but with easy familiarity, as if they were equal. They held hands in broad daylight, not hiding from anyone, and everyone else seemed to find this completely normal.

After a little while I took my coat off; I thought I might stick out less. I still had on a headscarf and a long skirt, but it was the most uncovered I had been in public for many years. And yet I felt anonymous. There was no social control here. No eyes silently accused me of being a whore. No lecherous men called me to bed with them. No Brotherhood members threatened me with hellfire. I felt safe; I could follow my curiosity.

I walked until my feet hurt. Everything was so well kept. The grooves between the cobbles on the street were clean. The shopfronts gleamed. I remember thinking, "This is amazing, how can it be so?" I was used to heaps of stinking rubbish and streets pockmarked with huge potholes, where the dirt comes at you and nothing ever stays clean. In Nairobi, apart from a few wealthy enclaves reserved for superrich government officials and millionaire businessmen, people live on top of each other, in slum houses made of bare cinder block or cardboard and metal sheets. There are beggars and bag snatchers and orphans living on rubbish heaps; the traffic swerves and radios blare and *matatou* drivers beckon you into their buses. I felt as though I had been thrown into another world, calm and orderly, as in the novels I'd read and certain films, but somehow I had never really believed them before.

When I got back to the hotel Omar was very worried. He said it was already nine p.m. I said it couldn't be: it was still light outside. He sighed, and explained patiently that in Europe there is a season when it is warm, and then it is light until very late at night; and another season which is cold, when it's dark almost all the time. In Europe, he said, you can't tell the time by the sun. He gave me his watch and asked if I needed to be taught how to read it.

I felt crushed to have been so stupid. I could see that even the planets and solar system were different here. I was Alice in Wonderland.

Omar said Africans like us couldn't eat German food and took me to a Chinese restaurant. I tried to follow the route and realized that all the streets had their names helpfully written on little signposts. You didn't have to stop people constantly and ask them for directions. How pleasant and ingenious, I thought; in our neighborhood in Nairobi there were street signs on only a few main roads. I asked Omar who put them up. He just rolled his eyes and said, "This is a civilized country."

I met my relative, Mursal, the next day. He seemed embarrassed to admit it, but he told me he couldn't actually have me stay at his house. He had married a German woman who didn't take kindly to housing stray Somalis. So he had arranged for me to stay with another Osman Mahamud family, in Bonn. It wasn't far. Mursal said he would phone the Canadian Embassy every day to inquire whether my visa papers had arrived; I could just as easily wait at this other woman's house as at his.

They drove me there, after my luggage was politely delivered to my hotel by an airport van. We arrived at a whole field of identical houses—a housing estate owned by the government, they informed me. This woman in Bonn, Amina, was also an Osman Mahamud, of course. But Amina felt shunned by the other Osman Mahamud because she had married a Hawiye, and her children were Hawiye. Mursal had helped her a lot; he must have spent a huge portion of his income on fellow Somalis and their troubles.

There were TVs on in all the rooms, and lots of children. The oldest boy, Ahmed, was about fourteen; he volunteered to show me around Bonn. It was July, and therefore school vacation, and Ahmed, who had nothing to do, was eager to show off his superior knowledge of the city.

Though she had apparently lived in Germany for some time, I could see that Amina was still completely Somali. She couldn't find her way about on her own and took her son with her to buy groceries. Whereas when I went out walking with Ahmed the next day, I could see that I could probably manage to make my own way around, as he did. He explained how to use the subway; it wasn't that difficult.

These white people didn't frighten me. They seemed uninterested, but that was welcome. I had taken two airplanes on my own, I had wandered around the streets, and the world did not seem as dangerous as my mother and grandmother had warned me. Everyone was anonymous here, but it gave me a feeling of freedom and power to be managing my way around these strange places. I felt safe.

For months I had been thinking more and more frantically about how to undo the marriage my father had chosen for me. I didn't want to go to Canada and live with Osman Moussa and live the life that was preordained for me from the time I was born a girl—my mother's life. I had thought that when I got there I might purposely perform so badly as a wife that Osman Moussa would simply send me back home to my mother's house in Nairobi. There was a hitch to that: I might get pregnant. But that first afternoon in Bonn, a new idea crept up on me: I didn't even have to go to Canada. I could disappear here. I could escape it all, hide, and somehow make my own way, like someone in a book.

I didn't have any concrete plans of how, but I thought I would look for the right moment. I didn't worry about loneliness, or how I would live without my family. I didn't have a detailed plan, barely even an idea. I thought escape would be like quickly stepping off a *matatou* when it slowed for a traffic light, and then watching it lurch on down the road. I would find the right time and I would get away.

I wouldn't stay here, in Germany; it would be too easy for Mursal to find me. I would get to England. There I would be able to speak the language and understand the culture, with its meadows and cows, and the Queen, and Mayfair and Whitechapel—I knew it all, I thought, from books and Monopoly games. I would go there. I had my certificate from Valley Secretarial College with me; I would work, save money, study. Nobody would know where I was.

I didn't know how I would escape or what freedom might mean. But I knew what course my life would take if I went to Canada. I would have a life like my mother's, and Jawahir's, and like the life of this woman with whom I was staying in Bonn. I would not have put it this way in those days, but because I was born a woman, I could never become an adult. I would always be a minor, my decisions made for me. I would always be a unit in a vast beehive. I might have a decent life, but I would be dependent—always—on someone *treating me well*.

I knew that another kind of life was possible. I had read about it, and now I could see it, smell it in the air around me: the kind of life I had always wanted, with a real education, a real job, a real marriage. I wanted to make my own decisions. I wanted to become a person, an individual, with a life of my own.

Young Ahmed took me all over Bonn. He was friendly; we talked about all sorts of things. As we headed back to his house, I asked him, "Tell me, if I wanted to go to England, how would I do that?" Ahmed said it wouldn't be easy; there was sea between Germany and England, so you had to have a visa. The countries around Germany never checked you for visas, though. It would be easier, he said, to go to Holland or Belgium.

Where were we, exactly? All I could remember from geography lessons was a chapter on the wealthy Rhinelands: Germany, Holland, Belgium, was it? I recalled only that our teacher had pointed out that all put together, these places were smaller than Tanzania. I kicked myself for not paying more attention in class; if I had, at least I would know where I was.

But Holland—I knew someone in Holland. Someone who would help me. Fadumo, the wife of Mahamed Abdihalin, whom I had helped rescue from the refugee camp in Dhobley—she had claimed asylum in Holland. She was living there, in some kind of camp.

Young Ahmed told me Holland was easy, only one and a half hours away by train. You just bought a ticket and went there, no visa necessary.

That afternoon I went to the call box at the corner of the street and dialed the phone number of Fadumo's refugee center. She was so warm and cheerful, so happy to congratulate me on the news of my wedding. I broached the idea of paying her a visit; she was delighted.

I didn't tell her I was planning to run away, or give her a date. I didn't tell Ahmed either. I just told his mother that I wanted to visit a relative for a couple of days, and I asked Ahmed to take me to the train station and help me buy a ticket. I left my big suitcase behind at Amina's house; I took only a duffel bag, with my papers.

When I left the house, I took one last look at the suitcase filled with my trousseau: silk *dirhas* and frankincense, all kinds of Somali accoutrements that I was leaving behind. I had two long skirts with me, some tunics, my coat—what I could carry. I told myself I would explain it all one day to my father.

It was Friday, July 24, 1992, when I stepped on the train. Every year I think of it. I see it as my real birthday: the birth of me as a person, making decisions about my life on my own. I was not running away from Islam, or to democracy. I didn't have any big ideas then. I was just a young girl and wanted some way to be me; so I bolted into the unknown.

It was almost midnight when I arrived at Amsterdam Central Station. A young North African man came up and asked if he could help me. He took me to the counter where I could change some money and showed me the phone booth. He was very kind—perhaps it was the headscarf I was wearing, or the bewildered look on my face. He gave me his phone number in case I had any problems getting around.

I called Fadumo. She said it was far too late to make it to her refugee center in Almelo that evening. She gave me the phone number of her cousin Mudoh, who lived much closer, in Volendam. I called Mudoh: it was dark and I was in Amsterdam Central Station and had no idea what else to do. I said, "I am Ayaan, the daughter of Hirsi Magan, and I'm looking for a place to stay the night." Mudoh told me which bus to take, how much to pay, where to get off.

It was the middle of the night, and after a few stops I was the only person on the bus. I was very frightened. I kept asking the driver if it was Volendam yet, expecting something horrible to happen. He drove far, and fast. But he didn't carry me away and cut me into pieces or rape me, as I half-feared. He dropped me off near a green phone booth, at precisely the place that Mudoh had described.

Mudoh's husband picked me up. He was Dutch. Mudoh had not just married outside the clan, but also outside the Somali nation and outside Islam. She, a woman, had married a *gaalo* man. Even I was a bit taken aback by this. I had never met a Somali woman who had done such a thing. I asked Mudoh how her family had reacted when they learned of it. She said they called her filthy: they made her outcast. But after the collapse of Mogadishu, Mudoh told me, they became terribly polite. They asked constantly for help, and money. Mudoh gave help, but only to her closest family, her brothers. Apparently she had cut the clan out of her life.

I decided to trust Mudoh. I told her everything. I said I didn't want to go through with my marriage, I wanted to go to England. Mudoh said she wouldn't advise that. She said it would be too complicated to get there. I should stay in Holland, she told me. I could use my English here, too. She said I should ask for asylum, as Fadumo had; I should go to her and ask her how she'd done it.

I spent the weekend with Mudoh. She walked me around her neighborhood. All the houses were alike, and all the same color, laid out in rows like neat little cakes warm from the oven. They were all new homes with flouncy white lace curtains, and the grass in front was all green and mown evenly, to the same height, like a neat haircut. In Nairobi, except in the rich estates, colors were garish and houses were completely anarchic— a mansion, a half-built shanty hut, a vacant lot all jumbled together—so this, too, was new to me.

Mudoh put the trash out on the street on Sunday evening. All along the street people were doing the same thing. She explained that there were rules: you had to put the garbage containers out at the proper time, in the proper way. Brown was for organic waste; green was for plastic; and newspapers were something else entirely, some other time. If you faithfully observed these rules, the government came the next morning and whisked it all away for recycling. Wow, I thought. In Kenya you feared the government, and when it did come around to your house it was frightening. Garbage you hauled to a dump at the end of the road. This seemed like a life I could adjust to.

On Monday I went to Almelo to ask Fadumo how to go about becoming a refugee in Holland. Fadumo was so happy to see me; she hugged me and cried. Her camp didn't look anything like a refugee camp in the sense of Dhobley; these weren't tents, but houses—temporary, but adequate—and everything was orderly. Fadumo had one whole prefab to herself, with her five children; one, a baby just born.

We sat down to talk and I told her everything. Fadumo was horrified and asked me, pleaded with me, not to do it. "Think of your father," she begged. Fadumo was Osman Mahamud, so of course she felt it keenly: she must protect me from making a terrible error, something that would damage me forever and hurt the honor of the whole clan. Her marriage was arranged by her parents, she told me, and it was a happy one. Arranged marriages were best. An arranged marriage within the family with your father's blessing: that was the best destiny.

I made her tell me anyway. She said asking for asylum was easy. There were special receiving centers for refugees; the closest one was in Zwolle. You went there, and you asked to be a refugee. You had to go as quickly as possible and say you had recently run away from the civil war, and that you had only just got to Holland. There was a time limit.

I went to Zwolle. The center was easy to find. Everyone seemed to speak English, or at least want to understand it. There was a policeman in uniform, and I felt a sudden fear when I saw him, but he told me politely, "Our center is full, we're not taking any more refugees, but you can go to Zeewolde." He gave me a bus card and a train ticket and instructions for the journey. He said I should go to see Refugee Aid before I registered, and complimented me on my English.

Police to me were oppressors, demanders of bribes. They were never *helpful.* I asked him "Why are you helping me?" and he smiled and said, "Those are the rules." I asked, "And is every policeman this kind?" and he replied, "I sure hope so."

After this, anything was possible. To me, government was bad. It was crooked and duplicitous and it oppressed you. And here all these people were busy helping you and this for *foreigners.* How on earth did they treat their own clans?

On the bus to Zeewolde, I stared at the countryside around me. It was flat, with long farm roads and windmills and fat, cream-colored woolly sheep—more wool than sheep, I thought, accustomed to our scrawny black-headed herds. There were lines of water everywhere: dikes. Buses were sleek and clean; their doors opened by themselves. Near Zeewolde, the land seemed emptier and the vegetation drier, and the land was crisscrossed by wider ditches; it was a polder, new land that the Dutch were reclaiming from the sea, though at the time I had no idea of all that.

I was facing a huge opportunity, but it was daunting. At twenty-two years old, I was on my own for the first time. I would have to see if I could make it without falling into the hazards that my family, and most Muslims, think befall girls on their own: ending up in prostitution, or working as a maid, or marrying beneath your status to a man who will exploit you—out of haste, your name smeared.

Waiting to change buses, I noticed that the bus came precisely at the time it was supposed to, 2:37, to the minute. It had been the same with the buses in Bonn, and this eerie punctuality seemed positively uncanny. How on earth could anybody predict a bus would arrive at exactly 2:37? Did they also control the rules of time?

The Zeewolde Reception Center was a huge compound of bungalows, each one surrounded by a little hedge. There was a tennis court, and people playing volleyball, and close to the offices I saw a signpost for a swimming pool. It was all quite unbelievable.

I went into the little office near the gate and showed a man the paper I had received from the policeman in Zwolle. This man shook my hand, and said "Welcome," and told me he would take me to Admin. He picked up my duffel bag in one hand and two bags containing blankets and bedsheets and towels in the other, and led me to a bungalow.

All around us were asylum seekers. There were a lot of Kurds and Iraqis and quite a few Iranians, who all had pale faces, though the Dutch call them black. A large number of women were from Africa, dressed in minis and T-shirts; I guessed from the way they looked that they were from Liberia and Congo, two countries at civil war. There were a few huddled heaps of cloth: these were the Arab women, sitting on the ground with their robes around them, watching the men.

There were also a lot of people who were white; I asked the Dutch man who these people were and he said, "They are the Muslims." He saw my surprise, and added, "From Bosnia."

He took me to Bungalow 28 and said I would be sharing with three

Ethiopian girls. Every Thursday, he told me, I could take my sheets to the laundry and receive a clean set. I gaped at him. He explained that dinner would be at five-thirty in the canteen, and told me that tomorrow I would receive a fuller introduction; someone else would show me where the interview would take place, where the lawyer's office was, and the health center. Health care was free, he informed me, and so was room and board: it was all provided by the government. I would also receive a weekly allowance for my basic needs.

I had never heard of a welfare state. I had no idea why complete strangers were giving me so much. Where did they get the money from? Why didn't it run out?

The next morning I had to go to the immigration police. They finger-printed me and had me fill out forms, but it was utterly different from anything I had expected. It was "How are you, ma'am? Can I get you a cup of tea or coffee?" and every step of the procedure was explained; they even asked if I needed a translator. Then they gave me a green card, which made me an official asylum seeker, someone who had asked for an interview to be considered for refugee status.

The police sent me to the Refugee Aid office, where two women told me I was eligible for free legal advice and walked me through the pro-cedures. They asked why I wanted to live in Holland, and I told them my story, honestly: my father had obliged me to marry a man I didn't accept, and I didn't want to go to Canada to live with him. One of the women said, "It's horrible what has happened to you, but how many women from Somalia are married against their will?"

"It's our culture," I said. "Practically all of them."

"And what about other countries?" she asked me. "Does it happen elsewhere?"

"I think in every Muslim country," I told her.

"So you see?" she told me. "It's impossible to give refugee status to every woman who has been married off by her family." She read me the Geneva Convention on refugees, and said, "If your story is not true and not consistent, and if it does not fall into these categories, then your chances are slim. To be a refugee, you must prove you have a clear, spe-cific fear of persecution."

I went back to the bungalow. I had a meeting the next day with a government-supplied lawyer. I started drafting a story based on my experience leaving Mogadishu in 1991, and the experiences of the refugees in our house in Park Road. This story was detailed, consistent, but it was an invention. With hindsight I'm not proud of this fact, but yes, it is true that I did not tell my full story to get into Holland.

In addition, I didn't say my name was Ayaan Hirsi Magan; that would make it too easy for my family to track me down. I hit on my grandfather's birth name, Ali, the name his father gave him, before people called him The Protector. A modest name, a name easy to disappear with. I would be Ayaan Hirsi Ali, born November 13, 1967.

August 6 was my interview with the Dutch Immigration Service. My lawyer, a careful woman with long black hair, came with me. When I knocked on his office door the immigration official bounded out from behind his desk to shake my hand. He was polite, but I felt he was testing me, trying to catch me out. He kept probing my story, and I left feeling that he had seen through me. I would be rejected for sure.

After the interview I was in a constant state of tension. I thought Mursal would find me, or even Osman Moussa himself; both would be hunting for me now. I watched buses drive up to the center, filled with refugees from Bosnia. I watched CNN and the BBC on the TV at the asylum center and felt horrible. I was occupying a bed meant for someone deserving, someone from Liberia or Bosnia, who had suffered. I was a spoiled brat, stupid and ungrateful, who should thank her father for finding her a husband in a rich country.

I was carrying a huge weight of guilt over what had I done to our family. And I felt fear, not of being alone but of the unknown: What would become of me? But I also felt a sense of freedom. This was real life that I was experiencing. I remember thinking, in that refugee center, "If I fall down dead right now, then at least I've seen the world." I didn't for one moment ever seriously entertain the idea of going back to Germany and picking up my visa to Canada. That part of my life was over.

The Ethiopian girls with whom I shared the bungalow at first seemed frivolous and hopelessly silly. They said I was so lucky to be from a country mired in civil war, which meant I was far more likely than they were to get refugee status and be allowed to live in Europe. The time they spent getting dressed, and the clothes they wore! The makeup and the miniskirts, and lending each other belts—the whole procedure took forever, and then they went out uncovered, perfectly happy with themselves. Mina was the friendliest. One morning she told me, "Come *on,* take off the scarf and the long skirt. You're pretty."

"I will not!" I said. "I am a Muslim." This was precisely what people had always warned me about: the devil, in the form of Ethiopian girls, come to tempt me. But this Mina, who had been very welcoming and helpful and in every way agreeable up till now, asked me, "But why? Why do Muslims have to cover themselves and never have sex and all that? What is wrong with you?"

Growing up in Nairobi, everyone knew about Ethiopians: they seemed to have sex whenever they felt like it. There was a house of young Ethiopian refugees down the road from us, and people used to say that they went at it like goats, all the time. The Ethiopians would insult the Somalis in return, saying Somalis don't know how to enjoy sex and are all frustrated, that's why they're always fighting people. This kind of caricature very much informed how we felt about Christians, because Somalis and Ethiopians have always been at each other's throats, since time began.

"Why should I uncover my naked skin?" I asked Mina. "Don't you have any shame? What are you hoping to achieve walking around undressed? Don't you know how it affects men?"

"I wear these skirts because I like having pretty legs," said Mina. "They won't be pretty for long, and I want to enjoy them." She shook one at me and said, "If anyone else enjoys them, so much the better."

I couldn't believe it. I said, "This is *precisely* the opposite of what I have been brought up to believe." And all of them, because all the girls had gathered around by now, chimed in, "But *why*? Why are all you Muslims so difficult?"

"But if men see women dressed like you are now, with your arms bare and everything naked, then they will become confused and sexually tempted," I told them. "They will be blinded by desire."

The girls began laughing, and Mina said, "I don't think it's really like that. And you know, if they get tempted, that's not such a big deal."

By then I was wailing, because I could see what was coming, but I said, "But they won't be able to work, and the buses will crash, and there will be a state of total *fitna*!"

"So why is there not a state of total chaos everywhere around us, here, in Europe?" Mina asked.

It was true. All I had to do was use my eyes. Europe worked perfectly, every bus and clock of it. Not the first tremor of chaos was detectible. "I don't know," I said helplessly. "It must be because these are not really men."

"Oh? They are not really men, these big strong blond Dutch workers?" By this time the Ethiopian girls were almost weeping with laughter at the bumpkin that I was. They thought it was such Muslim bullshit. We

Muslims were always boasting about something or other, but our whole culture was sexually frustrated. And who on earth did I think I was to personally wreak *fitna* on the world? They were friendly, because they knew it wasn't my fault I felt this way, but they really let me have it.

I got up and put on my headscarf, and stood at the doorway of the bungalow. A group of Bosnian asylum seekers lived a little farther on, and they were talking in the sun. These women were supposed to be Muslim, but they were really almost naked, wearing short shorts and T-shirts with not even a bra, so you could see their nipples. Men worked nearby, or sat and talked to them quite normally, apparently not even noticing them. I stared at them for a long time, thinking, Could there be some truth to what the Ethiopian girls had said?

The next morning, I decided to stage an experiment. I would walk out of the door without a headscarf. I was in my long green skirt and a long tunic, and I had my scarf in a bag with me in case of trouble, but I would not cover my hair. I planned to see what would happen. I was sweating. This was really *haram,* and also the first time I had walked in a public space with my hair uncovered since I was sixteen.

Absolutely nothing happened. The gardeners kept trimming the hedges. Nobody went into a fit. Still, these were Dutch people, so perhaps not really men. I walked past Ethiopians and Zaireans, and no one paid any attention to me; but then, these people were not Muslims either. So I walked over to the group of Bosnians. Nobody looked at me. If anything, I attracted less attention than when I was covering my head. Not one man went into a frenzy.

Slowly, in the next few days, I shed the headscarf. I thought to myself, "I will tell Allah that I was careful. It didn't do anyone any harm." He didn't strike me with a thunderbolt. I concluded that when the Quran said women should cover their bodies, it must really just mean that they shouldn't attract attention to themselves. This way I didn't feel as though I was sinning. In fact, walking about with my hair in the air, I felt somehow taller.

From then on, the only thing I was careful about was trying to stay away from the Somali men. I knew they could recognize me as a Somali. One had already approached me to ask me about my clan. I had used the new name, Ayaan Hirsi Ali, and he had not been Darod, so he didn't instantly realize I was lying. Still, I knew it was only a matter of time before I was discovered.

*   *   *

One day the Ethiopians told me a friend of theirs was coming over to teach them to ride bicycles. He was an Ethiopian refugee and had bought them three secondhand bicycles with the 20-guilder living allowance we all received every week. They planned to ride into the village: it would be an adventure. So I went along.

I watched the Ethiopian girls straddling the saddles in their short skirts and sniffed at their wanton, typically Ethiopian behavior. All the same, I would have liked to ride a bicycle, too. But when I tried, in my long skirt, I could only perch sideways on the thing. "This isn't a horse, you know!" the Ethiopian man scoffed. "You'll have to wear trousers. Go buy yourself a pair of jeans."

I had just received my 150-guilder clothes allowance. The next day I walked to the village with Mina and tried on some cheap trousers. Only men's sizes were long enough to cover my legs, and I finally emerged with an enormous, baggy pair of men's jeans. They showed not one inch of the shape of my legs, and I wore them with a tunic that went halfway down my thighs. You couldn't have described this outfit as immodest. Then I tried the bicycle. Falling off it, I felt I was free.

I began having a huge amount of fun. Every day, the Ethiopian girls found something to do. One day they asked me, "Do you want to swim?" I said, "I can't. I'll drown," but they said, "Rubbish," and I could borrow a swimsuit at the pool. So, less than a month after I first arrived in Europe, I found myself in an ill-fitting swimsuit, in front of a crowd of other asylum seekers, women and men.

I cringed. I wasn't ready for this. Even while I was splashing in the pool I thought about Allah and the angels looking down at me. But when I looked around, none of the men was even noticing me. Every so often a man would look at me, but I in no way had the impression that because of me, any of them would end up in Hell or drowned at the bottom of the pool. The tall Bosnians, and the Zaireans, with their wonderful torsos: I found myself noticing them, too. But I was not going into any kind of fit either.

I kept coming back to it, arguing with myself, trying to justify what I was doing. I was supposed to cover myself because I was so beguiling that I would lead men astray; even the allure of perfume or high heels under a black *hidjab* could supposedly cause an intolerable chaos of desire. But this was clearly not true: everything was going on entirely the same.

I kept returning to the Bosnians. I found them fascinating, partly because all the Dutch workers at the center called them "the Muslims," as if all the rest of us weren't. I struck up a conversation with one Bosnian girl, who said of course she was a Muslim, though she never wore a headscarf; she had on a tiny T-shirt. She never read the Quran, either; she didn't even know how to say *Bism'Allah Al-Rahman Al-Raheem,* "In the name of Allah Most Gracious Most Merciful." I didn't see how this girl thought she qualified as a Muslim, but to her, apparently, Islam wasn't really a religious belief at all, more like an ethnicity. I found this mystifying.

At the end of August, I got an official letter from the Dutch refugee office. My heart sank; this must be my letter of rejection. I would be sent to Canada, or to Nairobi—it amounted to the same thing. I didn't deserve refugee status; it was over. When Mina saw my face, I confessed to her that I had lied to the authorities. She shrugged and said she had lied, too; the camp was full of people with manufactured stories quaking that they would be thrown out.

Mina opened the letter for me. It was a transfer. I was to go to Lunteren, to a long-stay center, to await the final answer.

I wrote to Haweya at a personal post office box that she had recently rented in Eastleigh. I gave her my address and told her to keep it to herself. She wrote back, "There was a lot of fracas here when you left. Father asked me to give him your address. I refused, and now we don't talk."

She went on, "Your husband is in Germany looking for you, and the whole search is being coordinated by father here. If you are going to run away, or meet him, it is up to you, but I am warning you, if you don't already know, that practically all the Osman Mahamud in that area are looking for you everywhere. Be warned." She also asked me to send her clothes and a passport so that she, too, could get out. My nightmare was coming true: I was being hunted.

I arrived in Lunteren at the end of August 1992. The train station was a sweet little building in the middle of a cobbled village with manicured front lawns. Everyone was white, well-dressed, and looked happy.

I had traveled there with another girl, Rhoda, who was claiming to be Somali though anyone could tell from her accent that she was from Djibouti. The center for asylum seekers was miles into the forest; there was nothing for us to do but start walking. When we arrived at the refugee center, a field of tiny green-and-pale-green houses on wheels, called caravans, and a white brick office, it was pitch dark.

We would be sharing a caravan with two Somali women, but when we knocked on the door they wouldn't let us in. These women were Hawiye and could tell I was Darod from my accent. They didn't want any Darod woman living with them. The social worker accompanying us was an Iranian man, and when he asked the Hawiye women to unlock the door they ignored him. He left, then returned with one of his Dutch colleagues, a woman called Sylvia, and two guards. Sylvia announced that she would break the door down and transfer the women if they couldn't obey the camp rules.

I thought it was such innocence. I explained to Sylvia that the Hawiye and the Darod were destroying each other and couldn't possibly live together in such a tiny, toylike place. But Sylvia said, "This is Holland. You will just have to ignore each other. You are four adult women and you will manage."

Finally the door opened. It emerged that one of the Hawiye women, Yasmin, had a grandmother who was Isse Mahamud, like my father's mother. I explained that I had grown up in Kenya and had no hostility toward her about clan. Yasmin said she felt the same way. Gradually we worked things out and became friends.

Yasmin had never meant to go to Holland. She had been on her way to the United States, with false papers, but she got caught at the Amsterdam airport. She claimed asylum when they caught her, and though she was my age, she told the officials she was a minor so she could stay in the country. She knew how it worked.

Yasmin didn't like Holland. She said the Dutch had treated her like a criminal at the airport. The air stank of cow dung and the language sounded stupid. She called the Dutch *gaalo,* and *kufr.* Being nice in Somali terms means when someone gives you what you ask for. So if someone politely said no, even if they explained why they couldn't do something, Yasmin and the others saw this as arrogance, or racism.

Like all the asylum seekers, I had to check in once a week to have my card stamped. September 1 was my first Tuesday in Lunteren, so that morning I went over to the police office at the asylum-seeker center. When I went to the desk, the policewoman looked at me and disappeared underneath the desk for a minute. She reemerged, cooing in English, "Oooh! Congratulations!" and waving a pink card instead of my green one. I didn't understand, but she shook my hand and said, "You can stay in Holland for the rest of your life. You are a recognized refugee, and now I will read you your rights."

Sweating, I thought, "Thank you Allah, thank you."

The policewoman told me that there is no better status than the A status I received. As an A-status refugee, I would never again have to check in to have my card stamped. I could work or register for unemployment benefits, I could buy or rent property, I could attend university, receive free health care, and after five years in the country I could apply for naturalization and vote. I didn't even know they had elections in Holland. What would they vote about? I thought. Everything seemed to work so perfectly.

"Do you have any more questions?" the policewoman asked me, and I said, "Yes. Why are you doing this?" She said, "The authorities have determined that you have a well-founded fear of persecution. It's the law."

She gave me a bus ticket to Ede, where I could register for municipal housing. There were so many refugees in Ede now that the city had waiting lists for municipal housing, but I could register for the waiting list and, in the meantime, still live at the Lunteren long-stay center. She apologized for this. And could I really go to the university? I asked. The policewoman said yes, although I would have to learn the language first, of course.

I left, floating, staring at the pink card with my photo, printed in indecipherable Dutch. Suddenly, I could stay in this country, with all these nice people. It was like a dream.

CHAPTER 11

A Trial by the Elders

At first, I felt an enormous sense of relief. The nightmare that I would be returned to Kenya, or sent back to Germany, receded, and I was euphoric. I registered in Ede with various offices, constantly taking buses; then Refugee Aid gave me a secondhand bicycle of my own. I bought another pair of jeans: I never wore long skirts any more. I was constantly cycling places, registering for things.

My first imperative was to learn Dutch. Now that I was a recognized refugee, I was eligible for lessons at the refugee center, taught once a week by a woman volunteer from the village. But once a week wasn't enough for me; I wanted more. This Dutch volunteer, blessed woman, persuaded a real language school in Ede to accept me, and she told me she would pay for the classes; I could pay her back in weekly installments out of my pocket money. So I began cycling three times a week to my Dutch class at Midlands College in Ede. The leaves were turning, I remember, and I felt so happy riding my bicycle through the forest, with a sense of purpose and an overpowering impression of good fortune.

Haweya's letters were full of her fights with Ma and the growing rift between Ma and Abeh, as well as constant requests for clothes. She said all the Somalis in Nairobi were shunning my mother, saying she was behind my disappearance. She refused to talk to anyone: the whole community—all the Farah Gouré family, my stepsisters, Arro and Ijaabo, everyone—thought Ma had plotted my escape to take her revenge on my father. They thought I was too docile to have come up with such an evil stratagem on my own. I felt horrible thinking about what Ma was going through.

It grew cold. The rain never stopped, and the caravans shook in the wind and froze on the outside at night. One day that was too wet to cycle, I waited at the bus stop, so cold I thought I might cry.

One gray November evening, the day I turned twenty-three, an Iranian asylum seeker set himself on fire in the canteen just as I was on my way to line up for dinner. Having received a negative decision on his appeal for refugee status, he poured paraffin over himself and ignited it as a kind of mad expression of his hopelessness. I felt horrible for him. Other, far more deserving people than I waited for years at this refugee center and received negative decisions. People from countries involved in civil wars were often accepted into Holland, usually with C status, a temporary right to stay on humanitarian grounds. But Iranians, Russians, Iraqis—most other asylum seekers—were more usually denied any right to stay in Holland at all.

I was lucky and felt guilty for getting refugee status so quickly, on false pretenses, when so many people were being turned down. I tried to be of service to people; it reassured me to feel that I was still a good person. I wanted to pay all this back in some way, and return goodness with goodness, which is how I understood Islam at the time. I registered with the center as a volunteer. I worked in the laundry office once a week and in the library. Sylvia, who worked at the center, asked me if I wanted to play volleyball; that was fun.

I liked the people who worked at the center, and they liked me. I was useful to them because I spoke English, the center's lingua franca. Any time a Somali was sick and couldn't make himself understood, or someone needed help filling in a form, they knew they could call on me to act as go-between, without going to all the bother of getting an official interpreter to come in. If there was trouble with a Somali—and there often was—I used to mediate. People who refused transfers, or who got into fights, or who wanted something—either the Somalis themselves or the staff would come for me.

Thankfully none of the Somalis in the center were Osman Mahamud, but they still regarded me and my jeans with undisguised hostility. To them, it seemed normal to lecture me, to try to make me conform. They were always telling me I must cover my hair and dress in long skirts. One man said, "You are putting us all to shame with your bicycle. When you ride toward us with your legs spread we can see your genitals."

I told him I was wearing the same trousers he was, and if they showed genitals then a man's would be more visible than mine; then I sped away as fast as my legs would take me. Sylvia had said that anyone who threatened me physically would be transferred, but other than that, I would have to defend myself. "The Somalis here are dependent on your goodwill," she told me. "They knock on your door and beg you to translate for them when they need something. *They* need *you.* Just tell them it's none of their business what you wear."

So I did. I used direct language. I stared right in their face when I said it. It was kind of thrilling to be able to say such things out loud.

Early in December, I received a letter from my father, addressed to the asylum-seeker center. He had tracked me down. "My Dearest Liver," he began. My father used to call me his liver, which in Somali is very meaningful, because without a liver, you cannot survive. (Haweya was his eyes. Mahad he called his heart.) "In our game of hide-and-seek I finally got you."

My father's letter was intended to persuade me to return to the proper path, but it was also couched in such a way that I could do this with my head high—and with his honor intact. He feigned to believe that I was still planning to live with the husband he'd chosen for me, that I'd somehow just made a short detour. And he told me that he needed $300 for an urgent operation on his eyes. "Although you have yet to get enough allowance, still I feel you can come up with a few hundred dollars because you are very influential," he wrote.

My father knew that I would become frantic at the news that his eyesight, always weak, was now failing. He assumed I would go straight to Osman Moussa to get the money: How else could I come up with such a sum? The husband is the maintainer of the wife—and, if necessary, the wife's family. Father ended his letter, "Your house shall be either a source of honor or a source of disgrace for me. . . . God be with you." He knew me, and he thought that to save his eyes, I would agree to go back to my husband.

Several days later, Osman Moussa called the asylum-seeker center. Someone came to the caravan and said I had a call from Canada. My legs shook. I went to the phone, and I spoke to him, and again I lied. I spun a tale. I pretended that I had never really disappeared, just gone to Holland for a few weeks to be with my dear friend Fadumo. He scolded me— "You can't just disappear like that"—and told me to get back to Germany as soon as possible. I said I would. Then I told Osman Moussa about Abeh's letter. He said he was constantly in touch with my father, and that he would deal with it. Apparently he sent the money.

Now I knew I was living on borrowed time. My father, my brother, and my husband all knew my address. There was nowhere else I could go. It was only a matter of time before they came to claim me. I was frightened—frightened of the physical violence that might mean. But I had no intention of going with them. That center in little Ede was my only chance to lead my own life, and I wasn't going to let go of it. Somehow, I thought, I would get out of this trap, too.

One crisp January afternoon, Yasmin and I went swimming in the covered pool at the nearby campsite, which was reserved for women once a week. We couldn't swim, but we splashed about, screaming with laughter. When we came home, I went straight to the shower to try to do something with my hair, which was becoming impossible. I had recently cut it short to try to minimize the upkeep.

Yasmin and I were in the middle of a noisy, happy conversation, with the radio blaring, when the door knocked loudly. Yasmin yelled at me to get it, so I emerged, with wet hair and red eyes, and opened the door. I found myself face-to-face with Osman Moussa, standing in the doorway of the caravan in the late afternoon sun with three other Somali men.

I stood there, my hair a fright, my skin blackened from the open air, in my jeans, at a total loss for words. It somehow yanked me back to the old Ayaan: the docile girl compelled by years of habit to offer hospitality. *"Asalaam Aleikum,"* I greeted him. "Would you like to come in?"

I stood aside as these four large men filled the living space of our caravan. I had no idea what to do. I grabbed a thermos flask and said, "Rest here, I will get us some tea." Then I disappeared into Yasmin's room and explained to her that this man was legally my husband. I begged her to look after the guests; I would be back as soon as I could. Before I left, I pulled on a headscarf.

I went first to Hasna's caravan. Hasna was a Somali woman in her forties who lived in a caravan nearby; she was a busybody, but I knew she understood the code of conduct and would know how to behave. Hasna said she would make tea for my guests at her place—it was larger—and began to bustle. With my duty as hostess taken care of, I went to Sylvia and told her everything. I said that I had lied to obtain my refugee status. I told her that in reality I was running away from a marriage that my father had arranged for me. Now my husband had come to pick me up and take me to Canada.

I thought Sylvia would be bound to tell me that I could no longer stay in Holland, that I must return to Kenya, or leave with this man. But Sylvia said, "What you did to obtain your refugee status is your business. Keep it to yourself. As for this man: if you don't want to go to Canada with him, then just tell him so. Even if you are married to him, he cannot make you do it. If he is violent with you, I will call the police."

I returned to my caravan feeling much more sure of myself. Hasna tactfully led Yasmin and the three Somali men away, leaving me alone with Osman Moussa. He swept his arm with contempt around the cramped little tin box that I lived in. "Is this it?" he asked scornfully. "Is this what you wanted?"

"This is it, yes," I said.

"Will you come with me now?" he asked.

"I will not."

I was quiet. There was no shouting or crying; no dramatics. I knew that for Osman I had become a cipher, but I could read him perfectly well. In his eyes I saw arrogance and disdain. This man was offering the moon to a foolish girl who chose to live in a squalid camp among strangers. He thought he had authority over me, that he owned me. But he didn't, I thought to myself. I knew now that I had rights in this country. I indicated that we should follow the others to Hasna's caravan, and I took the lead out of the door.

When we got there, Hasna said, "I will talk to her." She took me into her bedroom and lectured me. "Are you mad?" she asked. "Are you stupid? Retarded? This man is handsome and wealthy. What more could you want? What are you waiting for?"

I said, "Soon I will be able to rent my own place. I will work."

"Why are you doing this to yourself?" Hasna asked me. She told me I would be cursed, stricken with poverty and disease and thirty different kinds of damnation. I let her talk, and then I said, "This is too much for me right now."

Finally, Osman Moussa agreed to leave. I could see that he was at a loss for what to do. Here in Holland, in a center that was staffed with Dutch security guards, he could not use physical violence to force me to go with him. I was nervous, but also unexpectedly self-confident.

I was ready to confront my family. I had discovered an inner strength. I had tested my self-reliance, and I felt I could manage. I had become resilient, and I had discovered the rule of law. There were potential predators here, too, but I could avoid them. I could ask for help from the police and from Sylvia. She knew my story, and she didn't disapprove of what I had done; instead, she had offered to help me.

A few days later Osman returned. He said he had consulted Father and they had agreed to summon a *tolka,* a gathering of the oldest, most prominent men among our close relatives. The *tolka* would meet in the asylum-seeker center on January 26. I agreed.

In the next few days, every Darod woman in the camp must have come to my caravan to try to talk me into going to Canada. They made it clear I was making the biggest mistake of my life. My father had found me a splendid match. They would do anything for half my fortune. Here in Europe, on my own, I would be garbage. They told me spirit stories ending in horrible death and warned me that the djinns would be drawn to me if I disobeyed. They cited every case in recent Somali history in which girls ran from their families and became prostitutes, sick, barren, unmarriageable—because come on, think it through, you're twenty-three, you're not getting younger.

There was a huge, spontaneous uprising of pressure from all these people who did not know me. I just listened to them. I knew what I was going to do.

After two days of this, Hasna returned to my caravan. Hasna was from the Ogaden subclan but had been married to an Osman Mahamud; this made her my closest female relative in the camp, as well as my neighbor. She told me to get dressed: she would host the clan meeting in her caravan after dinner.

On the evening of January 26, Osman Moussa came with eight older Osman Mahamud men and two Macherten men; a huge crowd of men massed outside Hasna's caravan in the dark. Even though we were on Dutch soil, this would be a real, formal gathering of the elders of our clan. Because of the deep shame I had caused, the Osman Mahamud family could not permit me to decide my future on my own.

Hasna and I greeted them. Osman was following procedure by the letter. Some of the men he brought with him were great names, men I didn't even know were in Europe: my family elders, the nobility of the Osman Mahamud. We shared a fifth grandfather or an eighth grandfather. One man was even a Boqor, the direct descendant of the king for whom my grandfather Magan had fought.

For this full confrontation, I planned to obey the codes of good behavior. But I didn't dress in my long skirt. I wore jeans and a tunic. And I didn't cover my hair with a headscarf. My clothes were correct—they didn't display any skin—but my message was clear: things had changed.

The men trooped, stooping, into the tiny space, and settled down on the bench and a few chairs, their faces in shadows cast by Hasna's candle. Abdellahi Moussa Boqor, the man who was Crown Prince of all the Osman Mahamud of Somalia, began. He was regal: his authority seemed to fill the whole tiny caravan. He spoke for half an hour, first to explain the procedure that the gathering would follow, then about the values of the clan. He praised my father. He said how precious marriage is, how important our honor and our name. He appealed to me: the country is falling apart, this is not what we, from the higher-level clans, should be doing to each other. When he stopped, the next man spoke. All eight Osman Mahamud elders took their turn, according to rank.

I remained quiet, sitting up quite straight, and sipped with two hands from my tea. I had broken the most sacred rules of the clan—I had placed a hideous, irreparable stigma on my father—but I knew how to behave. I would not be rude. I would not stoop to hysterics or insults. I had my feet exactly so, as you are required to sit, and I was looking at the men's mouths, not their eyes, which would have been immodest—only once in a while glancing up, to show I was listening, and nodding. I knew this was now my trial. At stake was my right to rule my own life.

Then Abdellahi Moussa Boqor said, "Now I think Osman Moussa himself should say something." Osman Moussa went on and on about honor and family, about the clan and the war. He acknowledged that he didn't know me; he had been a little too sure of himself, not inquiring about me at all, taking everything for granted. But now, he said, he was really prepared to get to know me: who I was as an individual, not just as the daughter-of.

Then Abdellahi Moussa Boqor spoke to me directly. I had still not uttered a word. "You understand that even though this is not the proper place, this is a formal sitting?" he asked. I nodded. He said, "Now it is for you to think about your answer. We cannot permit you to say yes and then disappear again to the next country. If you say yes, you must mean it. Your answer will be final." I nodded again.

He said, "We will now pause so you can think about it. We are all prepared to come back tomorrow in order to hear your answer, or we will hold a gathering at my house, or at a house nearby." I knew that it was time for me to speak. I said, "I know my answer."

I looked into his face and said, "It is no." I surprised myself, I was so calm and determined. I have never felt so right about anything in my life. I said, "I don't want to stay married to Osman Moussa, although I respect him and he has not mistreated me in any way. I understand what you are doing for me and how extraordinary this is, and I understand that my answer is final."

The Boqor paused for a moment. He was clearly taken aback. He said, "May we ask you some questions?" and I agreed. He asked, "Has Osman Moussa been violent?" and I said, "No. He has always been completely correct in every way."

"Is he stingy?"

"No, he has been very generous."

"Do you know something about Osman that we don't know?"

"No, I don't know him at all."

"Is there someone else?"

I said, "No."

With every question, he was offering me a way to explain myself in a way that would justify my behavior and lessen the stigma on my honor and on my father's good name. But I was determined not to lie, not to claim that Osman Moussa had hurt or cheated me in any way. It would not have been fair. I simply didn't want him.

Finally Abdellahi Moussa Boqor asked, "So why are you doing this?"

I paused for a moment, and then the words just came out of my mouth. "It is the will of the soul," I said. "The soul cannot be coerced." The language I used was grandiloquent, not at all the language you'd expect from a woman, let alone a twenty-three-year-old. Abdellahi Moussa Boqor stared at me, and then he said, "I respect this answer. I believe all of us should respect it." He turned to Osman and said, "Do you accept it?"

Osman said, "I have to."

Then the Crown Prince told the gathering that Osman's acceptance should be seen as honorable and brave and should enhance his reputation for wisdom. He embraced Osman Moussa and patted his back. All the men present did the same.

I felt bad about what I had done to him. It wasn't this poor man's fault. I said, "I will pay you back one day, you know, for the air ticket and all the expense," because this had been bothering me.

Osman Moussa was deeply insulted. He said, "In addition to everything you have already done, this is really rubbing salt in the wound." According to the honor code, it was not required, but I had not meant to insult him. I said I was grateful.

All the men stood up then, and one after another each man cupped my hands in their two hands, and left. They were full of respect. There was no violence. We were Osman Mahamud, not Arabs, and the Osman Mahamud very rarely hit women. But I looked out of the caravan as they walked into the blackness of the night and I knew I had done something I could never, never undo. There was no regret, but I knew that I had cut myself off from everything that was meaningful and important to my family.

So much had changed in me in the space of a few months. In Nairobi I had been incapable of standing up for my right to refuse this man. I did tell my father I didn't want to marry him, but I felt unable to act on that. If I had, I would have been disowned, shunned, deprived of the invisible protection of the clan. My mother and sister would also, to a lesser extent, be punished. I would have been seen as prey, like Fawzia and other Somali women who were alone: begging for a roof, potentially a victim of every kind of predator. I just couldn't imagine having the strength to do it.

But now I had a refugee permit. I had a right to stay in Holland, and I knew I had other rights, too. Nobody could force me to go anywhere I didn't want to go. That pink piece of paper giving me refugee status had changed everything. Now I knew that, somehow, I would summon the strength to continue to defy them.

Still, I felt crushed by my guilt. I couldn't sleep that night for thinking about what I was doing to my father.

Early next morning, January 27, I went into my room and began writing the most difficult letter of my life. I began, "In the Name of Allah Most Gracious Most Merciful," and continued:

Dearest Father,

After very warm greetings, I will just get to the point and tell you that I have become a disappointment to you and I have decided to divorce Osman Moussa Isse. No amount of apologies or begging for forgiveness will make you feel any better, but I will just beg you to understand and I am very sorry. Of course I don't expect you to feel understanding towards me but that is that.

Osman telephoned you, and followed your advice to bring the matter to the attention of the male relations (tolka), and we have met and reached an agreement peacefully and honorably (if there can be anything honorable in such a situation). The agreement was that the DIVORCE goes through.

I am very sorry, Father, but that is that. I shall come back to Kenya as soon as I make enough money to pay for my ticket and as soon as I get a visa back. Right now, I go to school.

Father, I feel your unhappiness towards me but please reply and try, when your anger is over, to understand me and forgive me. Maybe it is too much to ask, but I also need your blessings.

Love, Ayaan, your loving daughter.

About a week later I received a letter from my father postmarked January 26, the night the *tolka* met. I suppose Osman had phoned him. "Dear Ayaan," I read. "I could not believe what Osman told me about you. If it is true, you made me and our family not only mean and disgraceful, but you cause me pain and grief. I could not pray nor could I sleep well since Osman phoned. Look, Ayaan, I cannot withstand this sort of situation any longer. Therefore, either you gracefully obey your husband, or you force me to come to Holland and I and you will decide the matter face-to-face."

I felt lashed by his rage, by how deeply I had damaged his reputation. And I felt real fear: if he came to Holland, my father could beat me, perhaps kill me. I had shamed him, and for that I knew that he had to punish me.

Then, two weeks after the clan gathering, I received another letter from my father. It was written on the pages of the letter I had sent him on January 27; he wrote in red ink—the color you use to write to your enemies. On the first page, he wrote, "As I shall not open your letters, never attempt to write." On the reverse side, across my signature, he wrote:

Dear deceitful fox,

You do not need me and I do not need you. I just invoked Allah to disgrace you as you have disgraced me. Amen! This is the last message you will receive from me, as your letter was the last message I was to accept from you. Go to Hell! and the Devil be with you.

He added, in angry capital letters, "MAY ALLAH PUNISH YOU FOR YOUR DECEPTION. AMEN! YOURS, THE FOOL!"

My fears that my father would kill me became less acute. For him, I was now already dead. And although I was physically intact, I felt as though I had been kicked in the stomach. I was outcast.

I bought a phone card and dialed the number of the Indian family who lived next door to us in Park Road. I asked them to get Haweya. I needed her badly. It was the first time I had spoken to her since I'd left. Haweya said she had read my letter to Abeh and she was proud of me. She said she was sorry for me, too, and she warned me to be careful: Abeh might still come after me. His fury was frightening, even to her.

I told Haweya to bring Ma to the neighbors' house next week. I wanted to talk to her, too. And I begged Haweya to try to persuade her not to reject me.

When I heard Ma's voice, the line crackled so much that it sounded as though she was on another planet. She said, "So you did what I suspected you would." Her voice rose, "Do you know how I am being treated here?" I said, "Haweya told me." Then my mother said, "You have made a terrible mistake, but you will always be my child." She went on, "Your father is very angry. Aren't you afraid that he is going to curse you? His curses are more effective than a mother's."

I said, "We shall have to see." My mother wished me good luck before we hung up. She was very kind. She promised we could speak again. Then the line went dead.

I felt as though I were living through the final episode of my life. I had cast off my father, and now I had disappointed my mother, too. I thought about dying, and waking up in the Hereafter, where you cannot hide from Allah's judgment. There was no end to my sins. I had shamed my parents, rejected a rightful husband, neglected my daily prayers; I was wearing men's clothes and had cut my hair. The book of misdeeds written by the angel on my left shoulder would surely weigh far more than the slim volume of my good works. My father had cursed me, and now I was damned.

CHAPTER 12

Haweya

For many months after receiving my father's letter, I felt very bleak. There was nothing I could do now but go forward, alone, in the direction that I had chosen. Slowly, the weather improved, and so did my grasp of the Dutch language. The staff at the center for asylum seekers began encouraging me to translate from Somali directly into Dutch, instead of into English. They patiently corrected my mistakes. It was like wobbling down the road on a bicycle—I found myself getting better at it.

Sylvia, in particular, encouraged me. She told me that I had a future. I could request that the Dutch government accept my Kenyan O-levels as a high school equivalency, and then I could study, perhaps even qualify to attend the university, if that was what I really wanted.

One day, a Somali girl asked me to go with her to the hospital; she had to have a gynecological exam. The doctor told me to explain that this girl would have to take off her clothes and that he would look at her uterus with a long silver tool. She told me, "I will do it, but I don't think he will be able to see my uterus." I understood: she was closed up, a scar.

I tried to tell the doctor, but he just retorted, "Do as I say." But when she climbed onto the table and he looked between her legs, he snapped back with shock, and swore. Then he angrily ripped his gloves off, because no steel tool was getting inside that. This girl had no genitals at all, just a completely smooth panel of scar tissue between her legs.

This was the *farooni,* the excision so extreme that the woman's whole genitals are scraped off and mend into a hard band of dark skin. I had never seen one—mostly only the Isaq girls from the North are excised in this way—but I knew what it was. The doctor, though, thought the girl had been burned. The whole medical team seemed shocked. It dawned on me that here in Europe, the excision of women was unheard of.

In May 1993, I received an official letter: I had housing. The municipality of Ede was able to offer me a one-room apartment. I would receive an unemployment allowance that would pay for the rent.

I welcomed the prospect of leaving the refugee center. Fights constantly broke out between asylum seekers, over politics or women, and there was constant gossip. But when I told Yasmin my news, she burst into tears, and asked, "So you're going to leave me here?"

Yasmin's claim to refugee status had been refused. But because she had declared she was a minor, she was allowed to remain in Holland. She had to live at the asylum-seeker center and attend a special school for foreigners, which she hated. I asked the housing office if Yasmin could live with me, but she couldn't: it was a one-room apartment. If I wanted a two-bedroom place, I would have to wait.

I thought about it. I had been so selfish. If I didn't stand by Yasmin now, I risked becoming a truly bad person. I turned the flat down and applied for a two-bedroom, with Yasmin.

I began making friends with some of the people who worked at the asylum-seeker center. A counselor a few years older than I, Hanneke, introduced me to her friend Ellen, who was my age and studying social work at the local Christian vocational college. We rented videos, went for walks, and arranged picnics—all sorts of girly things, which I loved doing. They introduced me to their friends and their families.

Both Hanneke and Ellen were Christians, and seemed to take their religion seriously, but they still went to pubs. The first time Hanneke persuaded me to come along, I thought Allah truly might strike me down. It had been a long time since I last prayed, but going to a bar—this was really *haram*. In fact, a pub turned out to be just a place where people stood up for hours in a crowd of other people, drinking alcohol and smoking and shouting at each other over loud music. I could never understand much of what was going on. The custom was mystifying.

I kept going there, however, because the others liked it. I didn't drink, but still, sometimes when I came home I would feel bad about it. How could I be going to places like this, places that had once seemed so evil? I would tell myself, "I didn't do anything wrong. I didn't seduce or encourage anyone, just drank a Coca-Cola, wearing jeans. There's nothing wrong with that." If I wasn't doing anything wrong, then surely Allah wouldn't punish me.

Actually, I didn't get why people needed to go to a noisy place to talk. Ede was a nice, conservative, Protestant small town, a very peaceful, predictable place. There wasn't any bad behavior in pubs. People got drinks, and the people who were together in a group stood facing each other in a small circle and shouted at each other over the music. When they were choosing which pub to go to, people always picked the one that was already packed. There was no logic to it.

I was having difficulty figuring out the Dutch. I imagined going home and telling Haweya, "From sunrise to sunset they seem normal, but they have some weird habits in the evenings."

Hanneke thought it was important for me to see more of Holland. One spring weekend she decided to take me to Amsterdam for the day. There, we strolled around the elegant houses around the Herengracht, the Gentlemen's Canal, with its tiny, delicate bridges. Every Dutch city, it seemed, had a center that was ancient and lovely, and such a lot of thought had been given to preserving it. You could walk undisturbed in the streets at night; it was orderly and clean. Everything seemed to function so beautifully in this country, while a few hours away there was so much conflict and filth and hardship.

Hanneke also walked me through the red-light district near the Central Station, just to show me what it was like. I remember feeling as if I'd been hit in the stomach by the sight of women standing behind glass, naked or strung together in obscenely sexual clothes. It made me think of animal parts hanging off hooks at the butcher's stall in Kariokor market. This was exploitation: I recoiled from it. Hanneke couldn't persuade me that these women were doing it voluntarily, as an honest day's work.

But this unpleasant side of Dutch society seemed also to have no connection with the Holland I knew. Ordinary Dutch people were not depraved in this way. Perhaps I had more connection with them than most foreigners did, but I was convinced that the Dutch were not the licentious monsters that many Somali asylum seekers perceived.

Ellen and I had numerous conversations about her Christian beliefs. Her relationship with God seemed to be about dialogue and love, a striking contrast to the fear and submission I had been taught to show. Ellen had been brought up a fundamentalist Protestant; her parents were from a strict Dutch Reformed denomination. They went to church twice every Sunday and made her wear long skirts; Ellen was searching for her own way to relate to God, and this troubled her. Still, her beliefs seemed far less restrictive than Islam as I knew it. In fact, I thought they were much too pleasant and convenient to be true.

Ellen said she prayed to God only when she felt like it. She said her

Christian God was a kind, fatherly figure, though, mystifyingly, he seemed not to help her directly—apparently he wanted Ellen to help herself. She told me, "In your religion there is so much Hell, and you pray because you have to. This is a master-slave relationship."

Ellen had a boyfriend. She was in love with one of the Iranian asylum seekers, Badal Zadeh. But she wanted to start marriage as a virgin. She and her boyfriend used to kiss on the mouth quite openly, even in front of people. Ellen used to tell me, "But this is normal!" And it was true: young people did this all the time on the street. I had noticed it the minute I got off the plane, and all the Somalis said this was what the filthy *gaalo* always did. And yet Ellen still wanted to be a virgin?

One day the four of us were sitting around watching TV in the apartment that Hanneke and Ellen shared in Ede. The program was called *All You Need Is Love*. Dutch men and women declared their love for someone, in front of the whole nation, and the presenter played Cupid. After a commercial break the viewers got to see if this love was mutual or not. It seemed completely barbaric to Yasmin and me.

Ellen and I started talking about love, courtship, and virginity. To me, as a Somali, being a virgin meant being excised, physically sewn shut. I had already figured out that Dutch people didn't do that, so I asked, "How will your husband find out whether you're a virgin or not? Isn't there a test?"

Ellen replied, "Of course not. He'll know I'm a virgin because I say I am." My question seemed weird to her, so she asked, "You have a test?" I told her: we are cut, and sewn shut, so that the skin is closed, and when a man penetrates you there is blood. There can be no pretending.

Ellen and Hanneke were disgusted, appalled. They asked, "And this happened to you?" Yasmin and I both said yes, and Yasmin, who was a snob, added, "If you're not cut, you're not pure, are you?" Very innocently, with her big blue eyes wide, Ellen asked, "Pure from what?"

Pure from what. Pure from what, exactly? I thought about it for a long time, and realized I had no answer. It wasn't completely because of Islam that we were cut: not all Muslim women are excised. But in Somalia and the other Muslim countries, it was clear that the Islamic culture of virginity encouraged it. I knew of no *fatwa* denouncing female genital mutilation; on the contrary, suppressing the sexuality of women was a big theme with imams. Boqol Sawm and the other *ma'alims* had always preached endlessly about how women should become aware of their sexual powers; they must cover themselves and stay indoors. They went into minute detail about this, yet somehow they never got around to saying that it is wrong to cut girls and sew them up.

What were we being kept pure from? Somebody owned us. What was between my legs was not mine to give. I was branded.

I found I had no answer for Ellen. I just gaped at her and said, "It's our tradition." And because Ellen truly was a believer, she said, "But you believe God created you, don't you?" I said yes, of course. Ellen said, "So the way God made us is the way God wants us to be. Why shouldn't we stay like that? Why does your culture feel we should improve on God's work? Isn't that blasphemy?" I stared at her. There really seemed to be something to what Ellen was saying.

Ellen said Dutch women were never circumcised, and neither were Dutch men. Yasmin curled up her face in disgust at that. The minute we left, Yasmin started rubbing her skin; when she got home she washed for hours. "I sat in their house and ate off their plates, and they are not puri-fied!" Yasmin said. "She is filthy. This whole country is filthy."

I thought about it. Ellen wasn't filthy, and neither was Holland. In fact, it was a lot cleaner than Somalia or anywhere else I had lived. I couldn't understand how Yasmin could perceive Holland as evil, even though all around us were Dutch people treating us with kindness and hospitality. I was beginning to see that the Dutch value system was more consistent, more honest, and gave more people more happiness than the one with which we had been brought up. Unfortunately, many of these Dutch ideas seemed not to be congruent with Islam.

I replied, "Yasmin, you know what? You'd better get used to it. Because your teacher in school is not circumcised, the person cooking your lunch is not circumcised. If you want to remain completely pure here you will have to lock yourself away and never have any contact with a white person."

But Yasmin said, "There is a difference, and that is why the Quran tells us never to make unbelievers our friends."

In July 1993, I finally was allotted a two-room apartment in Ede. It cost 600 guilders a month, but I would receive a 5,000-guilder loan for furni-ture, which I would have to pay back, and a monthly unemployment allowance of 1,200 guilders. Yasmin, who the Dutch believed to be only fifteen, would be released into my guardianship.

The flat was in James Wattstraat, a neighborhood of low-rise brick buildings—maybe a little shabby, but not squalid by any means. I thought it was nice. But in the building next door to ours, a Turkish woman was beaten almost every night. We heard all of it. We heard her smashing against the wall of our living room and crying for mercy. Ellen and Hanneke told us we should call the police. We did, but the police phoned us back, very politely, to say there was nothing they could do. They had visited the apartment, and the woman in question hadn't filed a complaint. The next night she was screaming again.

Her husband used to turn the TV up loud so people couldn't hear her. I saw this woman in the street very rarely; she almost never left the house. I think what she felt was shame; the whole neighborhood knew about her. She cringed and scuttled.

One day the refugee officer from the asylum-seeker center came to check on our progress. He said to me, "Ayaan, how is it possible that your Dutch has become worse since you left us?" Ever since I had moved to town, I had almost stopped speaking Dutch. I spoke Somali with Yasmin and English with Ellen and Hanneke. I understood simple Dutch, but it didn't yet come out of my mouth right; it embarrassed me.

The refugee officer offered to put a notice up in his church, to find someone who would agree to give us a free hour of conversation in Dutch every week. That was how, about a year after I arrived in Holland, I met Johanna.

Johanna became like a mother to me, as I gradually began to adapt to this strange but pleasant country. Yasmin and I went to Johanna's house once a week, then twice, then as often as we felt like it. We would just drop by, as if we were in Somalia. We cooked in her kitchen and played with her children. Johanna taught us so much more than language. She taught us how to live in the West.

There were the little things. How to be economical: look for the cheaper items on the lower shelves at the supermarket; turn down the heat and wear a sweater indoors. How to navigate through society: in Holland, you open a present in front of the giver, and even if you are a woman, you must look people straight in the eye.

Johanna taught us other important things, too. She told us to speak to people directly, not pussyfoot around, just get to the point. If you had no money, you admitted it, then you looked at why you'd overspent. There was no honor, no shame, no complex preamble: you admitted the problem clearly, and you learned your lesson. She taught us to be self-reliant, and to deal with problems squarely. All my life I had watched my mother veer off and pretend problems weren't there, hoping Allah would just make them disappear on their own. But Johanna faced things. She said what she wanted; she was clear and direct instead of avoiding issues that were difficult. She would tell us, "There's nothing rude about saying no."

Johanna's house was modern, a gray-brick home with a carefully tended garden. It was small, but put together so that everything fit. The gadgets were fascinating. There was a special spoke in the garden that fanned out when you needed to dry the laundry and folded up when you didn't need it. Even the cheese slicer seemed ingenious.

Johanna's husband, Maarten, was not the boss of the household. The two of them talked things over together; they asked each other's advice. The children were allowed to interrupt them, too, and Maarten and Johanna listened to their opinions. And Maarten helped with the housework.

The kids went to bed every night at eight and not a minute later. It was a very structured life, and a lot of thought had gone into building that structure. Johanna was always consulting books on child development, and though she punished her children if they misbehaved, I don't think she ever hit them. Her family was very like the whole country: so well-kept, so well-planned, so smoothly run and attractive. It seemed nothing could go unnoticed in such a place. Sometimes that felt constricting, but it also seemed welcoming, and safe. It was a much more attractive model than any family I'd seen in the world I came from.

And most important, this family was warm to me. They took me in. Johanna was wise and skeptical, with a dry sense of humor and enormous capacity for openness and love. I began looking on her as a confidante, a guide.

I told Johanna how selfish I felt about what I had done to my parents. But Johanna didn't think there was anything wrong with putting myself first. She said it wasn't selfish to do what you wanted with your life—everyone should pursue her own happiness. She said I had done the right thing, and made me feel that I might still be a good person.

Every Islamic value I had been taught instructed me to put myself last. Life on earth is a test, and if you manage to put yourself last in this life, you are serving Allah; your place will be first in the Hereafter. The more deeply you submit your will, the more virtuous that makes you. But Johanna, Ellen, and everyone else in Holland seemed to think that it was natural to seek one's own personal happiness on earth, in the here and now.

*   *   *

After Yasmin and I moved to our apartment in Ede, I resolved that I would go out to work. Being on welfare shamed me. Sylvia and the other workers at the center had taken the time to answer my incessant questions, and I now understood roughly what a welfare state was: the able contributing to help the needy. I was able: I had arms and legs. I didn't want to keep taking and never give.

I went first to the government employment bureau. The woman there registered me, but she said there wouldn't be much point in my working. I wanted to keep on with my Dutch classes, and whatever I earned in sporadic, temporary jobs would be subtracted from my welfare payment; I would be allowed to keep only the surplus, if there was one.

I decided that I must try to work anyway, and that afternoon I registered with all the temp agencies in town. I said I was qualified as a secretary and wanted a job. My Dutch was completely inadequate, but the agency staff put my name in their data banks. Two days later a woman called from Temp Team: the Riedel orange juice factory in Ede needed a temporary cleaner.

I was supposed to clean the factory from six to eight in the morning, before the workers' shift started. The factory floor, the canteen, the toilets. It wasn't nice, but it wasn't difficult. Another job I did was packing huge rolls of thread into a flatbox at a dye manufacturer, Akzo Nobel. The boxes were taped shut by the next worker down the assembly line. In another, similar position at a biscuit factory, Delacre, I packed cookies into plastic containers. I did these two jobs several times, replacing people who were ill or on holiday for a few weeks; I also did a number of stints putting letters into envelopes at the housing corporation.

There was nothing noble about these jobs, but they weren't dishonorable either. They were mundane, but they paid money, and they were convenient: if I took the morning shifts, I could attend Dutch class in the late afternoon. I saw them as stepping stones: if I worked enough, I could earn more than my welfare benefit, and the surplus helped pay for my rent and classes.

Working at factories gave me a chance to see another social class of Dutch people. So far I had met only social workers and middle-class people who volunteered at the refugee camp. Working-class people spoke differently, and their interaction with migrants was not as easygoing. At the biscuit factory almost all the workers were women, and they divided clearly into ethnic groups: Dutch women on the one hand, and Moroccan and Turkish women on the other. They kept apart in the lunch room and on the factory floor as well. If a Moroccan woman was paired with a native Dutch woman, the work would be done shoddily and there would be constant conflict, with packages piling up and falling on the floor, whereas if Moroccans worked together they made an effort to get the job done right. It was mutual xenophobia: the Dutch thought the Moroccans were lazy and unpleasant, and the Moroccans said the Dutch stank and dressed like whores. Both groups saw themselves as superior.

The dye factory was almost all Dutch. Some of the workers had been employed there for ten, even twenty years. They liked their jobs, they told me, and I saw that they expected to work hard and get it done efficiently, that there was a kind of pleasure in doing even a lowly job well.

Gradually I was changing, learning how to adapt to this new country, to manage time, and work, and go to school, alone.

Six months after I first registered at the government labor agency, they called me in to take an IQ test. The test was very long, and I'm sure it was extremely expensive. A lot of it was math, which I have always been hopeless at; the rest of it was psychological tests and language skills— Dutch language, of course. My results were poor.

The job counselor told me I was eligible to attend a medium-level vocational course, something administrative, like bookkeeping or training to be a receptionist. Something with very little theory, which would swiftly prepare me to work. I told her that I wanted to study political science, and she said I couldn't: political science was a university course, and I could never hope to get in.

The job counselor sent me to learn bookkeeping in Wageningen, a village close to Ede. That was a very expensive course, too, but it seemed to her to be the only option. I suppose she thought that the universal language of numbers would be easier for a foreigner to grasp.

I did horribly. After four weeks my debit side had never once matched my credit side. The teacher sighed and said, "This is really not for you." I said, "I *told* them that." So he wrote a letter saying I was not suitable for bookkeeping, and I stopped attending class.

I still wanted more than this life. I had decided I wanted to study political science. If that required going to university, then that's where I would go. Ellen and Hanneke thought I was mad: a degree, sure, that was a fine ambition, but in *political science*? I tried to explain that I wanted to understand why life in Holland was so different from life in Africa. Why there was so much peace, security, and wealth in Europe. What the causes of war were, and how you built peace.

I didn't have any answers, just questions. I thought about it all the time. Every contact I had with government, I thought, "How do you get to have a government like this?" I watched Hanneke and Ellen draw up schedules with the other girls they shared their flat with—lists of who would do the cleaning and the grocery shopping and cooking. And it was like the bus timetable: all the girls actually did all the chores. Amazingly, there wasn't even any conflict about it. How did you get to be this way?

There were rules about everything in Holland. I got stopped by a policeman one evening for cycling without my lights on and I froze, assuming something horrible was going to happen. But all I got was a firm but courteous lecture and a fine of twenty-five guilders. Moreover, the policeman said I wasn't supposed to pay the fine right away; it would come in the mail. Sure enough, a month later I received a detailed bill. I thought about this system, how cleverly it prevented you ever giving a policeman money, so he never got tempted to pocket it.

Government was very present in this country. It could be bureaucratic, sometimes stupidly complex, but it also seemed very beneficial. I wanted to know how you do that. This was an infidel country, whose way of life we Muslims were supposed to oppose and reject. Why was it, then, so much better run, better led, and made for such better lives than the places we came from? Shouldn't the places where Allah was worshipped and His laws obeyed have been at peace and wealthy, and the unbelievers' countries ignorant, poor, and at war?

I wanted to understand conflict. In 1992 and 1993, it seemed as if the whole world outside the West was breaking out in civil wars and tribal conflicts. The end of the cold war had unfrozen old fault lines of hatred. And of all the countries where war had broken out, so many seemed to be Muslim. What was wrong with us? Why should infidels have peace, and Muslims be killing each other, when we were the ones who worshipped the true God? If I studied political science, I thought, I would understand that.

It wasn't going to be easy to qualify. The government had accepted my O-levels and Kenyan secretarial course as equivalent to a Havo Plus school diploma, but even this was stretching it. To get into the university, I would need another qualification called a *propadeuse*. I panicked: I thought I could never pass the math. With Ellen's help, I figured out that the easiest way for me to pass the *propadeuse* would be to study social work in a vocational college, as Ellen and Hanneke did. That way, after a year I could transfer to the university, and I could avoid encountering too much math.

I announced to my language school that I wanted to register for the Dutch language test that I would need to pass in order to attend the vocational college. My teacher was kind but told me condescendingly that it was far too early, I had been studying Dutch for only a year. People took three years; I was being impatient and irresponsible. It would be a waste of my money even to apply.

Ellen told me the teacher had no right to prevent me—it was my money. So I went to the exam center in Nijmegen and registered to take the Dutch test anyway. And I passed. Vocational college would be my next step.

All this time, I had mostly avoided other Somalis. Even when we were still living in the asylum center, I hadn't had much fun with them. Everyone who hung out in Hasna's caravan seemed to spend all their time complaining, especially the people who lived outside the asylum center, who had been in Holland for years and were simply visiting. These Somalis weren't integrating into Dutch society. They weren't working. They had nothing to do but hang about the asylum center and cadge meals. There were a few individuals who learned to cycle, who were ambitious and studied and worked—I wasn't unique—but those people had no time to socialize. The others just chewed *qat* all night and sat around talking about how horrible Holland was.

We were all facing the same confusion. We had always been sure that we, as Muslims and Somalis, were superior to unbelievers, and here we were, not superior at all. In day-to-day life, we didn't know how the cash machines worked or that you had to push a button to order the bus to stop. One time I took a bus together with Dhahabo, another Somali asylum seeker. When it hurtled right on past where we wanted to go, Dhahabo yelled "STOP!" and everyone stared at us. It was embarrassing.

Many people withdrew from such embarrassment into an enclave of shared Somaliness. Their reaction was to create a fantasy that they as Somalis knew better about everything than these inferior white people. "You don't need to teach me how to use a thermometer, our Somali thermometers are much more advanced"—that kind of attitude. "His breath smells of pig. He's only a bus driver. How dare he think he can tell me how to behave."

In my first weeks at the asylum center, as I was standing in a crowd of Somalis just outside Hasna's caravan, someone called out to us, "There's a man crying on TV!" We rushed to the television; it was a program called

I'm Sorry, where people confessed things. A huge broad-shouldered Dutch man, red-faced and squeaky-voiced, was weeping—weeping tears—over something he'd done. He whimpered, "I'm so sorry," and we stared at each other in horror and wonder. I'm sure none of us had ever seen a man cry. Then we burst out laughing. This country was so strange to us.

By the time I moved to Ede, I had come to understand Holland better. It irritated me now when Somalis who had lived in Holland for a long time complained that they were offered only lowly jobs. They wanted honorable professions: airline pilot, lawyer. When I pointed out that they had no qualifications for such work, their attitude was that everything was Holland's fault. The Europeans had colonized Somalia, which was why we all had no qualifications and were in this mess to begin with. I thought that was so clearly nonsense. We had torn ourselves apart, all on our own.

It was the same sort of defensive, arrogant attitude that I had often seen among people from rural areas who emigrated to the city, whether Mogadishu or Nairobi. Here in Holland the claim was always that we were held back by racism. Everyone seemed to be in a constant simmer of anger about how we were discriminated against because we were black. If a shopkeeper wouldn't bargain over the price of a T-shirt, Yasmin said there were special, discount prices only for white people. She and Hasna told me they often didn't bother paying for buses; they just invented appointments in town, and if the refugee office didn't give them a ticket they said they were being racist.

"If you tell a Dutch person it's racist he will give you whatever you want," Hasna once told me with satisfaction. There is discrimination in Holland—I would never deny that—but the claim of racism can also be strategic.

Sometimes it did feel good to be around Somalis, to relax with people I completely understood. Adapting to Dutch people was still a huge effort for me. But the minute I said "I'm sorry, tomorrow morning I have to wake up early," the Somalis were at me. I was acting white, who did I think I was, I looked down on them, I had become *gaalo*.

Somali young men constantly approached me on the street as if they had some kind of right to me. They made obscene suggestions; to them I was obviously immoral, and therefore available. Somali women always tried to wheedle money out of me. I didn't give it them. I used to say,

"Why should I?" I thought if they needed more money they could do factory work, too.

I felt embarrassed and even let down by the way so many Somalis accepted welfare money and then turned on the society that gave it to them. There was still a lot of clan feeling in me; I felt somehow responsible for their actions. I didn't like how they denied misdeeds, even if they were caught red-handed. I didn't like how they boasted, or the myths and transparently false conspiracy theories they propagated. I didn't like the endless gossiping or the constant complaints that they were victims of external factors. Somalis never said "Sorry" or "I made a mistake" or "I don't know": they invented excuses. All these group strategies to avoid confronting reality depressed me. Reality is not easy, but all this make-believe doesn't make it easier.

So I spent my time with Ellen and Hanneke. But that left Yasmin all alone after her school ended, which was at about three every day. A bunch of Isaq and Hawiye boys from the asylum center began coming to our apartment in the afternoons, to chew qat. (Somalis are extremely good at getting things done when they want to, and somehow there were fresh qat leaves available, even in little Ede.) Yasmin used to cook for these men, so when I came home they would all be reclining on a mat in the living room with the leaves and stalks on the floor.

For a while I crept around in my own house, feeling invaded. Among Somalis it is dishonorable to turn a guest out of your house. Finally, though, I did it the Dutch way: I told Yasmin to stop it. I didn't want these men in my place. I told Yasmin that when they rang the doorbell we would pretend to be out. After that, on the street, I got a name as the awful Darod woman who was snooty to the Isaq and the Hawiye, and that was fine by me. I didn't want to observe the code of honor any more.

The relationship between Yasmin and me began deteriorating. One night she walked out. I didn't even realize she was gone till two days later, not until I found out that my bank card and my A-status refugee papers were missing. She had just given me three hundred guilders for the month's rent, and that was gone, too. A few days later I got a letter from her. She said she was in Italy, but the letter was postmarked Denmark. She said she was sorry, and she hadn't used the bank card; the three hundred guilders wasn't really stealing because it was hers. She said she was lonely, and hated living in Holland. She said the phone bill might be high, but she had needed her family.

About a month later I received a 2,500-guilder phone bill and went berserk. I was beyond bankrupt. Johanna helped me call the phone company. They sent a detailed bill, and it was Australia, Canada, Kenya, Somalia—I had no idea Yasmin knew so many people. Johanna said, "Take Yasmin's letter to her social worker, because it proves that she made all these calls, and they will look after the bill." I did, and Yasmin's social work agency paid about two thousand guilders.

One morning in January 1994 the phone rang. It was Haweya. She was standing in a phone booth at the Frankfurt airport. It had been months since I had last called home. Now my sister was here, in Europe. She had just arrived! A huge wave of joy rushed over me. I asked Haweya if this was a just a visit, or more, and she said "More." I said, "Come to Holland—come and live with me."

I called my friends Jan and Greetje. Jan was in his late fifties and a volunteer at Refugee Aid. He suggested that Haweya take a train to the German border; he would meet her there and drive her into Holland by car, to avoid any checkpoints. That way Haweya could claim she had traveled directly to Holland. It meant she could ask for asylum in Holland instead of in Germany.

When Jan's car finally drove up with Haweya inside, we hugged and screamed and jumped and laughed and hugged again. But after a while Haweya slumped into a chair and started crying. Finally, she told me she had had an abortion in Nairobi. A man who was from Trinidad, who worked for the UN, who was divorced—she had loved this man, and she had become pregnant.

A man from Trinidad—uncircumcised, not even a Muslim. Flat-nosed, round-faced, kinky-haired. My mother would have seen such a man as subhuman, like the Kenyans. What Haweya had done was, in clan terms, unforgivable. Running away from your husband was one thing, but getting pregnant out of wedlock, and with such a person—it was as if the whole Osman Mahamud family had been impregnated by somebody from Trinidad.

Haweya's lover arranged for her to have an abortion, discreetly, with an Indian doctor. Afterward, when she felt so rocky, he said, "Take time off, go to Holland, see your sister."

I choked back the Somali in me, which was appalled by the whole story. I told her to stop crying. I said these weren't the right circumstances to have a child, be sensible, don't torture yourself. I said the sorts of things Johanna would say, and then I put Haweya to bed in Yasmin's old room, just as Johanna would have done.

But Haweya didn't spring back to life. She was dreamy, absent-minded, unfocused. She couldn't sleep. She said the fights at home with Ma had gotten completely out of hand. She had come to me with no plan, no idea of what to do next.

I was so eager to have my sister live with me. I helped her cook up a story that would get her refugee status. Haweya registered as an asylum seeker in Lunteren, and the refugee center agreed to allow her to stay with me as long as she signed in once a week.

Haweya started Dutch lessons, but it was just one lesson every week at the refugee center with a volunteer, because she wasn't allowed to take proper classes until she was given refugee papers. I took her out with me and my friends. We took long walks together, and watched all the films we wanted to without fear of punishment. We took trips to Amsterdam; I taught her to cycle. We had many happy moments. But so often, Haweya didn't seem to want to be anywhere. She spent most of the time lying on the sofa, watching TV until the programs turned to snow. She had bouts of crying: tears simply rolled down her cheeks. She tramped off on long walks on her own.

We called Ma from time to time, always using her Indian neighbors' phone. Our conversations were predictable. Ma would always tell us to pray, to fast, to read the Quran. Or she would complain. She constantly told me she had sacrificed her whole life for her children and all of us had let her down. Her legs were covered with open sores from her psoriasis. Her head hurt. We had left her to die like this; it was our fault. Mahad didn't look after her and never held down a job; he thought he was too good for anything he was qualified to do. Calling Ma was not always pleasant, but I did it, and I sent money, because it was my duty.

The months went by. Haweya began spending much more time at the asylum center, seeking companionship. I found out she was having a relationship with a Somali boy there, and I suspected that they were sleeping together. One day Haweya told me she was pregnant again. Here I had cut almost all ties with Somalia and my sister was reviving them.

I got really angry with her. I hate to think about it now. I yelled, "Is this going to be a habit? To get pregnant once may be forgivable, but now you are in Holland! Condoms are free at the refugee center!" I told Haweya, "You can't have another abortion—this is murder. You'll have the baby, and I will look after it."

I moralized. Haweya insisted she wanted an abortion anyway. We had a huge fight. I went with her to the refugee center to ask for medical assistance. I asked the social work counselor, Josée, to talk to Haweya, because I was worried about her.

To my surprise, Josée said Haweya had already approached her. She said, "There are deep problems. But don't worry about your sister. I see her every week and I believe it's helping." I had no idea that Haweya was in any kind of psychotherapy. Josée said this was because Haweya was afraid of my judgment.

So Haweya had the abortion, and after she received her refugee status, she began attending proper language school. Something brightened about her for a while; my little sister's sparky, quick wit began flashing through again. She could be charming, sharp, funny, stylish. But then she would slump again and stop looking after her clothes and her hair. Or she would turn on people; she could be very aggressive. She still wasn't sleeping well.

I couldn't register for the same course in social work as Ellen and Hanneke, although their college was in Ede. It was a Christian school: you had to acknowledge the existence of the Trinity to attend classes there. For me, at the time, that was absolute blasphemy. To associate Allah with other unities and say he had a child—you would burn in Hell for saying this. Allah is not begotten, nor does he beget. It was out of the question that I attend such a place.

I wanted to apply to a secular vocational college in Arnhem, but an official at Refugee Aid told me I wouldn't be happy there: I should go to Driebergen, which was also a secular college but much more *multicultural,* a code word for ethnically mixed. Again, the advice was well-meaning but it was based on preconceived notions about where I, as an immigrant, would feel comfortable. And of course such advice only reinforced the immigrants' urge to build enclaves.

When I went to Driebergen to apply, the administrator told me I would have to pass an admissions exam. There would be papers in Dutch, history, and civics. Reeling, I asked, "Where are the books to study for them?" The administrator said they had a class that helped students prepare for the exam. This preexam class lasted for four months: I could start in February 1994 and take the exam in June.

I went back to the government Labor Bureau and said I had found what I wanted to do. As I had dropped bookkeeping, could they now kindly pay for this precollege course in Dutch history? But the Labor Bureau refused: they couldn't finance something that wasn't authorized by the IQ test I'd taken. They said I would have to apply for a student grant, which I wouldn't be eligible for until I was actually admitted to the college itself. So I paid for the preparation on my own.

It was nothing like school in Kenya. We sat in a circle and called the teacher by his first name. There was no "Good morning, Mrs. Nyere" in unison, and no uniform. If you failed the exams you got a second chance, which seemed a little foolish, but still, kind. And it was only three hundred guilders. For this, I didn't mind scrimping.

The most fascinating class was history. Every week we discussed a chapter in the textbook, which covered not just Holland but the history of the modern world. Each country had a chapter, and I read every word of all of them. There was Germany: how it became a state, then the Weimar Republic, the rise of Hitler, the Second World War. The Russian Revolution: tsars, Bolsheviks, Stalin. The American civil rights movement, the Vietnam War. Each country had a life; it struggled and took form, systems rose and fell—it was like a story.

The book told a very romantic, optimistic view of modern history. There was a chapter on "Colonization and Decolonization," which ended with prospects for a bright future for Africa. There was the end of the cold war and the fall of the Berlin Wall, which brought an end to communism. There was the story of the United Nations. I was completely absorbed.

I realized this text was just an overview to give us a grip on what happened where. I wanted more. I wanted to study further why so many of the decolonized countries had fallen apart, and why the countries that I had lived in weren't working.

That history book taught me Dutch. The civics class, on the other hand, was full of terms I didn't understand, like *municipality* and *upper chamber*. I scraped through it. I failed the Dutch class by just one point: I still couldn't write proper grammar. But because I had my Dutch equivalency exam, they let me enroll in Driebergen Vocational College anyway. By the skin of my teeth, I had made it.

I could start attending college in Driebergen in September. I applied for, and received, a student loan; then, at the end of August, I was called to an introductory weekend. The other girls—they were mostly girls in the social work course—were friendly and open, but they were much younger than I. At twenty-four years old, I was gawky, wore ill-fitting clothes, and cut my hair really short, like a boy's.

I liked it that way. Looking after long hair, braiding and oiling it, was so difficult to do in Holland. Dutch hairdressers couldn't understand my hair. With it shorn, I felt free of all the bother, and much more. I couldn't feel anyone's eyes boring into me. With no headscarf, with short hair and jeans, I was nobody's thing. No Somalis attended the vocational college, so nobody felt he could tell me what to do. There were a few Moroccans and Turks, but I was not their responsibility.

I felt under intense pressure: I really had to prove to myself that I could make it. Social work didn't appeal to me that much in itself—for me it was the simplest way to get into political science—but I was unexpectedly thrilled by the course in psychology. The idea of taking some distance from yourself, of thinking in a systematic way about who you are and how the mind is built up, gave me a whole new way of looking at life.

Meeting Freud put me in contact with an alternative moral system. In Nairobi I had had plenty of contact with Christianity, and had heard of Buddhists and Hindus. But I didn't for one instant imagine that a moral framework for humanity could exist that wasn't religious. There was always a God. Not having one was immoral. If you didn't accept God, then you couldn't have a morality. This is why the words *infidel* and *apostate* are so hideous to a Muslim: they are synonymous with immorality in the deepest way.

But here was psychology, a story with no religious roots. It was about drives, the passion to eat, have sex, excrete, kill, and how you mastered those drives by learning to understand them. When I read the first week's assignment I thought, "Are they trying to make people become unbelievers?" But the material was fascinating. I recognized so much of myself and my family in it. I learned about Rogers and Skinner and Pavlov, and reveled in these theories about what makes human individuals tick.

I also found clear explanations of sexuality, which had tortured me so much as an adolescent. Gradually I began to see that the way I had been brought up didn't work. Excision of my genitals didn't eliminate the human sex drive, and neither did the fear of hellfire. Repression only led to hypocrisy and lying, strategies that corrupt the human individual, and it failed to protect people from unwanted pregnancy and disease.

The Dutch apparently did things differently. They explained puberty to their children, and told them that sexual feelings would come along with the physical changes. Dutch teenagers were apparently expected to experiment with their sexual feelings, but they did so using their reason, with more information than I had ever dreamed was available.

I also took a class in child development, which was again entirely new to me. I wondered how I could be even vaguely balanced when my parents had paid attention to none of this: the cognitive development, the emotional security, the motor skills, the social skills, all of which were supposed to be vital to creating a well-formed human being.

I read that bullying could destroy a child's self-confidence, making him withdrawn and antisocial, and remembered how pitilessly Haweya was bullied in primary school. It didn't occur to me at the time to think of excision as a kind of a trauma, but I thought about the way Ma beat us. I didn't want to judge my mother. I love her. Everyone I knew in Nairobi hit their kids. But to discipline us without ever explaining anything—according to the books, this was damaging, and wrong.

I made friends with Naima, a Moroccan girl in my class who cycled to Ede Station every morning and rode the same train as I to Driebergen. Naima was my age, and with her I felt something of the easy familiarity of being among the Somalis, with none of the sharpness of their disapproval. We cooked for each other, and her food was very much like mine. During Ramadan, both of us fasted. With Naima there was none of the punctuality you had to observe with Dutch people, which was a relief, too.

Naima was married. She had come to Holland as a child and had lived here all her life. She didn't wear a headscarf but was active in a Moroccan women's group at her local community center, and they danced and ate together. When she took me there, it reminded me of being with Halwa and her sisters.

Naima came in one morning with a black eye. I asked, "What happened to you?" She said her husband beat her; she was totally matter-of-fact about it. Over the next few weeks she got beaten again and again. I told her she was mad to let him do it. I told her she could leave her husband. In this country, she could file for divorce.

But Naima knew that I understood why she couldn't do it. Her husband was from her father's village. She had not met him before they were betrothed. That was how she had always lived. Even in Holland, where it was easily possible, Naima felt she simply couldn't just break away. Leaving her husband would mean leaving her family. It would shame them and leave her homeless. Where could she go? Where could she hide? I had managed to disappear in Holland, but Naima's family lived here: they would find her.

Naima complained constantly, but it was about the Dutch. She was always insisting that shopkeepers looked askance at her because they were racist, and they didn't want Moroccans in their shop. Personally, I thought they were staring at her bruises, and told her so. They never looked strangely at me, and I was far darker than Naima. She said it was different for me because I was a refugee, and Dutch people thought refugees were romantic. I thought this was illogical: How could anyone tell that I was a refugee?

But in the train, when the conductor came to check our student transport cards, Naima would fume that he had stared at her card longer than at the white girls'. She never complained about the violence and humiliation she suffered at home, only about Dutch racism. I think now that this obsession with identifying racism, which I saw so often among Somalis too, was really a comfort mechanism, to keep people from feeling personally inadequate and to externalize the causes of their unhappiness.

Naima was right about one thing: it didn't seem fair to expect the same from her as from my Dutch schoolmates, who had nothing to do except study and worry about whether people liked them enough. Her circumstances were so much less nurturing.

I would read psychology books all afternoon and then look up at Haweya on the sofa. She seemed like an object case of every kind of neurosis there was. All psychology students feel this way about their flatmates, but not all of them are clumsy enough to say so. I did, though. I was always telling Haweya what I thought was wrong with her. I also told her she should stop therapy with Josée. I thought my friend Hanneke would be a far better choice.

Haweya felt assaulted by all of this. She felt that I was implying that she had some kind of mental illness. She switched counselors, but she thought Hanneke was too shallow to understand her. Soon after she began seeing her, Haweya stopped going to therapy at all. After that, she became impossible to live with. She stopped attending school and would sit all day on the couch, watching TV day and night, letting dishes pile up in the sink. Her dirty clothes were strewn on the floor. Sometimes she would barely look up when I came in. She used to cry for days about the way she had mistreated Ma, and how she would burn in Hell for it. Ma had not wished her good-bye, and Haweya had left telling her, "I hate you. From now on you are no longer my mother."

I sympathized with Haweya, but we quarreled. I couldn't stand the way she was living, lying on the sofa all day like some vacant life form. One time I got so angry I pulled the TV plug out of the wall and kicked the TV down the stairs. Haweya just stared at me, then locked the front door shut against me. She wouldn't let me back in, though I pleaded.

I was barefoot, and it was cold outside, but I ended up walking to Johanna and Maarten's house. Johanna and Maarten had been telling me for a long time that Haweya and I should stop living together. They knew how much we bickered, and they thought I was looking after Haweya too much, destroying my chances of doing well in school. They drove me home, and Johanna laid down the law to Haweya: she should move out.

Haweya liked the idea. There was a one-room apartment available in a building near where Ellen and Hanneke lived, ten minutes away by bicycle. We joked that this way no one would bother her about doing the dishes. We could invite each other over. Johanna lent Haweya the money to pay the guarantee on the flat; Maarten helped us move and built her new furniture.

After Haweya moved out, she went back to language school. She seemed to take charge of her life again. We saw each other often, in the beginning. She seemed to crave my company. It was almost as if we could be more friendly now that we were slightly apart. A Dutch girl moved into my flat; life became more peaceful.

In May 1995, Sylvia, the social worker at the asylum center, persuaded me to try to become an official Somali-Dutch interpreter. She said my Dutch was far better than most of the official interpreters she worked with, and the work paid well. The Immigration Service paid its interpreters forty-four guilders an hour, plus twenty-two guilders for time spent in transport, compared to the thirteen guilders an hour I earned at the biscuit factory. I was still attending vocational college at the time, but Sylvia said translating would be ideal: I could do it in my free time, after school.

I went to the Immigration Service headquarters in Zwolle and applied. They tested my Dutch (though not my Somali) and said I could try out the job for a couple of months and they would see how it went. They suggested I get a pager. Everyone at college thought I was so cool when the pager beeped and I had to rush off to a phone.

I bought myself some professional clothes: a black knee-length skirt, a long, tailored shirt, and some pumps. My first job was to translate for a

Somali asylum seeker at a police station. For me, it was a momentous occasion.

It was just like my own experience asking for asylum, only now, less than three years later, my position had changed completely. The asylum seeker was a Darod man with a little beard and ankle-length trousers. When I came in, he scrutinized me and asked, "Are you the translator?". When I said yes, he sneered at me. He said, "But you're naked. I want a real translator." So I translated that, and the Dutch civil servant told the man, "I decide who translates, you don't."

The atmosphere had certainly shifted from my own courteous tea and coffee. It was all business. The Darod man tried to find out my ancestry, who I was, but the civil servant put a stop to it. Neither of them even looked at me while the interview went on. I was just a part of the process, like a typewriter. I found this soothing. Although the Somali man's contempt bothered me, I knew I must learn to control my emotions if I was to become a professional. This was my work, a simple transaction, no different from packing boxes at a factory. And anyway, *he* needed *me*.

Afterward, the policeman handed me a form with the time I had worked and the amount I would earn all filled in. I walked out, thrilled.

My next assignment was in a reception center in Schalkhaar. I would be interpreting for a Galla woman who had lived near Afgoye. The Hawiye fighters had taken her and put her with other Galla women in a compound. They were there to be raped, although they also were made to cook and clean and get firewood for the soldiers. Telling her story, this woman began shaking. She spoke in small, short, quiet sentences, and as I tried to pass them on, I couldn't control my tears.

I said to the civil servant, who was a woman, "I know I'm messing up. I've only just started working and I'm so sorry. I just need to take a minute to wash my face." But when the Dutch woman looked at me, I saw she was crying, too.

The girl's story was so horrible. She had become pregnant and given birth. The baby was always with her. Then one night one of the Hawiye soldiers picked the baby off her and threw it in the fire. He forced her to watch as the child burned.

She was thin. She said she was twenty-eight or twenty-nine, but she looked over fifty. She kept talking about all the other Galla women with whom she had been kept captive. She had escaped when another Hawiye subclan took over the compound; she didn't know what had happened to the others.

Two months later I went back to Schalkhaar for another job. That same civil servant caught sight of me and rushed over to tell me that the Galla woman had been given refugee status. We smiled and congratulated each other. Still, by then I knew how many others failed to get asylum in Holland.

There are so many different kinds of suffering in this world. Many times while I was working as an interpreter I wished someone would give these people a chance—especially the women, who could really make something of their lives here. But I knew when I was translating a story that would not qualify the person as a refugee.

I translated for men who had killed, who were clearly soldiers; I even translated for a man who was a notorious torturer in the Godka, Siad Barré's torture center in Mogadishu. Now family members of the people he had tortured were hunting him down. I didn't say anything: I was just the interpreter. I don't know if he got in.

At the end of June, I took my first-year finals at the vocational college, and I passed. I had a *propadeuse.* Now I could claim my right to attend the oldest and finest university in Holland: the University of Leiden.

CHAPTER 13

Leiden

I could study political science in just three universities: Amsterdam, Nijmegen, or Leiden. In Nijmegen the courses didn't interest me; it was all public administration—land use and waterways—and social geography. Amsterdam appeared chaotic: I had heard that students marked their own exams and demanded equality with professors. But Leiden, Holland's oldest university, had rigorous standards. And when I visited the old city, with the tiny canals and flocks of students careering around on bicycles, I wanted with all my heart to be a part of it.

Leiden was so pretty it was like walking through an illustration from the Ladybird books of fairy tales with which I'd learned English in Nairobi. Houses had long-necked bell towers, stepping-stone roofs, and curiously tiny, twisted staircases that I always found so perilous to navigate, each little step much thinner than your foot. Every staircase made me feel more foreign, yet I marveled at this dollhouse of a city.

So, midway through my year at the vocational college, I had applied to Leiden. That was not a happy experience. The woman at the desk told me she was legally obliged to register my application, but made it clear that she thought it most unwise. She sent me to talk to the dean of students, who also seemed dubious. She told me I would do far better to return to vocational college and complete my three-year social work course there: it would qualify me for a real job right away. I might fail a degree in political science in Leiden. It was perhaps too abstract to be useful. Better to stay where I was, it might suit me better. I told her I wanted to apply anyway. I was determined to try, at least.

Now that I had my *propadeuse,* the condition for my entry, I could begin classes in Leiden. Almost immediately, I was swamped. The first three courses were basic: Introduction to Political Science, Introduction to History, Introduction to Public Administration. There were piles of books to read every week: books on the art of governance, books about what is a state, books about the history of Holland and Europe. We didn't have to memorize them, but we needed to know the themes, the theories, and—this was new—we needed to develop our own opinion. We were always asked what *we* thought.

In spite of everyone telling me what a poor choice political science was, I loved it. To others it might seem dry, but not to me. From birth I had been fed shards of this story: democracy, justice, nation, war. Now, with kind and thoughtful teaching, good governance was making sense to me as a process, something that had grown.

European history was a gripping chronicle, which began with chaos. Holland came from nothing: mud and poverty and foreign rule. Even the land was constructed by a collective effort. The sea tides roaring over half the country were too powerful to confront individually, so the Dutch learned to be clever and work together. They cut channels through the silt to control the flooding and built new land where the sea had been. They learned to be resourceful and persistent. They learned negotiation. They learned that reason is better than force. Above all, they learned to compromise.

Half of Holland was Protestant, half Catholic. In every other European country, that was a recipe for massacre, but in Holland, people worked it out. After a period of oppression and bloodshed, they learned that you cannot win a civil war: everyone loses. They set up a system so people could be separate *and* equal. Two big blocs developed in Dutch society, Protestants and Catholics. Later a third bloc developed for social democrats, who were both Protestant and Catholic, and there was also a much smaller group of nonreligious, secular people called the liberals. These blocs were the "pillars," the foundation of Dutch society.

These pillars operated just like clans. For generations, Dutch Catholics and Protestants went to separate schools, hospitals, clubs, shops; they even had separate channels on TV and separate radio stations. As late as 1995, in Leiden, the pillars at least partly defined who you were and who you knew, as the clans did in Somalia. But here everything was negotiated and shared out in apparently seamless equanimity.

I came to realize how deeply the Dutch are attached to freedom, and why. Holland was in many ways the capital of the European Enlightenment. Four hundred years ago, when European thinkers severed the hard bands of church dogma that had constrained people's minds, Holland was the center of free thought. The Enlightenment cut European culture from its roots in old fixed ideas of magic, kingship, social hierarchy, and the domination of priests, and regrafted it onto a great strong trunk that supported the equality of each individual, and his right to free opinions and self-rule—so long as he did not threaten civic peace and the freedom of others. Here, in Leiden, was where the Enlightenment had taken hold. Here, the Dutch let each other be free. And here, this commitment to freedom took hold of me, too.

Sometimes I could almost sense a little shutter clicking shut in my brain, so that I could keep reading my textbooks without struggling to align their content with my belief in Islam. Sometimes it seemed as if almost every page I read challenged me as a Muslim. Drinking wine and wearing trousers were nothing compared to reading the history of ideas.

People had contested the whole basis of the idea of God's power on earth, and they had done it with reasoning that was beautiful and compelling. Darwin said creation stories were a fairy tale. Freud said we had power over ourselves. Spinoza said there were no miracles, no angels, no need to pray to anything outside ourselves: God was us, and nature. Emil Durkheim said humans fantasized religion to give themselves a sense of security. I read all this, and then had to try to stuff it all behind the little shutter in my brain.

In every way, to read these books of Western history was sinning. Even the history of how modern states formed confronted me with the contradictions of my belief in Allah. The European separation of God's world from the state was itself *haram*. The Quran says there can be no government without God; the Quran is Allah's book of laws for the conduct of worldly affairs.

In February 1995 there were huge floods across Holland. When Somalis are faced with catastrophic weather, drought and flooding, they all get together and pray. Natural disasters are signs from God, to show humans they are misbehaving on earth. But the Dutch blamed their government for failing to maintain the dikes properly. I didn't see anybody praying.

It was such a strange paradox. In Holland everything had been founded on people's religion, but the whole nation, at its core, seemed so ungodly. Here one could (and many did) contest the very existence of God at every turn. People openly disbelieved every aspect of religion. The very shape of Holland seemed like a challenge to Allah. Reclaiming land from the sea, controlling flooding with canals—it was like defying God.

Almost everything was secular here. God was mocked everywhere. The most common expletive used in Dutch is *Godverdomme*. I heard it all the time—"God damn me," to me the worst thing possible—and yet nobody was struck by a thunderbolt. Society worked without reference to God, and it seemed to function perfectly. This man-made system of government was so much more stable, peaceful, prosperous, and happy than the supposedly God-devised systems I had been taught to respect.

Sometimes the shutter wouldn't close any more: I had stuffed too many ideas behind it. I would have an attack of guilt, and take stock of myself: the trousers, the hair, the books, the ideas. I would think about Sister Aziza's angels, who were certainly still on my shoulders, watching me, recording it all. I would tell myself, weakly, that I was pursuing knowledge. If Allah had predetermined everything, he must have foreseen me doing this.

I told myself that, one day, when I had developed the willpower, when I was back in a Muslim environment, I would find the strength to repent and truly obey God's laws. Meanwhile, I would be honest. I would try not to harm anyone. I would not myself adopt the ideas I was reading about. But I would keep reading them.

With the exception of statistics, which I failed repeatedly, I enjoyed every subject at Leiden, particularly political philosophy. Humans have made so many observations; I felt so lucky that I didn't have to think of all of this by myself. It was such a privilege to watch people thinking, page after page. Everything in the books was so beautifully put together, so rational. We learned to define, to think clearly about what we were saying, to set out our thinking in building blocks and argue with data. In that way we improved on older theories and expanded our understanding of the world.

Most of those first courses in Leiden stressed the empirical. Just the facts: the facts themselves are a beautiful idea. They were about method and reason. There was no place here for emotions and irrationality.

Sometimes, reading history or philosophy books, I would actually get goose bumps. I remember this happening when I read the story of the First World War. At the end of the nineteenth century, science brought industry, wealth, and medicine to Europe. Then, as the century turned, countries become suspicious of each other. They formed alliances and stocked arms. They sought power and territory. War broke out, and a whole generation of young men, who had just recently escaped from poverty and disease, were mowed down in the trenches. People came back to their senses and stopped the war, only to repeat it twenty years later. It was appalling, but also completely gripping to me, like a novel, and it bore so many parallels with what I had known in other countries.

When I turned and looked at the kids sitting next to me, they clearly didn't feel the same thrill I did. To them, it was a story they knew by heart already, just another grade. Most of the students in Leiden were eighteen years old, and this was their first experience of living away from their parents.

All the students in Leiden seemed to be white, with blond hair and light blue eyes. There were clear clan distinctions among them, however. There were the girls with their hair in stiff little bobs, who wore blue eye makeup and sweaters that said Benetton on them; they were the clones. The girls who colored their hair and let the roots show were trash. And girls whose hair was oily and unwashed were sleazy; they did drugs. As soon as a girl who looked slightly different left a group of students, the others gossiped about her. Although these girls identified each other by dress and accent—by class, not clan—it was just like being among Somalis, trying to figure out if everyone was Osman Mahamud and then all feeling comfortable to talk about the Hawiye.

Sometimes I would remark during a lesson that something was a class issue. People would always say, "We have no class problems in Holland. We are an egalitarian society." I didn't believe it for a second.

Top people sent their children to Leiden, CEOs and people in the government. These children had their own upper-class fraternity, Minerva, within which they divided into old money—the old Dutch nobility—and the nouveaux riches. They all gathered in the grand old Minerva student house, and their social lives circulated within the club. Most of them did law or banking. If they were doing social science, they studied government. Political science was apparently considered left-wing.

There were all sorts of fraternities. Catena was for nonconformists, kids from intellectual families in Amsterdam who didn't want to go through a week of hazing. They had multiply pierced ears, wore dirty clothes, and organized environmental protests. Quintus was for people who couldn't get into Minerva and wished they had. In my first few weeks people took me around to these fraternities. When they told me about the de-greening week—that's the Dutch phrase for hazing—I told them I had already lost my bloom. I was twenty-five; this was not for me. I had been "de-greened" by life.

I wasn't tempted either by the student dorm I visited when I first arrived in Leiden. It was filthy. So I rented a room from a lovely woman, Chantal, who had a big house in the suburbs. I bought a brand-new bicycle, which I still have a decade later, and rode it to class every morning.

For the first few months, I didn't socialize much. When I wasn't studying I was working as a translator. I had now registered as a Somali interpreter, and I worked all the time. In the morning, if I didn't have class, I would leave my beeper on. I bought my own phone so I could be available for phone translations from all over the country until late at night. I was called by police, by hospitals, by law courts, by all kinds of shelters.

The worst calls were when I had to break the news to someone that, no, the authorities won't allow your wife and children to come to Holland to be with you. No, we cannot give you the opportunity to go back to Somalia and get your children, even though you have been raped and your husband has been killed and four of your fingers have been cut off. Or, I have to inform you that you have HIV/AIDS. Sometimes I would put the phone down in my little room and shake with the feelings I had just translated.

One Somali girl lived in an asylum center, just as I had, and she had an Ethiopian girlfriend, just like me. This Somali girl got in a car with four men; she thought she was meeting her girlfriend at a party. She was raped repeatedly, then ran away from the house and was found in the village, which was when the police called me. I sat in my little room in the attic of Chantal's lovely home and tried to translate what they were telling her. I explained to this girl that she must not wash herself, because the sperm and blood that were still trailing between her thighs were evidence. I couldn't ask if she had been infibulated because the rules are you can't insert your own questions and opinions, you are purely a machine. I could only try to calm her down.

The girl was completely hysterical. She was frantic that the other people in the asylum center would shun her because she was defiled. The policewoman I was translating for had me talk the girl through her story and persuade her to give evidence. She told her that in six months they would give her an HIV test, if she wanted one. I asked the policewoman if it would be possible to have her transferred to another refugee center, so there would be no shame; she agreed. The girl grew calmer.

I put the phone down, blown to pieces by this horrible world, and then I had to walk downstairs to have dinner with Chantal. There could not have been a greater contrast with her tidy, gentle, pleasant life. Sometimes it was hard even to talk about what I had been doing. When I told Chantal my stories, she was horrified. She said these things were unheard of in Holland.

It didn't occur to me then, but this was also another kind of education—an education in suffering, abuse, pain, misery, and the evils of ignorance.

I did abortion clinic translations. If it was a phone translation, then mostly I had to explain to the girl what abortion means, translate a few questions: Does the father know? Have you thought about keeping the baby? I knew the form by heart. Then, when I put the phone down, I would know that this girl would now have an abortion, and I had been instrumental in this sinful act. I would stuff it all behind the shutter in my brain and go on to my next class or appointment.

Sometimes I would have to go to the abortion clinic and explain to the girl that because her scar was still almost completely closed up, she would have to have complete anesthesia to cut it open and remove the baby. The girl would always be horrified and insist, "Then you must resew me afterward." Mostly the doctors would nod, but they never did it. One young doctor asked me to explain. "It's unnecessary and dangerous for you, and we in Holland don't do these things," he told me to tell the girl. She just cried, helplessly.

When I went to the awful places—the police stations, the prisons, the abortion clinics and penal courts, the unemployment offices and the shelters for battered women—I began to notice how many dark faces looked back at me. It was not something you could avoid noticing, coming straight in from creamy-blond Leiden. I began to wonder why so many immigrants—so many Muslims—were there.

It was particularly striking when I visited women's shelters—terrible, depressing places. The addresses were supposed to be secret. Perhaps thirty women, but sometimes as many as a hundred, would live in each shelter, and children ran everywhere in the living space. There were hardly any white women: only women from Morocco, from Turkey, from Afghanistan—Muslim countries—alongside some Hindu women from Surinam.

The Somali cases were almost always the same, again and again. The husband took all the welfare money, spent it on *qat,* and when the wife hid the money he would beat her until finally the police intervened.

One Somali woman was about my age, from a rural area. She couldn't read or write Somali or speak a word of Dutch. She had been married in Somalia, to a man who had come to visit, looking for a wife, and who then brought her straight to Holland. She almost never left the apartment on her own: she was frightened of the foreign streets. Her husband beat her; finally, the police brought her, horribly bruised and cut, to the women's shelter. This woman was not only homeless in Holland; she could not go back to her family in Somalia either. She told me it was Allah's will. "Allah gave me these circumstances and, if I am patient, Allah will remove this misery."

Women like this never pressed charges. The prospect of making their way alone seemed to them impossible. They were convinced that by accepting systematic, really merciless abuse, they were serving Allah and earning a place in Heaven. They always went back to their husband.

I was only a translator, but I absorbed these stories and had to confront the unfairness of it. The social workers would always ask the women, "Do you have family here? Can they help you?" The women would say to me, "But they support my husband, of course!" You must obey your husband if you are Muslim. If you refuse your husband and he rapes you, that is your fault. Allah says husbands should beat their wives if they misbehave; it's in the Quran.

This attitude made me angry. I knew that many Dutch women were abused, too. But their community and their family didn't approve of it. Nobody blamed them for the violence, or told them to obey better.

I went to prisons, to the penitentiaries in Rotterdam and The Hague. Mostly they were violent assault cases; Somalis weren't usually involved in stealing or dealing drugs. But if Somali men disagree, losing their temper and grabbing a weapon is almost second nature. One man had hit his landlord on the head with a hammer when he came to the flat to ask for the rent. Social services sent the man to counseling, but I don't believe there was jail time.

I went to remedial schools, schools for children with learning disabilities, schools for the mentally handicapped and the deaf. Once, I was called to a school to help a teacher explain to some parents that their seven-year-old was extremely aggressive. If he beat up one more child he would have to be sent to a special school for aggression treatment. I had trouble even finding the words in Somali to explain what aggression *treatment* might be.

The child told his side of the story: a kid stuck his tongue out at him and called him a bad name, so he beat him up. Doing this was completely congruent with his upbringing. In Somalia, you attack. You hit first. If you wait to be hit, you'll only be bullied more. I was taught that, too.

Having heard the kid's story, the parents said, "See: the other child started it!" The teacher, who was a young woman, said, "But this other child didn't hit." And the parents, in chorus, exclaimed, "You don't wait to be hit!"

I had to ask to be released from the rule of strict translation so I could explain things. I told the teacher, "Where we come from, aggression is a survival tactic: we teach our children to hit first. You will have to explain more."

The teacher looked at me as though I was mad. She explained that if all the children were allowed to hit each other, then it would be survival of the fittest: the strongest would bully the others. And the parents nodded. This satisfied them, because they wanted their child to be the strongest.

Finally, I said to the parents, "Look, in Holland, if you hit people, then they think something is wrong with you. Here, they solve disagreements by talking. If your son continues to hit, he will be taken to a place where the children are mentally unwell, to be treated for an illness."

So then they listened. They made all sorts of agreements and arrangements to meet again. When the meeting ended, all three of them said how illuminating it had been for them, to see that such an unusual culture could exist.

I cycled home thinking, "This is why Somalia is having a civil war and Holland isn't." It was all there. People in Holland agree that violence is bad. They make a huge effort to teach their children to channel aggression and resolve their disputes verbally. They had analyzed conflict and set up institutions to regulate it. This was what it meant, to be citizens.

I wasn't strong enough to think all these things through just yet. I didn't feel ready to step back and ask myself why so many immigrants—so many Muslim immigrants—were violent, on welfare, poor. I just absorbed the facts. But I was beginning to see that Muslims in Holland were being allowed to form their own pillar in Dutch society, with their own schools and their own way of life, just like Catholics and Jews. They were being left politely alone to live in their own world. The idea was that immigrants needed self-respect, which would come from a strong sense of membership in their community. They should be permitted to set up Quranic schools on Dutch soil. There should be government subsidies for Muslim community groups. To force Muslims to adapt to Dutch values was thought to conflict with those values; people ought to be free to believe and behave as they wish.

The Dutch adopted these policies because they wanted to be good people. Their country had behaved unspeakably in Indonesia, and didn't (much) resist Hitler; in Holland, a greater percentage of Jews were deported during the Second World War than in any other country in Western Europe. Dutch people felt guilty about this recent past. When massive immigration began in Holland, which wasn't until the 1980s, there was a sense among the Dutch that society should behave with decency and understanding toward these people and accept their differences and beliefs.

But the result was that immigrants lived apart, studied apart, socialized apart. They went to separate schools—special Muslim schools or ordinary schools in the inner city, which other families fled.

At the Muslim schools there were no children from Dutch families. The little girls were veiled and often separated from the boys, either in the classroom or during prayer and sports. The schools taught geography and physics just like any school in Holland, but they avoided subjects that ran contrary to Islamic doctrine. Children weren't encouraged to ask questions, and their creativity was not stimulated. They were taught to keep their distance from unbelievers and to obey.

This compassion for immigrants and their struggles in a new country resulted in attitudes and policies that perpetuated cruelty. Thousands of Muslim women and children in Holland were being systematically abused, and there was no escaping this fact. Little children were excised on kitchen tables—I knew this from Somalis for whom I translated. Girls who chose their own boyfriends and lovers were beaten half to death or even killed; many more were regularly slapped around. The suffering of all these women was unspeakable. And while the Dutch were generously contributing money to international aid organizations, they were also ignoring the silent suffering of Muslim women and children in their own backyard.

Holland's multiculturalism—its respect for Muslims' way of doing things—wasn't working. It was depriving many women and children of their rights. Holland was trying to be tolerant for the sake of consensus, but the consensus was empty. The immigrants' culture was being preserved at the expense of their women and children and to the detriment of the immigrants' integration into Holland. Many Muslims never learned Dutch and rejected Dutch values of tolerance and personal liberty. They married relatives from their home villages and stayed, inside Holland, in their tiny bubble of Morocco or Mogadishu.

I worked every day as an interpreter, before class, after class, on weekends. At night I translated documents, often reports on children with suspected learning disabilities. The child would be three years old, not talking, unable to play with educational toys like blocks and puzzles, did not recognize a pen. The mother would be young, uneducated, barely able to speak Dutch. There were medical reports on battered women or social workers' recommendations that children should be removed from their parents' homes. Twenty-five cents a word made seventy-five guilders a page. I could easily have quit school and made a very good living as a Somali interpreter for the rest of my life, but I didn't think of it for one minute.

I was worried about Haweya. While I was picking my way through my textbooks in Leiden, dictionary in hand, Haweya seemed to be falling apart. She could be charming, but her mood swings had become much more intense. They made her seem harsh and hostile, and many people were afraid of her.

At first, Haweya's guilt over her abortion seemed natural to me. She told me Allah would never forgive her: she had killed, not once, but twice. But then one day when we went out together, she put on a headscarf. She told me, "I have to be careful in this country. It's Godless. It will turn us into unbelievers."

I said, "But Haweya, you were never religious before." She told me, "It's true, but I need to become religious now, because otherwise I risk losing my religion completely."

Haweya thought she was going to Hell. Perhaps the dissonance between what she saw and what she thought she should believe was so severe that she couldn't stand it. Perhaps she couldn't deal with individual freedom. Perhaps it was simply a reaction to her abortion. At first, I couldn't figure out what was going on; I thought this must be some kind of phase.

Haweya began praying every day. She had exactly the same questions as I did: Why was it that Holland could give its people so much better a life than any Muslim country we had seen? But Haweya answered those questions by going back into religion. She started reading Hasan al-Banna and Sayyid Qutb, Islamic thinkers I had once devoured in Nairobi. Haweya had not been in the Brotherhood as I had, or seen the misery I translated every day, and she sought her answers in the Quran.

To me, seeking answers in the Quran had only led to more questions. Once I told her, "I don't think you'll find the answers to your questions there." She turned on me: "Are you saying Allah doesn't have the answers and you do?" I became confused. I wasn't in any way challenging Allah. I couldn't do that.

I told her, "Look at Holland: it's not perfect, and the Dutch complain a lot, but it's orderly, it's humane, it's prosperous, everybody seems to be basically happy. And we from Muslim countries are pouring into places like Holland, so you must admit they must be doing something right. If you want to do things as Allah says, then look at Iran. Want to live there?"

"Iran is Shia," Haweya said.

"So, did you prefer Saudi Arabia?" I asked. I said the Quran might be God's truth, as a spiritual guide, but it seemed to me that, in terms of building governments, it was the Godless, Western theories that gave better answers.

Haweya told me I had become *kufr*. It had started with the language and the way I dressed, and now it had reached my brain. I was a traitor. She made me feel horribly guilty about the way I had abandoned prayer and my obedience to Allah. She described my Western ideas as a sort of virus that was slowly destroying my moral values.

But the more I read Western books, the more I wanted to read them. The more I learned about government, about the development of the individual, about systems of thought like social democracy and liberalism, the one the product of the other, the more I preferred things this way. The concept of individual choice improved people's lives so visibly, as did equality between men and women. I was enamored of the idea that you should think precisely and question everything and build your own theories.

I was not blind to the disadvantages of all these freedoms. I felt the loneliness and sometimes even the emptiness of our lives. It was sometimes tiresome to have to find out everything by myself, instead of relying on the comfortable, clear lines of doctrine and detailed rules. At times I, too, feared the limitless freedoms of Holland.

So I understood why Haweya was fleeing into religion. But I saw the joy in living in the West. Here I could satisfy my curiosity. When I felt interested in something, I could try it, and was wiser for that. I could draw my own conclusions.

Haweya did like the efficiency in Holland, and that she didn't have to pay bribes. She thought it was wonderful to be able to say no: "No, thank you, I'm not coming." "No, I won't be there tonight." She used to say, "This is the one great thing here. They are frank, they are honest."

But mostly she existed on welfare. She wasn't well. She had no discipline. My sister wanted contradictory things: to be a good, practicing Muslim and to be a news anchor on CNN, but she couldn't get out of bed. There were months when Haweya didn't seem to wash her clothes or clean her dishes. She would grow plump, then scarily thin. Showering once a day seemed to cost all her energy. Sometimes she would lie in bed for three days on end without getting up. Suddenly she would have a series of bright months, in which she could be generous, interesting, tell funny stories. She would have energy, attend class, impress her teachers. But just as suddenly she could turn rude, harsh, low, and would sink back again into lethargy and outbursts of crying.

By the early months of 1996, Haweya began saying things like "Please turn the mirror to the wall." I would ask why, and she would say, "When it faces me I see things in it." I would yell at her, "Stop making yourself crazy, get a grip on yourself," but she started sleeping with the lights on. She would call me to come and see her—she needed me now, right away—but when I arrived, after traveling for hours, she would dismiss me, saying, "I can't bear company now, so go."

I wasn't a hermit in Leiden. I saw my friends in Ede quite regularly, and gradually made new ones. Geeske was a first-year political science student, like me, and had a vivid energy. She used to take me to the cinema and student cafés, which were more relaxed than the pubs in Ede, though no less crowded and smoky, but now that I could understand people, I enjoyed them more. People sat outside and ate and listened to music.

It became a kind of joke that I didn't drink alcohol. The first time I finally did, I felt woozy and the room swayed. There were no thunderbolts of any kind, but it was far too late to cycle home to Chantal's place, and I had to stay the night with another friend of mine, Evelien. When I woke next morning I felt I had crossed a horrible line, from stretching Allah's rules to really breaking them.

I didn't think Chantal liked me coming home late to her house, and I felt awkward about inviting friends there. Meanwhile, Geeske lived with sixteen other students in a vast, run-down old canal house, and she was always talking about how much fun it was living there. When a room in her student house became free, Geeske suggested I apply for it. She told me I would never understand Holland if I didn't experience student life properly.

There was a whole selection procedure. All the people who lived in this house got together to interview the candidates over a bottle of wine. They asked us what kind of music we liked, what we liked doing on vacation, what were our hobbies, what kind of student jobs we had. I said my hobby was reading and I had never been on vacation. All these kids were young, all of them were white, and most of them had lived in the same house all their lives. They asked me where I'd lived, and just listing the countries—Somalia, Saudi Arabia, Ethiopia, Kenya—I saw their eyes widen. When I said I was an interpreter, one boy said, "Wow, you must earn a ton of money." I said yes, I did.

Geeske was frantic that her housemates would find me boring, or weird—or worse still, old—but she lobbied them so hard that they chose me anyway. So I moved into a tiny room in a Dutch student house, a place I would share with boys, where there would be alcohol, perhaps even drugs. I armed myself with courage.

I moved to Geeske's student house in March 1996. Before I fell asleep that first night, I had managed to get all my furniture into my new room, except for my desk, which Chantal had given me. It was large, old, and beautiful, and it wouldn't fit in the door. So the next morning I got up early to try to take it apart with a screwdriver. I was underneath this desk, in my yellow pajamas, when everyone headed off to class. One, an older boy called Marco, put his head under the desk and introduced himself as he headed out.

At lunchtime, when Marco reappeared, I was still under there, still in pajamas. In between I had done three phone translations, but of course he didn't know that. He said, "It can't be true! This is unbelievable! Get out of there," and he got the whole thing neatly taken apart in fifteen minutes. Then he moved it into my room, put it back together again, and admired my computer. Then my phone rang for another translation.

As he left, Marco invited me to have dinner with him that evening in the kitchen. He explained that the people who lived in the student house often shopped and cooked together, to save money. "At last there's someone interesting in this place," he said, smiling. "I was tired of all these eighteen-year-old know-it-alls."

Marco was a year older than I, and he worked; he was a reporter for a Dutch science magazine. He had lived in this student house as a biology student; after he graduated and found a job, he stayed on, though he wasn't supposed to. Rents in Leiden were very high. Marco, like so many Dutch people, loved traveling. He spent all his spare cash on long journeys to exotic places like Egypt and Syria. We took to having dinner together several times a week.

I went on working, but it was more fun now that I was surrounded by other young people. Still, I knew I was strange to them. I would emerge from my room and tell the others what I had just translated—announcing to someone that he had HIV, counseling a woman who had been beaten—and my housemates would be mesmerized. To them, the lives I came in contact with were on another planet. Almost all my housemates had grown up in the same town as their grandparents, sometimes even in the same house. They had very limited experience of the unpleasantness of the world.

Another thing about these kids fascinated me: everything was about the self—what they liked, expressing their style, treating themselves to something they felt they deserved. There was a whole culture of self that I had never known in Africa. In my childhood, the self was ignored. You pretended to be obedient, good, and pious for the approval of others; you never sought to express yourself. Here people sought their own pleasure, just because they felt like it.

Marco was handsome, with light brown hair and big blue innocent eyes; there was always a smile in the corner of his mouth. We were interested in each other—not quite just friends—but neither one of us made a move.

One summer afternoon my friend Tamara came to visit me, along with her mother, who was visiting from Canada. The weather was so surprisingly lovely that I invited them up to the roof terrace of our student house and suggested we eat there. Coincidentally, Marco had a friend over, too, and he also had hit on the idea of a rooftop picnic. (These picnics were forbidden, but we ignored that.)

We all ended up eating together, in an improvised private feast. As the evening progressed Marco and I kept getting closer to each other. The attraction between us, which had been latent for months, flared up and released a kind of energy that caught the others, too. Tamara's mother pulled out her camera and took a photograph of us. We posed; Marco put his arm around my shoulder and drew me to him. I still have that photo: it looks so natural, as if we had already been together for a thousand years. And it felt so wonderful—surprising and good.

We didn't kiss or anything. We just held hands for a moment and stayed close to each other, talking, all evening, as more friends of Marco's turned up: Giovanni, Olivier, and Marcel. But the next day, Marco invited me to a friend's place down the road; he was looking after someone's cat while they were traveling. We bought some groceries and cooked there. We both knew something would happen.

Marco was tender and patient. At first I felt frozen. I felt that Allah and the two angels were in bed with us, too, judging me. I was sinning. But it didn't feel like sin. As the months went by I grew certain that I wanted to spend the rest of my life with this man; I trusted him. Eventually I managed to peel the angels off my shoulders and pry them out of our bed.

Marco and I almost never spent a night apart for five years. We were inseparable. We were equals, we laughed together, we were all the other needed. Midway through 1996 I registered at the housing corporation for an apartment, and after only six months I received a letter informing me that I was eligible to rent a flat on the Langegracht, in central Leiden, for only 800 guilders. Marco and I decided to move in there together. We could pick up the keys on January 1.

We welcomed the New Year of 1997 together with Haweya. She had recently moved to a student house in Nijmegen, two and a half hours from Leiden, and had begun working for a degree in public administration there. A whole gang of us rented a house on an island off northern Holland for a couple of days. Haweya seemed tense around Marco's friends, but she loved the long walks when the weather cleared. I remember her running along the beach one afternoon, chasing the gulls, her arms waving for joy. I thought she was fine.

But a few days after Marco and I moved into our new apartment, I received a call from Tamara. Tamara and Haweya liked each other and often met for dinner or a movie. Tamara told me she had called Haweya's student house in Nijmegen to cancel an appointment, and one of Haweya's flatmates told her that Haweya had been taken to the hospital.

She had been shouting in Arabic in her room, throwing herself against the walls and the floor; the police had had to smash down her door. Haweya was taken away in a straitjacket.

I went to the psychiatric ward in Nijmegen with Marco. My sister looked frightening. Her hair was wild, standing straight off her head; she'd been pulling clumps of it out all night long. Her face was almost unrecognizable, and she had a huge wound on her forehead from banging her head on the wall. She had black-and-blue bruises all the way up her legs and was heavily sedated. I asked, "Were you beaten?" Haweya said, "No. I was throwing myself on the ground all the time and I hurt myself."

When I arrived she seemed calm, but as she told me what had happened, she started seeing things, things that were not there. She told me she was hearing voices. She became very blurry and began talking about

Jesus in some kind of religious mania. As I sat there she began talking louder. She got up and began pacing from one end of the room to the other, faster and faster, chanting *Allah Akbar, Allah Akbar, Allah Akbar,* louder and faster with every step. I couldn't catch her, she just flung me away, onto the bed. She seemed to have enormous strength.

Two nurses came in. They held her down and gave her an injection and yanked me outside. They told me I had to leave. I could come back the next day to talk to the psychiatrist.

The psychiatrist said Haweya was having a psychotic episode, but she was responding well to medication. They would keep her for a week, for observation. Everything might be fine.

I went to see Haweya every day. Classes, translations—nothing else mattered. And after a few days she seemed to get better. She went back to wearing a headscarf, and she seemed not to remember what had happened. All she said was "I was a little off balance. Holland affects me this way." She said she didn't want medication; she was perfectly fine now.

After a week, a judge came to the ward to discuss whether Haweya should continue to be hospitalized against her will. She convinced him that there was nothing fundamentally wrong with her. I took her back to her flat and settled her in. But three days later, when I went to see her again, Haweya was visibly not all right. She kept muttering under her breath, she was talking loudly again, like a preacher. She took out Sayyid Qutb's book and said "Ayaan, you must repent, return to Allah." Suddenly she began taking off her clothes.

I yelled at her to stop, and she did, looking shamefaced. I said, "Do you realize you were whispering to yourself?" Haweya said, "Not to myself. There's a voice in my head. It keeps on asking me to behave like a child, so I was telling it, 'Now is not the right moment. When Ayaan is gone I will do it.' "

The next morning I headed straight to the Leiden library. I was trying to figure out what was going on. Over the course of the next few weeks I came to see that the voice was like a little Haweya. Her memories, her feelings about religion as a little child, her recollections of school and our parents were all swirling around inside her, mixing into her adult life as if they were real.

I saw that my sister was ill in her mind. Physical illness is easy to understand: you are sick, you take medicine. But mental illness is frightening: you can't see the wound. Marco was a biologist, so he helped educate me in the chemistry of the brain. I talked to a psychiatrist. Rationally,

I could understand it. I told myself, "It's a chemical inside her that is unbalanced. My sister is not cursed. It's not because she has been disobedient to Allah or to my mother." But emotionally, I was devastated. My sister was disintegrating right in front of me, and all I could do was watch. I felt helpless, and guilty that I had not seen the signs and somehow prevented this illness by providing her with a stable, supportive environment.

Haweya was not made mentally ill by Islam. Her delusions were religious, but it would be dishonest to say they were Islam's fault. She went to the Quran seeking peace of mind, but the unrest inside her was chemical. I think perhaps it had something to do with the limitlessness of Holland; she used to say it was like being in a room without walls. One time she told me, "I was so used to fighting with everybody for every little thing, and suddenly there is nothing to fight for—everything is possible." In Europe, Haweya lost her road map, and the lack of guidance became unbearable.

Haweya hid her pills. She became delusional and raved. She thought she was cursed. Late one night she took a taxi from Nijmegen to Ede to see Hasna, the Somali woman who was a refugee in Ede. Hasna paid for the taxi and put her to bed, but next morning Haweya picked up Hasna's baby daughter and refused to let her go. She tried to suckle the child; now she thought she was Mary, the mother of Jesus. Hasna called the police: there was no choice. They gently pried the baby away from Haweya and took her to the hospital.

She was placed in a padded room, where everything was gray and soft and only dimly lit. For a while I wasn't allowed to visit her. They medicated her again. The drugs leveled her out, but they had side effects. She began walking jerkily, throwing her arms around. She got more medicine; she became lethargic, and slipped back into depression.

Haweya stayed in the hospital for six months. I visited her constantly. One time I found she already had a visitor, Yassin Moussa Boqor, the younger brother of the Boqor who had presided over the clan meeting about me in the refugee center in Ede. This man, who was a prince of the Osman Mahamud, greeted me courteously. He was there to check on Haweya on behalf of my father and the clan: the news had spread.

A few weeks later, the phone rang at my apartment. It was Marco who answered. He turned to me and I saw that he was crying. He said, "Ayaan, this is a special call." I took the phone and my father said, "Abeh, Abeh," in a voice like a little girl, as I used to.

I screamed, "Abeh! You've forgiven me!" I even flung the phone away. I screamed, and jumped, and did a little dance around the living room before I picked up the phone again.

My father said Yassin Moussa Boqor had told him how I had been looking after my sister. He had told my father that any man should feel blessed with such a child. In this country, so gray and cloudy and depressing, here was this young Somali girl, behaving so dutifully, working so hard, and studying. The prince had respectfully suggested that my father should forgive me.

His voice was tender. I was overwhelmed with joy; it was one of the happiest moments of my life. We avoided discussing the whole issue of my marriage and my flight; we wanted to say only good things to each other. My father told me he was living in Somalia again, with his third wife and his little daughter. He said he had everything he needed, but he obviously didn't have his own phone. I said, "I want to call you and I want you to pick up the phone," and I sent him the money to have one installed. After that I called my father at least once a month. He said we must pray to Allah to cure Haweya, but he told her also to take her medication.

Haweya seemed to improve. She was moved to the long-stay section of the hospital and was permitted to go out during the day. I threatened to have her committed again if she didn't return at night as she was supposed to. Over the next few weeks, she seemed occasionally to recognize that she was ill. She said once, "Suffering is so lonely. Nobody can possibly understand what is going through my head." It broke my heart to hear it. But Haweya insisted that it was Holland that was making her sick. If she left Holland she would be all right. I knew that was nonsense. If Haweya went home to Nairobi she would stop receiving the medication that was preventing the terrible psychotic attacks.

When she was released from the hospital, in June, I moved Haweya into the flat I shared with Marco in the Langegracht. It didn't go well. She had become extremely unpredictable, and I spent all my time persuading her to take her pills. Although Marco was supportive, he and Haweya fought all the time; both of them were very headstrong. I was torn between my translation jobs, my classes, and the sister I was nursing at home: there was barely any room in my life for Marco, let alone for my friends.

Haweya was determined to go home to Kenya. She phoned our mother, who agreed with her. Ma told me, "Of course Haweya went mad in that *kufr* country. Ayaan, you should come home, too, before you also go mad."

My father, Johanna, and everyone else told me I had no right to prevent Haweya from going back, if that was what she wanted. In July, she left.

It was a relief to be able to focus again on my studies, although I felt guilty to admit it to myself. I had fallen behind; constantly traveling to Nijmegen took so much time, and so did my translation work, which I needed to pay for Haweya's upkeep and to send money to Ma.

The classes in Leiden were small, and could be intense. The teachers used to lay out three or four theories on something abstract—charismatic leadership, or middle-class support for revolution, or the need for proportional representation—and ask us to analyze whether the data backed up the argument, whether there were gaps, and then form our own theories. If we couldn't develop an alternative theory, they said we were incurious and not fit to become scientists. We had to devise a proper theory, with proper methodology; if not, what we said was dismissed as pub talk, not science. We were encouraged to read widely, outside the curriculum. I loved it, but it was hard to keep up with it all.

In September 1997 I became eligible for Dutch citizenship. I had been in Holland for five years. I could barely wait; in fact, I had registered my application months before. On a practical level, I wanted a Dutch passport so I could travel more easily; it was so difficult to move around as a refugee. I also still thought the authorities might find out I had lied and retract my refugee status. Once I became a Dutch citizen, I thought I would be safe from that. I had been a refugee all my life, since I left Mogadishu when I was eight. Now I wanted to become a real, participating member of a living democracy. I wanted to belong.

On August 21, 1997, I received a letter: five years, almost to the day, since I'd first received my refugee status in Lunteren, the queen of Holland had accepted my application to become Dutch. I would have to wait for two weeks to pick up my new passport at Leiden City Council.

When I got to the front of the line, my heart was pounding. "I'm here for my naturalization," I told the dumpy blond woman behind the desk, and showed her my letter. She looked up and said, "Okay. You can pay over there." The cashier took my money and handed me something: a Dutch passport. It had my photo in it, and my name, Ayaan Hirsi Ali, a name that by now had come to seem normal. There was no speech, no lecture of my rights and obligations. Receiving it was the least momentous occasion in the world.

Marco and I had a party to celebrate and I told everyone, "I'm Dutch!"

Nobody snickered exactly, but they looked at me strangely. It wasn't that I was black and claiming Dutchness; that was fine. It was because being Dutch meant absolutely nothing to these people. If anything, my Dutch friends seemed uncomfortable with the symbols of Dutchness: the flag and the monarchy. These things seemed to them to hark back to the treacherous days of the Second World War. They saw nationalism as almost the same thing as racism. Nobody seemed *proud* of being Dutch.

At first, Haweya seemed to be doing well in Kenya. We spoke on the phone every ten days or so, and she seemed happy; she even talked about getting a job. Then in October, she clearly became ill again. On the phone, she rambled incoherently, lacing every conversation with religious ravings. She was hearing voices.

I suggested that she come back to Leiden, but she said she was afraid of Holland. Then, the next time I called, she said she wanted to come back to Holland but she'd lost her passport. She begged me to come and get her out somehow without one. She said Ma tied her up sometimes, and Mahad beat her. She wailed, "I'm wasting time, I'm getting older, I'm in a mess, I'm pregnant."

After that, Haweya never came to the phone again. I spoke only to Ma, who told me Haweya was becoming more violent. Ma knew Haweya was pregnant. When I brought it up, she just said "Allah has willed it" with bitter resignation. I sent money.

At the beginning of December, I called again, and Ma told me Haweya was ill. She said, "If you want to see your sister alive, come now." It was exam time in Leiden, and I didn't take Ma seriously. I thought about going to Nairobi during the Christmas vacation. But I had fallen so far behind with my studies in the months I had been looking after Haweya. I ended up deciding that I must use the holiday break to finish writing several papers.

A few days after the New Year celebrations, on January 8, 1998, my father called, and it was the worst news of my life. "Haweya was taken by Allah to her final destination," he said.

She had been sick for a week; then she died. I couldn't believe it. It was as if someone had just sucked all the air out of the room. I burst out crying and my father said, "No, Ayaan. We must not cry for Haweya. From Allah we come and to Allah we return. She is with God. All of us still have to struggle through life on earth to attain what she has. She rests in peace."

I just kept on crying. I took the first flight. When I left for the airport,

I put on a black coat and a headscarf—the same outfit I had worn when I arrived in Europe.

About an hour before I landed in Nairobi, they buried Haweya. I never got to see her body, never got to say good-bye. Muslims must bury people within twenty-four hours. There might perhaps be a dispensation for a father or a husband. But my father didn't come to the funeral—he was in Somalia—and nobody even thought about asking for a dispensation for me.

So when I came Haweya was already in the ground. I just sat in the squalid little room that my mother was now living in, on a filthy street in Eastleigh, and listened to her stories about living with Haweya for the past six months. I looked at the thin window bars, dented when Haweya threw herself at them, and the windows she'd smashed, still broken.

Ma and Haweya had lived here, in this awful place. This was where they slept, cooked, washed. It was the most depressing room imaginable. Decades of charcoal fires stained the peeling walls.

Ma told me how Haweya died. Her psychotic episodes had become much worse. Sometimes several men had to tie her down; Ma couldn't even go near her. A doctor came to give her injections, and she seemed calmer. Then one night there was a thunderstorm. Haweya was standing at the window, watching the deluge. Suddenly she said she saw Allah in the lightning and ran out of the door. She ran barefoot into the road in the dark, sprinting across the potholes, and when Ma screamed for help, two Somali men ran after her. When they brought Haweya back, she was bleeding from her knees and from between her legs.

She died a week after her miscarriage. I suppose it was an infection. I don't know if she even saw a doctor.

I was speechless, and horrified, and I was also frightened of my mother. It occurred to me that she might try to take away my passport and keep me in Nairobi. I went to sleep that night, on the mattress that had been Haweya's, with my passport tied tightly around my waist.

When Haweya died, I prayed. I robed and bowed for prayer, as Ma told me to, for the sake of peace in the household, but those prayers were empty of content. More important, I sat by myself and begged Allah to give Haweya peace, because she had Hell on earth. The idea that she was now no longer in pain, but resting peacefully, was surprisingly comforting.

My mother was bitter, a spent force. There was nothing left of the proud young woman who had left her family in the *miyé* to go to Aden, who married the man of her choice, and who struggled to save her family under dictatorship. Her dreams had turned into nightmares. My grandmother had left, to go and live with my mother's youngest sister in Somalia. My mother was living in Eastleigh, a neighborhood she despised, in a country and a city she had always hated, and she was not on speaking terms with barely anyone in the community. Her family was no more: Mahad had disappointed her; one daughter had deserted her; and the other had gone mad, then become pregnant. That was my mother's worst nightmare come true. It was much worse than Haweya dying.

On the afternoon of the next day, my mother began railing, "Why has Allah done this to me? How could your sister do this to me?" I couldn't bear that, hearing Haweya being blamed for hurting Ma. I thought of all the abuse, all the beatings my sister received when we were little. It didn't seem to occur to Ma that she might have had a role in what went wrong. I thought of how my mother had persuaded Haweya to leave her doctors and her medication in Holland and come back to Nairobi, to this ugly room, this utter squalor.

I tried to sit Ma down and tell her this. I wanted to have a real conversation with her, perhaps the first in my life. But there was nothing left of the towering mother I remembered. Ma not just thin now; she was *worn,* and I took pity on her. She was skin and bones, her legs were open scabs from the psoriasis, and she was so unhappy.

I had $1,000 with me, and I gave it to my mother. I said, "I want you to get out of this room immediately. I'll send you the money. I want you to go to Somalia. Go to your brothers and sisters, your clan. There is nothing more in Nairobi. Haweya is gone, Mahad has no plans, and I won't be coming back here. You have no friends, you're fighting with everyone. You should leave."

I felt I was the authority in the household now. I told Ma, "I want you to go yourself to the grocery store, to pick up the money when it comes. I don't want Mahad to be involved." I told her how much money I had sent Mahad for her—easily over $10,000, which he had told me he was using to rent her a house in Westlands—and she came to life a bit, with anger.

I went to visit Halwa. She was still living in her father's house, still sleeping in the same bedroom, but it was as if a ghost had taken out her soul. A few months after I left Nairobi in 1992 to live with Osman Moussa, Halwa was finally married to her cousin from Yemen. He ordered her around and expected her to serve him, though he was primitive and had never learned to read. Halwa hated her husband, but she became pregnant. When her daughter was born, she pleaded with her father to allow her to divorce. Her father reluctantly paid out a settlement, and Halwa's husband returned to Yemen. Now she hardly ever went out of her father's house. Her daughter was four years old; she was Halwa's only joy in life.

The next day I went to visit Mahad's newborn son. I liked Sha'a, Mahad's young wife, very much. She seemed neglected: Mahad obviously wasn't spending much time with her. When I cornered Mahad, he said he was angry with Sha'a for getting pregnant. I asked if he had by any chance been using contraception, and he said no, Sha'a was supposed to count the days. I couldn't help it: I told Mahad how facile it was for him, a male, to always blame women for his problems. But when I saw him getting angry in return, I gritted my teeth to avoid another outburst: this wasn't the right time for that.

Then I asked about the money I had sent him. Mahad told me he had invested it in a business, but the man absconded to Oman. As usual, he was the victim.

I walked around. Nairobi was a shell of the city I had lived in. Roads were wrecked, telephones barely worked. The economy was in ruins; such a huge increase in poverty in so short a time seemed obscene. Violence had become routine on the streets. Under Daniel Arap Moi, larceny and corruption on a truly massive scale was draining the whole country of any sense of energy and hope. Everything was chaos and no one seemed to have any hope of making it better. It seemed like the end of the line.

The night before I flew back to Holland, I couldn't sleep. I listened to the cars rumbling down the road in the early morning and realized I would never live here again. My life, or what I would make of it, would be in Holland now, for good.

When I got back to Leiden after Haweya's funeral, I was on autopilot. My feelings had gone dead. I executed daily tasks and somehow got things done. Gradually, life took shape. I had missed several exams and papers, so I had work to do. Marco was very good to me: that helped.

My old boyfriend, Abshir Abdi Aynab, the imam from Somalia, called me to express his condolences. He told me he was living in Switzerland and wanted to visit me. I brushed him off. I wanted nothing more to do with my old life.

CHAPTER 14

Leaving God

I was becoming integrated into student society, and that society was nowhere near as predictable or as sedate as my circle in Ede. Geeske and my other friends in Leiden were either agnostics or atheists. Elroy, Marco's best friend, was homosexual.

For example, Marco's friend Giovanni and his girlfriend, Mirjam, broke up after Giovanni went to Israel to do biology research for three months. In his absence, Mirjam fell in love with Olivier, one of Giovanni's friends. When Giovanni returned, he was upset—they had been together for years—but there was no honor killing, not even a hint of violence. Mirjam had a perfect right to fall in love with someone else. Even her mother thought so, though she'd adored Giovanni. I was fascinated by this vision of a completely different moral system.

In May 1998, there were elections. Now that I was Dutch, I could vote. I gave it a lot of thought. Actually to have the ability to choose the government of Holland—it felt like a momentous responsibility. I voted, like most of my friends, for Wim Kok from the Labor Party, a social democrat. My heart was on the left. I chose Kok because of his fairness and honesty, because he promised jobs and I believed him; he had experience, and I liked his track record. Although I was a political science student working as a translator, it had not occurred to me yet to analyze any party's stance on immigration and integration. I was not yet questioning the government's role in why immigrants were so overrepresented in crime statistics, unemployment, and other social problems.

In January 2000, the political commentator Paul Scheffer published an article, "The Multicultural Drama," in the *NRC Handelsblad,* a well-respected evening newspaper. It instantly became the talk of Holland. Everybody had an opinion about it. Scheffer said a new ethnic underclass of immigrants had formed, and it was much too insular, rejecting the values that knit together Dutch society and creating new, damaging social divisions. There wasn't enough insistence on immigrants adapting; teachers even questioned the relevance of teaching immigrant children Dutch history, and a whole generation of these children were being written off under a pretence of tolerance. Scheffer said there was no place in Holland for a culture that rejected the separation of church and state and denied rights to women and homosexuals. He foresaw social unrest.

At the time, I pooh-poohed Scheffer's concerns. To me, it seemed that the Dutch lived in an absolute paradise and tended to call any small problem a crisis. I thought of Holland in the 1990s as a country living through an Embarrassment of Riches, like its Golden Age in the 1600s. It was a trim little country, where everybody was always nice. The economy was booming. Trains arrived on time, although markedly less so since they had been privatized. Politics were collegial and even friendly. There were women and homosexuals in the cabinet, and everyone respected them enormously. I didn't believe the country could really have problems. To me, the words Scheffer used—crisis, social upheaval—seemed just newspaper chatter.

In my final year, I had to focus on completing my thesis. I had chosen to examine the drift toward making law in the courts instead of in Parliament. Politicians in Holland were failing to take responsibility and act decisively; because they were so driven to seek consensus and electoral gains, they were letting judges take charge of issues that they deemed too controversial to touch. I thought I might go on to do a doctorate after I graduated, and perhaps teach.

In the spring of 2000 my father, by then almost blind from cataracts, managed to get a visa to go to Germany for an operation on his eyes, for which I gladly helped him pay. I visited him in Düsseldorf, driving all the way in my Peugeot 206 with Mirjam. Marco and Ellen joined us a day later. Marco wanted badly to meet my father, and we agreed that Ellen and he should pretend to be a couple because I wasn't ready to discuss with my father the fact that I was living in sin. Not yet.

Abeh embraced me. He looked much older, but he smelled exactly the same. It felt deeply good to be enfolded by him again. At first we just talked about general things: what I was studying, politics. All my father wanted to talk about was Somalia, the great state Somalia could one day become. And he clearly said he wanted an Islamic government, a rule by Allah's laws. Any system of politics devised by man was bound to go wrong.

I took the opposite stance. I surprised myself: I spoke sharply. I said Divine Law wouldn't be fair to everyone who wasn't Muslim. Even within Islam, not everyone thought the same way. Who would make the law? I told my father, "The rule of clerics is totalitarian. It means people can't choose. Humanity is varied, and we should celebrate that instead of suppressing it."

My father just said, "We must all work hard to convert everyone to Islam." He disappointed me with this simple-minded logic and his depressing lack of realism.

My father had decided to arrange for my divorce. I didn't feel the slightest bit married; Osman Moussa was just a vague memory for me. But to my father, it was vital. He told me that he shouldn't have obliged me to marry against my will. I should be free to choose the husband I wanted. I think he wanted to think of himself as someone who accorded freedom; there was still a democrat buried inside him, after all.

Abeh told me he was sad to see changes in me. He said I was becoming too worldly, not spiritual enough. He said, "I won't ask you to wear a headscarf, but please, grow your hair." I told him I would, and I have. When he asked me if I still prayed, I said of course I did. In some sense this was still true. I had all sorts of un-Muslim ideas, and yet, in those days, I did still think of myself as being, in some larger, more important way, a believer.

When I graduated from Leiden, in September 2000, I was almost thirty years old. It had taken me an extra year to get my master's degree, but I had made it. I told myself I should be proud. I had solid qualifications, a rocky but intimate relationship, and strong friendships. I was earning my own money. I had made myself a place in Holland with my own hands and legs and brain.

I was thrilled to be graduating after so many years. I tried to get a visa for my father to attend the ceremony, but it was turned down. I phoned my mother, to tell her I was getting my Master of Science degree. She made an awkward remark about how odd it was that it should be me, of her three children, who would graduate from the university. She probably meant no harm by it. In her eyes, I was still the dumbest of the three of us.

Marco and I threw a party at the Café Einstein, which many Leiden students frequented. Johanna and Maarten came from Ede with their kids, Irene and Jan, whom I adore as if they were my own little brother and sister. Maarten climbed on a chair and started telling funny stories about what I was like when I first arrived. Geeske was the master of ceremonies, and Mirjam's parents made lots of little hors d'oeuvres, which touched me hugely. When Mirjam and Olivier walked in I tensed, waiting for some dispute to break out with Giovanni, but Mirjam hit it off perfectly with Giovanni's new girlfriend, Albertine.

A whole group of people around me wished me well, but I also needed to think about what I was going to do next. I wanted to get a proper job and earn money, so that Marco and I could afford a nicer apartment. I hated our dank council housing on the Langegracht, which gave me allergies. Before the Eid festival, some of our neighbors, who were Moroccan and Turkish, slaughtered sheep in the basement, where we kept our bicycles. The entrails stayed in the trash for days before the garbage was picked up; it was like being in Eastleigh. There was noise at all hours. I wanted to get out of there, even though Marco said we couldn't afford it yet. He was so frugal, I complained. I couldn't see the point of waiting any longer than we had to.

I decided against continuing my university studies. I could have gone on for a doctorate and received some kind of stipend as a teaching assistant, but that wasn't much better than minimum wage. It wouldn't get us out of the Langegracht, or go far toward supporting my family in Africa. I would have to work. But I didn't want just to continue as a translator, which I saw as my student job, not a permanent career. I also wanted to gain more experience before shifting from being a student to research and teaching. I still had a great deal to learn, but I feared that in the private sector everyone would say I was too old for an entry-level job. I was so nervous about it that I took the first post I was offered, with Glaxo, the pharmaceutical company.

I had applied because Glaxo's business was helping people. Glaxo spent millions on AIDS and malaria research: by working there, I would somehow be participating. It was a big company; you came in on the sales force but you could move, and rise, with time. The job came with a good starting salary, a company car, and two weeks of training that was like a crash course in medicine, with an emphasis on headaches and the respiratory system. It was also an education in how to sell things to people, which was a real eye-opener.

I was supposed to sell Imigran, a migraine medication, to doctors. The Glaxo people taught us techniques to outwit doctors' secretaries and get an appointment. They taught us to evaluate someone's personality type and pitch our sales techniques precisely to that kind of person, so that every appointment would get us a sale. If you sensed a doctor was the authoritarian type, you had to keep your pitch short and make it clear how clever you thought he was. You let him talk a lot, then when you pitched the medication, you used the exact same words that he had. With analytical personalities you didn't mention the medication at all, at first; you went straight into a long discussion of all the different kinds of migraine headaches. It was manipulative and to me a waste of doctors' precious time, so after a few weeks I gave back the car, the phone, and the laptop. That was it for me and business.

Next I signed up at a temp agency, which sent me to work as an office manager in the housing department of the Oegstgeest City Council. It was the same pleasant residential community outside Leiden where I had first lived with Chantal. I worked there for two or three months; I thought it would give me the opportunity to see government from within.

For every application for a permit to build an attic or change a few windows, a whole group of people in this office had to work together, but they seemed to dislike each other. There were more civil servants than there were tasks to do, and they spent their days bickering. Every permit had to be countersigned by directors and directors of the directors, and everything was unbelievably slow. I had applied for a job at the Interior Ministry a year before and it had taken six months to process my application: now friends who worked in government ministries confirmed that government work was slow, with no imagination or satisfaction. So I ruled out government. I didn't want to work in the civil service for the rest of my life.

I began looking around, with a sense of growing panic, for what I was going to do. One morning in March, Marco looked up from the newspaper and crowed, "This job's perfect for you: your name is written all over it." He showed me the ad. The Wiardi Beckman Institute, the political bureau of Wim Kok's Labor Party, was looking for a junior researcher.

It paid less than Glaxo, but it was only four days a week, and I could translate the rest of the time to supplement my income. More important, it sounded truly interesting. I would be researching issues that were politically and socially relevant, for a party to which I already belonged. A think tank would not be bureaucratic at all. It would be small, intellectually agile, challenging.

The Wiardi Beckman Institute offered me the job in June 2001. I was thrilled. I was supposed to start work the first of September. I instantly quit the city council job and went back to translating; this earned me much more money, which Marco and I would need to buy a house.

I was determined to find us another place to live, and at first Marco went along with me. But whenever I found somewhere I liked, Marco would balk, claiming it was too expensive or too far away from the center of town for him. Marco didn't want to move, didn't want to be ensnared in a huge bank loan. He wanted to spend all his spare cash on roaming the world. I thought that was immature. He said I was too impatient and a spendthrift.

Our relationship was deteriorating. We had been fighting for years over small, stupid things: time management and household expenses. He needed to plan everything; I hated that constriction. He had a temper; I have never liked yelling or being yelled at. I had already started thinking about breaking up when I saw a perfect, if run-down house on a tree-lined street, close to the train station, with wooden floors and fireplaces. Marco said renovating it would cost too much.

I decided to buy the house anyway, without Marco. We could still be friends—maybe he could still be my boyfriend—but it was time for me to move out, before things got any worse between us. Ellen had split up with her husband, Badal Zadeh, and, after a certain amount of soul-searching, she agreed to come live in Leiden and share the house, and mortgage, with me. We went to the bank: both of us earned good money. In April, Ellen and I moved in together.

One evening we were watching TV when an item came on about gay schoolteachers being harassed by Moroccan kids. This sort of thing was often in the news in those days; you would open the newspaper and think "What, Moroccan boys again? What's wrong with them?" So when an imam came on, wearing traditional clothes and with the imam manner about him, speaking Arabic, I turned up the volume. He looked at the camera with great authority and explained that homosexuality was a contagious disease that could infect schoolchildren. It was, he said, a threat to humanity.

I remember standing up and saying, "This is so backward. He is so stupid!" To the Somali in me, this attitude was familiar; but the Dutch person in me was shocked. The interview caused a commotion, and I sat down and wrote an article and sent it to the *NRC Handelsblad*. I wrote that this attitude was much larger than just one imam: it was systemic in Islam, because this was a religion that had never gone through a process of Enlightenment that would lead people to question its rigid approach to individual freedom. Moreover, I wrote, Islam didn't oppose only the right of homosexuals to live undisturbed. Anyone who had been to an abortion clinic or a women's center could readily see that the sexual morals of Islam can only lead to suffering.

It was spontaneous indignation: I found myself discovering my opinions as I typed. The article was edited into a short letter couched in nice, politically correct language, and was published in May. But that was my political coming out.

Ellen and I spent two months fixing up the house. Then I settled back to enjoy life. We had dinner parties. Ellen was going through a period of religious turmoil, looking for her bearings, and she talked about which church she should join. Even Marco and I were getting along very well; we considered getting back together again. It was a summer of cooking for people, independence, a happy time.

On September 3, I started work. The Labor Party's think tank was a small office, and I was just a junior researcher. My first task was to work on immigration, which I was beginning to see as the most important question facing Holland in the twenty-first century. I wasn't looking at Islam as a central question yet but studying migration, its causes, and the implications for a welfare state of absorbing all these new migrants. Should the Labor Party support more restrictive policies on immigration?

Holland wanted to keep its welfare state, but it clearly could not afford to offer its benefits to the whole world. They had to have some kind of restrictions on entry; the question was what. I planned to arrange a discussion among experts and organize their papers into a book. I was not writing policy, but I was required to nurture and expand the think tank's network of experts and do research for them; they would deliver a road map on how to deal with the question. How did other countries manage immigration, and how much migration could a welfare state absorb and still remain a welfare state?

One afternoon, in my second week of working at the Labor Party, I was reading old reports when a commotion erupted downstairs. I walked down to see what could be making so much noise, determined to tell these people to be quiet.

A clump of people huddled around the TV, which was tuned to CNN. I sighed. In those days I was prejudiced against America, and the American media. At Leiden I had even written a paper on media hype, using the Monica Lewinsky debacle as an example. During Bill Clinton's impeachment, CNN had constantly reported LIVE with BREAKING NEWS on completely trivial aspects of Clinton's sex life; the holier-than-thou manner of Kenneth Starr, Clinton's nemesis, always reminded me disagreeably of Ijaabo. Simply by devoting so much attention to this issue the media had made it seem important, and the whole episode left me with the impression that Americans were hysterical.

So when I saw the BREAKING NEWS banner that afternoon, I thought CNN had unearthed another minor event to bang its drum about. But as I stood there the second plane hit the World Trade Center. The anchorwoman was saying that it might not be an accident—that the two crashes might be a deliberate attack. Again and again we watched the horrific footage of planes hitting the towers. I found myself screwing my eyes tight shut and thinking, in Somali, "Oh Allah, please let it not be Muslims who did this."

I knew this could ignite a major world conflict. When I got home from work I told Ellen, "The Americans are going to retaliate. They are not like the Dutch—they are not going to say, 'Let's sit down and talk about this.' It will be the third world war." Ellen told me not to get so overwrought.

But that night we saw news footage that shocked me further. In Holland itself—in Ede, in the town I had lived in—a camera crew who happened to be filming on the streets just after the towers were hit recorded a group of Muslim kids jubilating. All of Holland was shaken by that, but I was far more frightened than most. Ellen kept telling me, "They were just kids, it's been overblown, if the cameras hadn't been there it wouldn't have happened." But I knew, inside, that the cameras just caught a part of it. If there had been more cameras in other neighborhoods they would have seen it there, too.

The morning after the 9/11 attacks, after getting off my commuter train, I found myself walking to the office with Ruud Koole, the chairman of the Labor Party. Ruud had been one of my teachers at Leiden. He greeted me by my first name—there isn't much hierarchy in Holland—and, like everyone in the world, we began talking about the Twin Towers attack. Ruud shook his head sadly about it all. He said, "It's so weird, isn't it, all these people saying this has to do with Islam?"

I couldn't help myself. Just before we reached the office, I blurted out, "But it *is* about Islam. This is based in belief. This is Islam."

Ruud said, "Ayaan, of course these people may have been Muslims, but they are a lunatic fringe. We have extremist Christians, too, who interpret the Bible literally. Most Muslims do not believe these things. To say so is to disparage a faith which is the second largest religion in world, and which is civilized, and peaceful."

I walked into the office thinking, "I have to wake these people up." It wasn't just Koole by any means. Holland, this fortunate country where nothing ever happens, was trying to pretend nothing had happened again. The Dutch had forgotten that it was possible for people to stand up and wage war, destroy property, imprison, kill, impose laws of virtue because of the call of God. That kind of religion hadn't been present in Holland for centuries.

It was not a lunatic fringe who felt this way about America and the West. I knew that a vast mass of Muslims would see the attacks as justified retaliation against the infidel enemies of Islam. War had been declared in the name of Islam, my religion, and now I had to make a choice. Which side was I on? I found I couldn't avoid the question. Was this really Islam? Did Islam permit, even call for, this kind of slaughter? Did I, as a Muslim, approve of the attack? And if I didn't, where did I stand on Islam?

I walked around with these questions for weeks; I couldn't get them out of my head. I became fixated on the 9/11 attacks. I combed through newspapers, searched the Internet. I saw how many demonstrations around the world took place, actively in open support of Osama Bin Laden. In northern Nigeria, hundreds of people were killed in communal riots. World leaders hurried to TV stations, calling on Muslims to condemn the attacks. There seemed to be a huge appeal to the morals of Islam. All sorts of articles called on Muslims to stand up and say that Islam does not permit this sort of slaughter of noncombatants. When I read them, I felt as though these articles were talking to me.

Mohamed Atta, the hijackers' leader, had instructed them on how to "die as a good Muslim." He used the prayer every Muslim utters when he is dying: he asks Allah to stand by him as he comes to Him. I read it and I recognized it. Everything about the tone and substance of that letter was familiar to me. This was not just Islam, this was the core of Islam. Mohamed Atta believed that he was giving his life for Allah.

Mohamed Atta was exactly my age. I felt as though I knew him, and in fact, I did know many people just like him. The people in the debating center I had attended in Nairobi, for example: they would have written that letter, if they had had the courage to do what Atta did. If I had remained with them, perhaps I could have done it, or perhaps Ijaabo would have. There were tens of thousands of people, in Africa, the Middle East—even in Holland—who thought this way. Every devout Muslim who aspired to practice genuine Islam—the Muslim Brotherhood Islam, the Islam of the Medina Quran schools—even if they didn't actively support the attacks, they must at least have approved of them. This wasn't just a band of frustrated Egyptian architects in Hamburg. It was much bigger than that, and it had nothing to do with frustration. It was about belief.

Infuriatingly stupid analysts—especially people who called themselves Arabists, yet who seemed to know next to nothing about the reality of the Islamic world—wrote reams of commentary. Their articles were all about Islam saving Aristotle and the zero, which medieval Muslim scholars had done more than eight hundred years ago; about Islam being a religion of peace and tolerance, not the slightest bit violent. These were fairy tales, nothing to do with the real world I knew.

Everything in the newspapers was "Yes, but": yes, it's terrible to kill people, *but.* People theorized beautifully about poverty pushing people to terrorism; about colonialism and consumerism, pop culture and Western decadence eating away at people's culture and therefore causing the carnage. But Africa is the poorest continent, I knew, and poverty doesn't cause terrorism; truly poor people can't look further than their next meal, and more intellectual people are usually angry at their own governments; they flock to the West. I read rants by antiracist bureaus claiming that a terrible wave of Islamophobia had been unleashed in Holland, that Holland's inner racist attitude was now apparent. None of this pseudointellectualizing had anything to do with reality.

Other articles blamed the Americans' "blind" support for Israel and opined that there would be more 9/11's until the Israeli-Palestinian conflict was resolved. I didn't completely believe this either. I myself, as a teenager, might have cheered the World Trade Center and Pentagon attacks, and the Palestinian dispute was completely abstract to me in Nairobi. If the hijackers had been nineteen Palestinian men, then I might have given this argument more weight, but they weren't. None of them was poor. None of them left a letter saying there would be more attacks until Palestine was liberated. This was belief, I thought. Not frustration, poverty, colonialism, or Israel: it was about religious belief, a one-way ticket to Heaven.

Most articles analyzing Bin Laden and his movement were scrutinizing a symptom, a little like analyzing Lenin and Stalin without looking at the works of Karl Marx. The Prophet Muhammad was the moral guide, not Bin Laden, and it was the Prophet's guidance that should be evaluated. But what if I didn't like the outcome of that analysis? What would I do then?

Videotapes of old interviews with Osama Bin Laden began running on CNN and Al-Jazeera. They were filled with justification for total war on America, which, together with the Jews, he perceived as leading a new Crusade on Islam. Sitting in a dainty house in picture-perfect Leiden, I thought it sounded far-fetched, like the ravings of a madman, but Bin Laden's quotes from the Quran resonated in my brain: "When you meet the unbelievers, strike them in the neck." "If you do not go out and fight, God will punish you severely and put others in your place." "Wherever you find the polytheists, kill them, seize them, besiege them, ambush them." "You who believe, do not take the Jews and Christians as friends; they are allies only to each other. Anyone who takes them as an ally becomes one of them." Bin Laden quoted the *hadith*: "The Hour [of Judgment] will not come until the Muslims fight the Jews and kill them."

I didn't want to do it, but I had to: I picked up the Quran and the *hadith* and started looking through them, to check. I hated to do it, because I knew that I would find Bin Laden's quotations in there, and I didn't want to question God's word. But I needed to ask: Did the 9/11 attacks stem from true belief in true Islam? And if so, what did *I* think about Islam?

Osama Bin Laden said, "Either you are with the Crusade, or you are with Islam," and I felt that Islam all over the world was now in a truly terrible crisis. Surely, no Muslim could continue to ignore the clash between reason and our religion? For centuries we had been behaving as though all knowledge was in the Quran, refusing to question anything, refusing to progress. We had been hiding from reason for so long because we were incapable of facing up to the need to integrate it into our beliefs. And this was not working; it was leading to hideous pain and monstrous behavior.

We Muslims had been taught to define life on earth as a passage, a test that precedes real life in the Hereafter. In that test, everyone should ideally live in a manner resembling, as closely as possible, the followers of the Prophet. Didn't this inhibit investment in improving daily life? Was innovation therefore forbidden to Muslims? Were human rights, progress, women's rights all foreign to Islam?

By declaring our Prophet infallible and not permitting ourselves to question him, we Muslims had set up a static tyranny. The Prophet

Muhammad attempted to legislate every aspect of life. By adhering to his rules of what is permitted and what is forbidden, we Muslims suppressed the freedom to think for ourselves and to act as we chose. We froze the moral outlook of billions of people into the mind-set of the Arab desert in the seventh century. We were not just servants of Allah, we were slaves.

The little shutter at the back of my mind, where I pushed all my dissonant thoughts, snapped open after the 9/11 attacks, and it refused to close again. I found myself thinking that the Quran is not a holy document. It is a historical record, written by humans. It is one version of events, as perceived by the men who wrote it 150 years after the Prophet Muhammad died. And it is a very tribal and Arab version of events. It spreads a culture that is brutal, bigoted, fixated on controlling women, and harsh in war.

The Prophet did teach us a lot of good things. I found it spiritually appealing to believe in a Hereafter. My life was enriched by the Quranic injunctions to be compassionate and show charity to others. There were times when I, like many other Muslims, found it too complicated to deal with the whole issue of war against the unbelievers. Most Muslims never delve into theology, and we rarely read the Quran; we are taught it in Arabic, which most Muslims can't speak. As a result, most people *think* that Islam is about peace. It is from these people, honest and kind, that the fallacy has arisen that Islam is peaceful and tolerant.

But I could no longer avoid seeing the totalitarianism, the pure moral framework that is Islam. It regulates every detail of life and subjugates free will. True Islam, as a rigid belief system and a moral framework, leads to cruelty. The inhuman act of those nineteen hijackers was the logical outcome of this detailed system for regulating human behavior. Their world is divided between "Us" and "Them"—if you don't accept Islam you should perish.

It didn't have to be this way. The West underwent a period of religious warfare and persecution, but then society freed itself from the grip of violent organized religion. I assumed—I still assume—that the same process could occur among the millions of Muslims. We Muslims could shed our attachment to those dogmas that clearly lead to ignorance and oppression. In fact, I thought, we were lucky: there were now so many books that Muslims could read them and leapfrog the Enlightenment, just as the Japanese have done. We could hold our dogmas up to the light, scrutinize them, and then infuse traditions that are rigid and inhumane with the values of progress and modernity. We could come to terms with individual expression.

For me to think this way, of course, I had to make the leap to believing that the Quran was relative—not absolute, not the literal syllables pronounced by God, but just another book. I also had to reject the idea of Hell, whose looming prospect had always frightened me from making any criticism of Islam. I found myself thinking one night, "But if that is so, then what do I believe, truly, about God?"

Around this time, Abshir, the young imam from Somalia, once again contacted me. He had been living in Switzerland for some years, and had just been hospitalized; he was set to undergo heart surgery the next day.

We talked about September 11, of course. I told Abshir, "All these statements that Bin Laden and his people quote from the Quran to justify the attacks—I looked them up; they are there. If the Quran is timeless, then it applies to every Muslim today. This is how Muslims may behave if they are at war with infidels. It isn't just about the battles of Uhud and Badr in the seventh century."

Abshir said, "You're right, and I'm just as confused as you. I'm being operated on for my heart, but it's my head that's hurting." He told me he had begun attending talks on Islam in Geneva by the French Islamic philosopher Tarek Ramadan. Ramadan is the grandson of Hasan al-Banna, who founded the Muslim Brotherhood. After these talks, Abshir said, "I find I'm even more confused. He talks in circles. He says things like 'The Prophet has declared Islam is peace, therefore it's peace.' "

I said, "Yes, but those verses about peace in the Quran apply only to life among the Muslims. The Prophet also said 'Wage war on the unbelievers.' Who are the unbelievers, and who gives the signal to wage war?"

"It's certainly not Bin Laden who's the authority," Abshir said. "We can't wage war against a whole hemisphere where Muslims aren't in control."

I broke in, "Abshir, if we say the Quran is not timeless, then it's not holy, is it?"

He said, "What are you talking about?"

I told him, "I'm sorry, but I think I'm on the brink of becoming an apostate. I'm finding it more and more difficult to believe."

There was silence on the other end of the phone. Then Abshir said, "This thing has confused us all. You're living with a lot of stress. It's always difficult to maintain perspective in the context of a non-Islamic country. Give yourself a break, take some time off. You need to get back in touch with our family, with our kinsmen. You're too isolated from the Osman Mahamud. Ayaan, if you think about this, you risk Hell."

I said, "But if I'm questioning the holiness of the Quran, that means I also question the existence of Hell and Heaven."

Abshir said, "That's impossible."

I told him, "It's not just that. All these angels and djinns—I may be very underdeveloped in my understanding of the exact sciences, but I still see no proof of their existence. Abshir, looking at the paintings here in the West, are these the angels, beings in white dresses with chubby cheeks?"

Abshir said, "No, Muslim angels are totally different. They don't have wings."

I said, "You know I am now going to ask you what they look like, and you will tell me you don't know, because Allah reveals things in His time."

Abshir said, "I love you. I, too, am confused. This has had a huge impact on all of us. Please, don't do this, Ayaan. Give yourself a break."

I wished him lots of luck and the moral strength to find a way out of this dilemma. Abshir was intelligent, compassionate, and generous, but he was scared. Scared of the angel who would visit him after he died to interrogate him on his loyalty to Allah and the Prophet. He was scared of failing that exam, and of the endless hellfire that would await him. We hung up awkwardly. I knew I wouldn't be talking to him again.

In November 2001, I attended a debate at The Balie, a discussion house in Amsterdam. It was organized by *Letter and Spirit,* the review section of the newspaper *Trouw,* which was run by two men, Jaffe Vink and Chris Rutenfrans, and was fast becoming something of a forum for discussion of the relationship between Islam and the West. *Letter and Spirit* published all kinds of articles by people who didn't necessarily share the mainstream view that Islam was a peaceful, Aristotle-rescuing movement. At The Balie, the discussion was entitled "The West or Islam: Who Needs a Voltaire?"

The speakers, one after another, supported the premise that another Voltaire is needed in the West. They pointed out everything that is wrong with the West: the arrogance of invading other countries, and neocolonialism, and the decadence of a system that had created societies that only consume, and so on. It was the usual. Then came Afshin Ellian, from Iran, a professor of penal law at Amsterdam University, who eloquently proposed that Islam needed critical renewal.

It was time for general debate in the audience. Most people seemed to agree with the speakers who had criticized the West in some aspect or other. I decided to speak. I raised my hand for the microphone and said, "Look at how many Voltaires the West has. Don't deny us the right to have our Voltaire, too. Look at our women, and look at our countries. Look at how we are all fleeing and asking for refuge here, and how people are now flying planes into buildings in their madness. Allow us a Voltaire, because we are truly living in the Dark Ages."

When I finished, the room was full of raised hands, many of them Muslim. This was Amsterdam; lots of people attend these talks, so their presence at this debate was natural. But almost all of them seemed very angry with me and Afshin Ellian. They went on about Averroes and saving Aristotle, and how Islam discovered the zero, and so on. It was irritating. So what has happened in Islamic civilization since the year 1200? But I couldn't just take charge of the microphone; I could only roll my eyes and curl my lip.

When the debate ended, Afshin came up to me and said, "You're a little Voltaire yourself. Where did you spring from?"

I said, "I'm from Somalia," and Afshin said, "I just *know* our Muslim civilization will be saved by a woman." He was very nice. He was a refugee himself.

While we were talking, Chris Rutenfrans, one of the editors of the *Trouw* supplement, came up to us. He introduced himself and said to me, "Why don't you write us an article about these ideas, just as you said them here?"

I said I would be delighted, and in the next few days I worked furiously. But I was not allowed to publish articles without showing them to my boss at the Wiardi Beckman office, because the newspaper would identify me as a researcher there. A few days later, I showed my draft of the article to my director, Paul Kalma. He was annoyed. We were a think tank, we were paid to think, and of course he was in favor of freedom of expression, he told me; but I couldn't possibly say such things. It would harm the Labor Party. Even if I signed it with just my name, no affiliation to the Institute at all, the minute a Muslim published such an article, all the racists and Islamophobes would seize on it.

I told Paul, "That's not relevant, because when something is true, it is true." But it was a sensitive time in Dutch politics. Pim Fortuyn, a complete unknown in Dutch politics, had begun a meteoric rise in popularity on the basis of his accurate observation that ethnic minorities didn't sufficiently espouse Dutch values. Fortuyn pointed out that Muslims would soon be the majority in most of Holland's major cities; he said they mostly failed to accept the rights of women and homosexuals, as well as the basic principles that underlie democracy. Rather than dealing forthrightly with the issues that Fortuyn raised, the Labor Party had basically decided to avoid them.

Paul Kalma was honest, and a good person; there was a lot of affection between us. He was seeking to protect me, to prevent me from pandering to racists by voicing right-wing views. So he edited my article until he was comfortable that potential racists would not be able to abuse it.

In those days, especially in Labor Party circles, people were always positive about Islam. If Muslims wanted mosques and separate graveyards and ritual slaughterhouses, such things were built. Community centers were provided. Islamic fundamentalist ideas were swelling in such centers, but Labor Party people usually dismissed this as a natural reaction. These immigrants had been uprooted, they said; they were clinging, temporarily, to traditional ideas, which would gradually fade away. They forgot how long it had taken Europe to shake off obscurantism and intolerance, and how difficult that struggle was.

When Somalis told me they didn't want to live in *gaalo* neighborhoods, I knew they wanted to avoid contact with the ungodliness of Holland. But Dutch officials always saw it as a natural desire to form a community. When Muslims wanted their own school, I saw it as forcing children to obey ideas unquestioningly; the Dutch saw no harm in funding them. When satellite dishes began bristling from every apartment in municipal housing projects, tuned to Moroccan and Turkish TV, my Labor Party colleagues saw this as a natural desire to maintain contact with home.

But with the dishes came preaching, indoctrination. There were door-to-door preachers passing out cassettes in most Dutch cities, just like Boqol Sawm did in Eastleigh. Most migrant neighborhoods had shops selling traditional clothes and carpets and tapes, DVDs, and books on how to be a good Muslim in infidel territory. When the number of women wearing headscarves on the street became impossible to ignore, my Labor Party colleagues thought it was only recent immigrants, who would soon abandon the practice. They failed to realize that it was the second generation, who were rediscovering their "roots," brainwashed by jargon I recognized: *tawheed, kufr,* the evil Jews.

After my article was published I received dozens of letters from readers applauding me: "How wonderful that someone like you exists. Have you heard of Spinoza?" I received an invitation to speak at a symposium on Spinoza at the Thomas Mann Institute. I went back to my Enlightenment textbooks and read about Spinoza and figured people were probably connecting us because we were both refugees. (Spinoza's family emigrated to Holland in the 1600s to flee the Inquisition in Portugal.)

I received several other invitations to speak, one of which was in the little Dutch city of Hengelo; they invited me to give their fiftieth annual freedom and human rights speech in December. The title of the evening was "Should We Fear Islam?" I told Paul Kalma about it, and he said, "What is your answer?" I said, "Well, it's yes and no," and he said Fine, I should attend.

I was nervous. I had never written a speech before. I showed what I had written to Chris Rutenfrans from *Trouw*. He wanted to publish it; I asked him to let me give the speech first. But when I asked Paul for permission, and showed him what I'd said, he went scarlet. He told me I was personally attacking the minister for integration, and even the mayor of Amsterdam, Job Cohen, who was prominent in our own Labor Party. (Actually, my intent was more like teasing them for being so silly as to think that Muslims would integrate best if the Dutch indulged every kind of Muslim self-segregation.) Paul said he had a duty to protect me from writing this right-wing stuff.

Everything I wrote about Islam turned out to be much more sensitive than any other topic I could have chosen to write about. I changed a couple of terms: I was learning that in these extremely civilized circles, conflict is dealt with in a very ornate and hypocritical manner.

When I told Chris Rutenfrans I had another draft, he realized right away that my boss had advised me to tone it down. He called Paul, and they had a shouting match. The next weekend, the revised article appeared in *Trouw*. But a week later Jaffe Vink, Rutenfrans's coeditor at the supplement, wrote an article about the quarrel. He quoted all the material that Paul made me remove, such as comparing Job Cohen to an ayatollah.

Two days later there was a board meeting at the Wiardi Beckman Institute, with Job Cohen himself, and my article—and Vink's piece in *Trouw*—was on the agenda. I just kept quiet. Paul Kalma told the board, "Ayaan is just starting out. She's sharp, but she shouldn't have gone so far." Cohen asked him, "This description of your quarrel in *Trouw*, is it true?" Paul said, "Of course I didn't want her to write this sort of personal attack. We're members of the same party. A conflict of opinion should be solved behind closed doors, not in a newspaper."

Cohen snapped, "If she wants to write it she should write it. I don't mind in the least being called an ayatollah; what I mind is censorship." He looked at me and said, "I've read what you said, and I want the opportunity to say I don't agree with you. This is an institute for thought. As long as it's well argued, you should be able to write what you want." He blew me away with his open-mindedness.

Cohen went on to say that the Labor Party needed more thinking about these subjects. He had been the junior minister for migration policy, and he said immigration wasn't so much the issue: people should be focusing now on the shocking deficit in integrating the children and grandchildren of immigrants into Dutch society. He said, "Ayaan, why don't you look into that for us?" I thought he was a hero.

I began reading everything I could lay my hands on about immigration and integration. Basically, I saw the problem as similar to those of the *miyé*—the rural, poor lands—being brought to the city. European societies, with their thrilling technology, easy money, and bright lights, were decadent and tempting and unassailable, their codes a cipher. The question was how to adapt.

In February I attended a conference on Islam in Europe held by the European Social Democrat Parties in Granada, Spain. All present seemed to think that it would be easy to set up the institutions for a European Islam in peace and harmony. They seemed clouded by wishful thinking rather than operating with rigorous analysis. A tiny community of so-called experts on immigration in Europe had been quoting each other for decades, it appeared: they shared an approach that was essentially socioeconomic. I thought we also needed a broader, cultural analysis of immigrant integration. In the past, Dutch social democrats had blamed the Catholic Church for keeping people poor and ignorant. I was only a junior researcher, but I thought to myself, "When are they going to look at Islam?"

Surely Islam was some kind of influence in the underperforming segregation of so many immigrants in Holland? As I went on doing research, it became painfully apparent that of all the non-Western immigrants in Holland, the least integrated are Muslims. Among immigrants, unemployment is highest for Moroccans and Turks, the largest Muslim groups, although their average level of skills is roughly the same as all the other immigrant populations. Taken as a whole, Muslims in Holland make disproportionately heavy claims on social welfare and disability benefits and are disproportionately involved in crime.

If Muslim immigrants lagged so far behind even other immigrant groups, then wasn't it possible that one of the reasons could be Islam? Islam influences every aspect of believers' lives. Women are denied their social and economic rights in the name of Islam, and ignorant women bring up ignorant children. Sons brought up watching their mother being beaten will use violence. Why was it racist to ask this question? Why was it antiracist to indulge people's attachment to their old ideas and perpetuate this misery? The passive, *Insh'Allah* attitude so prevalent in Islam—"if Allah wills it"—couldn't this also be said to affect people's energy and their will to change and improve the world? If you believe that Allah predestines all, and life on earth is simply a waiting room for the Hereafter, does that belief have no link to the fatalism that so often reinforces poverty?

I recommended that the think tank organize a body of experts to look more deeply into whether high unemployment, crime, and social problems among migrants were also caused by cultural issues—including Islam. Once we perceived these cultural causes of immigrants' misery, we could try to shift this mentality through open debate and real education.

Most women in Holland could walk the streets on their own, wear more or less what they liked, work and enjoy their own salaries, and choose the man they wished to marry. They could attend a university, travel, purchase property. And most Muslim women in Holland simply couldn't. How could you say that Islam had nothing to do with that situation? And how could that situation be in any way acceptable?

When people tell me it is wrong to make this argument—that it is offensive, that it is inopportune at this particular moment—my sense of basic justice is outraged. When, exactly, will it be the right time? Dutch parents breed their daughters to be self-reliant; many, perhaps most, Muslim parents breed them to be docile and submissive. As a result, immigrants' children and grandchildren don't perform in the same way as Dutch young people.

I thought about Johanna and how she explained things to her children, showed them how to make good decisions and stand up for themselves. Her husband was involved in their upbringing; Johanna was a self-reliant woman who chose her own partner and how many children they would have, and when. Clearly she was a very different kind of mother from a twenty-year-old Somali woman in a housing project. Why were we not allowed to look into the impact of such factors on children?

The Dutch government urgently needed to stop funding Quran-based schools, I thought. Muslim schools reject the values of universal human rights. All humans are not equal in a Muslim school. Moreover, there can be no freedom of expression or conscience. These schools fail to develop creativity—art, drama, music—and they suppress the critical faculties that can lead children to question their beliefs. They neglect subjects that conflict with Islamic teachings, such as evolution and sexuality. They teach by rote, not question, and they instill subservience in girls. They also fail to socialize children to the wider community.

That raised a dilemma. Holland's constitution itself permits faith-based schools, in Article 23. If the authorities were to close down only Muslim schools, permitting other forms of private schooling to continue, that would be discrimination. I thought it was time to start a debate on the funding of all faith-based schools. Holland has become an immigrant society, with citizens from all kinds of non-Western backgrounds: Hindu, Buddhist, Muslim. Perhaps everyone, native Dutch children, too, should learn to understand and grow up alongside children from all other backgrounds. Perhaps Article 23 of the Constitution should be abolished. Government funds would be better used setting up schools that are ideologically neutral and encourage kids to question and respect pluralism.

I was making Paul Kalma nervous about my views on education. I no longer sounded right-wing to him; I sounded positively communist. "Do you realize what Article 23 of the Constitution means to Holland, and to the feelings of the average Dutch person?" he asked me. "Don't you know the history of conflict that preceded it? Do you honestly imagine that article will be modified just because of the integration question?"

I said, "Oh, so we are no longer a think tank? Aren't we supposed to think things through? The arrival of migrants in this country is going to affect the heart of Dutch society, and it's time to face that."

I miss those days—those sharp but friendly discussions.

In May 2002, Ellen and I decided to go on vacation. Perhaps Abshir had been right, I thought: I did need a break. We went to Corfu, and I took along with me a little brown book, *The Atheist Manifesto,* which Marco had handed me one day during an argument we were having.

When Marco gave it to me, I felt as if he were handing me his holy book, as if I had pressed the Quran on him, and it put me off. But now I wanted to read it. I wanted to think this thing through. My questions were taboo. According to my upbringing, if I was not a follower of God, I must be a follower of Satan. But I couldn't be spouting answers for Holland's problems when I still had questions about my own religious faith.

Before we left, I told Ellen, "I have huge doubts about God's existence, and the Hereafter. I'm planning to read this book while we're away, and think about it. Are you offended?" Ellen grew quiet. She said, "I'm not offended. I understand completely. I'll be there for you, like you were there for me when I was asking these questions."

I read the book, marveling at the clarity and naughtiness of its author. But I really didn't have to. Just looking at it, just wanting to read it—that already meant I doubted, and I knew that. Before I'd read four pages I already knew my answer. I had left God behind years ago. I was an atheist.

I had no one to talk to about this. One night in that Greek hotel I looked in the mirror and said out loud, "I don't believe in God." I said it slowly, enunciating it carefully, in Somali. And I felt relief.

It felt right. There was no pain, but a real clarity. The long process of seeing the flaws in my belief structure and carefully tiptoeing around the frayed edges as parts of it were torn out, piece by piece—that was all over. The angels, watching from my shoulders; the mental tension about having sex without marriage, and drinking alcohol, and not observing any religious obligations—they were gone. The ever-present prospect of hellfire lifted, and my horizon seemed broader. God, Satan, angels: these were all figments of human imagination. From now on I could step firmly on the ground that was under my feet and navigate based on my own reason and self-respect. My moral compass was within myself, not in the pages of a sacred book.

When we got back from Corfu, I began going to museums. I needed to see ruins and mummies and old dead people, to look at the reality of the bones and to absorb the realization that, when I die, I will become just a bunch of bones. I was on a psychological mission to accept living without a God, which means accepting that I give my life its own meaning. I was looking for a deeper sense of morality. In Islam you are Allah's slave: you submit, and thus, ideally, you are devoid of personal will. You are not a free individual. You behave well because you fear Hell; you have no personal ethic. If God meant only that which is good, and Satan that which is evil, then both were in me. I wanted to develop the good side of me—discipline, generosity, love—and suppress the bad: anger, envy, laziness, cruelty.

I didn't want any more imaginary guides telling me what to do, but I needed to believe I was still moral. Now I read the works of the great thinkers of the Enlightenment—Spinoza, Locke, Kant, Mill, Voltaire—and the modern ones, Russell and Popper, with my full attention, not just as a class assignment. All life is problem solving, Popper says. There are no absolutes; progress comes through critical thought. Popper admired Kant and Spinoza but criticized them when he felt their arguments were weak. I wanted to be like Popper: free of constraint, recognizing greatness but unafraid to detect its flaws.

Three hundred and fifty years ago, when Europe was still steeped in religious dogma and thinkers were persecuted—just as they are today in the Muslim world—Spinoza was clear-minded and fearless. He was the first modern European to state clearly that the world is not ordained by a separate God. Nature created itself, Spinoza said. Reason, not obedience, should guide our lives. Though it took centuries to crumble, the entire ossified cage of European social hierarchy—from kings to serfs, and between men and women, all of it shored up by the Catholic Church—was destroyed by this thought.

Now, surely, it was Islam's turn to be tested.

Humans themselves are the source of good and evil, I thought. We must think for ourselves; we are responsible for our own morality. I arrived at the conclusion that I couldn't be honest with others unless I was honest with myself. I wanted to comply with the goals of religion, which are to be a better and more generous person, without suppressing my will and forcing it to obey inhuman rules. I would no longer lie, to myself or others. I had had enough of lying. I was no longer afraid of the Hereafter.

CHAPTER 15

Threats

In March 2002 Pim Fortuyn won a huge victory in local elections in Rotterdam. An almost total newcomer, he booted the Labor Party out of power in Holland's biggest city, and the world's largest port, for the first time since the Second World War. National elections were to be held in May, and Labor went into a flutter of panic.

Personally, I wasn't surprised or frightened by Pim Fortuyn's popularity. To me, he seemed like a fresh voice, and some of the things he said were the plain truth. Fortuyn could certainly be irritating, but I thought there was nothing racist about him. He was a gay man standing up for his right to be gay in his country, where homosexuals have rights. He was a provocateur, which is a very Dutch thing to be. People called him an extreme right-winger, but to me, many of Fortuyn's policies seemed more like liberal socialism. Though I would never have voted for him, I saw Fortuyn as mostly attached to a secular society's ideals of justice and freedom.

Pim Fortuyn was a symptom of the failure of the Labor Party and the other established parties in politics to take a clear look at the social situation of immigrants. Although I didn't always agree with his views, I was grateful, actually, that it was Fortuyn talking about some of these issues and not some real racist.

It wasn't clear yet, but a rift was opening within the Dutch Left, and within left-wing parties all over Europe. Former left-wingers, like Paul Scheffer, Arie van der Zwan, and Pim Fortuyn, began criticizing the moral and cultural relativism of the leftist parties. Paul Cliteur, one of my professors at Leiden, a staunch believer in reason and a sharp debater, dared early on to criticize both multiculturalism and Islam. The media dubbed him a right-wing conservative, which simply wasn't true.

Dutch politics was becoming a mess. Citizens generally felt that established politicians weren't listening to what they really wanted, which was a better health care system, less bureaucracy, and a response to the social problems of immigrants. The Dutch government of the day had sent troops to the UN peacekeeping force in the former Yugoslavia, troops who turned a blind eye to the Serbian massacres at Srebrenitsa. Yet not one politician resigned over it. What did political responsibility mean, if nobody suffered for a decision that caused thousands of deaths? How could politicians be surprised that people stopped voting for parties that behaved this way?

In May, Fortuyn declared that he would permit asylum seekers who had been living in Holland for a long time to remain in the country, even if their appeals had failed. It was front-page news, and I welcomed it. Paul Kalma and I had been pleading with the Labor Party to agree to just such an amnesty.

Sitting in a coffee shop in Berlin after a symposium on Europe and immigration, I wailed at Paul, "Why didn't Labor go for this? Pim Fortuyn tells right-wing audiences what they want to hear, which is that the current situation is failing to integrate migrants, and he tells left-wing audiences what they want to hear, which is that an amnesty is inevitable and humane."

The elections were due in just nine days, and Fortuyn was now so high in the polls that he could even become prime minister. I felt, however, that even if he did take over the government, it wouldn't last long; he didn't have the experience to handle the job. His own political party was a mess—it didn't even have a proper name—and I had learned in Leiden that in party systems, such one-man candidacies are almost always a flash in the pan.

Two days later, Fortuyn was shot dead in a parking lot outside Holland's largest TV and radio studios. Everyone was appalled. Such a thing hadn't happened in Holland since the brothers de Witt were lynched in the streets of The Hague in 1672. In modern times, all Dutch politicians cycled or rode the trains or drove themselves to work just like everyone else. The murder of a political leader for his opinions was simply unthinkable, and the scale of the country's emotional reaction was almost impossible to exaggerate.

The minute I heard about Fortuyn's murder I found myself thinking again, "Oh, Allah, please let it not be a Muslim who did this." I was not alone. There was a general sense that if Fortuyn's assassin was a Muslim, hideous things could happen in reprisal: killings, burnings. When we heard that a white animal-rights activist was apparently responsible for the shooting, it seemed as if the whole country let out a collective sigh of relief. Wim Kok decided to hold the elections regardless, and Pim Fortuyn's party entered Parliament with twenty-six seats. Labor lost big.

After that, Kok, the Labor leader I had voted for and admired, left politics. He had transformed Labor from a spendthrift, dogmatic, almost communist-style party to a third-way party, pretty much like Tony Blair's Labor Party in Britain. He was a real coalition builder: he found ways to respond to all kinds of different communities and was skilled at keeping all opposing parties happy. (This is a very difficult thing to do, and I have often fallen short of it.) I felt that Kok's departure was a blow to the country, and that when he left Dutch politics along with the Liberal leader Frits Bolkestein, a kind of self-evident leadership and thoughtful maturity went with them. The political arena became populated by people of much less stature and was reduced to personal squabbling and infighting of a kind that had not been seen before.

A few weeks before Fortuyn was killed, a documentary filmmaker, Karin Schagen, asked me if she could do a short film about my life as a refugee in Holland. Over the course of that summer, she drove me around to the office in Zeewolde where I had first asked for asylum, and the places I had lived. It had been ten years since I first arrived in Holland, and I gladly showed her around.

One evening Karin phoned my father. He was visiting my stepmother, Maryan, in London, where Maryan, too, had received refugee status. My father told Karin that he was receiving threats on my life. Somalis from Italy, from Scandinavia, from Holland were phoning him and warning, "Hirsi, if you don't do something fast to rein in your daughter, she is going to be killed."

At first Karin didn't tell me about that conversation. Later, when she did let me know, I didn't take it seriously. Who would bother to kill me?

In early August I was invited to appear on a Dutch TV program about women in Islam. There were a number of short items on girls in the Netherlands who had escaped their parents' abuse, and about girls who chose to walk about veiled even though they were living in Holland.

When I was asked for my opinion, I explained that Islam was like a mental cage. At first, when you open the door, the caged bird stays inside: it is frightened. It has internalized its imprisonment. It takes time for the bird to escape, even after someone has opened the doors to its cage.

A week after the show aired, my phone rang: it was my father. He said, "What on earth is happening, child? It's raining phone calls. In just one week I have been called by twenty people. What is all this stuff I'm hearing about you? What have you said about Islam?"

I told him, "Abeh, there are so many Muslim women in shelters here, who have been beaten. The men who beat them say these women must obey because Islam requires it. I am exposing this relationship between our faith and the behavior of our men."

My father said, "Islam does not say women should be beaten. Islam is a religion of freedom, and peace. You can fight the oppression of women, Ayaan, but you must not link it with Islam."

I couldn't bear to tell him directly that I no longer believed he was right. I spluttered, "No, it's not that," but my father cut me off. He told me he was praying for me, and he told me to pray; then he hung up.

A month later, on the first anniversary of the 9/11 attacks, I was invited to the most popular talk show on Dutch TV at the time, a live program that aired at 10:15 p.m. Early that morning my doorbell rang, and two huge men told me that the show had sent them to accompany me to work and all my appointments that day. It was a normal courtesy, they said.

I was only going to Amsterdam. The train station was right around the corner; it was a simple commute. I thanked the men and told them I didn't need their services, but Karin, who was still filming me, was encumbered by cameras; she was glad for the lift, so we accepted.

In the car, looking at all the communications equipment and the heavy doors, and the enormous backs of these two men, Karin went silent. Then she said quietly, "Ayaan, this is not standard procedure. Look at the size of these men. They are bodyguards. There's something wrong."

Before we needed to be at the TV studio, they accompanied us to the Felix Meritis discussion house in Amsterdam, where I had been invited to participate in a debate on the integration of Moroccan youth. Someone from the Liberal Party was also speaking, and a Moroccan woman who was alderman of an Amsterdam neighborhood. As the debate went on and we discussed the apathy and hostility of many migrants, it became clear that the Moroccan woman and I disagreed the most, and the Liberal and I agreed in essence.

I often found this to be the case. Especially in public, Muslim opinion leaders loudly denied the truth of what I was saying; yet in private, some Muslim women would agree with me. As for Dutch people, the Labor types usually felt uneasy about my critique of their multicultural tolerance of Islamic practices, but Liberals were often enthusiastic about my emphasis on the rights of the individual.

After the debate, my two drivers took us to Utrecht for another panel discussion about Islam and multiculturalism. This discussion took place in a café full of Moroccan young people. As I came in they booed loudly. I was astonished: Did all these people recognize me? Every time I opened my mouth they shouted, and others shouted back. A fault line seemed to divide the room between the native-born Dutch, who approved of my views, and the Muslims. One after another the Moroccan kids stood up, men and women, and told me, "You're a traitor. You sound like Pim Fortuyn. You know nothing about Islam. You're stigmatizing us."

The atmosphere was thick with personal insults and bad feeling, but I had to leave for the TV studio. In the car, I said, "Karin, what is going on with these people?"

Karin said, "Don't you realize how small this country is, and how explosive it is, what you're saying?"

Explosive? In a country where prostitution and soft drugs are licit, where euthanasia and abortion are practiced, where men cry on TV and naked people walk on the beach and the pope is joked about on national TV? Where the famous author Gerard Reve is renowned for having fantasized about making love with a donkey, an animal he used as a metaphor for God? Surely nothing I could say would be seen as anything close to "explosive" in such a context.

"These people have lived here for years," I told her. "The girls were all wearing tight trousers and T-shirts—they're Westernized. They attend debates. They're accustomed to criticism."

"You're wrong," Karin said, "If your name hadn't been on the flyers, they wouldn't have come. With you, there is something to discuss. They don't attend these things regularly—they've heard about you from TV. I don't think they are accustomed to this kind of criticism—not from someone who is a Muslim, like you."

We arrived just before the show was scheduled to air. Frits Barend and Henk Van Dorp, the hosts, told me they had received a threatening phone call about my appearance, and the police were taking it seriously. I was startled, but I had no room in my brain to deal with this information right now: it was time to go on the air.

After briefly introducing me, Frits Barend asked, "So, you came to Holland in 1992 as an asylum seeker. Did you lie, like everybody else did?" I answered that yes, I had lied, about my name and about my story, and I explained why: I was afraid of being sent back to my clan. They seemed to accept that, and after more questions, asked the big one of the day: "Do you agree with Pim Fortuyn that Islam is backward?"

I was taken aback, but answered, "According to the Arab Human Development Report of the UN, if you measure by three things—political freedom, education, and the status of women—then what Pim Fortuyn said is not an opinion, it's a fact." I thought I had been very deft. I had not actually repeated what Fortuyn had so controversially stated, but I was clear and, I thought, accurate. Aspects of Islam did slow a society's development, by curbing critical thinking and holding women back.

Next I was asked, "But are you still a Muslim?" Now I felt truly on the spot. And once again I avoided a direct repudiation of Islam, answering instead, "I am secularized."

I did not feel strong enough to face what would happen if I said, out loud, that I no longer believed. For a Muslim, to be an apostate is the worst thing possible. Christians can cease to believe in God; that is a personal matter that affects only their eternal soul. But for a Muslim to cease believing in Allah is a lethal offence. Apostates merit death: on that, the Quran and the *hadith* are clear. For a Muslim woman to abjure her faith is the worst kind of disobedience to God, because it comes from the lowest, most impure element in society. It cries out for God's punishment.

I had been invited to another debate the next day. There really was a public discussion of these issues under way, I thought, as I accepted every invitation to speak; it seemed as if the whole country was churning with debate. Again, this debate was televised, this time with mostly Muslim men and women present. Finally, I thought, Dutch TV is inviting Muslims to participate in discussions.

I was seated next to Naema Tahir, a beautiful young Pakistani woman who had been married off by her father. Naema had rejected that marriage and put herself through school to earn a master's degree in law. She and I were both dressed in light blue blouses, like schoolgirls, and we felt very much alike. All around us were men, and as the show went on, they began barking at us: screaming, shouting at us, cutting us off. Then one man yelled, "But you're not a Muslim! You said you're not a Muslim! You said Islam is backward! You're lying!"

I sat up and said, "It's my religion, too, and if I want to call it backward I will do so. Yes, Islam is backward."

Chaos broke out. As the atmosphere thickened at that debate, I found myself growing more tense. Men were glowering at me; one of them stormed out. I thought back to what Frits Barend had said the night before. There were no bodyguards around me now.

After the show, the moderator said to me, "You're not safe walking out of here by yourself." He told me the TV program would pay for a taxi to take me all the way back to Leiden. When I got home, the phone rang: it was Johanna and Maarten. They had watched the program and they were worried; they thought something might have happened to me after the filming and were relieved I was home. But Maarten was also angry. He told me I must be more careful. "What you're doing is wrong for you," he said. "You're putting yourself in danger. Try to find something else to talk about."

The next day was a Friday, a normal working day. I got up and took the train as usual to the think tank's office. This was daytime, in Holland: I wasn't frightened. I was, however, very motivated to prepare a proposal for our institute to put real money into investigating the situation of Muslim women in Holland, and I began working on a draft for a proposal. When I popped into Paul Kalma's office, he said to me, "I saw the show last night. You should be careful, Ayaan. I would advise you not to do these things any more. Television is too sensational. Writing opinion pieces may not be so bad after all!"

Everyone seemed to agree that doom was nigh and I was too dumb to have spotted it. I began to feel a little intimidated. A friend arrived at the office to escort me home that evening, and as we were talking together, I looked around nervously: *Did* anyone recognize me? Was I being followed? But no, everything seemed normal: people were cycling, chatting on cell phones, and they paid no special attention to me at all.

That evening Ellen sat me down for a talk. She told me quite frankly that I had lost my mind. I had bought the house with her fourteen months before and I was barely ever home. I worked all the time trying to become the female answer to Bin Laden, and as a result I was ruining my health and our friendship.

The next day, Saturday, Karin came over. We phoned my father again. Again, he told Karin there were threats against me, that he was truly afraid that people were planning to have me killed. Karin took notes on the conversation. But when I spoke to him, he didn't repeat it: I think my father wanted to protect me from fear. He just told me, "Be very careful." I asked "Careful of what?" and my father said again, "I'm getting warnings from everywhere. Don't say anything about Islam."

When I hung up, Karin said, "Your father wants me to look after you. He thinks you're going to be assassinated."

I said, "For heaven's sake. My father grew up far away, long ago. Come on, what have I done? I'm just a little pawn who earns sixteen hundred euros a month. You don't murder people for raising a small voice in a small country."

Then Marco called. He told me he had to see me. I said fine, I would cycle right over, and he said, "Don't do that—you can't go out on your own." I told him this was absurd, but he came by in his car and drove me to a sweet little village called Roelofsarendsveen, where the chance of encountering an angry radical Muslim was next to zero. Marco said, "Ayaan, something could happen to you. You have to be careful."

While we were talking, my phone rang. It was Leon de Winter, a famous Dutch writer. I asked "Oh, are you going to tell me to be careful?" because all these lectures from friends and colleagues were starting to get on my nerves. But de Winter said, "No, I am only going to say how much I admire you. I watched you on TV the past two evenings, and I really think what you're doing for us is great." He warmly invited me to dinner the next week, which was something like an American receiving an invitation from Philip Roth, except that in Holland everyone knows Leon de Winter. I accepted, of course, but I told him, "I'm a little ashamed, because I haven't read any of your books." He said, "No problem. I've read your articles."

The phone rang again, and now it was Jaffe Vink from *Trouw*, who said, "I want you to talk to this special policeman who works for the Dutch Secret Service, because something very bad is brewing. I think the threats against you are real. You can see him on Monday." I agreed to do it.

I spent that weekend at home with Ellen, doing chores and trying to mend our flagging friendship. On Monday morning I went to meet this special policeman. His office was like a prison: bars, and more bars, and every door with elaborate locks and cameras. I told the man, "I don't know what I did or said, but my father is afraid I will be assassinated, and all sorts of people seem to be terribly worried about me. I haven't received any threats directly, so I feel a little dumb, but it's beginning to frighten me."

He said, "You are a little dumb, because these threats are very real. We know about some of them. You'll need protection. Go to the police office in Leiden and file a complaint. And tell them about the stuff on the Internet."

I said, "Is there something about me on the Internet?"

He sighed and said, "A lot, and it's growing. We're monitoring it." This man was very Dutch, very avuncular and protective, and he told me to stop thinking I was an invisible nonentity. I had set off something that could be very big and very dangerous.

I went to the police station in Leiden, which I knew well from my work as a translator. A police officer who had already heard about me—and seemed, in fact, to know far more about my situation than I did—said police would evaluate the security of my house, and that Ellen and I would have to change the locks.

He asked, "How many people do you think know your address?" I showed him one of my business cards: my home address was printed on it. I'd given those cards out to people at debates all over the country. Networking was part of my job. Moreover, I said, Ellen and I were in the phone book. He groaned.

At another Wiardi Beckman Institute board meeting that night, I was on the agenda again, but nobody blamed me for anything. Again, Job Cohen was splendid. He said, "Whether I agree or disagree with Ayaan is irrelevant. Any threat against her for expressing a simple opinion is completely unacceptable to all of us."

I thought, "Why on earth isn't Cohen the leader of the Labor Party?" He was such a clear thinker; he had authority; he understood the rule of law better than anyone I knew. I felt slightly ashamed that I had once called him names in an article. After the meeting, Cohen came up to me and said, "Ayaan, you look exhausted. I want you to think long and hard about taking on this challenge. This could take a long time. Do you want to live like this? Go and eat something, and get some sleep, and think about it."

It was clear to everyone, apparently, that I shouldn't take the train to work again. It wasn't clear to me exactly what they thought I should be protected against, but all were adamant that any chance encounter might set off some kind of violence. So that night Karin drove me home, and the next morning she came with her crew and drove me to work. The following day, Paul Kalma called the hosts of the TV show and got the name of the private bodyguard service they had used to protect me. He decided to hire them to drive me to and from work.

My daily life became unbelievably complicated. When I was at work in

Amsterdam, the Amsterdam police were responsible for my safety. But once I got to Leiden, thirty miles away, I had to phone the Leiden police to let them know I was home, because now they were responsible for me. Moreover, the bodyguard service was expensive, and the Labor Party, having lost a number of votes, had just slashed the funding of our think tank. Paul Kalma asked me if I couldn't find an address in Amsterdam for a while, so the Amsterdam police could just walk me home every night.

A reporter called to talk to me. I said, "I can't. I just filed a complaint, and I'm not going to talk to the media any more." She put that in the paper; it became headline news that I was being forced into hiding. I received bags full of mail and lots of offers from people who wanted to hide me in their homes. One was my former professor of Methods of Social Research. He lived near the Labor Party office, and his duplex apartment included a granny flat with a kitchenette, which was empty.

We decided that I should move in there temporarily, after the weekend. When I told Ellen, I could feel the air stiffen with her disapproval. We had an argument; she accused me of abandoning my share of the housework and of our friendship. I told her she wasn't supportive when I needed her. It was ugly, and the bodyguards were honking impatiently. I left.

That evening I was supposed to have dinner at the Hilton in Amsterdam with Jaffe Vink, and Leon de Winter and his wife. We had just started the appetizer when suddenly the two bodyguards descended on me, caught my hands, wrapped themselves around me, and said, "We're leaving." I barely had time to put down my fork.

They took me out through the back doors. I didn't see anything, but as we drove away, fast, the bodyguards told me that cars packed with North African–looking men had begun arriving, one after another. They were dropping people off in the hotel parking lot and then heading off to get more people. Someone must have seen me walking into the hotel and cell-phoned his friends. The guards said they weren't equipped to deal with such numbers. I saw nothing, but now I was frightened.

We arrived at the Leiden police station where, an officer told me, they had been doing their own research and felt strongly it was unwise for me to continue sleeping at my house in Leiden. My address was too widely known; there was no way they could protect me. I said, "Are you saying I should sell my house?" The police officer said, "We can't tell you to do something like that, but we can tell you that you're not safe there."

I phoned my father. When he picked up the phone I said, "Hello, Abeh, this is Ayaan." There was a shuffle and a click. This happened a number of times. I had insulted that which he held most dear. Our relationship could never be mended.

When it was clear that my living situation had become untenable, Leon de Winter proposed that I go to a writers' retreat in California to take a break. I could return when things had calmed down in Holland. I didn't have the money for such a trip, but Paul Scheffer suggested that the Institute set up a nonprofit foundation and raise funds.

I had come to incarnate a situation that Holland was beginning to perceive and was shocked by. This peaceful country, which thought it had reached the peak of civilization and had nothing more to worry about except perhaps the dikes breaking one day, was waking up to the nightmare of citizens who completely disagreed with fundamental values like free speech—to the realities of airplane attacks and murdered politicians and death threats. The news that a young woman could have her life threatened merely for speaking the truth, as she saw it, on TV seemed to many people an important symbol.

People petitioned for my right to free expression. They sent flowers. My views became a subject for debate. Some people claimed that all the threats against me were just lies and hype, but many others, whom I didn't even know, seemed to be working now to gather support for me. Leon de Winter, Geert Mak, Harry van den Berg, and Paul Scheffer, all well-known Dutch writers; Job Cohen; Felix Rottenberg, a former leader of the Labor Party, and Paul Kalma, my boss; Tilly Hermans, now my Dutch book publisher, and Cisca Dresselhuys, a prominent feminist—all these extremely visible and important figures were involved in my case. They wanted me to be able to return to Holland safely, and under the protection of the elite police corps that protects well-known politicians and the royal family, instead of just under the eye of the local police.

In October 2002, I flew to California. It was the first time I had ever been in the United States, and I realized almost immediately that my preconceptions of America were completely ludicrous. I was expecting rednecks and fat people, with lots of guns, very aggressive police, and overt racism—a caricature of a caricature. In reality, of course, I saw people living perfectly well-ordered lives, jogging, and drinking coffee.

I loved the huge bookstores and spent hours in the Barnes & Noble in Santa Monica, where I was staying, buying crateloads of books. It was a relief to have the time to think and read again.

*   *   *

On October 16, 2002, the cabinet fell, after less than three months in power. Pim Fortuyn's group in Parliament was unable to manage a coalition with the Liberals and the Christian Democrats. The small universe of Dutch politics was agog: the country faced the prospect of yet another election, scheduled for January 2003.

Neelie Kroes, a prominent politician from the Liberal Party, which is known in Holland as the VVD, is a strong woman, very dignified and determined. Although we had never met, Neelie was outraged that someone in my position would have to leave the country to seek safety. She organized women politicians from all the main political parties in Holland to issue a statement in support of my right to speak freely, in safety.

Neelie believed that the Dutch Parliament needed more strong, bright women. When the cabinet fell and new elections were called, she thought of me, even though I was only a junior researcher from the Labor Party and she from the right-wing VVD. Neelie called Leon de Winter and told him she wanted me to stand (run) for Parliament for her party.

Far away in America, I thought about it. I wasn't horrified by the idea of being called right wing, as some people are. In Holland, all the political parties are in favor of an active, almost invasive degree of government intervention in the business of buying and selling, with high taxes and redistribution of wealth. In economic terms, the Liberal Party stands for less government interference and lower taxes; I felt comfortable with this. In terms of its principles, the Liberals were secular, careful to be neutral about religion. They stood for abortion rights, gay rights—the emancipation of the individual.

Moreover, I felt disappointed by the Labor Party. I had joined them originally because, in my mind, social democrats stood for reform. They sought to improve people's lives; they cared about suffering, which I thought should have meant they would care about the suffering of Muslim women. But in reality, the Labor Party in Holland appeared blinded by multiculturalism, overwhelmed by the imperative to be *sensitive* and *respectful* of immigrant culture, defending the moral relativists. When I said the position of Muslim women had to change—to change now—people were always telling me to wait, or calling me right wing. Was that what they told the mine workers in the nineteenth century when they fought for workers' rights?

Neelie was planning a trip to visit her son, who was living in San Francisco, and it was there that we actually met. I told her I was considering moving to the United States to pursue a PhD. We talked politics. She listened as I went on about the Enlightenment and John Stuart Mill and the cage of women's repression and then caught my eye with a decisive air and told me, "You're not a socialist. You are one of us."

Neelie said my dreams of academia were like a sinkhole; they would never go anywhere. No matter how wonderful a PhD thesis I wrote, it would disappear into a file drawer. It would never shift the lives of Muslim women by an inch. The most important thing I could do with my life was expose the reality of those women's lives to people in power and make sure that existing laws demanding equality between the sexes were applied. Mine was in a combat of action, not ideas. I should stand for Parliament, where I could truly have an effect on the emancipation of Muslim women and the integration of immigrants.

That night I thought about what Neelie had said. What was I trying to achieve? Three things: first, I wanted Holland to wake up and stop tolerating the oppression of Muslim women in its midst; the government must take action to protect them and punish their oppressors. Second, I wanted to spark a debate among Muslims about reforming aspects of Islam so that people could begin to question, and criticize, their own beliefs. This could happen only in the West, where Muslims may speak out; in no Muslim country can there be free discussion on such a subject.

Third, I wanted Muslim women to become more aware of just how bad, and how unacceptable, their suffering was. I wanted to help them develop the vocabulary of resistance. I was inspired by Mary Wollstonecraft, the pioneering feminist thinker who told women they had the same ability to reason as men did and deserved the same rights. Even after she published *A Vindication of the Rights of Women,* it took more than a century before the suffragettes marched for the vote. I knew that freeing Muslim women from their mental cage would take time, too. I didn't expect immediate waves of organized support among Muslim women. People who are conditioned to meekness, almost to the point where they have no mind of their own, sadly have no ability to organize, or will to express their opinion.

When I worked at the Labor Party think tank, trying to talk about these issues, people always accused me of failing to back up my arguments with data. But hard numbers were completely unavailable. When I tried to find out about honor killings, for instance—how many girls were killed every year in Holland by their fathers and brothers because of their precious family honor—civil servants at the Ministry of Justice would tell me, "We don't register murders based on that category of motivation. It would stigmatize one group in society." The Dutch government registered the number of drug-related killings and traffic accidents every year, but not the number of honor killings, because no Dutch official wanted to recognize that this kind of murder happened on a regular basis.

Even Amnesty International didn't keep statistics on how many women around the world were victims of honor killings. They could tell you how many men were imprisoned and tortured, but they couldn't keep tabs on the number of women flogged in public for fornication, or executed for adultery. That wasn't their subject.

I decided that if I were to become a member of the Dutch Parliament, it would become my holy mission to have these statistics registered. I wanted someone, somewhere, to take note every time a man in Holland murdered his child simply because she had a boyfriend. I wanted someone to register domestic violence by ethnic background—and sexual abuse, and incest—and to investigate the number of excisions of little girls that took place every year on Dutch kitchen tables. Once these figures were clear, the facts alone would shock the country. With one stroke, they would eliminate the complacent attitude of moral relativists who claimed that all cultures are equal. The excuse that *nobody knew* would be removed.

If I were in Parliament, I could try to act on my beliefs, not just spout them. And Neelie was right: although the Labor Party had come to seem the right party for me, and although I was truly loyal to Paul Kalma and Job Cohen, many things about me had never fit with Labor's ideas. Social democracy is grounded in the rights of groups of people, not individuals. The Liberal Party may not have been as cuddly as Labor, but its philosophy was grounded in the values of personal freedom. My ideas felt comfortable there.

I was a one-issue politician, I decided. I am still. I am also convinced that this is the largest, most important issue that our society and our planet will face in this century. Every society that is still in the rigid grip of Islam oppresses women and also lags behind in development. Most of these societies are poor; many are full of conflict and war. Societies that respect the rights of women and their freedom are wealthy and peaceful.

I decided I would go wherever I had the most ability to effect change. If the Liberal Party was offering me a platform to stand on, then so be it.

I phoned Paul Kalma and told him I would be leaving both the Labor Party and my job. He told me he thought it was a huge pity that I was switching parties, but he said, "You'll be pursuing your ideals, and I support you." He wished me luck.

Neelie Kroes and the Liberal Party leaders Frits Bolkestein and Gerrit Zalm wanted me to be given a high position on the Liberal list of candidates for the election. Dutch politics doesn't work on the basis of local constituencies. Everyone votes for one nationwide list of candidates, and seats in Parliament are portioned out to the top names on each list, depending on what proportion of the votes each list receives. Dutch political parties are all grounded in powerful local groups, which jostle for electable positions on the list.

I was a rank outsider. If I wanted to be elected to Parliament, I would have to make my case to the Party barons. But Neelie and Zalm wanted my participation in the election to remain confidential until the Liberal Party Congress on November 30. For a week, I traveled around Holland as unobtrusively as possible, shuttling from one local Liberal potentate to another.

The Party barons were mostly hostile at first, although some were curious about me. One elderly man said, "You're from Africa, and you've been threatened because of remarks you made about Islam, and you're a woman, and a member of the Labor Party—and now you want to be with us Liberals? We're entrepreneurs. What do you know about business? Are you even interested in us?"

I answered, "That depends who 'us' is." I said that I wanted to address the issues of immigrant women, especially Muslims, and explained how I thought that affected business. Businessmen had a strong motive to free Muslim women to participate fully in society. If girls and women are uneducated, oppressed, and psychologically demeaned, then their children are all stunted by their ignorance. If women are well educated and nurtured, they and their children make up a self-reliant, responsible citizenry and a productive workforce. I also talked about integration and social welfare. I said, "You know the history of Liberal ideas. The oppression of women in Holland is against the philosophy of your party. To uphold the values of your party you should support my membership of it, because I stand for your values."

Those meetings were honest grillings. Some of the Party leaders thought I was brazen; a few were flat-out hostile. Most told me, "Your cause is brave, and just, but you don't belong in our party." One woman, the baron of the Liberals in Leiden, grilled me for an hour and then said,

"I think I'm going to love you very much. You have a certain authenticity about you, and that is very much a part of our party."

To everyone who asked me, I made it clear that when I first arrived in Holland, I changed my story on my asylum application: I gave another name and didn't tell the whole truth. I said this on TV and in radio and newspaper interviews and told the VVD leadership about it when they asked me if I had anything in my past that might prevent me from functioning properly as a politician. It simply was never an issue.

In the end, Gerrit Zalm got enough support from the Party barons to put me on the VVD list as number sixteen. That meant I was almost certain to be elected.

That week, on the BBC, I listened to the news of riots that had erupted in Nigeria. A young woman journalist assigned to cover the Miss World competition there had written, "Muslims thought it was immoral to bring ninety-two women to Nigeria to ask them to revel in vanity. What would the Prophet Muhammad think? . . . He would probably have chosen a wife from one of them."

More than two hundred people were killed in the riots that broke out. The office of her newspaper was burned down, and the reporter was forced to leave the country. Now I listened to a snotty British woman who had organized the pageant. Instead of blaming the violence on the men who were burning down houses and murdering people, she blamed the young reporter for making "unfortunate remarks."

I was incensed by this excusing of fanaticism. That journalist had written nothing wrong. She was right: the Prophet married most of his wives because they caught his eye in one way or another. As a gesture of solidarity with that young journalist, I decided that when I got the chance, I would say publicly what I thought the Prophet Muhammad was really about.

That moment came just a few days later, when Arjan Visser, a Dutch journalist from *Trouw*, asked me to participate in a series of interviews he was doing, using the Ten Commandments as a framework to talk about the place of religion in people's lives. In the interview I told him what I thought was the real nature of the Prophet. In the next few weeks, the interview didn't run, and I forgot about it.

On November 30, the day of the Liberal Party Congress, I walked into a huge room full of security people. There was a wide bank of cameras

going flashflashflash at me. I was supposed to stand with the other candidates on a platform with a microphone, where each of us would introduce
ourselves, one by one. But I shivered and froze at the doorway. I
couldn't move. In front of me were all those cameras and behind me the
bodyguards. I felt hunted, trapped. I was shaking. Very softly, Gerrit
Zalm told me to be calm, to breathe, and not to worry.

One after the other, the candidates made their speeches, during which
the room was only moderately attentive. Candidate fourteen, candidate
fifteen. It was my turn. I had prepared a small speech with the help of
Neelie and her husband, the politician Bram Peper, but I got frightened
again, because when I stood up everybody in the audience stopped talking. Hundreds of people fell silent, and then the camera shutters all
started up again. I froze on the steps to the dais. Frits Huffnagel, who was
introducing the candidates, could see that I was shaking; he gave me his
hand and said, "Easy."

Somehow I managed to control myself and read my speech. Afterward,
walking down, I was swamped by the media. The camera people even followed me into the ladies' room. One Liberal MP, the former Olympic
swimmer Erika Terpstra, decided to protect me; she put her body around
me and pushed people away.

From that time on I could no longer have a normal relationship with
journalists. I could not simply say what I thought, like an ordinary person. I was now a politician: the media, rather than a source of information, was an instrument I must learn to use. Professional PR people
who dealt with press for the Liberal Party now screened my calls and
requests for interviews from journalists. They gave me a short bio of each
journalist and told me what each was likely to ask. I received a quick education in Liberal Party priorities: the election program, agriculture, housing taxes, and so on. Because I was a Liberal Party candidate, it was
normal that what I said to the media should roughly correspond to the
Party platform.

Most of the media thought switching political parties made me an
opportunist, and they were watching to see if I screwed up. My first interview was supposed to be a human interest story, but I was asked if I still
wanted to ban denominational, religious schools. It was the most sensitive issue in the Netherlands right then. If they won the elections, the Liberals were planning to govern with the Christian Democratic Party, and
for the Christian Democrats, faith-based schools were a holy cow. I said
I was opposed to this form of schooling. I explained how bad Muslim

schools are for education. This set off a small storm about how I wasn't toeing the Liberal Party line, and how I wouldn't make it to the elections.

Gerrit Zalm, the Liberal Party leader, was stalwart throughout my candidacy and my political career. As a professional politician, he was polished and effective, a real example, and on a human level he proved himself to be clear-minded and direct. He didn't support me just because I could attract publicity for the Liberals and help them get elected; he never showed any sign of wanting to tidy me into some corner once the election was done, and he has stuck his neck out for me again and again. Throughout my political career, Zalm consistently led battles in support of my causes, from domestic violence to excision.

After that first interview, Zalm didn't flinch for a moment. He didn't say "This young woman has only just arrived in Holland and she doesn't understand the importance of these institutions to our society." He said, "I'm a Liberal, and there are good arguments for abolishing faith-based schools. But we can't do that right away, because we have to form a government with the Christian Democrats."

For me, the most sensitive issue was general amnesty for asylum seekers who had overstayed their legal residency in Holland. I wanted that amnesty. When I was with the Labor Party think tank, the Labor caucus in Parliament opposed it—but the Liberals opposed it even more. When interviewers asked me about it, I was clear about my views. I told Gerrit Zalm, "You know, I can't agree with everything the Liberals say." Zalm told me that was perfectly fine. I should just be myself. So long as I stuck to my own portfolio, which was integration, and so long as I voted with the Party once I was in Parliament, I could say what I thought.

During two months of campaigning, I went from one TV station to the next, from one speech to another. I sold tangerines in the market in Leiden; I shook hands on street corners. I met many citizens who surprised me with their apparently unconditional support for my ideas, and lots of Labor Party voters who said, "We deplore your choice of party, but your issue is so important that we will vote for you wherever you are." I met Frits Bolkestein, the aging lion of the Liberal Party; he was formal, but at the same time very kindly, paternal, and genuine. He took my ideas seriously and offered me good advice, and he insisted that I call on him whenever I needed help. I developed enormous respect for him.

Of course, I also encountered hostile reactions in campaigning. People called me names, even spat at me; I received more threats. The most remarkable people, to me, were those who apparently approved of everything I said but nonetheless wouldn't dream of voting for the Liberal Party. It reminded me of Somalia: they wouldn't vote outside their clan.

Now that I was a national politician receiving death threats, I was under the protection of the Royal and Diplomatic Protection Service, the DKDB. Everywhere I went I was under heavy guard, in a convoy of cars and armed men. They frightened me a little, at first, these strange men with their radios and weapons. Some of them stood very close and wanted to know every detail of what I was going to do a day in advance. I couldn't deviate from the schedule; every location had to be checked ahead of time. It was awkward going about my daily life under such scrutiny. The guards had to walk around me through the aisles of supermarkets when I went out for groceries. One afternoon, trying to buy pots and pans, I felt like an idiot, as if I ought to try to impress these men with my selection.

Sometimes the DKDB would inform me about a particular threat against my life. Mostly, though, they didn't. They felt it wasn't in my interest for me to obsess about the danger I was in. They were there to protect me; that was all I needed to know. In a way I agreed with them. Thinking about death threats all the time is no way to live.

Neelie Kroes found me a place to stay in The Hague, a lovely apartment that belonged to a friend of hers. But after I'd lived there two weeks, the local newspaper got wind of it from people in the neighborhood and published my address. At around lunchtime that day one of my bodyguards told me, "I'm sorry, but you won't be going back to the apartment. For tonight, we'll take you to a hotel, but you'll have to look for somewhere else to live." I didn't even get to go back to pack; they sent police officers to go through my drawers and pack my clothes and books.

Neelie went through her inexhaustible mental Rolodex and arranged for me to live for a few weeks in an apartment at the top of the phone company building in The Hague, where the director of the phone company could sleep when he was working late. I couldn't stay there for long, though. After two months, it was agreed that I could rent one of the houses on the phone company's grounds for up to a year, until I found a place of my own. It was wonderful, with a fireplace and gardens, and the rent was affordable; I thought that at last I would be able to settle down again. I planned to move in during the last weekend in January.

January 22 was the election. The Liberal Party rented a hall in Utrecht with a big screen; everyone congratulated each other in front of the cameras as the results came in. In reality, however, the Party's gains were quite modest. The Christian Democrats and Labor were the big winners and seemed likely to form a coalition government together. (Governments in Holland are always coalitions.) The Liberals won only 18 percent of the vote—not enough, in principle, to claim the right to govern. Still, we had twenty-seven seats in Parliament, which meant that, as number sixteen, I had been elected.

In Holland, voters for each list may, if they wish, indicate a preference for particular candidates. This makes for a complicated calculation, because if many voters indicate their support for a candidate, that person can move up on the electoral list. I was sixteenth on the list, but sixth in terms of voters' individual preference—a high score for a newcomer. To be precise, 37,058 Liberal voters picked me to represent them. I felt a rush of strength at this support for my ideas. My combat was legitimate. I could make a difference. I felt the weight of real responsibility.

CHAPTER 16

Politics

On the last Saturday in January 2003, Johanna and Maarten came to help me move into my new house. The new Parliament would take its seats on January 30, and I wanted to be in some sense settled before the opening ceremony. That morning I didn't even turn on the radio, just set about packing my boxes.

But Johanna and Maarten were woken up by the news: "Hirsi Ali Calls Prophet Muhammad a Pervert." *Trouw* had just run the interview about religion that I had given weeks before. In the interview I talked about the Ten Commandments in the Quran, the version of the Ten Commandments passed on to Muslims by the Prophet Muhammad. I described him as a cruel man who demanded absolute power and who stunted creativity by limiting the imagination to only what was permitted. I discussed aspects of his life. Conveniently, Allah helpfully indicated that Muhammad should marry the wife of his adopted son, Zayd. He also allowed the Prophet to marry the six-year-old daughter of his friend Abu Bakr, and to consummate that marriage when the girl, Aisha, was only nine. Aisha's description of the scene is truly pathetic; she was playing on her swing in the garden when her mother called her and placed her on the Prophet's fifty-four-year-old lap. I said, "By our Western standards, Muhammad is a perverse man, and a tyrant."

Admittedly, I let rip in that interview. Now, weeks later, it was published, and Maarten and Johanna were appalled. I didn't know it yet, but hundreds of people were already heading for police stations across the country to demand that I be punished for saying these things. The country was in an uproar, and I hadn't even been sworn in.

Ellen called and told me she had received an angry message on the answering machine at our house. A man with an accent said, "This is the last straw," and threatened to blow the place up. The Leiden police took her complaint and stepped up their rounds. Everyone was nervous.

After we moved all my boxes I took Johanna and Maarten out for dinner, to thank them for helping me. As we were eating, one of the bodyguards came up and said, "The situation here is too dangerous. We're taking Ayaan out of here." They asked Johanna and Maarten to go home by themselves, then they took me out by the kitchen and rushed me back to the phone company flat. When I got there, the building was crawling with security, maybe a dozen policemen, in uniform and plainclothes. I realized that the situation was really serious.

I slept in the apartment, now almost empty. The next day a large group of security people came over, men who were higher up in the hierarchy of three different police and security agencies of the ministries of Justice and the Interior, and also a man from the Security Division of Parliament. We went to the house where I planned to move. The man from the agency that evaluates security risks, the ABB, announced that my risk level was "maximum." (There are three levels: maximum, medium, and minimal.) The man from the agency that does the actual protection, the DKDB, looked around and drew up a list of all the modifications and reinforcements that would have to be made for the house to pass the maximum security requirements. Reinforced glass, cameras—he said it would cost over a million euros.

I was a member of Parliament, so Parliament would have to pay the bill: those are the rules. The man from the Security Division of Parliament turned to me and asked, "How long are you planning to live in this new house of yours?" I told him I had a lease for a year. He said, "I'm sorry, but we can't do it. Parliament won't invest a million euros for just one year. You'll have to find another place."

When it came time for the pageantry of swearing in the members of the new Parliament on January 30, I was living in a hotel. For weeks I kept on moving. Every few days, people in the hotel would learn who I was and the security people would move me again. I went house hunting, but when I found a perfect house it was unacceptable to the security people: it was a row house, with a garden that connected to a whole street of gardens. Another house was acceptable, but there was no way I could pay the rent. It went on and on, a very unsettling situation.

I was nervous at the ceremony, of course, and felt enormous regret that my father would not be there. He would have been proud. To him I was an apostate, but still, I was following in his footsteps, committed to working for the well-being of others, just as he had always been. It pained me to phone him and have him hang up on me. But I was now also filled with a kind of hope. I had a mission. I was going to put the plight of Muslim women on my country's agenda.

At the first meeting of the Liberal caucus in Parliament, everyone had read the *Trouw* article and was furious. That morning Frank de Grave, a courtly man who had taken me under his wing, came into the office that I had been assigned in the old parliament building and told me, "When the meeting starts, you'll see, people will attack you. I want you to stay quiet. When it's your time to speak, you must say, 'This interview happened a long time ago, before I was even elected. I realize this is not how things work, and I apologize for causing such commotion. From now on I will consult the Party before coming out with such things.'"

When some of my Liberal colleagues in Parliament started saying nasty things—and it wasn't everybody—I did stay quiet. But then one man looked over at Gerrit Zalm and asked, "Don't you think we should protect her from herself?" I saw red. I said, "What surprises me is that not one person in this room has asked 'Is this true?' If the Prophet Muhammad went to bed with a nine-year-old, then according to Dutch law he is a pedophile. If you look at how the Prophet Muhammad ruled, he was a lone ruler, an autocrat, and that is tyranny. As for being protected from myself, that is condescending, and inexcusable."

Zalm finally calmed down the voices raised in uproar. He, Johan Remkes, Mark Rutte, and Henk Kamp supported me on the grounds of freedom of speech. They also said the threats against me were inexcusable; to have to live with bodyguards was virtually unheard of in Holland. After the meeting, Frank de Grave came up to me and said, "What have you done! Why did you say that?" I told him. "Because it's true. I'm not going to apologize for the truth."

Parliament was slow to start up; the winning parties had still not agreed to form a government. The Christian Democrats were mired in talks with Labor over forming a coalition. Weeks went by. The new Parliament was seated, but the old government that had ruled before the election was still in place—not making new policy, but keeping the country minimally governed while everyone waited for a new cabinet to be named.

The situation was surreal. Pim Fortuyn's ministers, some of whom had been decisively voted out of Parliament, were still running the nation. Poor Zalm; when he wasn't running the Liberal caucus meetings he was baby-sitting the Pim Fortuyn ministers, who behaved as if they hadn't left kindergarten. I promised myself to try to be less of a worry to him.

We, the Liberals, seemed certain to remain out of power. This left me room to try to shift our Party's mind-set on my issues, free of the need to form coalitions and garner support from other parties. First, I wanted the Liberal Party to throw its support behind a Labor move to give independent residence papers to women who came to Holland to marry legal immigrants.

This was achieved, in the end, with the help of the Labor Party. Frank de Grave and Gerrit Zalm helped me push it through the Liberals, which wasn't easy because the Liberals wanted to curb new immigration and thought giving out more residence permits was unwise. But I talked about the women themselves, brought to Holland by men they barely know, after arranged marriages, beaten until they end up in the hospital, but who cannot file for divorce because if they did, they would have to leave Holland and return to their families, where they would be punished. The motion was passed by a majority of the parties in Parliament, although we had to do without the Christian Democrat's vote. (So much for brotherly love.)

There was more money needed for women's shelters. Zalm was a member of the outgoing cabinet that was still running the country. Soon after I talked to him about it, the finance minister, Hans Hoogervorst, told me he would free up an initial thirty million euros, far from enough but better than nothing.

In May, the Labor Party suddenly announced it wouldn't participate in the government. After four months, their talks with the Christian Democrats had broken down. Now the Christian Democrats had to turn to the Liberals to govern in a coalition that they quickly cobbled together. Another, much smaller party, D-66, which had lost badly in three elections in a row, also agreed to join. That gave the new government a scant majority of just three seats in Parliament.

At the end of February, I found a permanent place to live in The Hague: a little brick house in a courtyard right behind the Israeli Embassy, just across the public square from the Binnenhof, where Parliament sits. The rent was high, but the location was already tightly guarded, it was very convenient to Parliament, and it was highly acceptable to the security people.

I was just glad to have a place of my own. Once I moved in, I was free of bodyguards hanging portable cameras and movement alarms in hotel corridors and watching every movement around me. I could close the door, say good-bye to them, and sit on my sofa in a horrible T-shirt, reading and eating.

One evening that March, Neelie and I were talking over dinner in her garden about why the new kind of fundamentalist Islam was so successful and so persuasive. I thought it was partly because the preachers used different kinds of media: videotapes of martyrs, cassette tapes of vivid sermons, websites reinforcing the message. The new Islam is about images, and its technology is very simple and usual.

It is time for people who want to reform Islam to try the same techniques. Political speeches are fine, but it's time now for satire, for art, for movies and books. Creative people with a dissident message need to get beyond the mental block that prevents them from treating religion like any other subject—and from treating Islam like any other religion. They need to get their own message across with pictures, not just with words, to people who don't, literally or metaphorically, speak their language.

I told Neelie I had been thinking about doing some kind of art exhibit to spark discussion of women's position in Islam, perhaps a roomful of plaster casts or wax mannequins of women. There would be a woman flogged for adultery, a woman beaten repeatedly, a women imprisoned inside her house. One of them would be wearing a transparent *hidjab,* and each would have words of the Quran written across her flesh. Beside each statue would be a note translating the Quranic verses and estimating how many women across the world suffer from that verdict from the Quran. The exhibit would illustrate with simple images the suffering endured by women in the name of Allah.

Many well-meaning Dutch people have told me in all earnestness that nothing in Islamic culture incites abuse of women, that this is just a terrible misunderstanding. Men all over the world beat their women, I am constantly informed. In reality, these Westerners are the ones who misunderstand Islam. The Quran mandates these punishments. It gives a legitimate basis for abuse, so that the perpetrators feel no shame and are not hounded by their conscience or their community. I wanted my art exhibit to make it difficult for people to look away from this problem. I wanted secular, non-Muslim people to stop kidding themselves that "Islam is peace and tolerance."

I knew that such an exhibit would be hard for many Muslims to deal with. When you have been brought up to believe that a religion and a holy book are absolute, it is difficult to accept that not everyone thinks that way, and that no book is completely holy. But this was my point: Muslims needed to think about their beliefs, and to think about what these beliefs actually do to human beings.

Neelie got me in touch with Wim van der Krimpen, who ran the City Museum in The Hague and seemed open to my idea for an exhibit, which I wanted to call Submission. He told me security for such an exhibition really wouldn't be the problem I envisaged; his museum was already very secure. He warned me, though, that purchasing mannequins was expensive. I should write up my proposal, and he would discuss it with his board.

I figured nothing would come of it. A member of Parliament writing verses from the Quran on mannequins? The idea was doomed, I thought, so I shelved it.

Jozias van Aartsen asked me to write a policy statement that would summarize my ideas and specific proposals on integration and the emancipation of Muslim women. This would be discussed by the Liberal Party in September, at the annual policy planning meeting. We were in power now, so the stakes were high. Everything I wanted to say had to be in that paper. I involved Arie van der Zwan, an economist whose work I admired, and Paul Scheffer, the critic. We worked on it through the summer and ended up with a twelve-page proposal that was very comprehensive.

In September, when the Liberal Party met to discuss policy planning, I was tense. My statement proposed that the Liberals should come out in favor of closing down existing Muslim schools and refusing to finance new ones, and that the Party should work toward abolishing Article 23 of the Dutch Constitution, which allows parents to set up their own schools based on religion. This would be a brave move, in political terms, especially for a party that, at least in Dutch terms, is right wing. I had also proposed dramatically reducing unemployment benefits and abolishing the minimum wage. From my experience as a translator with welfare cases, I knew that easy access to generous unemployment benefits leads to a poverty trap: people in Holland often make more money from welfare than they would in actual jobs. Everyone told me these ideas were far too right wing—meaning that they would lead to a society polarized between wealthy and poor, teeming with beggars and very rich people, with lots of violence and exploitation.

Various people raged against aspects of my paper at the meeting, but the alpha males and alpha females declared their support, so the beta males and females mostly subsided into grumbling. Van Aartsen ended the discussion by proposing that the subject of integration be rescheduled for a meeting of the parliamentary group, where my more senior supporters would be absent.

By the following March, when the much-revised report was finally released, things were already happening in the country. The question of ending support for religious schools was in hot debate, and there was much more attention devoted to Muslim women. There were newspaper articles quoting teachers and social workers about girls in Dutch kindergartens who had been excised. Secular, free-thinking intellectuals were bashing each other in the op-ed pages about the virtues and vices of the Prophet Muhammad. I had leaked bits and pieces of my policy document and used aspects of it in other debates, gradually building a coalition. I'd given parts of it to Gerrit Zalm, who was now finance minister, and Rita Verdonk, the integration minister, to use in their own policy documents. Other politicians, from other parties, began to be interested in these issues.

I wanted Parliament to pass a motion that would require the police to register how many honor killings took place in Holland each year. After weeks of wheeling and dealing in corridors, the minister of justice, Piet Donner, did agree to a motion that I had concocted with the Labor Party, but he said he wanted to try it out first, as a "pilot project," in just two police regions. Months later, when the results were announced, Parliament was shocked, and I felt a huge groundswell of support in the country. Between October 2004 and May 2005, eleven Muslim girls were killed by their families in just those two regions (there are twenty-five such regions in Holland). After that, people stopped telling me I was exaggerating.

Most of the letters of support I received were from white Dutch people. I did receive a very few letters of support from Muslim women. Many more were at least listening to what I said. As I myself know too well, it takes a long time to dissolve the bars of a mental cage. Almost all the angry letters I received were from Muslims. People called me an Uncle Tom, white on the inside, a traitor to my people. All these *ad hominem* attacks were basically distractions from the real issue, which wasn't me—it doesn't matter who I am. What matters is abuse, and how it is anchored in a religion that denies women their rights as humans.

What matters is that atrocities against women and children are carried out in Europe. What matters is that governments and societies must stop hiding behind a hollow pretense of tolerance so that they can recognize and deal with the problem.

When I read those angry letters, I could understand the people who wrote them. At one time, I could have written such a letter, too. When you think something is holy and special and you're told it's not, if you're not ready for that information—and especially if you're from an honor background—you feel offended. These individuals I understood, but I was angered by the huffing and puffing of the Muslim organizations funded by the government to look after the community.

These Muslim organizations in Holland are supposed to act as liaisons between Muslims and the local and national governments. But their leadership represents no one. They're not elected. They're comfortably bloated on subsidies and produce virtually no real programs. The men who run those Muslim groups are supposed to represent Muslim women. They know the issues, but they simply never address them. They called me a traitor, but it is they who betray Muslims—Muslim women and children.

One night in May 2004 my father called me. Someone had given him my phone number, and it was as if nothing had happened between us. I said, "Abeh, I'm so happy and grateful that you called me!"

"Ayaan, people say such nasty things about you," he said, sounding old and tired. "I pray for you. Do you pray?"

I asked him if he remembered a story he used to tell us, back when we lived together in Ethiopia, in the headquarters of the Somali opposition force, about a comrade whom my father had invited to prayer. This man answered, "Hirsi, do you see the head of a big bull hanging in the middle of the room?" and my father said no. The comrade responded that to him, God was like that invisible bull's head: he couldn't see it.

"Abeh, I am like that man," I told my father. "You tell me to pray, but when I stand on the mat, the room is empty."

"That man has repented," my father said. "He has just returned from a pilgrimage to Mecca. I have prayed for him, and I will pray for you. You, too, will return to the Straight Path."

"Abeh, if I ever return to the faith, you are the first person I will tell," I told him.

My father was quiet. Then he said, "Meanwhile, Ayaan, if anyone asks you 'Do you believe in God,' don't answer. Reply that it is a very rude question."

After a conversation that lasted about an hour, we said good-bye. We have not spoken since.

In February 2003, I met Theo van Gogh for the first time. I was at the house of Theodor Holman, a journalist, and the doorbell rang; a loud, disheveled man rushed up to me and gave me a bear hug. He said, "I'm Theo van Gogh, I voted for you," and flooded me with instructions on how to survive in politics. He stayed and chatted for a bit, then he left, as abruptly as he had stormed in.

I knew a little about van Gogh, one of those Amsterdam personalities, always on TV or in the papers. Theo had unkempt blond hair, he was fat, he smoked a lot, and talked nonstop. A well-known movie director, Theo had a kind of compulsive urge to goad and insult even his best friends, preferably on live TV. Many people seemed to hate him.

I didn't see van Gogh again for over a year; there was no reason to. But one afternoon in May 2004, I was attending a friend's wedding in the United States when Theo called on my cell phone. There had been no contact between us since our first encounter, but he'd gotten my number from a friend. There was no "How are you?" or anything like that—he just said, "Ya, van Gogh," and began talking indignantly about a run-in he'd had with a Lebanese Belgian man who called himself Abu Jahjah.

Abu Jahjah ran a group of young Arab men in Belgium he called the Arab European League, and he had been invited to a big debate in Amsterdam at the Happy Chaos Debating Club. Theo had been asked to chair the debate, but Abu Jahjah refused to participate if Theo was chairman. After some of Abu Jahjah's goons threatened him, Theo called Abu Jahjah "the Prophet's pimp" and hell broke loose.

I had no idea what Theo thought I could do about it all. I was sitting in the back of a taxi in New York with a clearly Muslim driver and no bodyguard; it was not an opportune moment for an in-depth chat. I said, "Theo, I can't talk right now. I'll come and see you next week, when I get back."

At the time, I was sheltering a Moroccan girl, Rashida, in my house. Rashida had contacted me in the summer of 2003; she needed help to escape from her father and brothers, who beat her because she had a Dutch boyfriend. At twenty-two, she wanted to become an actress, and I found something poignant about her—perhaps an echo of myself. I

wanted to help her, but I had no idea how someone would go about starting an acting career; now it occurred to me that I could take her with me
to meet Theo van Gogh, the famous Amsterdam filmmaker.

Theo's most recent film was *Najib and Julia,* about the relationship
between a native Dutch girl and a Moroccan boy. Theo had an open sen-
sibility, an antenna that picked up distress signals when most people in
Holland wanted to believe that everything was nice and cozy. He thought
there were too many things that people didn't dare say for fear of giving
offense. He saw himself as a Fassbinder character: the Lord of Misrule.
His house was a shambles, but he focused intensely on his work. He was
a mess of contradictions, an impossible man, a genius in some ways.

At that first meeting, Rashida and I stayed for about an hour. Theo
promised Rashida that if she finished acting school he would do a real
screen test for her. We discussed his complaint about Abu Jahjah. I said,
"Why get angry? You're a filmmaker. Why don't you make a movie
about it?"

Somehow we got onto my idea for an art exhibit on Muslim women.
Theo said, "Just do it in video. Write a screenplay. Any idiot can write a
screenplay. All you have to do is write 'Exterior, Day' and 'Interior,
Night.'"

He meant it. Theo was offering to make Submission as a short movie.
At first I didn't take it seriously, but he kept calling me over the next few
weeks, urging me to get going on a script. I could do it after Parliament
broke, he said. We could film it over the summer. I told Theo I would
give it a try.

A few days later, I had a meeting with a production group from a
uniquely Dutch TV show, *Summer Guests,* which had invited me to
appear at the end of August. On this show, people talk for three hours
about themselves and select TV clips that have been meaningful to them
personally. Some people show old sitcoms; others show historic sports
events or a fragment from a documentary or children's program. Viewers are caught up in the pleasure of remembering all these shared Dutch
experiences as the footage is shown. Having no shared Dutch experience
to speak of, I asked the production people whether they would consider
showing a short film on which Theo van Gogh and I were working. I said
we could have it ready by August 29, when the show taped. I showed them
an outline of the script. They said it would be unusual, but they agreed.

I called Theo, and we decided to give it a try.

*   *   *

The film Theo and I made, *Submission: Part One,* is first and foremost about the relation of the individual with Allah. In Islam, unlike in Christianity and Judaism, the relationship of the individual to God is one of total submission, slave to master. To Muslims, worship of God means total obedience to Allah's rules and total abstinence from the thoughts and deeds that He has declared forbidden in the Quran. To modernize Islam and adapt it to contemporary ideals would require a dialogue with God, even disagreement with God's rules; but as Islam is conceived, any kind of disagreement with Allah is insolence because it assumes equality with Him.

The Quran tells a vivid story about how Satan was expelled from the realm of angels after Allah created Adam. Allah ordered all the angels to bow to Adam, but Satan refused to obey. He talked back to Allah: Why should he, an elevated angel, bow down to a creature made of mud? Allah threw Satan out of Paradise, and from then on Satan has tried to lure Adam and his offspring from the Straight Path. For a human being to doubt any of Allah's rules is to fall into Satan's clutches.

Probably every Muslim is taught that story, and as a child I thought of it often. Now, as an adult, I felt that liberation of Muslim women must be preceded by liberation of the mind from this rigid, dogmatic obedience to Allah's dictates. Allah is constantly referred to in the Quran as "the most compassionate, the most merciful"; He also says several times that he has given us a will of our own. In that case, I wonder, why would He mind a little debate?

When I sat down to write the script for our film, I decided to use the format of prayer to bring about dialogue with Allah. I pictured a woman standing in the center of a room. In the four corners of the room, four women depict restrictive verses from the Quran. The woman in the middle of the room is veiled, but her veil is transparent at the front, opaque at the back. The transparency is necessary because it challenges Allah to look at what he created: the body of woman. On her torso is written the opening verse of the Quran, the "Sura Fatiha," which every Muslim is required to recite first, at every prayer:

> In the name of God, the merciful, the beneficent.
> Praise be to God, the Lord of the worlds, the merciful, the beneficent,
>   ruler of the day of judgment!
> Thee we serve and Thee we ask for aid.
> Guide us in the right path, the path of those to whom Thou art gracious;
>   not of those with whom Thou art wroth; nor of those who err.

The woman observes the rules of prayer: her head is lowered and her gaze is fixed on the front of the mat, where she will place her forehead when she bows to express total obedience. But after she recites the *Sura Fatiha,* she does something unusual: she raises her head. The camera pans to the first woman, who tells Allah that she has obeyed all his injunctions, but she now lies in a corner, bleeding. She has fallen in love, and for that she has been flogged. She ends, very simply, with the sentence, "I may no longer submit."

Another of the women is repelled by the odor of her husband. She has been forced to marry him and now is forced to submit to him sexually, for the Quran says, *When your wives have purified themselves, ye may approach them in any manner, time or place.* A third woman is beaten by her husband at least once a week: *As to those women on whose part you fear disloyalty and ill-conduct, admonish them, scourge them and banish them to beds apart.* A fourth is a young girl who lives cloistered in her own home. She has been raped by her uncle, and now she is pregnant; she will be punished for having sex outside marriage.

I called the film *Submission, Part One,* because submission to Islam causes many other kinds of suffering. I saw this as the first in a series of films that would tackle the master-slave relationship of God and the individual. My message was that the Quran is an act of man, not of God. We should be free to interpret it; we should be permitted to apply it to the modern era in a different way, instead of performing painful contortions to try to recreate the circumstances of a horrible distant past. My intention was to liberate Muslim minds so that Muslim women—and Muslim men, too—might be freer. Men, too, are forced to obey inhumane laws.

It was a simple film to make. Theo wasn't interested in writing up proposals for grants and subsidies: he said we should just make a ten-minute film and see what happened. I finished the script at the end of July. Theo rented a studio and hired an actress and a makeup woman, and a few props.

We did discuss the danger of making a film with this message. Having already spoken out about Islam, I knew how dangerous it was. I warned Theo; I wanted him to keep his name off the project. But Theo called himself the village idiot. He said, "Nobody shoots the village idiot." He believed that I was the one who would be attacked, and nobody would bother with him.

The movie almost didn't happen. We shot it on Monday, July 26.

Theo wanted me to cut the script and make it five minutes long; I insisted on ten. He lost his temper, and yelled, "I'm not here just to help you resolve your childhood traumas!" I stared at him and then walked away. He apologized.

Actually, Theo was probably right: five minutes would have been more effective. I called him a few weeks later, to tell him so, and he said, "No, the film's perfect. I'm proud of what I've done."

Before *Submission* aired on TV, I thought it would be courteous to show it to the leaders of the Liberal Party. I also wanted to persuade them that Theo should be given more security, because he insisted on keeping his name on the film.

They all reacted differently. Frits Bolkestein, the wise old leader of the Liberals, who was now almost seventy, paced up and down his office with worry. He said, "My God, Ayaan, you're in danger." I felt awful. I thought, "I shouldn't have shown it to him, I've worried this poor elderly man." In hindsight, Bolkestein really understood what was happening, as did Neelie. I tried to reassure both of them: nothing would happen to me, because the DKDB was protecting me; we only needed to worry about getting protection for Theo.

Gerrit Zalm was unmoved. He simply asked if all this stuff was really in the Quran; because it was, he concluded that there was no reason I shouldn't use it, although he thought it was unfortunate that our actress was half-naked. Johan Remkes, the minister of the interior, just said, "Couldn't you have found a better-looking chick?" Remkes thought it was a rather amateurish movie; he had no idea why I was making such a fuss about security. I said, "Will you make sure Theo van Gogh is safe?" and he said, "If that becomes necessary, Ayaan, we will, of course."

Then I showed *Submission* to the defense minister, Henk Kamp. He was emotionally caught up by the film itself. He said, "What a cruel world we live in." It was moving to see him so stirred by it. I asked him "What about security?" and Kamp said, "Muslims have had a lot to take this past year. They've been hardened—they won't react to this."

And it seemed to be true. *Submission* aired on August 29, and there was no huge reaction. Everything seemed to be calm.

CHAPTER 17

The Murder of Theo

In early September 2004 , a Moroccan man was arrested by the police after he posted my address on the Internet. He called on all the Followers of the Oneness of Allah to rejoice, because having shadowed my movements they had finally, with the help of God, acquired my address, which was in a courtyard behind the Israeli Embassy. His message was accompanied by two photographs of me and Theo and basically said we both had to die.

I learned about this from reporters, who began calling me. A few days later, two policemen came to see me and asked me to file a formal complaint against the man they had arrested. I did, and I told the policemen—and everyone else I could think of—that Theo must be protected.

After making *Submission,* Theo and I never actually met again, but we used to call each other from time to time. He ignored my pleas that he get protection, and even joked about it. He told me, "Ayaan, you have no idea. I've been threatened for fifteen years. Everyone has threatened me: the Jews, the Christians, the Social Democrats, the Muslims—they've done it the most—and nothing has ever happened to me. Nothing is going to happen."

By this time I had been protected by bodyguards for more than two years. Theo didn't want a security detail like mine. I worried that he would be trapped in an alley one night on the way home and beaten up, or maybe get rocks thrown through his windows, something like that. I didn't expect a man to slaughter him in broad daylight—to shoot him, and cut his throat, and stick a knife into his chest.

The weeks went by, and nothing noteworthy happened, to Theo or me. We didn't forget about *Submission.* We spoke whenever I was contacted by the foreign media who wanted to see the movie, but life seemed peaceful that autumn, as I settled down to my second session of Parliament. I had a house, a job that made a great deal of sense to me, a number of friends. I was slowly becoming more accepted in politics. I had a feeling—rather new to me since my entry into Dutch politics—of satisfaction.

As part of this newfound serenity, I had decided to come to better grips with my management of time. I was constantly late for every deadline: this had to stop. I had to learn to fix goals and do only projects that met them. I hired a trainer named Rik, and on Monday, November 1, Iris, my parliamentary assistant, and I developed a new working plan that started with coming in on time, listing priorities, and ignoring the cell phone during the formal weekly meetings that we solemnly vowed to schedule.

The next morning, Tuesday, November 2, I was in my office bright and early, in accordance with my resolution, with coffee and a stack of things to discuss. Iris and I waited for the Liberal Party press secretary, Ingrid, to arrive. My phone started flashing, and a number appeared on the screen: it was Hugo, my former parliamentary assistant, a young man who now worked for the Liberal municipal councilors in Amsterdam. I decided to be disciplined: I had resolved that I don't always have to answer calls. This new, focused me clicked the "still" button on the phone.

And again it flashed: Hugo. What was going on? And again. I kept clicking him off. I really wanted to demonstrate how committed I was to this new schedule of ours. Then Ingrid called, I figured to apologize for being late. "Hugo has been trying to reach you," she said. "He says something bad has happened to Theo van Gogh. There's been an attack."

I jumped to my feet and ran down the hall to the office of the Liberal caucus's secretary. Artha had a much bigger office, with a TV that she kept on teletext all day. I ran in and said, "Something has happened to Theo van Gogh, he's not well"—I didn't know what I was saying—and she turned to the news. The text said only that there had been a shooting incident in Amsterdam. I said, "There's probably nothing wrong," but I was shaking. Artha said, "Call your security people, they should know if something has happened." My security detail in those days left me at the door of Parliament—there was no need for them to stand outside my office—but as I started to phone Bram, the senior guard on duty, he appeared beside me, as if from nowhere.

I said, "I heard that something happened to Theo van Gogh."

"I can confirm it," Bram said.

I asked, "Is he all right?" and Bram answered, "No. Theo van Gogh is dead."

I started to cry. I ran back to Iris's room, closed the door, and tried to breathe. I felt so helpless and shocked, so horrified. Ingrid came rushing in with the security people, and they said, "We have to leave, now."

I said, "Sorry, please leave me alone. I'm staying here." But Ingrid said, "Ayaan, you have to get out." Bram was very curt—"We have to move"—and Iris was crying. She put her arms around me and whispered as though she were comforting a baby, "Ayaan, let's go." Iris had known Theo; since he and I started to work on *Submission*, they had to joked on the phone a lot—he made her laugh. Bram got me my coat, put it on me, and said, "We're leaving."

Bram and the other guards closed in on me. As we walked out of Parliament into the brick courtyard, more security people surrounded Ingrid and Iris and me. They were not relaxed, as they usually were. They had become grim, and bulletproof, and I saw they were deliberately showing just a small bit of their weapons. This was security to be seen. It was frightening.

We walked the fifty yards to my house, across the huge public square outside Parliament. Everywhere I looked there were security people: police in uniform, plainclothes officers, cars, guns.

What had happened to Theo? I turned on the news; the phone calls started. I was confused, shocked—shocked, above all—that Theo had been killed: this was unbelievable. Even the idea that something like that could happen—my mind refused to accept it. I just hoped it wasn't true. On TV there was just a repetition of the news: a shooting, images of a shape under a white sheet, Theo van Gogh killed. I couldn't tell myself, "Theo is lying under that sheet": it simply didn't seem possible.

As the morning went on, details began coming in. A man had been arrested. There were fifty witnesses to the murder. A woman said in English—it must have been on the BBC—"a man with a beard, in a Muslim robe." I rocked back in my chair. So it was a Muslim, and this had happened because of *Submission*. If we hadn't made *Submission,* Theo would still be alive. I felt responsible for his death.

I would not undo *Submission,* but I should have done it under my own name, alone.

I thought about the threat against the two of us on the Internet, back in September. Theo could have been protected from this. It was so stupid; it could so easily have been prevented. I was stricken with anger, and horror, and grief.

Then Ingrid heard from a reporter that it wasn't just a shooting. There were knives, Theo's throat was cut, she said; and the killer left a note. I said, "Ingrid, things are bad enough already. This is hysteria—people are fabricating stories."

I was numb. The shock seemed to have obliterated the thinking part of my brain. I could only compulsively watch the news. Ingrid, Iris, and the security people stayed in the house with me all day. Job Cohen called to ask how I was doing. Then, as mayor of Amsterdam, he issued a public call for a demonstration that evening in the Dam, the huge square in front of the royal palace. He called it a noise demonstration, because Theo was noisy; it would be stupid to have a silent march for Theo, Job Cohen said.

I wanted to attend the march, but Bram got instructions from the hierarchy that I had to stay indoors because, in such a volatile situation, the threat against my life was too high. Attending the demonstration would only increase risks for me and others. I felt I was already responsible for one death: I had done enough damage. I stayed in.

We were watching on television as thousands of people massed in Amsterdam for the demonstration that evening, when Bram said we had to leave the house. He had orders to find me somewhere else to spend the night. Ingrid suggested I go to her place. We sat together in her living room and watched the late-night talk shows about the murder. I was bundled up in a coat and lots of scarves, paralyzed with cold. Everyone on TV was outraged. The entire country felt a sense of shock that someone could be murdered this way—in Holland, of all places—just for making a film.

Then Bram got another call from his superiors at the DKDB, saying it would be too dangerous to stay at Ingrid's house. The best idea seemed to be to take me back to my current house behind the Israeli embassy, in the middle of the night.

The security people stayed inside my house all night, watching. That's when the bodyguards began standing guard outside my bedroom every night. At around four in the morning, the doorbell rang insistently. I was still awake. I got up and asked the woman guard who was on duty downstairs, "What's this?"

The security camera showed an Arab-looking man. He'd rung the bells of all the other buildings around the courtyard. A few days later, when the police picked him up, he claimed to have been looking for a prostitute he'd once visited; eventually, they let him go. But it reminded me of the Internet post about my address. Somebody had localized me to this courtyard.

After that, it was clear that I couldn't spend the next night in my house. But I couldn't stay in a hotel either, the DKDB had decided. My face and name were everywhere on TV; somebody would be bound to recognize me. I couldn't be safe in any hotel in Holland.

Could I stay at a friend's house? I asked. A place in the country, surrounded by woods? The higher-ups at the DKDB thought that would be too dangerous. "Nothing stays secret in Holland," I was told. "People will talk. Houses that seem hidden will only give you a false sense of security." In the end, no decision was taken, and I spent that Wednesday night in my own bed.

At night, alone, I couldn't stop thoughts from coming. Every time I closed my eyes, I saw the murder, could hear Theo pleading for his life. "Can't we talk about this?" he asked his killer. It was so Dutch, so sweet and innocent. Theo must have thought there was some kind of misunderstanding that could be worked out. He couldn't see that his killer was caught in a wholly different worldview. Nothing Theo could have said to him would have made any difference.

I thought about Theo's twelve-year-old son, whom I had met once and who was now fatherless because of me. When I was awake it was all I could think about, and when I fell asleep I had nightmares. A man in a traditional Muslim tunic, with a beard and a curved sword, was coming into my house through the front door to attack me; when I tried to jump out of the window there was a crowd of men there, too, yelling. I woke up panicked, unable to get back to sleep. I still have these horrible dreams.

The next morning the security people told me they had orders to evacuate me from the house right away. They hustled me into a convoy of cars and took me to a place I didn't recognize, some kind of air base. From now on, my location had to be completely secret, they warned me. They gave me a phone number to give to Iris, in case she had to call me, but they advised me not to use my phone. For security reasons, I couldn't even be permitted to know where I was staying.

On the way to the air base, we stopped at the office of the minister of the interior, Johan Remkes. Rita Verdonk, the minister for integration, was there, and her eyes were wet. Rita is tough, but she had always been kind to me, and when she hugged me, I couldn't help it, I cried again. After a while, Johan said, "There's something I have to show you, but are you ready for it?"

I said, "I'm shocked, I'm sad, I'm angry—with you, for not protecting Theo better—but my mind is clear." Johan handed me a photocopy of the letter. He didn't tell me it had been stabbed into Theo's chest by his killer, just gave me some pages written in Arabic and Dutch.

I read them. The letter was structured very precisely, like a *fatwa,* a religious verdict. It opened with *In the name of Allah Most Gracious Most Merciful,* followed by a quote from the Prophet Muhammad, the swordsman. Then there was a summary of all the "acts of crime" I had committed against Islam. Then came a verse from the Quran, and a challenge from the writer on the basis of that verse, asking me if I was prepared to die for my convictions, as he, the letter writer, was. He went on to curse the United States, Europe, Holland, and me, and signed with the name "Sword of the Faith."

I asked, "Who signed this?" I was gasping. This was evil. It didn't have a face. If the letter was written by somebody powerful, from outside Holland, somebody whose words command legions, then I had a lot to fear. Remkes told me the letter was found on Theo's body, along with a poem of martyrdom.

I spent that night and the next in the air force base, sleeping in a room on a disused floor of the barracks. It was dusty; there were two thin, metal beds with woolen blankets, to which I'm allergic. Tiny windows opened onto a corridor where security guards stood all night. The place was crawling with soldiers. I was told to keep the curtains drawn: nobody was supposed to know of my presence, not even the air base personnel.

That night a mosque under construction in Utrecht was burned down. The country was raging; in terms of Dutch history, this event was seismic. Emotions were frighteningly high. But I was numb. Since Theo's death, I had felt stunned. It was like a short circuit had happened: some thinking part of me blinked off.

I just did what I was told. I did things I ordinarily never would. I spent the next two and a half months alone with bodyguards. I had almost no contact with friends or even my colleagues in Parliament. I appeared calm. I agreed to everything. It was as if I had lost my will.

I could be killed; that was part of it. I was frightened. I have no desire to die. And I was also very grateful to these people who were protecting me, because it was no small thing they were doing. Even if I was angry that nobody had protected Theo, I wanted to do what these men told me, because it seemed like they knew what they were doing, and they might be saving my life.

Still, if my mind had been operating properly back then, I would have seen that after Theo's murder, the security services went into some kind of overdrive. They had seen threats on the Internet building up against Theo. But they hadn't properly tried to persuade him to accept a security detail, because they thought that if they did, they would have had to protect "everybody." The DKDB was mandated to protect only royalty, diplomats, and members of Parliament. The justice minister, Piet Hein Donner, had said on the news, "We can't have one half of the population protecting the other half of the population."

Now Theo was dead, and the country was in deep crisis. The security services were seeing threats everywhere. Nobody knew anything then about the scale of the conspiracy to assassinate Theo. If I had been killed in those immediate few days, Holland could perhaps even have gone up in flames as citizens took up arms against each other—what all governments fear could happen. So I suppose the order was given: "Keep her safe, no matter what."

Theo's funeral was to take place a week after he was killed. The security people told me that if I insisted on attending, they would make arrangements for it, but they said it could put other people in danger. I decided I couldn't possibly go. I had to live with the guilt that Theo died because he made *Submission* with me; I couldn't put other lives at risk.

But I wanted somehow to see Theo and say good-bye. The bodyguards agreed to take me to the hospital morgue in Amsterdam, with lots of cars, lots of armed men. Theo's best friend, Theodor Holman, and his producer, Gijs van Westerlaken, were in the room with Theo's body when I got there. There was no mark of any violence. Theo was dressed as he always was, in a roll-neck sweater and baggy trousers. I looked for any sign of cruelty, but his face was smooth; there wasn't even a bruise or a pimple. He had a little sardonic half-smile on his closed lips. He seemed peaceful, the only time I had ever known him to be quiet. I touched his shoulder, kissed his forehead. I told him, "I'm so sorry for what I did."

Theodor Holman said, "No, Ayaan. If he were alive Theo would be hurt, hearing you say that. He wouldn't have wanted to die in his bed. He felt like a knight on horseback about *Submission*. He died in a battle for free expression, and that's what he lived for. It would have been much worse if he was eaten away by cancer or got in a stupid car accident. This was a meaningful death. He was *my* friend, and I don't want you feeling sorry that Theo died like this."

It was kind of Theodor, to try to make me feel better. I said good-bye to Theo. He himself didn't believe in a Hereafter. I no longer believed in a Hereafter. And so this was it, I thought: this is the end.

Afterward, I had coffee with Theodor and Gijs in the hospital waiting room. They made jokes, trying to cheer me up; they had their own way of dealing with the loss of their dear and eccentric friend. They told me that they and Theo's other friends had been trying to contact me, but Iris must have given them a wrong number, they said, because it always answered, "Air Force Base Woensdrecht."

"So that's where I'm being kept," I thought. Woensdrecht Air Base, near the Belgian border. As we were getting ready to leave, I told the senior bodyguard, "I know where we're going. It's Woensdrecht." He just stared at me and said, "Not any more." He was angry when he found out that Theodor had my number. "Who gave you permission to give out that information?" From then on, nobody was allowed to have a phone number for me.

The night after I saw Theo's body in the morgue, I was taken to a police training center in Hoogerheide, near Woensdrecht. I slept in one of the cubicles for the trainees, with my nightmares and more woolen blankets, which made my head swell and my eyes water. On Monday morning I would have to move again; the police recruits would be arriving for their training, and they might see me. I was beginning to reel from all the moving around and not sleeping, and I pleaded to be allowed to stay. But the senior guard said, "No. We can't trust all these recruits. They're not policemen yet."

Early on Monday morning, the guards moved me to the Ministry of Foreign Affairs. Jozias van Aartsen, the Liberal caucus leader, had been the foreign minister, so he arranged for me to sit in an office there, which would be secure and free of the pressure of the press. My parliamentary assistant, Iris, was allowed to come and see me; other than that, I had only a phone and a TV.

They told me not to send e-mail, claiming it could be traced. (A few days later, they took away my cell phone—they said it, too, could be traced.) I summoned up the curiosity to ask, "Are you sure these people have the ability to do this kind of thing?" Islamic radicals in Holland seemed to me to be young disaffected immigrants—rather low-tech— and, I thought, you'd have to be pretty organized to buy the equipment to trace a cell phone. But the guards said, "We can't rule it out." It became a kind of mantra. "We're not ruling out anything."

I sat in that office, reading every letter in every newspaper, watching TV, trying to access my e-mail. Eight North African men had been arrested in Amsterdam; there was talk of a terrorist cell. Four mosques had burned over the weekend, and two churches. A Muslim primary school in Uden, close to Eindhoven, had been set on fire and burned down on Sunday night.

Theo was going to be cremated the next day. It was all I could think about.

That evening I was taken to the office of the junior minister for European affairs, which was on another floor in the Foreign Ministry building. Behind this office was a tiny bedroom, with a bathroom and a narrow bed. The junior minister left—he was very courteous—and the guards stayed outside. I was to sleep here. I pleaded to be allowed to sleep in my own house—it was just around the corner—but the guards said it wouldn't be secure.

The guards' behavior with me had changed completely. There was something urgent, very serious, in the air. I felt it, too. They thought I couldn't be allowed to know too much about my situation. The stakes were much higher than just me.

I lay awake all night sneezing from the woolen blankets, my mouth and tongue and throat alive with itching. Every evil possibility went through my head: the guards, just outside my door; the fear; mosques burning; Theo, dead.

The next day, Tuesday, I watched Theo's funeral ceremony live on TV. It was very moving. Bram Peper, the former minister of the interior and ex-husband of Neelie Kroes, spoke well. He said that Theo's death was a worse shock than a political assassination because it was the murder of someone with no political ambitions, who never desired to take office. Theo's father was humble but dignified in his sadness. Theo's mother was in a fighting mood. In her speech, she said that I had no reason to feel guilty about Theo's murder: he had been threatened for fifteen years. She called me by my first name and addressed me directly. She said that I must continue with my mission. I was touched that she thought of me at such a time. I felt so sorry for her, and for Theo's father, who broke down in tears, and most of all for the twelve-year-old son who would have to live without his father, murdered so cruelly.

I wrote a letter to Theo's family a few days later. The security people read the letter before they delivered it, looking for clues that might betray my whereabouts.

*   *   *

On Wednesday morning, the news opened with the police besieging an apartment building in The Hague, just a short walk from where I was sleeping. Someone inside the apartment threw a hand grenade at the police and wounded several officers. The neighborhood was evacuated. The airspace over the whole city was closed to civilian flights while special forces moved in. No one knew what was happening; it felt like The Hague was under siege.

For several days, Neelie Kroes and Jozias van Aartsen had been talking with various security people about what I should do next. They had decided that, as in 2002, when I began receiving death threats, I should make a brief trip to a foreign country. I could get some rest, give myself a chance to mourn, and lie low until the dust settled—by which time, presumably, all the various agencies would have come to some kind of agreement about just how dangerous the threats on my life were, and exactly how to approach them.

Now, while the siege of the apartment building in The Hague was still under way, my guards told me that I would be leaving for the United States. They drove me home; I had three hours to pack.

I didn't know what to bring; the security people just said I would be going to the United States. Would it be hot or cold? My brain had simply stopped functioning. I randomly shoved every piece of clothing I owned and dozens of books into suitcases and, when I ran out of suitcases, huge plastic zip bags. The whole thing was irrational, but nobody was there to tell me so. The guards just wordlessly crammed the bags into their armored cars.

I was driven to Valkenburg Air Base, near The Hague, where we parked on the runway. Facing us was a military transport and surveillance aircraft, an Orion. As I walked up the jetway, I told myself, like a schoolteacher, "Pay attention. This is a unique experience." I felt oddly disembodied, completely calm. All the shutters had been pulled down on the windows, and I was told not to go near them or the doors. The plane was full of soldiers in uniform; two DKDB bodyguards were still with me. The senior guard was Pete, whom I had asked for and trusted.

The pilots invited me to watch the takeoff from the cockpit. They explained their job and the technology of the airplane; I asked a few polite questions. It was very cold. They said I could lie down on one of the two flip-down beds, so high up on the wall that I couldn't roll over without my knees or shoulders hitting the ceiling. I lay there, thinking about Theo and the enormous guilt I would forever feel.

We landed at the air base in Portland, Maine. Two Dutch policemen, who usually dealt with criminals in the Dutch Witness Protection Program came to pick us up. They didn't treat me personally like a criminal; I was a member of Parliament under protection, not the usual drug dealer. But they treated the situation authoritatively, as they were used to—they were the experts. They determined what I could and couldn't do.

I was still frightened—they could see me looking around, startled at the slightest noise—and they tried to calm me down. First they took me to a nondescript roadside motel, where I showered and tried to sleep while a couple of the guards took my passport and dealt with officially entering me into the country.

Then we drove to Andover, Massachusetts. Again they got rooms in the same kind of dismal motel, surrounded by highways in an industrial area, with hardly any human beings. It was freezing cold. The security people had decided that I should become completely anonymous in this typically American place, where no Dutch person would recognize me. We ended up staying there for weeks.

All I wanted was to follow the news in Holland. I wanted to know what had happened to Theo's family, to his son, to Parliament; how the police siege in The Hague had ended. But there was no news about Holland in America, and my guards had removed the phone from my hotel room. They might not have been treating me precisely as they would a criminal, but they were at the very least treating me like a child, as if I were oblivious to the danger I faced. I argued with Koos, the man from Witness Protection. I wanted to phone; I wanted to talk with my friends. But he replied that they were in charge of my safety, and this was for my own protection. Nor was I allowed to go on the Internet; that, too, could be traced. I thought surely no one could trace me if I went only on news sites, but there were rules, apparently: no Internet.

Thankfully, my guard Pete was from the DKDB, not Witness Protection; he had been with the police for more than twenty years and knew the difference between what was life-threatening and what wasn't. Pete insisted that someone check out the Boston Library and see if I could log on to the Internet there. He said, "We're responsible for her safety, but it's no good to anyone if she has a breakdown."

While Koos went to Boston, Pete passed me his own phone and told me to be careful what I said. He walked to the other end of the room while I called Johanna, Iris, my friend Geeske. We talked guardedly about my going somewhere for a short while. They told me the news in Holland; the siege in The Hague had ended and seven people had been arrested around the country on suspicion of links with some kind of terrorist group.

When Koos got back, he reported, "It's no good. Boston is teeming with Dutch people and all kinds of Europeans. We can't rule anything out. You're not going."

The next day the guards decided to take me to a shopping mall to buy fake glasses. But Americans are so curious; they pepper you with questions, even for simple transactions in shops. The guards said, "Just tell them your name is Jill Steele and you're from South Africa."

I was a black woman in a baseball cap with four big white men around her, wanting to buy clear glasses with no prescription, with a ridiculous story about South Africa. I could feel everybody in that shopping mall scrutinizing me.

The next day was my thirty-fifth birthday. I had planned a party in Holland, with dozens of friends. Now, just a few of my closest friends would meet without me to talk about what I should do next. Meanwhile I had nothing to do. I had a laptop with me, but couldn't write. I had books, but I couldn't seem to take anything in.

Pete could tell things were not well with me. He said once, "The way they define keeping you safe, we might as well lock you in a World War Two bunker on the beach and pass plates of food through the door." I said, "That would be an improvement. I'd be on the beach in Holland, and I could invite friends for tea."

Pete's solution was physical exercise. Physical exhaustion was the only cure for sleeplessness, fear, and worry, he said. He drove me to a huge sports center and made me work out on machines. He was right; it helped.

In Holland, questions were building about my whereabouts. Since Theo's murder I had more or less disappeared from the face of the earth. My friends were told I wanted to be alone, but they didn't buy it; they knew that at such a time I would want to be with them or, at the very least, phone. In the absence of any information, all kinds of conspiracy theories sprouted. Some people said that I had been killed and my murder was being hushed up by the authorities.

After I had been in the United States for about ten days, the security people authorized Neelie Kroes to call me. She and Jozias van Aartsen were trying to make arrangements to see me, but so far the security people were saying it was impossible. I realized that she and Jozias had no idea how far away I was.

Henk Kamp, the minister of defense, called me, too. He said, "I'll come and see you and we'll go for a walk in the Zutphen forest." I said, "Henk, don't you know that I'm nowhere near the Zutphen forest?" It was like I was a one-woman state of emergency; even the minister of defense didn't know where I was.

Months later, when I saw Henk again and everything was back to normal, I asked him how he could have been kept in ignorance of my whereabouts. He told me, "Only the minister of justice was supposed to know where you were. Piet Hein Donner told the rest of the cabinet, 'Please don't ask about her location,' so we didn't."

Piet Hein Donner is not a bad man. He's not a strong leader, but he's a very decent person—just from some other era, and he doesn't micromanage his department. I expect Donner gave the order "Keep her safe"and let his civil servants deal with it. Those men had never been confronted with this kind of situation, but their jobs were at stake. So they made me utterly, utterly safe. I'm sure they meant well.

After two long and empty weeks passed, Neelie called again at the end of November. She told me I would be allowed to go back to Holland for a few days, to talk to a few people about my situation and see when I could be allowed to go back for good. I was so relieved.

On November 27, after twenty-five days in hiding, we drove to the Portland, Maine, airport in a heavy rain.

We landed at Eindhoven Air Base, and then I was driven around for what seemed like hours in a convoy. The cars all stopped on the side of a highway and I was moved into a much smaller, nondescript car. Koos, from the Witness Protection Program, drove me to a house in the countryside, somewhere near Zelhem.

When it was time to meet Neelie and Van Aartsen for dinner, I was driven out in the small Volkswagen; again, we switched to a convoy of BMWs in a country clearing. It was dark. Finally I arrived at a brick building somewhere in the middle of the woods. All the lights were out. The entryway stank of urine. One of the guards said it was the smell of the old holding cells; this was a disused police station. There was no electricity, just little plate-warmer candles for lights. Blotting paper was taped over all the windows. A table was laid with a paper cloth, some sandwiches, and a couple of bottles of water and juice.

We were in Holland, the fifteenth or sixteenth largest economy in the world, and I was meeting a European Union commissioner and the leader of a governing party here, skulking around in this weird Boy Scout fantasy. I'm grateful that I've been protected, grateful to be alive—but there was something excessive about all this security.

Neelie and van Aartsen arrived and were hustled in quickly. When I hugged Neelie, I felt like crying again. Jozias looked harassed. He was in the middle of preparing for a party congress the next day, and his life had been threatened, too; he was also living with bodyguards now. We sat facing each other in the room that had been prepared; Neelie raised her eyebrows and said, "Goodness."

You could tell from her whole tone that she thought all this cloak-and-dagger stuff was perfectly ridiculous. She said, "So it's safe here? Why couldn't we meet at my house?"

After the guards closed the door, Jozias asked where I'd been. I told him: a motel in an industrial area in the United States, between highways; no contact with friends, talking only to bodyguards. Neelie was livid. I said, "If I must go back there for a while longer, I want at least some way of communicating, a place to get some news and e-mail people. I need to spend more time with fellow human beings."

Two men from the Justice Ministry were supposed to be meeting us after dinner, the chief of the terror-fighting department and the chief of the unit of protection and security. Neelie and Jozias grilled them about why I had to live this way, in such total isolation, so far away. Exactly what kind of attack did they really expect?

Finally, after weeks of passive acceptance, something inside me sparked to life. I said to those men, "I will bow to your judgment about when I can come back permanently, because this is your job. But I'm not going back to that motel. In America nobody recognizes me. I want permission to go to a university. I want to be writing, reading, doing something with myself. I can't look at that highway for longer than a few more days."

Neelie swept them out with a pointed look and closed the door. She told me that my friends in Holland were agitating to find out what had happened to me. People wanted to know where I was. Newspapers were questioning the need for all the security. Part of bringing me to Holland was to quiet this sort of thing and show people that I was all right. We agreed that before I returned to America I would meet a very good friend of mine, Herman, and also a reporter from the daily paper *NRC Handelsblad*. Jozias suggested I also write a statement to make it clear that I was all right, which he would read to the assembled Party members the next day.

I spent that next day alone in the house in Zelhem, waiting for decisions to be made. Finally, I was told I would meet Neelie, have dinner with Herman, and then receive Frank Vermeulen from the *NRC* for an interview. They wouldn't tell me where I was going, though it was easy to recognize the Ministry of Finance when we drove in. They sat me down in a large, empty office, and Neelie arrived with a bottle of champagne. We settled down to write a text for Jozias to read to the assembled Liberals. Then Herman came in and I asked him to find a university in America where I could go that would be acceptable to the people at the Justice Ministry.

It was so good to see them, to talk. I was overwhelmed: two friends at once, after so long alone, felt almost too rich for me.

When Neelie's champagne was finished, Herman asked for another glass. I went to the guard at the door and asked, "Could we have a bottle of wine?" He said, "But after dinner you have an interview with a reporter! You can't drink wine!"

Herman said, "Jesus, what *is* this?" He couldn't believe the way I was living and being treated. I suppose I was already used to it, but now that I was back in Holland, it was starting to seem odd even to me.

At the *NRC* interview, one of the civil servants in charge of my security, Tjeerd, insisted on being present to assess whether I said anything that could endanger my security. When he walked in, Frank Vermeulen raised both eyebrows at the arrangement.

When the interview ended, I asked Tjeerd to leave and settled back just to talk to Frank as a friend. When the door closed, Frank asked, "How long is this going to go on? They can't keep you out of the country forever. It's madness. You're a member of Parliament and you've done nothing wrong, but you even have a minder listening in—it's like the old Soviet Union." I told him, "I don't understand half the stuff that happens. Sometimes it feels as if they don't trust me with my own life."

The next day, I was told, "You're going to a neighboring country, and then you're going back to Massachusetts." The guard shift had changed—they rotated every eight days—and I knew none of these new guards; they wouldn't tell me any more than that. We drove across the border, far into Germany, to a sordid, filthy hotel in a little town called Meckenheim, though I didn't know that at the time.

There, I decided I couldn't take it anymore. I needed to stand up for myself. I walked out. Just walked out of the hotel, to get coffee and some fresh air.

A junior DKDB officer, Robert, was on guard in the corridor. He looked at me as if I were in the throes of acute psychosis, ran after me and asked, "What do you think you're doing?" I told him, "I'm getting coffee," and kept walking. Robert was a trained police officer, trained to guard, so he walked after me. Outside the hotel, the road was deserted; it was freezing. I saw a sign. I said, "Okay, we're in Meckenheim, and that's in Germany. We'll follow the signs to the center of town."

A few feet behind me, Robert was on the phone with Hendrik; he was armed, but he was very nervous. I wasn't. The air was fresh and clean, and it felt good to walk. But it was a Sunday morning, and most places in Meckenheim are closed. I caught sight of a bar, peeked through, and asked, "Coffee?" Neither I nor Robert spoke German. The barman nodded.

He was Turkish; it was a Turkish coffee bar. Robert looked paralyzed with shock; I admit I, too, felt a little scared. But I sat down and pretended it was the most delicious coffee I had ever tasted. Deep in my heart I wanted to run away as quickly as I could, but I needed my dignity more. I needed to reclaim my life.

So I drank that coffee very slowly and ordered another cup. As more Turkish guest workers came in Robert moved his hand to his phone; he didn't want to have this fight on his own. But I told him, "These are innocent people. They have a business to run. They won't shoot their clients."

Finally I stood up, said *Danke,* and walked out. About five yards down the road we both burst out laughing. I said, "You're relieved, aren't you?" Robert said yes, and I said, "Me, too." He said, "See? There can be danger everywhere," and I said "No, they didn't do anything to us, just sold us coffee. Let's walk. We're not going to sit in that morgue of a hotel."

When we got back, I was swept off to a luxurious spa for rich old people, which was not what I wanted either. I wasn't demanding luxury, I just didn't want to sleep in a room that stank.

*   *   *

I was returned to Massachusetts, back to the horrible motel outside Andover. I decided to send Theo's son a present for Sinter-klaas, the Dutch Santa Claus, who brings gifts on December 5. Two weeks later my package was returned, unopened. Theo's son wanted nothing from me. That felt bad.

I was again very low. The days crept by with no news of any transfer. My new guards didn't want me leaving the hotel, even to go to the gym. I begged constantly for the phone: talking to friends was the only thing I could do, the only way I could stay sane. But there was a new rule: I wasn't to use the phone unless my guards were present, listening. It was like being imprisoned. I withdrew even further into myself and began spending most of the time alone, in my room.

Finally the news came: I was to be transferred to San Diego. I couldn't yet make use of the university facilities; that was still waiting for clearance. But it was warm there, and Pete was back on my security detail. He drove me to the beach and had me hike through the dunes, in the sharp sea air, for hours. He let me use his phone, and he kept his distance, so he wouldn't overhear my conversations.

I began to revive and to sleep properly, purely from physical exhaustion, for the first time since Theo died. The day before Christmas, Neelie called. We agreed I would go back to Holland on January 10.

When the day came, I was flown to Frankfurt, Germany, even though I wanted to be in Holland—I wanted to be home, preparing for the press conference that I was scheduled to give on January 18 in The Hague. But this wasn't allowed, for some reason. We went to one German hotel, then another. Why? Nobody ever explained it; it was just security. The second hotel had a computer, an Internet connection. I settled down to write the statements I would give when I returned to work. I wanted to e-mail a draft of my ideas to my friends, but the Internet connection in my room didn't work. So around midnight I asked the guards to accompany me to reception and ask if I could e-mail it from there.

The man at reception was Turkish. He looked at me and said, "Hey, are you by any chance that Somali woman who's a member of Parliament in the Netherlands, whose friend was murdered?"

In the months since Theo's death, I had seen a few people recognize me from time to time—I saw surprise on their faces—but this was the first time anyone had confronted me. I said, "What?" The clerk said, "You *are* her. There was a letter on his body threatening her and she disappeared, and it's you, isn't it?" I made a silly laugh and said, "Oh, no. Many people make that mistake, but I'm not her."

This was an absolute breach of security. This clerk was completely unknown to me, and he had my room number. I asked my guards, "Are you sure it's wise to stay here?" But Case, the senior guard, said, "Tomorrow I'll call the office. All this moving around—it's not good for your rest."

It could have been laughable, only my life was at stake. I went to my room and piled furniture and suitcases in front of the door and balanced the coffee machine and some cups and saucers on top, just in case I fell asleep, so I would hear if someone tried to come in. I spent the night awake, waiting for the noise and the man with the knife and the gun. Next morning Case got the order to transfer me to a hotel in Aachen, along with a reprimand for not having moved me immediately.

We were creeping closer to The Hague. I wasn't allowed to leave my hotel room now, because receptionists recognized me. I wanted to get in contact with Theo's parents before I went back to Holland, so I asked Case to arrange for me to call them. But he told me, "We've talked to their police contact person, and they don't want to have contact with you. When they're ready for contact they'll seek it."

I found out later this wasn't true; Theo's parents have been utterly warm and welcoming to me. They never told anyone such a thing. I guess someone at Justice couldn't be bothered to make the call.

I asked if I could meet with my friend Paul Scheffer, the critic, so he could help me with my text, which was too long and too emotional. I wanted to be professional and talk about my work, but I also wanted—needed—to say that I was sad about Theo, that I felt guilty he had died, and I wanted to convey the message that I, and Holland, had to move forward, not bow to terror.

I was driven into Holland on January 15. Paul and I met in a police station in Dreiberg and came up with a much shorter text. I spent the night in a military helicopter base in Soesterberg. It didn't matter now; we were nearly home. Just to be back in Holland felt good.

The next day was Sunday, and I was taken to Leon de Winter's house. I could barely contain my relief and happiness. Leon was there, and his wife, Jessica, and Afshin Ellian, the Iranian law professor I first met at The Balie, as well as Jaffe Vink and Chris Rutenfrans from *Trouw*. I was overcome with the need to touch, to hug them all.

On Tuesday morning, I returned to Parliament. When I stepped out of the car in the cobbled courtyard, a huge bank of cameras faced me. Every time I stepped forward they all moved back, in formation. The chairman of Parliament welcomed me back formally, in his office, and then I went to see Jozias van Aartsen, who greeted me warmly. We walked into the Liberal caucus meeting, the usual meeting that happens every Tuesday morning. Almost every Liberal MP came up and kissed me. All the envy and bad feeling seemed to have melted away.

The caucus meeting settled down to an interminable discussion of where committee meetings should be held: in a meeting room in Parliament, or at the offices of the Liberal Party. It was as if I had never been gone. I excused myself and spent the morning working on the text of my speech in my office and making phone calls, unhampered by listening ears.

At 2 p.m. I walked into the lower chamber of Parliament. It was full of reporters and MPs. All of them stood up and applauded, even the ones who had always disagreed with everything I said. The chairman made a short speech and the minister of defense, Henk Kamp, came over to shake my hand and welcome me home with real warmth in his eyes.

At 4 p.m. I walked over to the news center for my press conference. It's an easy walk, but the photographers and cameramen jostled each other, filming every step I took. The room was crammed with reporters. I took a deep breath and started to read my speech. I had been gone from Parliament for seventy-five days, but now I was home.

The Letter of the Law

It was sixteen months later—Monday evening, May 15, 2006—when Gerrit Zalm, the finance minister, came to my apartment in The Hague. With him was Willibrord van Beek, the new Liberal Party caucus leader. Both looked grim. They had a message for me.

My apartment was full of people, and the only place we could talk in private was among piles of laundry drying in my spare bedroom. I asked Gerrit, "Tell me the bad news first."

Looking me straight in the eye, he told me that the integration minister, Rita Verdonk, was planning to nullify my Dutch citizenship. I would receive the official letter from the Ministry of Justice sometime in the next half hour. Rita had assured him that she would not make the news public until the following day, when I would announce that I was resigning from Parliament.

I struggled not to show emotion, but Van Beek looked on the verge of tears as he said to me, "We won't let this happen." Gerrit said angrily that it was a farce, and I should get a good lawyer, and when they left, he looked so sad that I felt compelled to comfort him. "Don't worry," I said. "Everything will be fine."

I kept my tears back until they had gone.

Five minutes after Gerrit left, Rita called. Our conversation was brief and cold. She told me there was nothing personal about her decision. She said she couldn't do anything about it, her hands were tied. She had been forced to determine that my Dutch citizenship was invalid. Because I had given a false name and date of birth when I applied for my nationality in 1997, citizenship had never been granted me in the first place.

Ten minutes after Rita and I had said our clipped good-byes, the door-bell rang. It was one of the security guards from the DKDB, a friendly man who usually had a loopy grin. Only now he wasn't smiling. In his hand was a white envelope printed with the logo of Justice holding her scales.

"Dear Madam," the letter announced "I hereby inform you that in my judgment you have not received Dutch citizenship, due to the use of incorrect personal data during the naturalization process. The decree that naturalized you is void. You have six weeks to respond."

I had barely finished reading the letter when the TV news opened with a report that Rita Verdonk had declared that I had never been a Dutch citizen.

I was no longer Dutch.

This strange turn of events had actually begun weeks before, on April 27, the last Thursday before the parliamentary spring break. My schedule had been full of appointments all week and I was a bit frantic from it, but there was one I was looking forward to in particular. A documentary producer from a program called *Zembla* was coming to Parliament to talk to me about the places I had grown up in Kenya and Somalia and to show me some raw footage he had filmed there.

He set up a VCR. Once again, I saw the schools I had attended, and the house in Kariokor where we first lived, after Abeh left us. There was my brother, Mahad, thin and nervous, wrapped in sunglasses. I was surprised that this reporter had gone to such trouble, but I was warmed by nostalgia, as well as struck by the overwhelming number of Islamic headscarves now on the streets of Nairobi. When I was at Juja Road Primary School, our headmaster had refused to let my mother send us to school in headscarves; now it seemed they were in every corridor.

After he turned off the tape, the *Zembla* reporter peppered me with questions about my past, in an unmistakably hostile tone. I was taken aback and struggled to remain courteous as he said that Mahad had told him I had never been excised—he claimed that our family was much too progressive to mutilate children's genitals. I tried to explain that Mahad was trying to save face: he didn't want to admit to an outsider that his family practiced traditions that would seem barbaric to Westerners. My brother could say what he liked, but that didn't make it true.

The reporter went on: Was it true that when I first entered Holland, I lied on my asylum application? This was familiar ground; I had talked about it often. As soon as I entered Dutch politics, I had volunteered the fact that I had held back information on my asylum application, and subsequently, whenever I was asked about it, in private or in public, I admitted that I had lied and explained why. So, once again, I told this *Zembla* producer that when I applied for refugee status in 1992, I did not tell the whole truth.

The reporter had more questions, all with the same hostile tone, but my parliamentary assistant, Iris, knocked at the door. The head of the Unit for Security and Protection from the Justice Ministry had just arrived in my office, along with his deputy: I had to go. Still seething slightly from the tone of the interview, I walked in to find Arjan Jonge Vos from the Ministry with an unusually compassionate look on his normally expressionless face. "Sit down," he said. "Please have a glass of water."

Jonge Vos handed me a sheaf of legal papers. My neighbors had been suing the government to evict me from my apartment, claiming that the security around me deprived them of privacy and my presence made them unsafe. This had been going on for months, but I had never allowed myself to imagine seriously that I might lose the case. Jonge Vos told me the papers contained the decision of the appeals court that was considering my neighbors' case. I had just been evicted. I had four months to leave, till August 27, Jonge Vos kindly told me. He had gone to the trouble of working it out.

I was stunned. Where could I go? To a hotel? An air base? To some bulletproof hut in the forest? Where could I live—where, in Holland, could I find a place where I would have no neighbors? The Netherlands is a small country with a lot of people. How could I function if I kept having to move from place to place? It was a blow. It may sound trivial, but when I heard Jonge Vos's news, I felt something close to despair. Would my wandering never end?

A few days later, in early May, I was scheduled to fly to the United States on a long-planned trip to promote *The Caged Virgin,* a book of my essays. But I also intended to meet with Christopher DeMuth, the president of the American Enterprise Institute, a think tank in Washington that was interested in offering me a job. After two and a half years as a member of Parliament, I had become disenchanted and I wanted to leave Dutch politics. Months before, I had informed Gerrit Zalm that I didn't plan to run again. There were aspects of Parliament I loved, like the sharpness of some debates, the matching of blade against blade. A real Parliament in action can be a fine thing. But the legislative process is slow and frustrating. I didn't want to toe party lines and grow deeper in my understanding of Europe's Common Agricultural Policy and the transportation system around Rotterdam. I didn't want to waste ridiculous amounts of energy building coalitions with people who accepted my ideas but who wouldn't vote with me because I was in the Liberal Party. The media frenzies that blew up constantly at my every comment or misstep made it difficult to function. Although the media attention did, of course, give me a platform, it also intensified the animosity that so many parliamentarians clearly felt toward me and my political initiatives.

It also seemed to me that I had already achieved a big part of what I had set out to do. I had wanted Islam to be part of the political debate, and now it was. All kinds of opinion makers were now saying that it was irresponsible and indeed morally wrong to pretend that appeasing Islamic leaders would magically lead to social harmony. Dutch society was churning with discussion over how best to integrate Muslims, and Muslims in Holland also seemed largely aware now that they needed to choose between Western values and the old ways. Above all, Muslim women were now prominently on the agenda of the country.

When I had been approached for a think tank position in the United States, I thought that perhaps it could take my ideas to a larger platform and give me more time to develop them. And now I knew that I wanted to do it sooner than expected.

When the *Zembla* show aired in Holland on Thursday, May 11, under the title "The Holy Ayaan," I was still in the United States, but a Dutch journalist living in New York arranged for me to view it in a studio. The tone was unpleasant, and it was certainly intended as a character assassination. But friends of mine who phoned me didn't seem to think it was in any way seriously damaging. The reporter had apparently tracked down Osman Moussa, who was still living in Canada, and he had claimed that I had married him willingly. But as someone said to me, "Who *would* admit to marrying a girl who didn't want to be married to him?" It seemed pretty clear that the reporter had gone to Kenya and Somalia to try to dig up dirt about me; if this was all he could come up with, I thought, then I was doing fine.

But then the drum rolls began. As the minister in charge of immigration affairs, Rita Verdonk had in the past ordered that a number of asylum seekers be deported from Holland because they had lied on their residency applications. The day after the "Holy Ayaan" show aired, Rita faced taunts that she ought now to deport Ayaan Hirsi Ali just as she would any other lying immigrant.

Rita was my friend. Known to others as Iron Rita, she was found to be rigid, and they constantly taunted her about her former job as a prison warden. I, however, had always found her to be warm, even motherly. Although we frequently disagreed about policy, she was often my ally in our Party and in Parliament; we exchanged ideas often, and she used bits and pieces of my proposals. I also intervened with her frequently on behalf of asylum seekers she was planning to have deported. Rita was one of the people who had comforted me after Theo's death. In a caucus where I had few friends, she had gone to a lot of trouble on my behalf.

And Rita knew very well that I had lied on my asylum application. Even if she hadn't read my interviews on the subject (and why should she have), we had spoken of it several times, most recently just a few weeks before, after she had decided to deport an eighteen-year-old girl from Kosovo, Taida Pasic, although she was due to take her final high school exams. I had phoned Rita from Leon de Winter's house, where I was having dinner, and pleaded with her to reconsider the girl's case, but Rita was adamant.

"She lied," Rita told me then. "My hands are tied."

"But Rita, I lied, too!" I said. Leon heard me.

Rita's words: "If I had been the minister when you applied for asylum, then I would have deported you as well."

On Friday, the day after the broadcast of the documentary, Rita publicly announced that I had nothing to fear from her. But Rita was running hard to be elected leader of the Liberal Party. The vote was scheduled for May 30. She could not afford to look weak. "Rules are rules" was her mantra, and she was adamant that she could not make any exceptions. And so, on Saturday morning—the day after calls began demanding that she examine my status as a lying asylum seeker—Rita let it be known that she was investigating my immigration file.

I suddenly felt like that foolish, trusting nomad from the tales Grandma used to tell me as a child.

By Sunday I had heard rumors that Rita was planning to retract my citizenship. So had everyone in the country: it was in the newspapers. My passport could be taken away. If I was no longer Dutch, I couldn't vote; it went without saying that I was no longer a member of Parliament. Would I even be allowed to remain in the country? Without a passport, would I be able to travel? If I were no longer in Parliament, would I have bodyguards? I was incredulous. Even when Gerrit Zalm walked into my apartment that Monday night and told me it was really happening, and I received the letter from the Ministry—even then, the whole thing still seemed completely unreal.

When I woke up on Tuesday morning, my voicemail was overflowing with calls. Hundreds of e-mails jammed my inbox. Due to hold a press conference that afternoon, I settled in to think about what I was going to say. The manuscript pages of my memoir were scattered across my printer: "I am Ayaan, the daughter of Hirsi, the son of Magan," I read.

How could this be happening, when I had so repeatedly told the truth about my real past? Yes, I should have told the whole truth in 1992 when I arrived in Holland, even though I was frightened of being sent home. In time, as I learned not to be afraid, I learned that it was wrong not to tell the truth.

Now, having been truthful, I had no idea what my citizenship was, or even if I could remain in Holland. The only thing that was clear to me was that I should resign from Parliament earlier than I had planned.

That afternoon, I walked into the news center beside Parliament and faced the cameras again. I announced that I was leaving politics and that I would be leaving Holland. I thanked various people for their support and tried to sum up what I thought I had achieved. My hands were shaking and my throat was dry. A few hours later, Christopher DeMuth called from the American Enterprise Institute and confirmed that I would have a job there in September.

My press conference that Tuesday was at two p.m.; by 4:45, Rita Verdonk was in Parliament answering questions from my angry colleagues. For over three years I had worked with these men and women—eaten with them, socialized, made alliances, traded votes. Now, after an internal inquiry that had lasted just four days, I was no longer a Dutch citizen and, as a result, I had been stripped of my position beside them. Many members of Parliament were outraged, and they made no secret of it.

At around eleven that night, under heavy questioning in parliament, Rita stumbled. She said I had never been Dutch. Then she claimed that I was now Dutch for a six-week waiting period, even though I had never been Dutch in the first place. She claimed to have no idea that I had lied on my asylum application. She said she had never heard of me using another name despite the fact that there were dozens of examples where I had. Whether it was in the press, in earlier publications, or even in simple everyday parts of my life (such as my e-mail address in Parliament, which was magan@tweedekamer.nl—the Dutch equivalent of "parliament-dot-Netherlands"), I had made no secret that in my youth my family name was Hirsi Magan.

Rita's support in the lower chamber of Parliament began falling away. The calculus of self-interest that hums just beneath the surface of politics was in action now, and this was no longer about me. Rita Verdonk would have been a strong leader of the VVD, and so the VVD's opponents wanted her destroyed. Within our own Liberal Party, too, there were people who were prepared, even delighted, to sacrifice her, whether on this pretext or some other.

By this time, millions of Dutch people were tuned in to the parliamentary debate on live TV. They watched as Rita was slowly torn to pieces in the arena. Leaders of the governing coalition began edging away from her on the podium. Two motions instructing her to review my case were tabled. Sometime around 2:30 in the morning, the chairman of the Parliament apparently passed her a note warning her that she must accept the next motion or she would be forced to step down from government. Abruptly, at around three in the morning, she agreed to reopen my case and review my naturalization. I would receive a decision within six weeks.

From this point on, the whole situation became a farce. I found a lawyer, who told me that because I used the name Ali, which was the birth name of my grandfather known as Magan, I hadn't in fact fraudulently filled in any forms. She also filed a document analyzing Somali law, which showed that I had a right to use any name in the long list of my male ancestors as my family name. (I hadn't known that.) Because I was unable to procure birth certificates for my grandfather, father, and mother, as requested, I obtained a statement from my brother confirming that my grandfather Magan was named Ali at his birth. Then I settled back to wait.

As the weeks passed, I heard the rumors, like everyone else: Jan Peter Balkenende, the prime minister, wanted Rita to retract her decision and reinstate me as an honorable Dutch citizen, but Rita didn't want to lose face. Finally, just two days before Parliament was due to break up for the summer, Balkenende scheduled a meeting with her late on Monday night, June 26, and insisted that she inform Parliament that she was retracting her decision, making me Dutch again.

When I learned about this meeting, just before it happened, I was in Washington, in the office of the lawyer who was helping me with my U.S.

immigration. My phone rang at about three p.m. It was my Dutch lawyer telling me that I must urgently fax a declaration stating that I would henceforth always use Ali as my name, and not another name like Magan. Once I did that, everything would be fine with my Dutch citizenship. I had to find a FedEx office in downtown Washington to send it immediately—it was too urgent to wait.

A few hours later, a real estate broker was showing me around an apartment for rent in Washington when the phone rang again. There was another declaration that I must sign before everything could be resolved. I should state that I was to blame for the entire business, because I had told reporters that I had lied when I called myself Ali, when in actual fact I hadn't lied—I was legally permitted to use the name.

I wanted to get the whole thing behind me. I no longer had a home in Holland. Without Dutch citizenship, I would be stalled in my application for a U.S. visa. Not to sign this statement could lead to years of insecurity and legal battles. My lawyers, who were in constant contact with The Hague, told me that I was not allowed to change a word in the statement—I had to take it or leave it. I did however manage to get one change put through. I took out "I am sorry" and replaced it with "I regret." (Apparently, Prime Minister Balkenende made Rita promise in return never again to say "Rules are rules.")

The next day, Tuesday, I was at the office of the American Enterprise Institute when Dutch reporters began arriving with camera equipment. I hadn't received any notification yet, but they had heard that Rita had agreed to reinstate my Dutch citizenship. I simply said how glad I was. That was it; I just wanted the matter closed. But the reporters told me a debate had already been scheduled in Parliament for Wednesday evening, just before Parliament broke for the summer. People in The Hague were saying that I had been blackmailed into writing the letter accepting blame and that it was shameful behavior by Rita Verdonk.

There was no blackmail, and I told the reporters so. There was only the pressure of time. I wanted the whole thing finished, so I could put it behind me.

When the debate in Parliament opened at eight p.m. on Wednesday night, June 28, Rita Verdonk and Prime Minister Balkenende came under attack almost immediately. Rita had notified Balkenende by voice mail of her original decision to take away my naturalization, and then never got back to him before it was announced. What kind of leadership was that? It was also obvious that many members of Parliament felt that the government was insulting their intelligence by claiming that the whole thing was essentially my fault.

In the early hours of the morning, Balkenende was asked in Parliament if I had been obligated to put my signature to a document taking blame for the whole affair—whether that had been a precondition for me to get back my citizenship. He said yes, it was a precondition: Rita had insisted that I should sign the statement or there was no deal. The floor of Parliament erupted in a frenzy as members rushed for the microphone.

At 4:30 a.m., the Green Party called for a motion of no confidence in Rita Verdonk. Many people across the country were still up and watching on TV. When the votes were counted, sixty-six members supported it and seventy-nine were against, which meant that D-66, a small party that was one of the three partners in the governing coalition, had voted no confidence in the government's minister. Either Rita would have to resign or there was no longer a coalition, and the government would collapse.

It was now June 29, the last day of the parliamentary term. At nine a.m., there was an emergency meeting of the cabinet. The prime minister emerged after lunch and told the press that Rita would stay on as minister: it was up to D-66 to decide what to do about it. Their six members quit the coalition that evening.

Balkenende's government had fallen. New elections would have to be called in the fall.

As the drama unfolded, I was kept abreast of it by text message. Friends of mine on the parliamentary staff, as well as my former colleagues, sent me hundreds of them. When the government collapsed, I received more than fifty messages almost simultaneously.

By that point, I was in Aspen, Colorado, where I had been invited to attend a conference at the Aspen Institute with a constellation of American politicians and heads of corporations. I was taken aback by how many people kept coming up to me to tell me how angry they were with the Dutch government. I found myself constantly explaining that Holland wasn't a xenophobic country and had not suddenly kicked me out.

I tried to tell people that I very much regretted the collapse of Balkenende's cabinet, because a government should not fall apart over such a minor issue. It leads to voter cynicism: people elect their leaders to make tough, big decisions, and this was a very small one. Above all, I told these people that Holland is a peaceful country, open and tolerant and free. It was in Holland that I became a free individual, and I am Dutch—completely Dutch again, and very glad to be.

*   *   *

Whatever your feelings on the subject, the United States is the leader of the free world. By taking my ideas to the United States, I don't feel in any way that I am selling out. At the American Enterprise Institute in Washington, I will have more time to think than when I was a member of Parliament in The Hague, trying to wheel and deal programs in the legislative process. At the risk of repeating myself, I am not leaving Holland because of the issue of my Dutch citizenship: it is an entirely personal decision, made long before the citizenship saga came about.

Years ago, fresh out of Leiden, I thought that politics was a truly noble pursuit, and that the institutions of democracy were humanity's means to better the world. I still think that's true. But I have learned that, like every other kind of human pursuit, politics can be an ugly game: clan against clan, party against party, candidate against candidate, with governments falling over trivial issues. Watching power will, I hope, be more agreeable than practicing it.

The freedom of expression that I found in Holland—the freedom to think—is unknown where I come from. It is a right and practice that I always dreamed of having as I was growing up. Whatever its flaws, no nation understands the principle of free expression better than the Dutch. It runs so deep in Dutch culture that Holland has chosen to protect me against death threats, even though members of the government constantly tell me how much they disagree with my ideas. I must say how grateful I am: I am lucky and privileged to be Dutch.

Muhammad Bouyeri, Theo's murderer, and others like him don't realize how deeply people in the West are committed to the idea of an open society. Even though the open society is vulnerable, it is also stubborn. It is the place I ran to for safety and freedom. I would like to keep it that way: safe and free.

People are always asking me what it's like to live with death threats. It's like being diagnosed with a chronic disease. It may flare up and kill you, but it may not. It could happen in a week, or not for decades.

The people who ask me this usually have grown up in rich countries, Western Europe and America, after the Second World War. They take life for granted. Where I grew up, death is a constant visitor. A virus, bacteria, a parasite; drought and famine; soldiers, and torturers; could bring it to anyone, any time. Death comes riding on raindrops that turned to floods. It catches the imagination of men in positions of authority who order their subordinates to hunt, torture, and kill people they imagine to be enemies. Death lures many others to take their own lives in order to escape a dismal reality. For many women, because of the perception of lost honor, death comes at the hands of a father, brother, or husband. Death comes to young women giving birth to new life, leaving the newborn orphaned in the hands of strangers.

For those who live in anarchy and civil war, as in the country of my birth, Somalia, death is everywhere.

When I was born, my mother initially thought death had taken me away. But it didn't. When I got malaria and pneumonia, I recovered. When my genitals were cut, the wound healed. When a bandit held a knife to my throat, he decided not to slit it. When my Quran teacher fractured my skull, the doctor who treated me kept death at bay.

Even with bodyguards and death threats I feel privileged to be alive and free. When I took the train to Amsterdam thirteen years ago, I took a chance at a life in freedom, a life in which I would be free from bondage to someone I had not chosen, and in which my mind, too, could be free.

I first encountered the full strength of Islam as a young child in Saudi Arabia. It was very different from the diluted religion of my grandmother, which was mixed with magical practices and pre-Islamic beliefs. Saudi Arabia is the source of Islam and its quintessence. It is the place where the Muslim religion is practiced in its purest form, and it is the origin of much of the fundamentalist vision that has, in my lifetime, spread far beyond its borders. In Saudi Arabia, every breath, every step we took, was infused with concepts of purity or sinning, and with fear. Wishful thinking about the peaceful tolerance of Islam cannot interpret away this reality: hands are still cut off, women still stoned and enslaved, just as the Prophet Muhammad decided centuries ago.

The kind of thinking I saw in Saudi Arabia, and among the Muslim Brotherhood in Kenya and Somalia, is incompatible with human rights and liberal values. It preserves a feudal mind-set based on tribal concepts of honor and shame. It rests on self-deception, hypocrisy, and double standards. It relies on the technological advances of the West while pretending to ignore their origin in Western thinking. This mind-set makes the transition to modernity very painful for all who practice Islam.

It is always difficult to make the transition to a modern world. It was difficult for my grandmother, and for all my relatives from the *miyé*. It was difficult for me, too. I moved from the world of faith to the world of reason—from the world of excision and forced marriage to the world of sexual emancipation. Having made that journey, I know that one of those worlds is simply better than the other. Not because of its flashy gadgets, but fundamentally, because of its values.

The message of this book, if it must have a message, is that we in the West would be wrong to prolong the pain of that transition unnecessarily, by elevating cultures full of bigotry and hatred toward women to the stature of respectable alternative ways of life.

People accuse me of having interiorized a feeling of racial inferiority, so that I attack my own culture out of self-hatred, because I want to be white. This is a tiresome argument. Tell me, is freedom then only for white people? Is it self-love to adhere to my ancestors' traditions and mutilate my daughters? To agree to be humiliated and powerless? To watch passively as my countrymen abuse women and slaughter each other in pointless disputes? When I came to a new culture, where I saw for the first time that human relations could be different, would it have been self-love to see that as a foreign cult, which Muslims are forbidden to practice?

Life is better in Europe than it is in the Muslim world because human relations are better, and one reason human relations are better is that in the West, life on earth is valued in the here and now, and individuals enjoy rights and freedoms that are recognized and protected by the state. To accept subordination and abuse because Allah willed it—that, for me, would be self-hatred.

The decision to write this book didn't come to me easily. Why would I expose such private memories to the world? I don't want my arguments to be considered sacrosanct because I have had horrible experiences; I haven't. In reality, my life has been marked by enormous good fortune. How many girls born in Digfeer Hospital in Mogadishu in November 1969 are even alive today? And how many have a real voice?

I also don't want my reasoning to be dismissed as the bizarre ranting of someone who has been somehow damaged by her experiences and who is lashing out. People often imply that I am angry because I was excised, or because my father married me off. They never fail to add that such things are rare in the modern Muslim world. The fact is that hundreds of millions of women around the world live in forced marriages, and six thousand small girls are excised every day. My excision in no way damaged my mental capacities; and I would like to be judged on the validity of my arguments, not as a victim.

My central, motivating concern is that women in Islam are oppressed.

That oppression of women causes Muslim women and Muslim men, too, to lag behind the West. It creates a culture that generates more backwardness with every generation. It would be better for everyone—for Muslims, above all—if this situation could change.

When people say that the values of Islam are compassion, tolerance, and freedom, I look at reality, at real cultures and governments, and I see that it simply isn't so. People in the West swallow this sort of thing because they have learned not to examine the religions or cultures of minorities too critically, for fear of being called racist. It fascinates them that I am not afraid to do so.

In March 2005, *Time* magazine informed me that I would be named one of its one hundred "most influential people in the world today." I went straight out to buy a copy of the magazine, of course, but I was weeks early; that issue wouldn't come out until mid-April. So the magazine I bought wasn't about me, it was about poverty in Africa. The woman on the cover was young and thin, with three small children. She was wrapped in the same kind of cloth my grandmother used to wear, and the look in her eyes was hopeless.

It threw me back to Somalia, to Kenya, to poverty and disease and fear. I thought about the woman in that photograph, and about the millions of women who must live as she does. *Time* had just named me to their category "Leaders and Revolutionaries." What do you do with a responsibility like that?

Perhaps I could start by telling people that values matter. The values of my parents' world generate and preserve poverty and tyranny, for example, in their oppression of women. A clear look at this would be tremendously beneficial. In simple terms, for those of us who were brought up with Islam, if we face up to the terrible reality we are in, we can change our destiny.

Why am I not in Kenya, squatting at a charcoal brazier making *angellos*? Why have I been instead a representative in the Dutch Parliament, making law? I have been lucky, and not many women are lucky in the places I come from. In some sense, I owe them something. Like the Galla woman I once translated for in Schalkhaar, I need to seek out the other women held captive in the compound of irrationality and superstition and persuade them to take their lives into their own hands.

Sister Aziza used to warn us of the decadence of the West: the corrupt, licentious, perverted, idolatrous, money-grubbing, soulless countries of Europe. But to me, there is far worse moral corruption in Islamic countries. In those societies, cruelty is implacable and inequality is the law of the land. Dissidents are tortured. Women are policed both by the state and by their families to whom the state gives the power to rule their lives.

In the past fifty years the Muslim world has been catapulted into modernity. From my grandmother to me is a journey of just two generations, but the reality of that voyage is millennial. Even today you can take a truck across the border into Somalia and find you have gone back thousands of years in time.

People adapt. People who never sat on chairs before can learn to drive cars and operate complex machinery; they master these skills very quickly. Similarly, Muslims don't have to take six hundred years to go through a reformation in the way they think about equality and individual rights.

When I approached Theo to help me make *Submission,* I had three messages to get across. First, men, and even women, may look up and speak to Allah: it is possible for believers to have a dialogue with God and look closely at Him. Second, the rigid interpretation of the Quran in Islam today causes intolerable misery for women. Through globalization, more and more people who hold these ideas have traveled to Europe with the women they own and brutalize, and it is no longer possible for Europeans and other Westerners to pretend that severe violations of human rights occur only far away. The third message is the film's final phrase: "I may no longer submit." It is possible to free oneself—to adapt one's faith, to examine it critically, and to think about the degree to which that faith is itself at the root of oppression.

I am told that *Submission* is too aggressive a film. Its criticism of Islam is apparently too painful for Muslims to bear. Tell me, how much more painful is it to be these women, trapped in that cage?

Acknowledgments

I was born in a country torn apart by war and grew up in a continent mostly known for what goes wrong rather than right. Measured by the standards of Somalia and Africa I am privileged to be alive and thriving, a privilege I never can and never shall take for granted. For without the help and sacrifice of family, tutors, and friends, I would not have been any different from my peers who struggle just to survive.

I wish to start with my mother who held me close and refused to believe that I would die for being born too early and underweight. My grandmother who taught me the art of survival. My father who insisted that I go to school. My late sister for her friendship, her laughter, her sense of adventure. My brother for his never-ending sense of hope.

I want to acknowledge my teachers at Juja Road who, besides the regular curriculum, were dedicated to instilling discipline in us, and some of my teachers at the Muslim Girls' School, such as Mrs. Mumtaz, Mrs. Kataka, Mrs. Owour, Mrs. Choudry, and Mrs. Karim, who "saw something in me."

A special thanks to Jim'o Musse and the Italian doctor at Nairobi hospital whose name I have forgotten but whose face I shall never forget—together they saved my life. I am grateful to my stepmother, half-sisters, cousins, aunts, and uncles who welcomed me to their homes, counseled me, and pampered me for nine long months in Mogadishu.

I would not have become the woman I am without the openness, hospitality, and opportunity that Holland offered me as a nation. The kindness and civility with which I was welcomed into Holland was profound. I felt at home from the very beginning. The INS officials, the police, the social workers at the refugee centers, my language teachers, the volunteers, the landlords, and many more who helped me when I first entered Holland left a deep impression on me of how civilized a nation can be. My

351

deepest gratitude goes to my "Dutch family"—Johanna, Maarten, Irene, and Jan—who offered me a real home in my new country. Also, they helped me learn how to become a self-sufficient Dutch citizen and overcome my own cultural prejudices.

Maarten van der Linde, my first professor at Hoge School in Driebergen, will remain dear to me for his devotion to giving vocations to as many nonnative Dutch as possible. Without Maarten I would not have taken those admissions exams, let alone pass them.

My tutors at Leiden introduced me to my faculty of reason. I particularly enjoyed the classes given by Professor Rudy Andeweg, Professor Paul 't Hart, and Professor Henk Dekker. Dr. Henk Kern's history workshops were both a challenge and a pleasure to attend. Professor Paul Cliteur made Introduction to Law seem like an entertainment class, and I am grateful that he and his wife, Carla, later became very good friends. I have since discovered he is better at law than cooking.

For all our disagreements on issues of multiculturalism, Islam, and integration and religion, I will remember Paul Kalma for his honesty and help. He protected me from the threats of the Islamists and from the pen of those who tried to slander me. I thank Margo Trappenburg, Bart Tromp, and especially Arie van der Zwan.

I want to acknowledge leading Dutch feminists: Cisca Dresselhuys, Nahed Selim, Naema Tahir, Adelheid Roosen, and Jeltje van Nieuwenhoven, who welcomed me as one of them and provided me inspiration in the debate to help improve Muslim women's rights.

Many people have stood up for me when freedom of speech was at issue. My special thanks to Betsy Udink, Nelleke Noordervliet, Max Pam, Joost Zwagerman, and Peter van Ingen for their support.

I am grateful to Gijs van de Westelaken and Theodor Holman and anyone else who contributed to *Submission, Part 1.*

I owe deep gratitude to Gerrit Zalm, Neelie Kroes, Jozias van Aartsen, and Henk Kamp. They were instrumental in boosting and preserving my political career. They believed in me, took a stand for me, and coached me throughout my years in Dutch Parliament, and continue to do so.

Frits Bolkestein was my intellectual mentor—he and his wife, Femke Boersma, opened their home to me and offered me comfort and support in my hours of need.

Special thanks to:

De Herenclub—the Gents' club—Chris, Chris, Hans, Herman, Jaffe, Leon, Paul, Sylvain: for your ideas and inspiring conversations. You taught me so much and always had the courage to criticize me when you thought I was wrong.

Leon, Jessica, Mo, and Mo: you are anchors of strength and I can never thank you enough.

The Van Gogh family.

The two I's—Iris and Ingrid—and Peter: without your guidance and levelheadedness I would have lost my mind many a time in the past few years. It is great to have you by my side.

My publishers around the world, in particular Tilly, for your commitment and friendship, and Leslie and Chris for your insights and support that helped me complete this book.

Ruth, for all your help in writing this book. Your patience, your inquisitive mind, your sensitivity, were all crucial to making this book happen. I know at times your pretty face frowned when I got behind in my work. I know that sometimes you wanted to pull out that wonderfully thick hair of yours. But you always had a kind word. And you always held out your hand to encourage me along.

Susanna, my agent, my friend, my sister—and even sometimes my Jewish mother! Thank you and your team for your unfailing calm, conscientiousness, and confidence.

The entire staff of the Dutch Royal and Diplomatic Protection Service (DKDB).

Annejet, Anne Louise, Britta, Corin, David, Evelyn and Rose, Evelyn, Frederique, Frédérique, Geeske, Giovanni, Hans, Hein, Isabella, Joachim, Marco, Mirjam, Nina, Olivia, Olivier, Roeland, Ruben, Sebastian, Tamara . . . I have been so fortunate over the years to have had so many friends who have supported me through thick and thin. I cannot name you all, and I would hate to forget someone, but you know who you are. Thank you for always surrounding me with your warmth, love, and understanding.

About the Author

AYAAN HIRSI ALI was born in Somalia, was raised Muslim, and spent her childhood and young adulthood in Africa and Saudi Arabia. In 1992, Hirsi Ali fled to the Netherlands as a refugee, escaping a forced marriage to a distant cousin she had never met. She learned Dutch and worked as an interpreter in abortion clinics and shelters for battered women. After earning her college degree in political science, she was elected to Parliament, where she worked to raise awareness of the plight of Muslim women in Europe. Hirsi Ali was named one of *Time* magazine's 100 Most Influential People of 2005, one of the *Glamour* Heroes of 2005, and *Reader's Digest*'s European of the Year, and she has received numerous human rights awards. She is author of *The Caged Virgin: An Emancipation Proclamation for Women and Islam,* and works for the American Enterprise Institute in the United States. If you would like to contribute to Ayaan Hirsi Ali's security trust, please visit www.AyaanHirsiAli.org.

INFIDEL

Ayaan Hirsi Ali

Reading Group Guide

ABOUT THIS GUIDE

The following reading group guide is intended to help you find interesting and rewarding approaches to your reading of *Infidel*. We hope this enhances your enjoyment and appreciation of the book.

Infidel Reading Group Guide

Discussion Questions

1. Hirsi Ali tells us that this book is "the story of what I have experienced, what I've seen, and why I think the way I do" (page xxii). Which experiences does she highlight as being integral to forming her current views on Islam?

2. "No eyes silently accused me of being a whore. No lecherous men called me to bed with them. No Brotherhood members threatened me with hellfire. I felt safe; I could follow my curiosity" (page 185). This passage refers to Hirsi Ali's initial impression of walking the streets in Germany. What other significant differences between the West and Islamic Africa did she observe during her first days in Europe? Upon arriving in Holland, what were her initial impressions of the Dutch people and the Dutch government? Did these change significantly while she lived there?

3. How did Hirsi Ali's immigration experience and integration into Dutch society differ from those of other Somalians?

4. Discuss the differences that Hirsi Ali noticed between raising children in Muslim countries and raising children in the West. In particular, what did she notice about Johanna's parenting? How were Muslim parents different from Dutch parents in their instructions to their children on the playground? (See page 245.)

5. In Hirsi Ali's words, "A Muslim girl does not make her own decisions or seek control. She is trained to be docile. If you are a Muslim girl, you disappear, until there is almost no you inside you" (page 94). How do the three generations of women in Hirsi Ali's family differ in their willingness to "submit" to this doctrine?

6. As seen through Hirsi Ali's eyes, what factors contributed to Haweya's death? How might members of her family describe events differently?

7. Although Hirsi Ali mostly refrains from criticizing her father, she publishes the personal letter he wrote her upon her divorce. Why do you think she included this letter? Were you surprised by any other intimate details of her life that she revealed in the book?

8. The events of September 11 caused Hirsi Ali to reread sections of the Quran and to evaluate the role of violence in Islam. Consequently, her interpretation of September 11 differs from those around her. What does she conclude? Do you agree with her analysis?

9. On page 295, Hirsi Ali lists the three goals she wished to accomplish by joining Parliament. By the book's end, has she accomplished all three? How did her views of the Dutch government change over time?

10. Examine Hirsi Ali's relationship with her brother. How did Mahad's and Abeh's reactions to her political work differ?

11. Throughout her political career, Hirsi Ali has made several bold statements challenging the Muslim world. In your opinion, were these declarations worth the risk?

12. Has this book changed the way you view Islam? According to Hirsi Ali, is Islam compatible with Western values and culture? Do you agree with her?

Enhancing Your Book Club

1. Visit the Web site of the American Enterprise Institute for Public Policy Research, the Washington, D.C., think tank that Hirsi Ali joined upon leaving Holland. Take a look at the articles that she has posted, and bring one to share. The Web site is located at www.aei.org.

2. Go to www.youtube.com to watch a version of Theo van Gogh and Hirsi Ali's film, *Submission: Part One*.

3. Research the Quran before your group meeting and choose a passage to examine together.

4. Take a look on the Web for Hirsi Ali's most recent statements about freedom of speech, women's rights, or religion in schools. (For example, in April 2006 she publicly stated her support of the Danish cartoonists' right to publish images of Muhammad.) Bring in a copy of any interviews you find and share with your group.

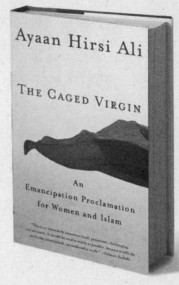